Sebastian de Grazia

OF TIME, WORK
AND LEISURE

Sebastian de Grazia, political philosopher and writer, is the author of *The Political Community, Of Time, Work and Leisure,* and *Machiavelli in Hell,* which won the Pulitzer Prize for Biography in 1989.

OF TIME
WORK
AND
LEISURE

Sebastian de Grazia

VINTAGE BOOKS

A DIVISION OF RANDOM HOUSE, INC.

NEW YORK

FIRST VINTAGE BOOKS EDITION, JANUARY 1994

Copyright © 1962 by Sebastian de Grazia
Copyright renewed 1990 by Sebastian de Grazia

Library of Congress Cataloging-in-Publication Data
De Grazia, Sebastian.
Of time, work, and leisure / Sebastian de Grazia. — 1st Vintage Books ed.
p. cm.
Originally published: New York: Twentieth Century Fund, 1962.
Includes index.
ISBN 0-679-74343-X (pbk.)
1. Leisure. 2. Work. I. Title.
BJ1498.D37 1993
174—dc20 92-50595
CIP

Manufactured in the United States of America
10 9 8 7 6 5 4 3 2 1

*Men come together to keep alive;
they stay together to live a good life.*
—Aristotle, *Politics*

ACKNOWLEDGMENTS

The author extends his appreciation to the Trustees of the Twentieth Century Fund for their generous support, and to the Fund's staff, on whose help he counted many times, and who never failed to respond with interest and dispatch.

CONTENTS

Of Time
Work
and
Leisure

The Background of Leisure

ARISTOTLE in the *Politics* says a curious thing. The Spartans remained secure as long as they were at war; they collapsed as soon as they acquired an empire. They did not know how to use the leisure that peace brought.

In Aristotle the words "peace" and "leisure" come together often. They repeat his thesis that wars are fought to have peace, and peace is needed for leisure. Sparta trained its citizens for war. It designed its laws principally with war in mind. Leisure and peace were used to prepare for war. The Spartans made another mistake. A well-ordered state manages to secure leisure or freedom from the necessity of labor. Now the Spartans did obtain leisure, but in a wrong way. They wrung it from a system of serfdom. What leisure could there be when Helots lay in ambush waiting for a chance at their masters? The moral is plain. Sparta had not discovered the best mode of governing for a life of leisure.

One more charge against Sparta: the men by their military life were educated to discipline, which at least tided them along in times of peace and leisure, but the women were given absolutely no education in self-control. With the men absent for long periods, the women abandoned themselves to license and luxury.

Legislators like Lycurgus tried to bring them, as well as the men, within range of the law, but they opposed him and he had to abandon the attempt. The results brought misfortune to Sparta — the growth of luxuriousness, avarice, maldistribution of property, shortage of warriors, and a female population that in war caused more confusion than the enemy.

These then are the charges. A citizenry unprepared for leisure will degenerate in prosperous times. Women, too, are liable to fall on evil ways. Furthermore, leisure based on serfdom is so insecure as to be no leisure at all.

The Greeks took the question of leisure seriously. Their ideas are worth attention for they not only examined many of the problems confronting us today but asked questions we have not dared to ask ourselves. Who today would say that a nation could collapse because it didn't know how to use its leisure? Who today so predicts the downfall of the United States or of China? But Aristotle not only lived in but was preceded by a century interested in leisure. His Greece, his Athens, pulled back the curtains to offer the West an ideal.

The etymological root of *scholē* meant to halt or cease, hence to have quiet or peace. Later it meant to have time to spare or, specially, time for oneself. Of the great Greeks, Aristotle was the one who most often used the word *scholē*. For him life could be divided into different parts — action and leisure, war and peace. Citizens must be capable of a life of action and war, but even more able to lead a life of leisure and peace. Warlike states are safe only while they are fighting. A sword resting unused in the scabbard loses its temper. In any case it never had a temper for peace. Courage in battle is a virtue of limited use in peacetime. The legislator is to blame if he does not educate citizens to those other virtues needed for the proper use of leisure. A greater emphasis on temperance and justice should be taught them for times when they are faring exceptionally well and enjoying all that the world holds to be happiness. In war the virtues of men come forth for a united effort; in peace and prosperity men lose their temperance and justice toward one another and become overbearing. The greater the abundance of blessings that fall to men, the greater will be their need for wisdom, and wisdom is the virtue that cannot appear except in leisure.

So, the dangerous period is peace. Yet for Aristotle it was self-evident that just as a person would not want to be fighting all his life, so a state would not want to make war all the time. The end could never be war. It had to be peace. The good thing about peace was that it allowed leisure. But what was this precious leisure? If the legislator was to provide for it, he had to know what it was. Or how was he to keep leisure in mind with regard not only to what wars are fought for, but to all problems pertaining to the state?

In some cases it seems that leisure is another word for spare or free time. For example the well-to-do, says Aristotle, if they must attend to their private affairs have little leisure for politics and absent themselves from the assembly and the courts. In common usage *scholē* seems to have had this meaning. Aristotle apparently uses the same sense when he says the Spartans used their leisure to prepare for war. But one senses a different element, an ethical note, a hint that spare time when misused is not leisure. The case of the Helots who lived for one day only, the day on which they would massacre their masters, reveals that free time if shot through with fear is not leisure. Yet the clearest of the charges against Sparta is that against the women, whose time, though all free, became not leisure but license. Obviously time on one's hands is not enough to make leisure.

At one point Aristotle gives a rough equivalent of leisure. He speaks of it and then adds, "or in other words, freedom from the necessity of labor." This at a glance seems similar to the modern idea of free time — time off the job — but we would be well advised to go slowly here. The differences, though mainly in the nuances of words, reflect a different world. We can note to start that free time accentuates time; it sets aside a unit of time free of the job. In Aristotle's short definition time has no role. Leisure is a condition or a state — the state of being free from the necessity to labor.

Elsewhere Aristotle mentioned not labor but action as a contrast to leisure. He spoke of the life of leisure versus the life of action. By action here he intended activities toward other persons or objects in order to effect some purpose. He was using "action" in a common meaning, but, as he often makes clear, for himself a living being can hardly be anything but active. The gods live and therefore they too are active. Though invisible, even thought moves, even pure speculation, and so does contemplation, the activity of the gods. Indeed, thoughts and those who hold them are active in the fullest measure since it is they that move persons and things to the outward, visible kind of activity.

Leisure is active, then, though not necessarily a highly visible kind of activity. But what had Aristotle against labor that he made it almost the contrary of leisure? In Greek there are two common words for labor or work. One is *ponos,* which has the connotations of toil in our sense, that is, the sense of fatiguing, sweating, almost painful, manual effort. The other is *ascholia,* which is more like our idea of work or occupation in that it has less of the painful physical element. In origin the word really denotes the absence of leisure for its root is *scholē,* before which an *a-* is placed to signify a want or a lack. It thus means un-leisure or the state of being busy or occupied. This being at unleisure, though it seems a roundabout way of putting things, may be the closest to our phrase of being occupied or at work. The Spartan women, however, were free of the necessity of working, and still they had no true leisure.

The idea of occupation here is somewhat different from ours. We come closer to it when we speak of being occupied or busy, for the noun forms, both occupation and business (originally busyness), are further away from the idea, having come to be associated with work and the job. We can now rewrite the original definition thus: Leisure is freedom from the necessity of being occupied. This includes freedom from the necessity to labor, but it could also embrace any activity one finds necessary to perform, but would fain be free of. Here again we seem to be near a modern notion of leisure, as time in which a person can do as he pleases, time, perhaps, for amusement or recreation.

We would still do well to proceed cautiously. When Aristotle uses the word occupation, he cuts out the idea of "do as one pleases." An occupation is activity pursued for a purpose. If the purpose were not necessary, the activity would not occur. Therefore no occupation can be leisure, not even the self-employer's, whose purpose is self-chosen. Nor can leisure be anything related to an occupation. Amusement (*paidia*) and recreation (*anapausis*) are necessary because of work. They are not ends in themselves. Happiness does not lie in amusements, the things children do. In the *Ethics,* Aristotle says, "To exert oneself and work for the sake of amusement seems silly and utterly childish." Rather is it the reverse, that we take to amusements as relaxation. We need relaxation, for we cannot work constantly. We need amusements and recreation to restore, to re-create ourselves for our occupation. But the goal of being occupied should only be to attain leisure.

The distinguishing mark now begins to appear. Leisure is a state of being in which activity is performed for its own sake or as its own end. What Aristotle means by an end in itself or a final end he himself has demonstrated in the *Ethics:* clearly not all goals are final goals, though the chief good evidently is. Therefore, if there is only one final goal, this will be what we seek; if there are more than one, what we shall seek is the most final among them. Now that which is in itself worthy of pursuit we call more final than that pursued for the sake of something else, and that which is desirable not for the sake of something else we should say is more final than things that are desired partly for themselves and partly for the sake of some other thing. And we call final without reservation that which is always desirable in itself and never for the sake of something else.

Leisure stands in the last class by itself. It is not exaggerating to say that, as Aristotle is a philosopher of happiness, he is also a philosopher of leisure. Happiness can appear only in leisure. The capacity to use leisure rightly, he repeats, is the basis of the free man's whole life.

We can better see the logic of this conception if we ask, What is one to do in leisure? To play would be impossible. Play — at least for adults — belongs to the side of occupation: it relaxes the worker. It produces not happiness but the pleasant feeling of relief from exertion and tension. "Leisure is a different matter," Aristotle holds in the *Politics*. "We think of it as having in itself intrinsic pleasure, intrinsic happiness, intrinsic felicity. Happiness of that order does not belong to occupation: it belongs to those who have leisure." Occupations aim at some end as yet unattained; felicity is a present end and is attained by leisure in its every act and very moment. When Aristotle himself puts the question, it is clear that play is out, for he says, "With what kind of activity should we do (*skolēn agein*) our leisure?" We do not *do* our leisure with play, yet we do not *do* it with work. An occupation is not taken on as an end in itself, and play for adults is needed only to relieve work. Aristotle has an answer for his question. There are two activities he cites as worthy of the name leisure — music and contemplation.

These two things are not so limited as they may seem. To understand what Aristotle meant we shall have to go back to Plato. Aristotle was his pupil for twenty years, until Plato died as a matter of fact, and often — particularly in the case of contemplation — he neglects to give an introduction to a subject that Plato has already discussed fully.

But let us take music first, the subject of almost the whole of the last book of Aristotle's *Politics*. The matter at hand is education. Aristotle, we remember, was interested in education for leisure. He makes short shrift of reading and writing: they are useful for money-making, for housekeeping, for acquiring knowledge, and for some political activities. As for gymnastics: it fosters only the virtue of courage. Drawing: it helps men judge paintings correctly and thus buy them prudently. They are useful, these studies, but at the same time that is their defect: they are mainly useful. All branches of learning ought to be studied with a view to the proper use of leisure in cultivating the mind. Studies pursued with an eye to an occupation are to be regarded merely as a means or a matter of necessity. Now what purpose can the teaching of music have?

The first argument for music is tradition, an important argument for Aristotle as for Plato. Their forefathers made music a part of education, but neither because it was necessary — it is not — nor because it was useful. We are left with its value for cultivation of the mind in leisure. It ranks as part of the culture proper to free men. Homer's lines testify that only those should be summoned to the bountiful banquet who "call with them a minstrel, to please all men with his music." Amusingly enough, Aristotle almost rejects drawing as a leisure pursuit because it may be held *useful* in saving people from mistakes in their private purchases of works of art. Later, however, he admits it because it helps develop in the young an eye observant to beauty in form and figure. He relents generally on the other subjects too, for they also *can* be pursued in a liberal spirit. But the emphasis remains on music.

Plato is just as insistent. Whoever cannot hold his place in the chorus, he asserts in the *Laws*, is not really an educated man. To hold one's place meant to be able to sing and dance at the same time. In the *Republic* he fondly recalls the ancient times when education consisted of gymnastics for the body and music for the soul. For Plato music often signified the dominion of the Muses. For the ancients it was generally restricted to the vocal and instrumental, but in both cases the word music covered a much broader field than it does now. Today we think of the Greeks as philosophers and mathematicians. We remember their scientific side. In considering their artistic side we recall their poetry, architecture, and sculpture. We forget that we see their statues without color, that culture and education in Greece were more artistic than scientific, that mathematics declined, and the arts, both literary and plastic, bowed before music. Above all, the Greeks were and wished to be musicians. Music was for them almost a synonym for culture. Music in the dance gave the beat to gymnastics; in song it carried the meter of poetry, the only form archaic literature took; and in the march, Plutarch says, "It was a majestic and terrible sight that of the Spartan army marching to the attack to the sound of the flute."

Up to the sixth century B.C. Sparta was the musical capital of Greece, and by no means for martial music alone. Its magnificent calendar of holidays served up music in every refinement, admired in all Greece. It is difficult for us to realize the shame that Themistocles, the Athenian general and statesman, felt at a banquet when the lyre was passed around and he didn't know how to play it. Themistocles was a parvenu and had never received the fostering in poetry and music that Plato and Aristotle and Pindar told of. Book learning was far from their minds. To learn to play the lyre the pupil sat face to face with the musicmaster. He did not decipher flyspecks on a sheet of paper; he followed the dexterity of the master's fingers. In the classical epoch the child went to three masters. To the original two, the masters of gymnastics and music, a third was added — the master of letters, of the reading and writing and arithmetic that Aristotle depreciatingly called useful. But this third master eventually won out over the others to become, without further qualification, "the master" or "the instructor."

As yet, in the period of Socrates, Plato, and Aristotle, the adult educational forum to which a youth aspired was the symposium, the banquet, the club of friends. Here he conversed, ate, and then drank into the evening. And to every dinner partner, one by one, passed the myrtle branch to show each that his turn had come, tortuously but inevitably, to sing his song, the *scholion*, the fundamental, lyrical, literary genre to which other arts came round in intermezzi of the lyre, the pipes, and the dance.

Leisure or *scholē*, believed Newman, the student of Aristotle, meant being occupied in something desirable for its own sake — the hearing of noble music and noble poetry, intercourse with friends chosen for their own worth, and above all the exercise, alone or in company, of the speculative faculty. From what we have learned of those musicians, the Greeks, we would agree with him, though we would make explicit the *playing* of music, the *reciting* of poetry, and the *composing* of both. All these things fit the word Aristotle uses occasionally to describe the activities of leisure, namely, the cultivation of the mind (*diagōgē*). He used the word leisure in at least two senses, as we have seen — one as available time, the other as absence of the necessity of being occupied. It is not immediately clear whether in talking about *diagōgē* he is saying that in leisure you should cultivate your mind or that in the true state of leisure you cannot do anything but cultivate your mind.

So far I have not discussed contemplation, or what Newman described as above all the exercise of the speculative faculty. By going into this idea, we shall get a firmer grasp on what Aristotle meant by the cultivation of the mind and "freedom from necessity" in leisure, and the relation between the two. Contemplation in the Greek sense is so close to leisure that in describing one and the other repetition is inevitable. Plato first developed the idea in the *Republic*. His models were the Ionian philosophers, whose absorption in knowledge for its own sake inspired Plato's academy and Aristotle's Peripatetic school. Thales of Miletus was one of these philosophers. Plato has told us his story, of how gazing at the stars he fell into a well, and of the little maid who, standing by, laughed at the sport. The idea of contemplation itself in those days seemed to be groping for its true meaning. Our word comes from the Latin but the Latin is a translation from the Greek *theorein,* to behold, to look upon. *Theōria* was also the word for theory, and was used in the phrase "the theoretical life," which in Latin became "the contemplative life," both of which have a fast friendship with the life of leisure.

Contemplation for Plato and Aristotle was the best way of

truth-finding. They prized it above all other activities. It was the only activity in which they could picture the gods. The contemplator looks upon the world and man with the calm eye of one who has no design on them. In one sense he feels himself to be close to all nature. He has not the aggressive detachment or unfeeling isolation that comes from scrutinizing men and objects with a will to exploiting them. In another sense he is truly detached because he looks on none of them with intent to manipulate or control or change, on neither man nor beast nor nature. Whoever does look on the world with design, who wishes to subdue or seduce others, to gain money, to win fame, cannot see much beyond the slice he is cutting. His aim on the world puts lenses before his eyes. He doesn't even know his sight is distorted.

When Plato describes the ideal education of those who should be the rulers of the country, he has them passing every test and trial with honors, so that finally they can "lift up the eye of the soul and fix it upon that which gives light to all things." In contemplation they can see the essence of the good and take it for their pattern. They can see things and how they fit together so well because, as rulers, they are free of all necessity to take an oblique view. They do not have the compulsion of those who must make money or win honors. Take the mechanic or anyone who has to work for his living. He is the one who must watch his job and tools and his boss, who must have relief from toil and calculate how best to sell his wares or his services, and who gets caught up in a futile flurry of activities that lead nowhere. How can he see true and carry truth forward to the outer reaches of the cosmos circled by man's eye?

Contemplation, like leisure, or being itself leisure, brings felicity. Aristotle in the *Ethics* contends that happiness extends only so far as contemplation does. Those who can contemplate are the most truly happy. Indeed, happiness must be some form of contemplation. The activity of God, surpassing all others in blessedness, must be contemplative. Those men who most cultivate the mind are most akin to the gods and therefore dearest to them. The man in contemplation is a free man. He needs nothing. Therefore nothing determines or distorts his thought. He does whatever he loves to do, and what he does is done for its own sake.

There is one more Greek philosopher whose influence on the contemplative life was great, Epicurus, but his contribution comes in better at a later stage of our study. Thus far we can see how philosophers, in an interplay of *scholē* and the contemplative life, transformed a word meaning simple spare time into the classical ideal of leisure with all its sense of freedom, superiority, and learning for its own sake.

We begin to grasp how leisure is related to politics. If a man is at leisure only when he is free, the good state must exist to give him leisure. What he does in this leisure can be equated with what we today call the good life. Surprisingly few political philosophers have seen the connection between freedom and leisure as ends of the state. The prevalence of work in modern times, as we shall see, partly explains the oversight. Aristotle took it for granted: the life of leisure was the only life fit for a Greek.

FROM GREECE TO ROME

The ideal of leisure went into Rome, carried there largely through the works of Plato and Aristotle and Epicurus. In Latin the word for leisure was *otium,* and as in Greece its verbal opposite was formed by a negative prefix, *negotium.* In most Roman writers the question of leisure is posed in the pendulum of *otium* and *negotium.* Leisure lured them; they sang its praises chiefly in terms of the *beata solitudo,* blessed solitude in the country. The way of conquest, of organizing and building, prefixed their thought so that even in the days of the Empire Rome found itself unable to shake off its Catonic heritage. Seneca first gave the ideal real consideration, and he almost alone among Romans carried the standard forward. Cicero, who in this matter is typical of most Roman writers, rarely if ever leaves the track of *otium/negotium*. A man is occupied — in the affairs of army, commerce, or state, whatever — and then he rests and re-creates himself. Old age itself is a peaceful well-earned rest from on-the-go of *negotium*. Aristotle would not have called this leisure. *Otium* thus conceived is not for its own but for *negotium's* sake. As Seneca conceives it, though, it comes close to the contemplation of Aristotle and Epicurus.

Seneca, who knew Cicero's world well, wrote of him that he took to leisure when he was in political difficulties or in a petulant mood at not being appreciated by his associates as he thought he deserved. Pliny makes another example: the active life is his meat but he also feels leisure's tug. Vanity and duty, both, make him a victim of the thousand-things-to-do. He winds up wishing for leisure rather than enjoying it, and worries often of how to avoid the crime of inertia (*inertiae crimen*). Pliny likes the retreat in the country for cool reflection, the charms of nature, study, the hunt, and distraction and freedom from the city's demands — for the pleasures, after all, of nobles. He advises others to alternate *otium* and *negotium:* when tired of one, take to the other. So in one of his letters, Pliny reports that the city is in tumultuous holiday, and that during these wild days he finds his leisure in letters, which the others in their madcap pursuits miss. Pliny's pleasure comes actually from the external things around him, his notebooks and pamphlets. The sentimentalism of the atmosphere he expresses is philosophical rhetoric. Some of Martial's epigrams set a similar tone. The calm retreat by the sea, the house on the shore, the wood, the lake: with these he had had leisure to court the Muses. But greatest Rome wears him out. "Here when is a day my own?" he complains. "I am tossed on the high sea of city, and life is lost in sterile work."

Seneca sees through all the postures. He doesn't consider among the leisured the one who is a finical collector of Corinthian bronzes; or who flares up if the barber does not put his ringlets in place ("as if he were shearing a real man!"); or who gives banquets for which how diligently they tie up the tunics of pretty slave-boys, how anxiously they set out the silver plates, how carefully unhappy little lads wipe up the spittle of drunkards; or who bakes his body in the sun; or who becomes a laborious trifler over learning. It was a foible confined to the Greeks to inquire how many rowers Ulysses had, but now the passion had seized the Romans too, so that they asked such questions as, Who first induced the Romans to go on board ships? These are not the leisured, but mere busy idlers; they have only idle occupations, not leisure. Seneca touches Pliny and Martial more closely when he advises Lucilius by letter not to make bombast out of leisure. One way to make bombast is to hide out while letting everyone know you're hiding out and where. A man creates a legend about being a hermit, and the curious crowd mills around his retreat. If he wants to go into a retreat, it should not be to make people talk about him but to help him talk with himself for a change.

From thought and experience Seneca arrives at conclusions that bring him, though he was formally a Stoic, closer to Epicurus. In his essay on *The Shortness of Life* he gives examples of many busy persons, including Cicero, who seek *otium* not for itself but because they are fed up with *negotium,* who crawl up through a thousand indignities to the crowning dignity only to find that they have toiled for an inscription on a tomb. They cry out that they have been fools, and would henceforth live in leisure, but too late. All the great ones, like Augustus, long for leisure, acclaim it and prefer it to all their blessings. They can answer the prayers of mankind, yet their own prayer is for leisure. Augustus's conversation, even his correspondence with the Senate, kept reverting to his hope of leisure. Seneca concludes that the only men of leisure (*otiosi*) are those who take time for philosophy. They alone really live.

In later writings Seneca carries the theme further. From *Of Tranquillity* through *Of Leisure* to his *Letters,* the succession runs: first, a prelude to going into a life of leisure; second, the philosophical justification; third, the spirit of that life as it shines through to one who tries it. The young and the old, Seneca says, need leisure. No one can go without it. Only in leisure can one choose the model by which to direct his life. And he cites the case of Cato who threw himself into political life without realizing that liberty had already gone bad, that he was fighting only for a choice between tyrants, and that the winner could only be worse than the loser. In politics — we shall see later that the position, while different from both Stoicism and Epicureanism, yet has moved from the first toward the second — it is as if one were told the best life is to sail the seas, but then cautioned against ship-wrecks and sudden storms. In reality one is being instructed not to set sail. The wise man does not launch ship on the sea of politics: the state with its tempests is too likely to wreck him. This is true for the state to which one belongs by accident of birth. That other *res publica,* the universal one that embraces gods and men alike, that houses all corners of the world, that defines citizenship by the path of the sun — *that* one we can serve even in leisure, actually serve it even better in leisure. If this universal state we dream of can nowhere be found, leisure is necessary in spite of and without the state. For the perfect state, the one thing that might have been preferred to leisure, exists nowhere. What one should aim for is to be able to say, as Seneca expresses it in a letter, "I am free, Lucilius, free, and wherever I am I am myself."

In Seneca, the thought of the Greco-Roman world converges. Four centuries, from the second until the sixth, feel the influence of his drawing together and fusing Stoic thought with Greek writings on leisure and contemplation. Poetry and prose both profit from it. The emperor Julian, the last great defender of pagan ideals, solemnly declared that whoever tries to persuade us that the philosophical life, meaning the life of leisure and contemplation, is not superior to everything else, is trying to cheat us. We have reached, indeed gone beyond, the point where the trail leads back to Plato and then goes off through Plotinus and into Christianity and monasticism. Here the contemplative element was singled out. Yet leisure, with part of itself withdrawn into monasteries, still did not quit the garden for the cloister.

The ideal has had an enormous secular influence. One current runs through the Stoics, for they lived as though they were Epicureans, and from them into Cicero and Seneca who later pass northward, penetrating as far as the English schools to put a stamp on the English and on part, but a lesser part as we shall see, of the American character as well. Another current helped form the idea of the liberal arts out of that of the general culture. Much of the tenacity of the liberal arts (they survived the barbarian invasions) and their strange attraction (they won over Theodoric who was illiterate) comes from their freedom, the liberality of having their end in themselves.

We cannot follow all the ramifications. They would commit us to a world's history of leisure and contemplation. At best we can mention only some of the various figures and periods that touched the ideal, not so much leaving it with a distinct impress as taking away some of the brilliance to which the Greeks had polished it, and forgetting some of the bitter experiences the Romans sought to drown in it.

THE CHRISTIAN FOCUS

Christianity came into a world dominated by Rome; its book, the New Testament, was written in Greek. These obvious facts remind us of the innumerable contacts Christianity had with the Greco-Roman world. The Old Testament did not have a Greco-Roman heritage, so its chapters and verses need not be recalled here. The Greeks discovered leisure. No other language seems to contain the word with the meaning the philosophers gave it in Hellas. For this reason the most we could hope to discover in places untouched by Greece would be conceptions of spare time or free time, a meaning that the Greek word had too, of course, but which it sped far beyond. Nor can we hope to find the con-

cept among primitives, and much less among preliterate and illiterate peoples. The following chapters will occasionally refer to
a custom or saying of different times and places, but only in those
that come after Greece can we say that leisure has ever existed.
Nor does it sound too improbable to say that without the ideal
the practice cannot come to light.

Early Christianity kept well in mind what Jesus Christ had
said about the birds of the air: "They sow not, neither do they
reap nor gather into barns; yet your Heavenly Father feedeth
them. Are ye not much better than they?" (Matthew, vi : 26).
Christians were not to waste their time thinking, planning, and
working for the morrow. Is one not to work then, but to live in
leisure? "Consider the lilies of the fields, how they grow; they
toil not, neither do they spin." No. Work and wealth, true, can
be bad because their doing and getting fill the mind with cares
and leave no time or strength for the service of God. It is not Jesus'
warnings about work that affect the idea of leisure but His turning of men's hope toward God and the coming of the Kingdom.

The Greeks had said that the activity of leisure was contemplation, the highest of all activities because it was the part in man
that was godlike, that most distinguished him from the animals.
Contemplating is divine then because it is an activity like God's.
In Christianity the activity remains important less because of
itself than because of its focus. The contemplator is now divine
not because he contemplates but because he seeks to contemplate
God, even though as Bonaventura in speaking of the last step of
the *Itinerary of the Mind in God* says, "It is indubitable truth:
man cannot see Me and live." The result is that contemplation
becomes more specifically a seeking of religious truth, and less
of what Plato had in mind when he spoke of using the good discovered in contemplation as a model for the *polis*. For Plato,
though good and God cannot be separated, neither can the *polis*
be set apart. The good man thinks of the *polis*. For Jesus Christ
the *polis* was less important, being of this world, not the next.
Augustine in *De beata vita* says that the blessed life is to have

God, namely the Knowing God, the only one who had said, I am the truth. To have God, therefore, is to have the truth. The need that urges us to seek God, to remember Him, to thirst after Him, flows from the very fountain of truth.

In Christianity the search for truth remains. Christians should try to participate in it by contemplating. Later the architecture of the church, the height and spaciousness, the opening up of the heavens in the dome — all lend aid in contemplation to the humble churchgoer. For the patristic age the end was salvation, the other life. The first thing was to save one's soul, to bring it closer to God. Work in a sense was something one did in his free time. Any activities other than those bearing on salvation were strictly speaking not essential. Everyone was to try to contemplate, though not gifted for it. This too remains, that the activity of contemplation is the highest of all.

The monks, whose missions after the fall of Rome we shall look into in the next chapter, had ideas of work different from those of the pagans. Work, manual work in particular, became an instrument of self-purification, of repentance, or for helping others in charity. When the Kingdom did not appear as quickly as the earliest Christians believed it would, the organization of Christians on this earth called for attention. Work and the morrow received fuller consideration from learned men. Augustine considered that work best that distracted the least — handwork, tilling, small business. (Big business leads too easily to forgetting God.) The order in monasteries reflected a growing Christian doctrine, particularly among the Benedictines. The monks, though sometimes of noble station, worked with their hands. A hierarchy existed, however, that differed little from the ancient world's. Manual work went to the lay brothers, who were prohibited from spiritual work. Intellectual and artistic activity such as reading or illustrating manuscripts was most honored outside the monastery. It was greatly honored within the walls too, but high above it came pure contemplation, meditation on the divine.

In Romanesque cathedrals the figures of stone carved on the façade portray these beliefs in telling fashion. Those who work with their hands — the peasant reaping, the smith hammering, the wagoner leading oxen — fill the niches at the portals. High above them stand the exalted, stiffer statues, the images of contemplation and learning. Thomas Aquinas, summarizing the age in the *Summa Theologica*, draws this very scheme of things. Religious activity stands above secular activity, but contemplation above all else. The act in itself crowns man's highest faculty, the power to know the truth. The act by itself delights the actor. A man contemplates because he loves the truth and wishes to know and understand it. Since man's ultimate aim is to contemplate God face to face, an act that would give him perfect happiness, man in contemplating, in gazing on God in his mind, has an intimation of real happiness.

Thomas believed work to be a necessary part of nature. But given a surplus, a condition in which people can maintain themselves without all of them having to work, then a man is under no obligation to toil. Material work confines the worker to a small piece of the world. Contemplation — not all have the gift, of course — enables a man to see the divinity in the cosmos.

ALL HANDS SET TO MOTION

Between the Middle Ages and the Renaissance lies an arbitrary border, wide and blurry, drawn by historians. The end of one age and the beginning of the other show few clear-cut differences. The later Middle Ages, partly because they no longer could hope for the millennium, sought to work miracles of their own. Out of these times came an enormous production of magic, medicine, astrology, and alchemy. Men urgently wanted to know the earth, to understand its deepest structure, so as to transform it. In magic they first combine "to know" and "to do," and try the strangest experiments to discover nature's hidden affairs. A fragment of Epicurus's writings tells us that the wise man finds happiness in contemplating the order in immortal nature that never grows old. "Even though you are mortal by nature and limited by fate to a span of time," he wrote to his follower Metrodorus, "remember that by your reason you have reached infinite and eternal nature and contemplated that which is, that which will be, and that which was." In late medieval times, instead of delightedly accepting the eternal harmonious order to be discovered through contemplation, men intrude on nature actively, seeking to learn its laws and subvert the order, to move the stars from their course, to change the living and revive the dead, to win back that hope the world lost when religious miracles ceased. The wise man will dominate the stars, read a favorite inscription of thirteenth-century astrological texts. Almost gone was the voice of humility of an earlier Christianity, preaching to men to leave the stars to their Creator, not to try to know too much by thrusting their face at the sky, as if they yearned to climb the heavens, to keep in mind that *Scientia inflat, charitas aedificat,* that science blows up everything full of air, while love and charity build on solid foundations. The humble order founded by Francis of Assisi, the poet of *The Little Flowers,* counted among its friars Roger Bacon and William of Ockham, two indeed powerful proclaimers of man and the world's plasticity. From the twelfth to the fourteenth century men came to grips with the stars, stones, sand, plants, and animals, and, in experiment, sought their transformation.

The Renaissance by the fifteenth century was ready to turn these ideas into mature doctrine, a new and great one for the Western world. Thomas Aquinas had held that work on materials limited one's view. The Florentines, specially Marsilio Ficino, Alberti, Cellini, along with their close neighbor Leonardo and the southerner Giordano Bruno, express a diverse sentiment. The world exists to be transformed. Man's greatness, his divinity, lies not in his capacity for contemplation, but in his ability to subdue nature and bend her to his will. Work on materials is work on the world in microcosm. By his hands and tools man leaves behind the animal realm and draws nearer his higher spirit. Some writers have found this outlook in times prior to the Renaissance, particularly in Vergil. In the *Georgics,* it is true, the poet has told the tale of the rule of two gods. Under Saturn the earth was so bountiful that men didn't have to work and fell in a stupor. Later, with Jove, life became hard, rousing men from their dullness; necessity stirred them to work and invention, to lose not a minute, to furrow Mother Earth with iron and bring the fields to obedience. But the *Georgics,* it must be remembered, was an apologetic, written to help Augustus keep families from leaving the farm. Toil conquered all, Vergil said, but he could not refrain from placing an adjective after the word *labor — improbus —* "*wicked* toil."

The men of the Renaissance did have an independent and in many ways a conquering spirit. Their idea of work expresses their confidence and exuberance. Unwittingly, it sings the praises of the kind of work at which they excelled — the individual, craftsmanlike, artistic — be it as *condottiere,* sculptor, painter, architect or scientist. Their work required that hands touch materials. It was this non-agricultural manual labor they rescued from the contempt in which the ancient world had left it. They gave work the dignity the word craftsmanship carries still.

This concept of work did not make up the only thinking on the subject nor was it at first able to dominate the times. Another doctrine issued from the period's great love and admiration for the classics. In the Renaissance the intent to copy, to imitate, to preserve, the ancient world was as impressive as their failure to do so, yet the terms of the ancient debate bow onto the intellectual stage again. Besides *scholia/ascholia* and *otium/negotium,* another pair appears that suits the religious environment the concept had been living in. Cristoforo Landino brings out the subject in an imaginary dialogue between Lorenzo the Magnificent and Leon Battista Alberti — *vita contemplativa* versus *vita activa.* The discussion is set in the monastery at Camaldoli during four days in the summer of 1468. On the first day (which takes up the first book of the *Disputationes Camaldulenses*) the speakers, making use of the figures of Mary and Martha, reach agreement on the contemplative and the active life. The former must alternate with the latter and be its guide. With the second proposition Plato and Aristotle would have agreed; with the first, Cicero, Pliny, and Martial. Leisure, secular leisure, though still garbed in Biblical allusions, is back on the scene.

The sixteenth century rolls around. Increasing numbers have learned to admire, have acquired taste, marvel at creation. The well-born keep their hands as far away from common clay as did the Greeks. The classic tradition persists: if the many work, a few have leisure. Hadn't Thomas Aquinas held that, if it was not necessary, there was no obligation to work?

The decisive break appears in an unexpected quarter, the utopias. The time is ripe for it. The kingdom of God is no longer awaited on earth. The world's physical laws seem more malleable than when, a thousand years earlier, Bishop John Chrysostom wrote an energetic lady of Constantinople that peace was not to be found in becoming involved with the immutable laws of nature, which it had not been given us to force and change at our pleasure; instead it was given us to govern our will in its free speculations. The Renaissance was showing more progress each day in taming shrewish nature and changing her into a compliant beauty. A chancellor of Henry VIII's takes a step. He creates a land, *Utopia,* where no one works more than six hours a day. The shorter work week has arrived. But there is a catch. All must work. And take turns at all kinds of work, and do work both of the head and of the hand. There's no working of 6.05 hours by the majority, the .05 hours being added so that a handful don't have to work at all. The Work Society is on the horizon. After work the day is for rest or whatever one wishes. Free time has arrived too, it seems. A century later there is less work and more free time in Utopia. A Calabrian friar, Tommaso Campanella, founds the imaginary *City of the Sun,* where no one works more than four hours a day. Here too everyone works. Furthermore, everyone is trained in mechanical and manual labor. After work, people are free within the limits of the solar city's laws to play or study as they wish.

The great change has begun. The classical side of Renaissance thought gradually loses weight. The eighteenth century, a humane century, civilized, too, until its last decades, contributed to leisure the Venice of Canaletto and Guardi, whose refinement and luxury, life and art, attracted all of Europe. In the same century there also lived a Scottish philosopher named Adam Smith, and the succeeding century came over to his side. His book, *The Wealth of Nations,* advanced the thesis that an act is truly productive if it takes raw material and makes it into something useful to man. Work like this is actually the beginning of wealth. The real producers are the workers. The idle produce nothing.

Adam Smith's notion resembles that of the Florentines, but Smith had seen factories. In his time power machinery had already taken hold. The way work was changing would not have pleased Leonardo, nor Cellini, not if they themselves had to be the workers. It was a kind of work they had not bargained for — tied to other men as in galleys, tied to machines by the clock, and paced by an unseen boss. This was the new order of things. The classical economists and democrats took over the idea, the anarchists found it just right, the socialists embraced it — all varieties of socialists: the communists, the Christian, utopian, and scientific. Of course, each used a different emphasis, but for all work was good or would become so, was the right of every man, and a duty as well. The philosophic doctrine they held in common was that through work and work alone does man produce and know. The doctrine was that of the Renaissance, the actual time was that of the nineteenth century; the ideal of leisure had long before taken its exit.

As this brief review has indicated, and later chapters will show, no one has thought about leisure so well as the Greeks. If this were the only sphere in which they were so capable, we could ask ourselves how it happened that they were able to go so far with the idea. But they excelled in so many things that the question would soon evaporate into the whole of Greek culture. A similar limit applies to what has already been said about the great thinkers and their ideas. Leisure as a concept plays so basic a role in their systems of thought — Aristotle and Seneca of course are good examples — that to extract it even for a moment may distort the meaning for the reader. To some extent I hope to correct or at least lessen the inadequacies by further reference to the history of leisure and work both as ideal and practice. The emphasis now changes. The stress is on work.

Toward the Work Society

The existence of slavery in ancient Greece must be faced. Still, it would be a mistake to jump to the conclusion that the ideal of leisure was far from the practice, or to deride it as hypocrisy. Slavery was part of the very foundation of the ideal. The classical Greeks wanted to be wise. To be wise one had to have leisure. Not everyone could have leisure. The body needs food and shelter and to get them requires work. But work is neither the noblest nor the most distinguished activity of man. All animals seek food and shelter. Man alone can think, reason, and invent. If some men at least could be freed from mundane occupations, they might soar to remarkable heights, and at the same time help lift up to a higher level even those whose workaday life kept them pinned to the ground, where vision is limited.

The free males of Athens, the citizens, numbered about 25,000. The slaves were four times that many. This did not mean that each citizen was a man of leisure supported by four slaves. Many slaves were taken into factories, mines, and the lower public offices as well as into rich households as private servants. The poor citizen had no slaves. He would have found the maintenance to say nothing of the purchase of one out of his reach. As

Aristotle remarks at the close of the *Politics,* the only slave the
poor man had was his wife.

Athenian policemen were slaves. There were slaves who lived
by themselves and paid their masters only an annual rent. In the
factory system of the day there were gangs of slaves, supervised
by slaves, who split their profits after paying their master his
rent. The poor free man might be a farmer, shoemaker, carpenter or trader. Like the slave, though in lesser degree, he was
bound to his work. Whoever has to work for a living is blocked
on the road to wisdom and suffers, as far as leisure is concerned,
the fate of slaves.

Thus when Aristotle states his case for slavery (which might
well have been a case against slavery, so moderate is it for the
times), we can treat his argument as similar to that he would
have made for the man who was free but too poor to own slaves
or property. There are men born to toil and others born to live
the life of leisure. If the two groups are linked by a moral bond
as in the family or household, then even those who work receive
the benefits of those who do not. To be attached to a master is
the best thing that can happen. The master, detached from lowly
cares, is free for higher things; the slave receives from him —
from the musician, the statesman, the thinker — what he could
never himself create. As a result he is brought into a life more
human, more refined, than ever he could have reached himself.
The gain the slave and worker receive is so great that payment
for it by toil is negligible in comparison. They are beneficiaries
of the partnership.

The slave was not a Greek. Typically he was imported from
Asia Minor and brought to Attica by the slave traders. Since the
Greeks considered Asia Minor to be an inferior culture, they
found it easy to believe their slave was by nature inferior. But
they did not mark him by emblems or dress to an inferior status,
nor did the state leave him unprotected from ill treatment.
Emancipation was not difficult; slaves sometimes bought their
own freedom. Many of them were used in households as tutors

for the young. In fact, before the coming of public schools, the method of early education was typically composed of instruction by household slaves.

Slavery was accepted in Greece in a way difficult for us to comprehend. The word did not have for the Greeks the connotations our experience has given us. Politically slavery was almost a neutral matter. Without touching on it, one could favor a monarchy, a tyranny, or a democracy. Plato, for example, remarks that in democracy the slaves become as lax as their masters. If the master is shameless and impudent, so is the slave. There was obviously no great gulf separating master and slave.

In Rome, too, slaves were used as tutors. Often they were Greeks, so one could say the Romans had better tutors than the Greeks had. The slave's lot in Rome, however, was a harder one. The Romans did not have two simple classes of "us" versus "barbarians-fit-for-slavery." The Greeks were clearly not barbarians. The Romans had to make finer distinctions among their slaves. By and large their treatment of slaves differed widely and according to distinctions of culture, learning, and skill.

One can imagine the life of the Greek or Roman free farmer or worker: much like that of a European farmer or *metayer* today in an area where mechanization of farming has not yet taken over, or like the life of an artisan — an ironworker, carpenter or bookbinder, perhaps — working with tools similar to those in use in colonial America. In parts of the world many such farmers and craftsmen yet exist. Hesiod, the Greek poet, described the life of the farmer. It has a special interest. His *Works and Days* reveals a world far from the city, and a way of life that took little from the city.

Hesiod precedes Aristotle in time, which means that he appears on the Greek scene at an earlier point in the evolution of the Greek city-state. We can take from him, then, an inkling of the meaning of work and leisure in a rural agricultural economy. It is not what Aristotle talked about. He who farms the land with his bare hands and animals works hard. He never expects a life of leisure. The mere idea is alien to his way of thinking. Leisure is something that can be attained by man's ingenuity, but the farmer expects to have only such spare time as weather and seasons allow him. Hesiod sings a song to this life, but it remains a life tied to necessity. If food is what men need, someone will have to farm for it. Without farming, we cannot live.

Socrates seems closer to Hesiod than Aristotle. This is the impression Xenophon gives in his *Recollections of Socrates,* which, at least for the philosopher's everyday side, drew a faithful likeness. Socrates is full of advice on how by doing some work we can resolve problems. He quotes the poet Epichamus: The gods sell us all good things for labor. He cites the story of Hercules who had to choose between easy Vice and hard Virtue. He quotes Hesiod: Vice can be found with ease, but before the temple of Virtue the immortal gods have placed labor. In fact it was, among other things, a verse of Hesiod's that got Socrates into trouble: "Work is no disgrace, but idleness *is.*" In the use of this ground to help condemn to death a well-known man the temper of Greek times reveals something of itself. Artisans and artists fascinated Socrates. He liked to wander in and out of their shops, questioning and concluding and pressing on to further questions, and always to talk with others about carpenters, shoemakers, and smiths. When he counseled persons to stoop to work, the tone changed: try a little work; it won't hurt you as much as you think, and just a little of it may solve your problem. But Socrates did not glorify work; he sometimes recommended it in small doses. He himself did no work, large or small.

Hesiod in singing the life of the soil goes further than Socrates would have gone, and he praises virtues other than those loved by Homer. The fighting man and the hunter and their virtues are outside Hesiod's world. Yet one can live, as well as die, by fighting and hunting. Between the battle and the hunt the warrior and hunter take their ease and pleasure. In Homer's world there is the cup filled to the brim, there are maids to bathe heroes, there is music, song and dancing, games with balls, lances, and weights, boxing, wrestling, running, fencing, and that noblest sport of all, chariot racing. They are not free of necessity, though, these warriors, any more than the farmer. The battle does not always go their way: the *Iliad* reports the games held in honor of Patroclus, at his funeral.

The farmer's life is dominated more by the elements. He cannot escape them to join the city dweller in companionable life, indoors, free of the fear of frost or blight and of not getting the crops in on time. The farmer lives his life taking time whenever he can. Since he cannot master the elements on which he depends, he cannot be free for leisure. His work is important for those who have leisure, and all others beside — and so Hesiod lauds it. But he laments it too. In the Socrates of Xenophon work is an expedient. In Vergil's *Georgics* it is a necessity, and a mock heroism. In Hesiod's *Works and Days* it is a necessity too, and, worse yet, a curse.

To the authors of the Bible also work is necessary because of a divine curse. Through Adam's fall the world was become a workhouse. Paradise was where there was no toil. This is the feeling about work one encounters in most of history's years. Unavoidable, but nonetheless a curse. God himself worked to produce the world, or so King James's translators rendered the passage in the Old Testament, but this working had another meaning. To work can mean to fashion, as God fashioned or formed the earth, and fashioning can require rest, as God needed rest after His self-appointed task.

The word we use today to signify exerting oneself to gain a livelihood has become broader and lighter. The term more in evidence years and centuries ago was labor. Today "labor" has the sense of strenuous exertion; in the past that is what it meant. "Toil" has an almost painful sense to it, and that, too, was what the word meant in centuries gone by. Work, on the other hand, had many meanings and could be used to refer to religious "good works," to "works of art," or to the "working" of wine. Not until the late nineteenth century did it become the comprehensive word it is today, containing in one bushel basket all forms of exertion. The English word "work" has so wide and rich a range and so varied a past that a mere catalogue of its senses would be several pages long. The encroachment of work was gradual. In Mark Twain's day the word had not yet been applied enough to the field of politics so that he could use the phrase "a political worker" without adding quotes.

Before the nineteenth century's close, if you worked, you labored or toiled, and if you did other than these, you did not *do* something; you did not work as you do today; you *were* something — a carpenter, mason, soldier, physician. One's work then was rarely called work. The various things people did conveyed no such unity of feeling. Evidently they were so different they were not grouped under the one label of work. In common usage today, however, work is the generic term. It takes in all washing. Moreover, unless accompanied by the proper adjectives, the word no longer calls forth the image of sweat and pain, of labor under the sun. The old expression "a working-day face" has little sure meaning for us; we would hesitate before associating it with doleful madrigals. Even God can work today because work has also lost its odor of inferior status.

THE MEDIEVAL FRONTIER

Certainly machines have lightened man's burden, and this makes one good reason for the change in the meaning of the word work. The working-day world has fewer briers than it had before. But the word began to change long before the load was lightened. In Egypt, Greece, and Rome, the sense of work remained labor and toil. Undoubtedly the word had its ups and downs — in commercial times work often climbs in esteem — but the ups and downs were of small amplitude compared to the wide sweep we are now tracing.

Perhaps it was first in the Middle Ages that the fermentation began. The world had once more been brought back to a rural condition. The cities had fallen and been reduced. Along with its aqueducts, Rome's population fell. In the second century A.D. it had been over 1,200,000. By the early Middle Ages it had dropped to twenty or thirty thousand. People lived under frontier conditions, and frontier life demands work — of men, women, and children.

The monasteries, it seems, led the way. In the West the most influential order was that of St. Benedict. His rule for monks, composed in the early sixth century, commanded them to engage in steady manual labor, thereby establishing a precedent in monastic history. "Idleness is the enemy of the soul" begins Rule XLVIII. "And therefore, at fixed times, the brothers ought to be occupied in manual labor, and, again at fixed times, in sacred reading." Work in those days usually meant laboring in the fields. Monks were not to grieve if the needs of the place or poverty demanded they labor at the harvest. If they lived by the labor of their hands, as did their fathers and the apostles, then were they truly monks. Under the rule of St. Benedict work took a more important place than it did under St. Pachomius or St. Basil. Directly religious duties can scarcely have taken more than four or five hours on weekdays. The remaining hours on a daily average numbered about six for labor and four for reading. Benedict was not a fanatic, however; his rule was marked by reasonableness. Let all things be done with moderation, he would say, because of the fainthearted. And while work came to occupy more time than church service, the celebration of canonical office was the monks' first duty. Nothing preceded it.

The Middle Ages were a time of pioneering. Although the drama of the destruction of the aqueducts to Rome is what leads us to picture a world collapsing dramatically to barbarian invasions, the deterioration of the Empire had long been going on. Without water Rome could not sustain its huge population. But in the West the turning back of the clock to a rural society had begun long before.

Decentralization began with the Empire still on its feet. The great landowners, influential with the Senate, indeed part and parcel of it, through privileged tax positions and other means, swelled their holdings at the expense of the city dwellers and small farmers. Little by little many of the newly propertyless were absorbed in huge rural estates, whose landlords, the *potentiores*, were thus supplied with small armies and a fixed labor supply. Others of the dispossessed went over to live with the barbarians, preferring their hard justice to the Roman government's corruption. As early as A.D. 328, Constantine had admitted that the most powerful *potentiores* could be checked only by the Pretorian Prefect and the emperor himself. At the end of that fourth century not even the imperial government could control them. By the middle of the fifth century, when the Marsilian priest Salvian was writing his *De Gubernatione Dei*, a fierce attack on the *potentiores*, the West was already cast in the feudal mold — on the one hand, great proprietors, on the other, tenants who lived on land not theirs, who performed services and paid taxes, most often in kind, and took their orders from their lords.

Though towns continued to exist in the West, and five centuries later new or rebuilt ones grew up, for a thousand years to come life and civilization was largely to be simple, agrarian, and rural. And at its dim beginnings there was very little to go on. Men had given up their freedom to gain food, shelter, and protection, the social security of an overlord. It was not really an exchange of freedom for serfdom, for when the exchange was made there was serfdom on both sides. Freedom and prosperity and a good life were mostly ancestral memories. The new world with a new religion and a new way of living had to go forward by itself, step by step, to win its own kind of freedom.

The first to push out were the monks. They had drunk more deeply than others of the new religion of Christianity. Perhaps the strength in Augustine's philosophy had affected them. Certainly the Rule for Monks fortified them, and certainly the Church in Rome remained as their background and symbol.

Conceive if you can of Europe without central political authority, of a Church better organized than the state, of the philosophy of Augustine which made of the state a junior partner, of the spirit of Christianity mobilized in a hierarchy of active bishops. Think also of vast rural areas where the Romans and Celts blended together with Germanic newcomers. Here was the first zone for the conversion of the pagan. Once the peasants had been won, the next field was ready to be tried, the vast terrain of Ireland, England, Scotland, Iceland, Germany and Scandinavia. The people here were often hostile and brutish, and life was nasty — certainly according to those who had memory of imperial Rome. The peasants, while perhaps no shorter on intelligence than anywhere else, had no ear for the notes of classical literature, nor for a learned theology, much less for the possible delights of a life of leisure according to Aristotle.

What was needed was men, legions of men, willing to take on the job of demonstrating a superior way of life. The cities were gone and could not serve as communication centers for the irradiating new spirit. The strategy called for these legions of men to scatter out over the map of Europe, self-reliant men who knew how to face danger and death, who could make do, who could take whatever religious feeling was at hand, be it in a pagan peasant or a pagan temple, and turn it to good use in teaching virtue and worship, not doctrine, and in showing what material advantages, too, the intelligent, energetic Christian held in his grasp.

Thus flew the spark toward a new ideal of work. Classical tradition played no part in it. Indeed a contrasting view took hold: labor, manual labor, too, is good for the soul. As the army of missionary monks went out to build monasteries among barbarians and wildernesses, they had to prove their superiority. They had to work with peasants, to share in the labors of plowing and planting, cleaning away forests, and building houses. Think again, this time of a landing party of monks, with a solid boat, their beginning to reclaim land and clear away trees, to build stone buildings in the Italian tradition, to plant vineyards, work metals finely, seek out herbal medicines, set up mills. Wouldn't such skill and zeal in labor be the talk of the countryside?

The beacon of Greco-Roman thought and learning never went out, of course, and burned its flickering brightest in Italy. But in the north it wavered feebly for long to come. Not that men glowing with missionary spirit had no access to it; they preferred to learn, develop, invent, or put to use other things — the wheeled plow, vaults and cupolas, the three-field system, horseshoes and collars, saddles and stirrups, water mills, the crank, seignioral government and a vast body of theoretical literature on the rights and freedoms of state, church, individuals, kings, princes, slaves, and women.

In Italy, where the Renaissance first appeared, classical learning seemed more essential to the energetic men of Florence. That imaginary dialog between Alberti and Lorenzo the Magnificent fits the classical mood. The fifteenth and sixteenth centuries looked on the gothic ones with contempt. So far had Renaissance men been freed by those prior centuries that they no longer acknowledged their debt, indeed saw their inheritance as chains, and looked to the glories of a remoter past for inspiration. Looked to, but, try as they might, they could never bring themselves to make a copy of their ancient models; so Leonardo, Galileo, Michelangelo, and Brunelleschi stooped to do things with their hands that only a mechanic in Greece would have done. The Renaissance, as the foregoing chapter told, brought forth a new philosophy of work, leaning more on *praxis* than *theoria,* moving away from *scientia contemplativa* to *scientia operativa.* The honorable position the monks gave labor could not be shed so quickly, not even in Italy, any more than could another monkish innovation that went so well with work — the clock.

Perhaps because they sensed that manual work was so unusual a demand to make of monks, the Benedictines worked out a regular system of work and prayer or meditation. To some monks, as to Frère Jacques of the time-honored round, the bed felt good in the cold, early morning. To others, contemplation, which did not die with the Greco-Roman world, seemed to be the more appropriate activity for a religious man. St. Thomas had insisted on it. So bells and clocks were used as never before to pull monks out of bed, to send them off to prayers and then to the fields, to mark off the time for work and prayer and contemplation.

To Luther, himself a monk, certain doctrines of the Church of Rome were dangerous for the soul, but not the praise of work that the monasteries had given to the world. Indeed the prospering monasteries by this time had begun to let manual work out to others. They had their own serfs, whose life, too, was now run by the bells. The original idea, though, was sound — to work is to serve God — sound not alone for Luther, but later for Calvin and Wesley as well.

The Reformation's ideas of work have been examined by many scholars. It was, in fact, one of the most intense areas of historical study in the first half of the twentieth century. Many points of controversy sprang up — whether religious ideas or industrial necessity first created the new idea of work, whether its first flowering was in Catholicism or in Protestantism, whether work is less prominent for the reformers than other doctrines were, and so on. With or without saying so explicitly, however, most students agreed that out of the Reformation came a new atmosphere. Labor commanded a new tone. Once, man worked for a livelihood, to be able to live. Now he worked for something beyond his daily bread. He worked because somehow it was the right or moral thing to do.

It is outside our limits to trace the spread of this work ethic or gospel of work, as it much later came to be called, over Germany, England, Scandinavia and elsewhere in Europe. We are chiefly interested in the fact that it eventually reached the United States, there to obtain the fullest expression. Perhaps the linking of work to God is no longer so clear as it once was, yet we can certainly see that the shadows of the great reformers fell over the idea of work in America. Here, all who can must work, and idleness is bad; too many holidays means nothing gets done, and by steady methodical work alone can we build a great and prosperous nation. Here, too, work is good for you, a remedy for pain, loneliness, the death of a dear one, a disappointment in love, or doubts about the purpose of life.

Today the American without a job is a misfit. To hold a job means to have status, to belong in the way of life. Between the ages of twenty-five and fifty-five, that is, after school age and before retirement age, nearly 95 per cent of all males work, and about 35 per cent of all females. Being without a job in prosperous times is bad enough, but being without one in a depression is worse yet. Then the American without work — or the German or Englishman — is a damned soul. Various studies have portrayed the unemployed man as confused, panicky, prone to suicide, mayhem, and revolt. Totalitarian regimes seem to know what unemployment can mean: they never permit it.

The modern doctrine of work affects all countries that try to solve their problems by industrialization. It has migrated to Russia, to China, India, and will make inroads on every modernizing nation, for work cannot be made methodical, rational or impersonal without the addition of some incentive besides the schoolbook triumvirate of food, clothing, and shelter. After the triumph of the United States in World War II — so heavily attributed to massive industrial productivity — the work ethic along with so many other things American was imported by countries all over the globe at an accelerated pace. In not a few nations new constitutions were drawn up. The very first article of one of these proclaims that the country is "a democratic republic based on work." It is hard to recognize from this definition the same Italy where the fervor of laboring monks had least shaken the Greco-Roman ideal of tranquillity, where Lorenzo and Alberti had agreed that the contemplative life must take an active life by the hand, where Thomas Aquinas had raised contemplation again to the skies, and where Venice had become the queen of serenity. Other countries have made similar constitutional provisions, as though the saying would make it so. The American influence was indirect; the more direct pressure for a work clause usually came from the communists or socialists. In Italy today even the newest recruits to an industrial life, unskilled workers coming up from the south to cluster in and around the big cities, will say almost in unison that what one has to do in this life to make one's way is, "work." The latest version of the bill of rights for mankind, the UNESCO Declaration of Human Rights to which almost all nations have put a signature, proclaims, "Everyone has the right to work."

THE WORKLESS

There have always been restraints to work, moral and legal brakes that have tried to prevent runaways at smash-up speed from destroying things people set store by. There have always been well-accepted canons of what work should not do to a man. It should not ruin his health, either physical or mental. Much of early labor legislation was designed to eliminate accidents and bad light or ventilation in work places. Nor should work ruin a man's family. Legislation against child labor or to protect pregnant working women falls in this category. Work also cannot be allowed to destroy existing communal loyalties with impunity. Working for the enemy, unless governed by legal formula like the Geneva convention, is dangerously close to treason. At times governments have prevented the exit of special workmen or technicians on pain of imprisonment or death. Furthermore, work cannot violate explicit religious precepts. One of the oldest and firmest is the injunction against working on the Sabbath.

Religion and the state have a voice in maintaining all these restrictions on work, in relaxing them in an emergency and in taking up the slack when health and family seem imperiled once again.

By and large, then, church and state protect things of greater importance from work's inroads. They have to use discretion, however. The range of this discretion is what makes so plausible the thesis that industrialism or capitalism could not develop without a change in religious emphasis. It also makes clear why a religious or state blessing on work is necessary in all countries that wish to modernize themselves. Practical theologians never lost their concern for the health and welfare of individual and family; different considerations simply came into play; otherwise — and this remains a problem today — some of the harmful results of work were not obvious. Admittedly sometimes there were none so blind as pastor and priest. Still, it often happens that the effects of working conditions are hard to see. Take sedentary work, for example. What are its effects on diet, the spinal column, length of life, or the forms of disease?

If sedentary work will serve as a health example, the case of working mothers will serve to illustrate how difficult it may be to see the effects of work on the family. Though we shall consider the case more fully later, it directs our attention for the moment to this question: If there are legal and moral restraints on work, can we see them reflected in the groups of people who do not work? Who in the United States today does not work?

One group we can discard as irrelevant to the purpose at hand — the unemployed. The unemployed in modern terms are those who seek work but for one reason or another have not found it. What of the young? Up to the age of fourteen they are not even counted as being in the labor force. The old, too, do not work. The proportion of persons in the labor force today after the age of sixty-five drops rapidly — from nearly all men between twenty-five and fifty-four years to about one third of those who have passed their sixty-fifth birthday. As for females, they are not as much a part of the working force as men. For every six of them working there are nearly ten men, and the men are more likely by far to be holding full-time jobs. Nor, of course, do the sick have to drag themselves off to work. The proportion of the labor force at home sick (the temporarily as well as the permanently disabled) is about 1⅓ per cent. Here then is where we find the workless: in the young, the old, the female, the invalid. We say "workless" instead of "unemployed" to emphasize that in the present case these persons do not seek work but are without work because it is part of the law or custom of the land that they should or need not work.

Outside of these groups, though, is there anyone who is workless because he wants to be workless? What of the rich? Offhand one can maintain that they too work, even though they don't have to for a living. To search for a workless man among one's friends and acquaintances makes for an illuminating experience. In Europe anybody can still name a dozen. In the United States one has to search as hard as Diogenes to discover even two. A workless man today is no easier to find than an honest man was in his time.

To back up these assertions with more than impressions is not easy. If, however, we take property other than real or personal to indicate no need to work for a livelihood, we can assume that most such property exists in the form of stocks, and then look to see whether among stockholders there are many who in the occupation column wrote "none." We find that, except for housewives, almost all stockholders have income from wages, salaries, or fees. Indeed, the great majority have greater income from work than from dividends. Those families whose other income is already over $10,000 make up over half of all stockholders. Nonemployed adults holding stock number about 30,000 out of 6.5 million stockholders, or about 0.4 per cent. Is this a leisure class, these "nonemployed adults"?

Another procedure would be to observe the rich families in the United States to see whether any of their offspring are lolling about, openly declaring their disinclination for work. Here too the search would not prove rewarding. They are all busy being bankers or lawyers or taking care of their investments and real estate or doing something equally productive. If they are not, they give that impression. If they gave any other impression, like that of spending their lives enjoying themselves, they would soon earn the appellation of playboy, a word nasty in itself and smacking of unAmericanism or at best the international set. Luther's denunciation of living on income or rents or interest as unworthy of the name work perhaps continues to have its effect.

There used to be a kind of person in America who openly proclaimed his aversion to work. The type, though not already gone from sight, seems to be going fast. He is or was called the hobo. He seems even to have had some intellectual justification for his way of life. Though the justification never reached a high level, it was undeniably based on the ancient idea that if one has not wealth, he might yet avoid work by cutting down his requirements of life. The hobo took pride in the fact that he only worked when he needed to to keep alive, or was forced to by superior strength. The hobo's numbers have been cut down by adverse changes in transportation and the law, by the elimination of boxcars and the applying of vagrancy ordinances. Diogenes today would have even further obstacles to contend with. If the barrel he lived in were to rest anywhere on ground, that ground would be private or public. In the first case he would be trespassing, in the second he would be obstructing traffic or disturbing the peace or violating the city's hygiene ordinances. But neither laws nor technical change can bottle up all modern aversion to work. Each generation will have its protestants: their names will change, and often their number; their ways of expression will change too in the effort to cope with the changing laws and technology of work.

Whether one is rich or poor the chance of escaping work today is slim. The pressures toward it are too great, the lack of comprehension of not working is too complete. One is not appalled or indignant on learning that another doesn't work; one simply does not understand, doesn't know where next to turn for conversation, cannot size up the ostensibly human object standing there. Thus can one appreciate the misery in which many aristocrats live in other countries well on their way to industrialization, the politely contained persistence with which they seek a post, the sense of futility they have in feeling they are fit for no job, the elation with which they tell, one fine day, that, hard as it may be to believe, they are working!

Of course, aristocrats once worked. Once they were under attack, however, whatever it was they did was redefined as being useless or nonproductive activity. Saint-Simon set things so straight for France at the beginning of the nineteenth century that Veblen, at its end, could state the same attitude for the United States. Saint-Simon was the first technocrat. He was the first to take to using the adjective *industriel* in phrases such as *la révolution industrielle*. His education was broader than Veblen's; so, consequently, were his heroes — the men of science, the fine arts, and the professions. Suppose that France suddenly lost the best of them all, he says, including also the best businessmen, farmers and artisans, whom he considered workers no less than manual laborers. France for a generation at least would be a corpse. These men are the flower of French society, contribute most to its glory and prosperity, are the most useful. Suppose now that France instead lost Monsieur the King's brother, Monseigneur le Duc de Berry, and so on down through Madame la Duchesse de Bourbon and Mademoiselle de Condé, all the great officers of the royal household, all the ministers without portfolio, all the councillors of state, all the chief magistrates, marshals, cardinals, archbishops, bishops, vicars-general, and canons, all the prefects and subprefects, all the civil servants, and judges, and, in addition, ten thousand of the richest proprietors who live in the style of nobles. Tender-hearted persons would grieve, but the loss would amount to nothing, for princes, bishops, prefects, and idle landowners contribute nothing. They hinder science, monopolize prestige, and eat up taxes. Their activities are of no use to the nation.

Aristocrats would not themselves have used the term work to describe their activities because the word's usage in their time was different. Boswell in his *London Journal* rarely uses the word work in any sense whatever, yet throughout almost all that period he was in the condition of what we would today call looking for a job. His daily writing we would today call work, and say that when he was "at work" on his journal he was "working." His intellectual pursuits we would also call work, for a professor works, so does a scientist. Boswell was seeking a commission in the Royal Footguards. Does an officer work? Here once more we come up against the fact that however much work may have become the touchstone of modern life, there is gold left that cannot be corrupted. It is true that we speak of a soldier or a clergyman as working, an artist, diplomat or physician too, yet would we call them job holders? We might, but with some uneasiness. These occupations somehow have too shady a past to have a clear work status.

To the job each person gives what he is paid to give. What comes out of it depends more or less on his own effort. Up to the diminishing returns of fatigue, the more one works the more one measurably produces. In the liberal pursuits or professions, a responsibility exists that goes beyond the money paid for the job, and though it may not go as far as claiming one's life, as Ruskin pointed out forcefully, at least it goes by the honorable name of duty. A soldier may have to die for his country no matter how poorly he is paid. How much money an artist gets will not make his effort a greater or lesser work of art. A physician or lawyer should fight for his patient's or client's life even if he is paid but two cents. A professor cannot teach what he does not himself profess; nor, paid more, teach better.

Besides the sense of responsibility in these pursuits there is another element that distinguishes them from mere job holding. What they do does not depend on themselves entirely. The scholar who works steadily is not necessarily better than the one who applies himself spasmodically. Hard work may be necessary in both cases but the touch that makes one a good scholar and the other a drone comes from another source than work. In the physician's case it may not usually be so simple as the view expressed in the proverb, God cures the patient, and the doctor collects the fees, yet the "something" in a good doctor does not depend entirely on his assiduousness in medical school — as particularly with the internist. Even clearer is the case of the playwright or painter. Hard work undoubtedly, but are the Muses a fiction? Why then speak of inspiration? Traces of these things are still discernible in word usage. The professions or liberal pursuits are compensated differently. Some would say they are compensated less, and this may often be the case, for reasons to be gone into later. But the doctor collects a fee; he does not work for wages nor get so much a piece. The artist is commissioned to do a work of art. The clergyman really receives living expenses, an honorarium. How much should he be worth in wages for ministering to souls? Salary, too, is a word that has honorific vestiges, originally being used to designate the Roman soldier's salt. Salary is now the ordinary remuneration of diplomat or professor, and of the clerical occupations, also, in a reflection of their historic link with the once rare skill of the scribe, the understanding of cryptic signs on flat surfaces.

MONKS IN THE FACTORY

If, then, in word usage, in the moral and legal restraints on work conditions, and in the actual composition of the labor force, we find opposition to the thesis that work towers over all else of value in the modern world, perhaps we should re-examine the work ethic to see just how pervasive it ever was or really is. Did it, as Max Weber once claimed, make every man a monk? That monks in general were model workers seems to be a fairly late Protestant notion. The Council of Trent debated how to correct their high and easy living, not their excessive industry. The mere mention of the *fabliaux* and the *Decameron* recalls what opinions circulated in Catholic countries, as far back as the late Middle Ages and early Renaissance, about monkish work habits.

A phrase yet current in Italy describes the monk as a cowled idler. To rephrase the question, then: Did the work ethic at any time ever permeate the working class?

Any question whatever about the sentiment of the working or poorer class at any time in history is difficult to answer. Until recently, a serious portrait of the poor, even in literature, was unheard of. As in Shakespeare's plays, they were usually put in to inject a note of levity or buffoonery. Today, with all the presumed improvements in methods of social investigation and research, the workers somehow defy detection and examination. In public opinion polls they are usually underestimated; in political studies they vanish into apathy; in sociological studies they prefer silence or evasion, leaving the stage to others more practiced in reading and writing. Like the slaves of antiquity, workers stay in the shadow of the public realm.

For this reason I regard with suspicion the contention that the gospel of work absorbed the working class. Its aim was to do that, of course, and, since it was expounded by persons of influence and position, no doubt many on the lower rungs paid it lip service. We can assert with greater certainty that a pious attitude toward work existed among the proprietors and the clerical classes. In attenuated form it exists among such classes today. The chapter to follow reveals this in its account of the length of the working day they put in. The worker probably never lost the idea of work as a means to a livelihood, though the work ethic may have infiltrated his class in the encouragement of regularity, honesty, application, and, certainly, respect for the clock. In 1848 when Charles A. Dana was in Paris as the *Tribune*'s correspondent the workers told him, "All we want is bread." He was a good reporter, fresh from another land, and although favoring the workers — "I had gone among the workers and ascertained the sentiments that animated them" — he had not gone overboard for them. Anyone who has punched a clock in a present-day factory can adduce current evidence to show that while there is more than bread on the workers' mind, there is little of the gospel of work.

In the factory, an underground life is lived under the noses of foremen, supervisors and time-study men. They may smell it but they find it hard to see or touch. The workers live in a world apart, on its negative side slow, restrictive, inimical to supervisors, management, and other outsiders; on its positive side inventive, ingenious, and loyal to co-workers. The experienced worker does everything possible, including purposely springing frames and burning up drills to put time-study men off their calculations and set a slower time estimate for the job. No mean dramatic ability comes to the fore in the effort: the worker jumps around the machine, steaming and sweating at every pore. Once management's man is out of range, the job goes back to the pace the workers themselves have decided to keep. They set a job at a certain pace, or fix an output quota, not only to keep from being speeded up but to avoid having their pay rates lowered. They often devise their own mechanical inventions and gimmicks which they apply to their machines once the cat is away. Anyone who tries to work faster than the informally set pace soon finds himself in Coventry — or even loses his job.

If the work ethic ever possessed such men, it has by now oozed away. No one maintains that this attitude characterizes every American worker: there are also the rate-busters. Great variations exist among workers, as any experienced foreman knows. Even their point of origin has importance — workers in a town full of Scotch-Irish descendants will work differently from those in a town with mixed nationalities. Workers newly arrived from the South or rural areas perform their job differently from those from other sections or the cities. The interesting thing at the moment is that to a surface observer these men, goldbrickers and ratebusters alike, might all seem to be hard at work, imbued with the zeal of missionary monks or Protestant reformers. Underneath the surface, there may be nothing of the sort. They may be plotting — all in the spirit of fun and fellowship — where to hide one another's wrenches or when to cut off the gas to the welder's line. This point will be returned to again when the history of modern work is considered in greater detail, and it will be seen that even the surface activity has a significance all its own.

For now, the question is why the job has such psychological significance. It is not uncommon today to expect a man at retirement to have problems so grave they may even lead to suicide. This does not seem consistent with the portrait of workers given above. In seeking an explanation we should first of all separate the job holder from those who are self-employed. Not only is the man who works his own business a property owner in many cases, he also sets his own pace and usually sees a direct relation between his effort and his gain. Moreover (this now is the important distinction), he sees his own operations as a whole quite clearly. Even if he employs others to work for him, their efforts lead toward an end, and this end the employer has well in mind. The job holder's situation is different. His knowledge of the end is limited. His work by its very title is a work in pieces. The origin of the word is still lost but "job" appears to come from the Middle English *jobbe* meaning a piece or a lump. In any case its early usage was to signify a piece of work, and our meaning — an employment — is so recent that Webster's dictionary still considers it colloquial. A job, then, is only a piece of work. The classic example in a classical text is Adam Smith's description of jobs in a pin factory. "One man draws out the wire, another straights it, and a third cuts it, a fourth points it, a fifth grinds it." Pinmaking introduces the reader to *The Wealth of Nations*.

Dividing work up into pieces has led to specialization and the division of labor. This last should be distinguished from cooperation. In cooperation one cannot help seeing the end one is working for, even though one works only on a minor part of it. The description in Cellini's *Autobiography* of the casting of the statue of Perseus is worth recalling for its picture of cooperation in the fifteenth-century shop of a fine artisan. By means of cables, pulleys, and levers Cellini had his men raise the mold and suspend it about a meter above the mouth of the furnace. He then set it down carefully in the bottom of the hole. Having seen that his journeymen could take it from there, he got other men to lay pine wood on the furnace. The shop caught fire, however, and spread until everyone was afraid the roof would fall in. The fire put out, Cellini who had been suffering all the time from fever, had to take to bed. He called together his assistants, about ten in all, including masters who melted bronze, helpers, men from the country, and his regular journeymen, and, putting them under the orders of one of these last, gave them instructions. There were too many difficulties, though; Cellini had to get out of bed again. He called out the remedy for each problem as it arose, and each man responded with the work of three men. This time an explosion hit the shop, throwing fire everywhere. Terrified, they saw that the cover of the furnace had blown off. The bronze was beginning to run. But everyone could see that it was running well and the mold was filling up. Cellini jumped here and there ordering, assisting, and praying. Prayers over, the mold a-cooling, he drank with them all and went joyfully back to bed — "for there were still two hours left to the night" — and got up next day at noon.

In the United States the great majority are employed by others. The percentage of self-employed has shrunk steadily, dropped from probably over one-fifth to under one-seventh of all the employed in just the twenty years from 1940 to 1960. It is not the moment yet to ask by whom employees are employed. We say, "employed by others," but these others are not necessarily either living or individual persons. Employees are hired by people who are themselves employees hired by other employees. This progression can go on indefinitely until finally a group of prime employers is reached. Even these are not employers but a board acting in name of a corporation. So, just as almost everyone works in the United States, almost everyone is a job holder.

THE JOB: TECHNICAL AND SOCIAL

Since a job entails working on a piece of a process or product for wages, the satisfaction of producing a whole object is lacking. For centuries this has been an argument against specialization. We should not expect the worker normally to get real satisfaction from a job on which he does a piece of the work, a task chosen and organized by others, under watchful eyes, at a pace not his own, at a time and place not his to say. This, one would venture, is the disagreeable part of the job — effort or exertion or exercise, physical or mental, under orders and supervision, constrained in time and place. Yet technically speaking this *is* the job. A job description with all its headings would be too long to quote and tedious to read. If I pick up the *Dictionary of Occupational Titles* and open at random, I learn that the "Sandblaster" cleans paint, scale, grease, tar, rust, and dirt from the surface of metal or hard-composition objects usually preparatory to machining, painting, polishing or plating, by directing a stream of sand, grit or steel shot and compressed air from a nozzle against the surface of the objects, and, further, that he wears heavy gloves to protect hands when holding objects in sandblast stream, and a helmet or hood as protection against breathing sand-laden air and to protect his eyes. The job description does have some relation to what goes on in the shop for eight hours a day but is by no means the full story, and for many purposes is the irrelevant story.

Apart from the worker's underground life of movement, adventure and cold war, there is an aboveboard life worth living too. In modern industry, where all men and many women work, no room is admitted for fellowship and leadership, and the play of a whole field of emotions. "Work is no place for courtship." This statement is no more observed than the one in the old days about flirting at Mass. "So the sermon ended, and the church broke up, and my amours ended also," confided Pepys to his diary. Love, matches, games, challenges, lunches, petty tyrannies, visits, are all managed on the job. This part of the job — together with the pay — is the agreeable part. Undoubtedly it is this and his basic status in society (which the job provides) that the man in retirement misses. When he is no longer on the job, he's alone. Everybody is at work except women and their babies. He has been put outside the network of both a useful and a social life. His only chance is to locate or slowly build for himself another necessarily minor network.

For clarity's sake this part of a job, the facility it offers for intercourse, should be separated from its technical element of work. Most studies that condemn the job have seen only the technical work aspects; studies that laud it have concentrated on the social rewards. Whether a job has the first and lacks the second may determine whether workers are satisfied with their lot.

With the introduction of the factory system, the old channels of intercourse were weakened. Previously, nonagricultural work was done at home or near home. Cities were small and towns smaller. Outside of artisans' shops, most of which gave onto well-traversed streets, intercourse took place in the market, the central square, and the home. The factory took men, women, and children out of the workshops and homes and put them under one roof and timed their movements to machines. The assembly-line process further geared the movements of man to machine, so that the expense, vulnerability to obsolescence, and fuel requirements of the factory dictated a regularity of human attendance. The artisan in his workshop could leave his bench, table, or lathe to go to the door to watch a passing procession, and afterwards perhaps take up with a friend to go to the tavern for a drink. Work waited until evening or the next day or the next few days. The machine can not be shut off so easily, and even when shut off, obsolescence gnaws away at it. The assembly line further meshed a man with gears so that if he left it for a moment, provision had to be made. Rigidity and interdependence are not so great as that lampooned by Chaplin in *Modern Times* or René Clair in *A Nous la Liberté*. But the gearing of men to machines and of machines to all other machines, and then nesting all machines and all men under one roof, obviously brought an unheard of degree of synchronizing and inflexibility of schedule.

For anyone in a factory to run to the window to see a parade pass is dangerous, for the machines do not wait. Even after 5:00 P.M. they wait impatiently for morning, silently depreciating away. Nor can wife or children be around in the work day. They would get in the way. If the worker sees a friend — and he does — he can't clap him on the shoulder and hale him off to the nearest pub. The walls would come tumbling down. The factory system and machinery brought the blessing of lighter labor, but also the curse of greater attentiveness over fixed stretches of time. In being paced by machines work took on a new concentration.

Work concentration usually lessens the chance for social relations on the job. By doing so, it deprives industrial work of perhaps its chief satisfaction. Studies of the origin of the gospel of work were themselves a query about the utility or naturalness or ethics of modern work. It should be noted that these studies began in Europe, where the classic views of work and leisure had tougher roots. The modern form of work had less resistance to overcome in the United States. Yet if it were unpleasant, doubts would be felt there too. In fact, in the second quarter of this century, a number of studies began which showed an increasing concern for the social side of work. Usually they overlooked that what they were studying was not the technical job so much (such study they now dubbed with the bad name "Taylorism," after the father of modern factory efficiency) as the collective life that the factory system brought with it by its very nature. As long as you bring people together under one roof, how can you keep them from a social life except by measures that will be felt as deprivation? As the old rule of etiquette goes, under the same roof no introduction is needed. The American studies concentrated on what grew to be called the "human relations" of the job. Studies of this kind spread out all over the world and especially in Europe, emigrating from American universities and publishing houses. To such an extent did these researches confuse the technical aspects of the job, that is, the piece of work itself, with its increment of social life, that it began to appear that persons were assembled in the factory as in the old public square, namely for reasons of society. Instead they are assembled for the job, and "the job must be done."

These various studies — those on the origin of the work ethic and those on the job's human relations — reflected questions, as we have already intimated, about the desirability of work, not so much in itself, but as it was organized and conceived. Did work have to be of such intense tediousness? Was there anything besides the job? The UNESCO Universal Declaration of Human Rights says that everyone has a right to work. It also says that everyone has a right to leisure.

Time Given, Time Taken Away

THAT a constitution could speak of a universal right to work would have surprised the Greek philosopher. That a constitution could speak of both a right to work and a right to leisure would have left him aghast.

In the preceding pages leisure took its stand on the other side of work, not necessity. For along the line of history, during the rough and tumble days of technology's growth, leisure disappeared under the avalanche of work. When it raised its head again it had changed form. It was now a matter of time free of work, time off the job. The quest for leisure had been transformed into the drive for free time. In its normal sense today leisure is often measured by the length of the work week. Being considered the opposite of work, and work being now calculated by time, leisure too must be figured the same way. The 48-hour week, for instance: day — 8 hours, ticked off by the clock; week — 6 days, marked off the calendar. The clock and the calendar became important now, for leisure is counted off in quantities of time.

The fact that leisure and free time are used interchangeably indicates that people consider time something concrete. If in conversation among literate persons the subject of leisure intrudes, the first remark may be cast in form of challenge, as, "Oh well, who knows what leisure is?," with the clear implication that no one in his right mind would venture to find agreement on its meaning. But let free time be proposed as a substitute for leisure, everyone knows what *that* is. Instead of one, there are now two words involved, indeed two words that have turned many philosophers into insomniacs: "free" and "time."

For the moment, time interests us. The idea that there is an exact hour everywhere, that all the world is on one time, must once have seemed revolutionary and the utmost in progress. Now, it seems so true as to be self-evident. Time is a moving belt on which all activities run off as on a sheet of teletype. It moves with perfect regularity, its pace is the same the world over and it never stops to back up and repeat itself. There's no turning back the clock. So much a part of us is this concept we find it difficult to believe that any other kind of time can be true or possible. Since its pace is uniform, time is measurable; one second in China is as long as another at the North Pole. Man is born with a limited but unspecified length of time stretched ahead. This length is measured off in seconds, minutes, hours, days, months, and years. Parts of it can be dedicated to this or that endeavor. These parts can be large or small. In the industrial world ten minutes is not an inconsequential amount of time, for in it one can make a sale, manufacture a bearing, or close a shop for the day. Under special circumstances — as in the synchronized movements of war and aeronautics — split seconds can make the difference between life and death, victory and defeat.

Leisure time (note how familiar is the association of leisure and time) has greatly increased today, it is said. Since free time is intended, and since free time means time off work or not related to work, it ought to be possible to verify or confirm this proposition. Has industrial society given more time to men? It would not be surprising, for from antiquity, a grant of free time has been a constant promise of the machine. Aristotle put it in the realm of imagination. "If every instrument could do its own work, if the shuttle could weave and the plectrum pluck the lyre without a guiding hand, foremen would not need workers, nor masters slaves."

Let time on the job, then, be considered work time. There are 168 hours to the week. If a man holds down a job of 40 hours a week, how much free time does he have — 128 hours? He would answer no. First of all he sleeps and eats, and these activities subtract a large sum from the total. Nor are they all he would subtract from the total before he arrived at free time. An early slogan of the shorter-hours movement in the United States proclaimed "8 hours for work, 8 hours for sleep, 8 hours for all the rest." The eight-hour remainder is not all free time, however. Instead it covers, as the pat phrase puts it, "all the rest" — shopping, grooming, chores, transportation, voting, making love, helping children with homework, reading the newspaper, getting the roof repaired, trying to locate the doctor, going to church, visiting relatives, and so on. Do all these activities rightly belong to free time?

We are confronted with one of the toughest problems in any statistical treatment of leisure and free time. The word leisure has always referred to something personal, a state of mind or a quality of feeling. It seemed that in changing from the term leisure to the term free time we had gone from a qualitative to a quantitative concept. We now had something that could be measured with ease. The subjective element, however, refused to be liquidated. It still lives in the "freeness" of free time. We said that free time is time off or not related to the job. We then subtracted sleeping and eating from it since it seemed likely that a man would not consider free the time spent on such necessities. But where should time spent in a weekly visit to the relatives be put? Or time spent in going to church? There seems to be a strong sense of obligation involved here, so that even if a person wished to spend his life differently, he was not free to do so. Until we have covered enough ground to thrash these problems out more thoroughly, we shall have to differentiate more or less arbitrarily as we go along.

A glance at the best figures available (Table 1) reveals that since 1850 the average work week has been reduced by about 31 hours. Thus, on the face of it, free time has increased by 31 hours a week. To this we should add something for the time involved in the so-called fringe benefits of paid vacations, holidays, and sick leave. Regular provision for them has been a recent phenomenon. As late as the 1920s only a small number of wage earners had paid vacations. Among salaried workers the paid vacation was more common. The national figures on these provisions do not go back much beyond the '20s or '30s. Indeed we know little of how many persons took vacations before then even when they were not paid for it. At any rate rough estimates today would set the number of days of paid vacations, holidays, and sick leave at about 15. So to our gain of 31 hours a week since 1850 we can add 2 or 2½ hours for "fringe benefits."

There are two more factors to take into account in considering the increase in free time nowadays. Both come in at the older end of the age scale. First, custom, law, and regulations have lowered the age of retirement to 60 or 65. For the individual this can free years of time. The second factor is the increase in life expectancy over the last century. This too can provide years free of work, for it means that after retirement men live more years than they used to. The two factors together, since 1900, have yielded an estimated 3 additional free years. All this reveals a situation not unlike that of a man going up on a "down" escalator. In 1900 at age 20 a man could expect to work about 39 years; now, in mid-century, he can expect to work an average of 43 years — 4 years longer. Yet we have seen above that he can now expect 3 more years of retirement. The result is he ends up working 4 more years to earn 3 extra years of free time. This seems an odd kind of progress over fifty years.

We could of course take the extra year of work and divide it into hours and subtract them from those of weekly free time gained over the half century. But the kind of time we are dealing with differs too radically from the work week to permit this or other kinds of weekly additions or subtractions. Vacations and holidays come within the working year and working span of life, and so may more justifiably be included. Let us omit from the accounting, then, the unexpected extra year of work. However, we should remember when judging men's life today as a whole that its lengthened span is not an unalloyed gain in free time. Earlier death may have taken away much free time in 1900 but it took away a larger share of work, also.

By using figures of the working life and retirement years expected at age 20, I have avoided the question whether school should be considered work time or free time. Children now go to school for a longer time than in 1900 or 1850. To which side of the balance should the additional years be added? With the tendency today to extend the application of the word work, we speak of schoolwork and homework. On this reasoning school attendance is work time. Our very word for school, though, comes from *scholē,* the Greek's word for leisure. With such a direct clash as this in view, let us simplify the problem by keeping youth under 20 outside our ken.

Still, taking all the years of a man's life together, it matters little where we put either school or retirement years. In 1900 for every two years of work in their active life men spent one year outside the labor force, and that same rough 2 : 1 ratio holds true today.

The hours of work within those years are also of importance, so back we return to our weekly figures. The gain there remains at 30 to 31½ hours per week. There was, however, one thing we overlooked. A year of work today does not equal a year of work decades ago, since the work week is shorter now by 31 hours. Each year there are 1,500 more free, awake hours, a gift of over one hundred days without nights for each of the 43 years of expected working life. Rather than calculate immediately how many summer years they add up to, let us look at these free 31 hours per week. We look back on 50 or 100 years ago as a period when life moved at a slower and calmer pace, when people had more time to themselves, when there was less tension — in short, a time when people, as we say, led a more leisurely life. While the picture of the 1850s that comes down to us from books and grandparents is one of life with an easier tempo, today many people seem hardly to enjoy their weekly lump of 31 clean, crisp new hours. They seemed harried, pushed and pulled, bounced off one thing onto another. Asked about leisure, they reply with a hollow laugh or a sneer, "*What* leisure?" Yet it is said that never before have Americans had so much time they can call their own.

There is no doubt that the amount of time that has to be put in on the job has been decreasing. What happens in the calculation is this: for every hour of physical presence on the job that is subtracted, add one hour to free time. If the work week is ten hours leaner than in 1920, it means that free time is ten hours fatter. From some time early in the 1950s the figure given for the average working week in the United States has been 39 to 40 hours. The gain in free time over the past fifty to one hundred years thus seems enormous. A closer look at the figures, though, reveals that somewhere along the line something has somehow slipped past us.

A MAN'S JOB, FULL TIME

Now when we speak of the length of the working week, we usually have in mind a man's full-time job. Most figures on the work week's duration include in their average the many part-time jobs in existence. They have become a more and more important distortion in recent times, since increasing numbers of teen-age youths and married women have sought these very occupations. Nineteen per cent of all persons at work now hold such part-time jobs, averaging 19 hours a week. If these are included, the average work week of all jobs declines more rapidly. Yet it certainly makes little sense here to throw an eighteen-year-old schoolboy's work in a drugstore in with that of a man in a steel mill. We are dealing with the full-time workers; the steelworker's or the executive's 40 hours, not the boy's 15, and it would be a statistical miscarriage to proclaim their combined 27.5 hours as the average work week. Part-time workers, those who put in less than 35 hours a week, should be kept out of the present estimate.

The statistics for part-time workers do not go back to 1850 or even 1900. We can assume such persons were then much less common, and in all probability were not included in regular estimates. The boy working part time peddling newspapers or jerking sodas in the ice-cream parlor was not considered a worker. Today once we remove the old lady who sits ten hours a week with babies, or the younger one who makes her Christmas money clerking over the holidays, or the student who works three hours a day checking out library books, we are dealing with the full-time worker's job, the kind of job that nearly all men in this country hold down. And when we add up their hours (regular and overtime) they come not to 39 or 40 but to 46 or 47 (Table 2). That is, the American worker puts in an average of nearly eight hours a day six days a week.

How this statistical switch ever got past honest statisticians is not hard to explain. A myth, I might point out, is not a lie. It is something almost everyone wants to believe. In believing it he sometimes embraces a cold figure too warmly.

The statisticians concerned with measuring the length of the work week were seeking a figure which, when multiplied by average employment, would yield total man hours worked. This, in turn, when multiplied by estimated output per man hour would yield an estimate of our gross national product. For their purpose an average work week that reflects the hours of all employed persons — full-time and part-time workers, men and women — is the appropriate figure. For measuring the amount of time on the job and the amount of time away from the job in the context of an examination of free time, however, an entirely different statistical measure is necessary. The more appropriate figure is the length of the work week of the average American male who works full time — that is, at least 35 hours a week. Many persons, concerned over the softening of pioneer fiber, may be pleased to learn that this individual works nearly 48 hours a week.

The news affects the good life of tomorrow too. In any revised projection of the trend, it will be clear that the rate of decline of the work week is slower than has been thought. The decline from 1948 to 1960 on the old basis was about 6 per cent; on the basis of only full-time workers the decline is about 3 per cent. Between the ages of 25 and 55, that is, after school age and before retiring age, nearly 95 per cent of all males work and about 35 per cent of all females. Labor force participation rates for these ages have never been so high, so it could just as well be said, "Never before have so many Americans had so *little* time to call their own."

Adjusting, then, for part time our rough calculation runs something like this:

69.7	work hours in 1850
— 39.5	work hours in 1956
30.2	gross free time
2.5	for vacation, etc.
32.7	
— 7.5	for correction to full-time employees
25.2	

The full-time worker's gain in free time since 1850 is thus closer to 25 hours.

The process of accounting is by no means finished. The first item is "moonlighting." Across the nation today many persons finding themselves with more time free of the job, go out and, as the phrase has it, work by the light of the moon. They tend gasoline pumps or bars, drive taxis, sell real estate or insurance, cut hair, fix TV sets, and clerk in stores. In 1950 an estimated 1.8 million persons, or 3 per cent of the total employed in the United States, held more than one job. At the end of 1959 the figures were 3 million, or about 5 per cent. Only those multiple job holders whose primary job takes 35 hours or more a week qualify as moonlighters. On their secondary job they average about 12 hours a week. The available figures do not try to establish a relationship between the decrease in work week and the increase in moonlighting, but a connection is apparent. In Akron the best guesses hold that 16 to 20 per cent of the rubber workers hold a second job, not a *part*-time but a *full*-time job. About another 40 per cent hold down a second, merely part-time, employment. Akron is the city with the longest experience in the short work day, having had a generation of trial with one of six hours. At the very least, moonlighting would be literally moonlighting if the primary job required 60 hours a week, as it did at the turn of the twentieth century. Those who moonlight today put in a working week of 47 hours at the inside and 60 hours at the outside.

The spread of moonlighting is undoubtedly greater than these figures convey. For various reasons the numbers involved are underestimated. An electrician employed full time by a company, if he works part time after the job in late afternoon or evening or on Saturday — Sunday is still held inviolable — can have many reasons for keeping quiet about it. He may wish to keep his extra earnings whole, away from the bite of the tax collector. His company may be against moonlighting on the theory it tires the employee out, rendering him less attentive to his regular job. The unions may not like the idea either because they have no control over the conditions of such jobs, which, from their point of view, might better go to needier union members, or which the moonlighter might be taking on for less than the union scale of wages, or which might lower his incentive to press for higher wages on the regular job. The union may even agree with the employer: moonlighting tires the employee out. If management then takes disciplinary steps and the worker insists he has a grievance, the union is caught in the middle.

Reasons like these make the extent of moonlighting hard to determine. Doubling the official figure would be making a conservative estimate. Eleven per cent of the work force, then, averaging 12 hours a week of moonlighting, takes away about 1⅓ hours a week from the free time of each employee. However, since some moonlighting is included in the estimate of average work week, an allowance of about one hour a week seems reasonable, bringing the change from 1850 down to 24.2 hours.

Whether a man holds one job or two, he has to get to the job. Almost all work is done outside home grounds. One does not have to go back to the crafts system or home industries to find a change in the length of time spent in getting to one's place of work. The journey to work in 1850 was probably much shorter than it is today for the simple reason that at that time about 85 per cent of the population was rural, living in places of fewer than 2,500 inhabitants. On a farm the journey to work counts as part of one's working hours. When one goes from house to barn or field, one is already at work. The same applies to the village. One goes to factory or shop or office there, but the time required to traverse the town is negligible, and work begins right after leaving the breakfast table. Today most people have a journey to make first, to get to work. Nearly two thirds of the population live in urban territory and one of these two thirds lives in or around cities of 100,000 or over. Urban concentration brings traffic problems.

Estimated average speed of traffic in big city rush hours is now down to 20 m.p.h. for motorists and to 13 m.p.h. for public transit systems. Traffic has slowed up in almost every city during rush hours, but we are still without the comprehensive figures that would permit setting an accurate average. A few studies exist that give an idea of the time involved, though it should be remarked that most of these studies err on the low side. For some reason people underestimate the length of their journey to work. They often report a precise transit time under good conditions, leaving out the bad scores and perhaps forgetting about the time spent waiting for the bus, or the days the commuter train broke down, or the time it takes to park the car and walk from it or the bus or subway to the place of work.

The rule of thumb reckons that men spend 10 to 20 per cent of their working life going back and forth between home and work. Nor does there seem to be much hope for improvement soon. The more approaches and parking lots, the more people drive their cars to work — the kind of situation where trying to improve things worsens them.

One study proved specially helpful for this chapter. It distributed a diary in 1954 to a national sample of Americans and asked them to record their time expenditures in it by 15-minute periods for the months of March and April (Table 3). For the purpose of estimating average hours of work it cannot be used here since there is no way of eliminating part-time workers. But from it we see that we can add three quarters of an hour traveling to and another three quarters of an hour traveling back from work. This would take seven or eight and one-half hours a week from free time, depending on whether the worker had a 5- or 6-day week. Those who make more than five work journeys each week include not only the workers who have a fixed 6-day schedule but also those who moonlight or work overtime on Saturdays. In fact we learn from the same study that American men work an average of over four hours on Saturday, so that to speak of a 2-day weekend in the United States is, to say the least, premature. Almost eight and one-half hours a week, then, are used for the journeys to work, which brings the change since 1850 down to not quite 16 (15.8) hours.

The length of the journey to work and its expense are two of the reasons why workers almost always prefer a 5- to a 6-day week, even when both weeks carry the same work-hour load. They often choose one job over another because "it's closer to work." There may be an objection at this point from the man who rides the 8:05 train and gets into New York at 8:55. The ride to and from work, he may say, is one of the high spots of the day; it's the only time available for nearly an hour of relaxing reading. Undoubtedly there are some who like to read at rush hours, and who actually ride comfortable trains or buses that do not jerk or sway and are neither crowded nor too hot or cold. There are also some who can sleep on such vehicles, although the private automobile must almost always exclude reading and sleeping, specially by drivers. But then there are automobile drivers who like to drive and who consider a spin in morning and evening rush hours to be a pleasant way of relaxing. Playing cards and having a drink or two on the returning 5:07 suburban train with steady partners comes closer to a pleasant way of passing the time until 6:39, since the movements of the vehicle are not violent enough to upset the cards, though they might be bothersome for reading. However, you must first find that train, and the proper partners, and like to play cards.

For everyone lucky enough to fit that picture there is perhaps one who reads over the business or financial sections of his paper on the ride to work and goes over office papers on the ride home, and still another one for whom the confinement, crowding, temperature, and motion of the vehicle are more tiring than the job itself. He arrives at work more tired than when he leaves for the day. By the time he reaches home, he's ready to throw in the towel for good.

Whatever it is you like to do on the way to work — whether read, play cards, or sleep — the key question is would you rather do it some place else, and be at work without having to make the journey? What data we have indicates that the journey to work is felt as constraint rather than pleasure and comfort. In the absence of sure answers to this question let us assume that for every one of those who find going to work and back a preferred way of spending free time there is another who works on the journey, and a third who finds the journey to work twice as great a hardship as shop or office. The loss by those in the third class would easily cancel out the gain of the first lucky ones.

Many of the moonlighting jobs are in the category of the service trades — TV and radio fixing, house painting and restoring, kitchen appliance repairs, carpeting, etc. These services are relatively expensive because of the high proportion of skilled labor they require. For many persons short of money there seem to be but two ways of handling these jobs: either leave home to become a beachcomber or do them yourself. The only safe choice seems to be do-it-yourself. Yet the working man home from work is entitled to his rest. Presumably he should not be called on to do other work, unpaid though it be. Besides he may not have the necessary skills. A new range of goods has sprung up to make his tasks easier and less fatiguing. These articles are broadly grouped under a heading entitled "The Do-It-Yourself Market" — the multipurpose bench tool, portable home-type tools, specially designed plywood, Fiberglass, aluminum, foam rubber, plastic upholstery material, plastic laminates, paint rollers and pressure cans, pretrimmed wallpaper, power lawnmowers, and so on.

We have the usual two difficulties here. How shall we classify these activities, as work or free time, and how much time do they take up? Classifying them as free time simply because they are unpaid would pass only the sleepyheads of an inefficient accounting system. If these jobs are not done the wood rots, iron rusts, the roof leaks, cold creeps in the cracks, food spoils, milk goes sour, the children get pneumonia, the family goes around unwashed and unironed, the lights go out forever. . . . If the jobs are done by paying someone else to do them, then it is clear: the time and money spent will appear in the other someone's work ledger. Apart from the high cost of skilled labor, the rise in the proportion of homeowners is often given as an explanation for the zooming of do-it-yourself sales.

Furthermore the houses in which there are these jobs to be done are bought by young couples. He is a graduate of the army or war plants where he learned something about woodworking and metalworking, and she is itching to make hers the home beautiful. One should remember that the word homeowner most often expresses a hope, not a fact — it should be "mortgaged-home owner." The mortgage on the old homestead which used to be the sword of Damocles and was always cut down as soon as possible is now blithely ignored. These young people must meet interest and principal each month, even though the mortgage holder is a friendly government agency. Free cash to go with their free time is scarce. Doing it oneself becomes a way of paying for the house by working longer hours. In many cases, too, the term should be "unfinished-home owner." The new house when bought is incomplete, to reduce costs, and work must be done to build the carport, finish the attic or basement. When old homes are bought, it is the renovating that calls for home work.

Of course some buy paints not in buckets but in paint sets. The purchase may include the outline of a landscape stretched on paper or canvas; the idea is to apply the colors (numbered 1, 2, 3) to the proper parts of the outline (also numbered 1, 2, 3). This should not be considered an activity of work time but of free time. The same applies for those who build model ships and airplanes. This is the hobby part of the market. We don't know what percentage of the total it amounts to. Nonetheless the bulk of the do-it-yourself market falls in the categories of structural home improvements, home painting and wallpapering, furniture making and finishing, slip-covering, home gardening and grounds maintenance, home dressmaking and sewing. It all has brought a rash of do-it-yourself activities — the plumbing, wiring, carpentry, painting, landscaping (to put it euphemistically) — that the man of the house suffers heroically.

Do-it-yourself work also extends to other parts of life — to shopping, for example. The customer has to learn how the supermarkets classify produce, meat, dairy products, groceries, and so forth — and then not only find the desired goods but sort them out properly for the checker who used to wait on the customer but now merely corrects his sorting! Nowadays the customer is not always right. Call it self-service or do-the-work-yourself, it all takes a lot more time and effort than having the grocer wait on you or the grocer's boy deliver your order on receipt of a note or a call. A similar system governs the sorting for collection of garbage and trash; it has become a do-it-yourself activity.

It is true that the young wife may like to see her house beautiful and that the young husband may have learned to use saw and plane at school, and that the two of them love to work on things together. If we classify such activities as part of free time, why, in history schoolbooks, do we consider the pioneer's lot such a hard one? He and his wife did all of these things. When we consider that these activities plus the husband's sports of hunting, fishing, and Indian-baiting made up the whole day, we may say that they had nothing but free time at their disposal. Further reasoning on the classifying of activities will have to wait until the next chapter where this chronic problem becomes acute.

What are the amounts of time involved in these do-it-yourself activities? We have nothing but scattered and incomplete information to go on. Surveys in six cities of the United States disclosed that 80 per cent of inside house painting and 60 per cent of the outside were done by people whose main job was not painting. The same people buy up most of the wallpapering and floor and wall tiling industries' production. About one out of every four homes has a workshop. Tenants undoubtedly spend less time in such activities than homeowners, yet three dwelling units are owner-occupied for every two that are tenant-occupied. The pile-up of time we can see calculated in the national diary survey (Table 3). Men put in on the average nearly five (4.8) hours a week in miscellaneous work (not hobbies) around the house. Five hours a week does not seem too much to allot householders for work in, around, or on the house, which they would not have done in 1850 because the skill required was too great, the materials too resistant, one's regular working hours too long, existing labor costs too low, and the numbers of homeowners not large enough. We stand now at a gain of about eleven (10.8) hours in free time over 1850.

WOMAN'S WORK

Another general factor. Let us assume that a man works a 48-hour week, which then is shortened to 40. The result is chalked up by the Bureau of Labor Statistics as a gain for the shorter work week. Suppose now that his wife decides to take a job, and finds one at 35 hours a week. That change also appears in official tallies as a gain for the short work week. Before there were none, now there are two with short work weeks and lots of free time.

Only 14 per cent of the households in the United States are composed of one person only. The rest have two or more, and we can assume that almost always, among these two or more are husband and wife, and when three or more, they include children. Since 1890 the size of households has been declining steadily. This reflects less the disappearance of children from the family than the disappearance of members of the extended family — grandparents, aunts, uncles, cousins. Keeping a house, as every woman knows, means work, even if there are no children. Anyway, the majority of households do have children, and, given the early age of marriage in the United States, most of these children are still dependent on their parents. Almost as soon as they reach majority, they prove it by getting married and quickly setting up their own household.

If in 1850 the men worked at their jobs 70 hours per week, they could not be called on to help keep house. The burden fell on the wife and whatever female help she could find. Women at that time worked outside the home more often before marriage than after. In 1890 18 per cent of the females over 14 had jobs. Today the proportion is about 36 per cent. Twice as many of these, now, are married as unmarried. In 1890 only 4 per cent of working women were married. It was possible then to get cheap domestic help. Some of the working women were undoubtedly in a position to help pay for help around the house. Since then domestic work, as a female occupation, has been disappearing. Yet two out of five women workers are mothers, and of them approximately one out of every three has children under 6 years, while the other two have children under 17. Of course, all women workers do not work full time. Indeed, as a group they hold the bulk of jobs under 35 hours. Even so, about half of them hold full-time jobs. We would expect mothers with children to seek and find those jobs that were part-time, were it not for the fact that a woman with just a husband to keep house for will want shorter hours too, and that working mothers would presumably have more need of the extra money to be gained from full-time jobs.

Let us now make a questionable assumption, namely, that whereas in 1850 housework fully occupied the housewife, today with labor- and time-saving devices it occupies her only about half time or 4 hours a day. We shall want to pick up this assumption again to challenge it. For the present it enables us to make some rough calculations.

To a woman's week of 40 hours full time and 20 hours part time, one would have to add the same daily travel time that men have. The married woman who works half time, say 20 hours a week, has to make up her travel and work hours each day by doing housework in the late afternoons or evenings and weekends. The married woman who works full time has to make up these same hours plus another twenty or so a week; she is saddled each day with a half-day's necessary housekeeping she cannot get around to. The day has only 24 hours. Married women with children under 6 we would say have a full-time job at home. They would have to make up even a half-time job at home. The mothers working full time would have to make up their whole time, for we cannot assume that having children under 6 takes less than full time. We can assume that mothers with children over 6 but under 17, like married women without children, have only a half day's work at home. So only that half of them with full-time jobs have a half day's work at home to make up. Thus only married women with children under 6 are assumed to have a full day's work at home on this basis. The score for millions of married working women in terms of weekly make-up hours of work at home would run close to two hundred million. The average would be over 20 hours per week to be made up by each of the 8½ million or more married working women.

Yet we started this section on women with the information that if they work a short work week, it registers somewhere in official totals as an addition to free time. How is this paradox resolved? Simply enough — by the men sharing in the housework. The husband finishes up at factory or office and pitches in with shopping or cooking or housekeeping or tending to the children, washing them, putting them to bed. Recently a number of writings have appeared lamenting the fact that men are stay-at-homes, that the dishpan hands that rock the cradle are likely to be theirs, that they are losing their identity as males by becoming domesticated and feminized. Women conversely are becoming masculinized, all business and work. Apparently there are some who feel that the physical difference between the sexes — which they have always cheered — is not going to be enough. The accounting of working hours given here reveals the source of much of the evidence. Women cannot bear the extra load by themselves. They are the doggedest fighters for the shorter work week. This fact has not been sufficiently appreciated.

Some writers have tried to laugh off women's concern with the shorter work week. They report that wives prefer not to have husbands at home another day of the week getting in the way around the house. This may be true of some women, specially those who do not have outside jobs. The working wife, however, has little such fear of the shorter work week. Pending its arrival, all she can do is look to her spouse for a hand with the housekeeping. Not all men help, yet many in fact do pitch in. On the average, men put in about two and a quarter (2.3) hours a week on household chores, housekeeping, and shopping, exclusive of preparing food (Table 3). Not much when spread out this way, but because of its very pervasiveness the phenomenon warrants attention. The hardship is greatest among working men with wives at work too. Farmers may help less than other American males, but then farmers' wives are rarely employed on outside jobs.

Aristotle had said, you may recall, that the only slave the poor man has is his wife. The times, it seems, have taken even that slave away from him. Perhaps his wife is a better wife now — I am no judge of that — but for his free time's sake, he could still use a slave.

We now have exactly 8.5 hours left of the 1850–1950 thirty-odd hours' gain in free time. A few general factors remain to be considered. One of them I discussed in the previous chapter — the concentrating and pacing of work by machines. In 1850 there was not much of a factory system; a higher percentage of persons were self-employed; the assembly line and Taylorism were not yet born. In one way or another most men were tied to the soil and the seasons; both exacted a pace of their own. Most families were close to productive self-sufficiency. Persons related by blood or marriage often lived close to one another. Those who lived in town had their work with its 10- or 12-hour day, but it could usually be interrupted at will for a chat with a caller or for watching interesting happenings from the window. Stores were at times left untended; neighbors knew where to find the proprietor in the rare case an urgent client came to the door. Laborers dug ditches and masons built houses, but there was no machinery to set their pace. Instead it was the sun. In the Europe of the time, too, respites of one kind or another were the rule. In Lyons, for example, around 5 o'clock men of all social standings would meet in cafés for a *casse-croûte,* a platter of pig's ears, tails, and chops. In the bistro men also took their *mâchon,* their chew of tripe and sausage. But in Europe the shift to a synchronized pace did not go as far as it did in the United States. Up to World War II the silk workers and others could be found, and still today many can be seen, taking a break in their long day to jab with their forks at the huge pork platter.

How shall we compare yesterday's work with that of today, synchronized with high-powered machines? The nearest thing to the old way now is found on the professional and executive levels in large corporations. There, to be sure, the day at work may be long, but the tempo is more or less one's own; machines play little or no part in it. The telephone is used for all kinds of friendly chats and shopping chores — many that help the wife out of her difficulties. Talk with colleagues is necessary, of course, and replete with jokes and stories. Visitors come and go. In fact it has become so difficult for these people to see each other after work, or out of the house in the evening, that the only time for a friend to visit them is during work hours. Then they can be found at their most relaxed and cordial, offering a cup of coffee without the gnawing fear that by talking they are taking away time from their wives and children. Lunch hours may be more difficult to use for social purposes, as they are usually taken up with business appointments.

To a certain extent free time on the job is available also to clerical or white-collar personnel. They eat lunch with colleagues or friends. The telephone is at their elbow and the conversations are usually long — thereby almost excluding the chance that they are business calls. The water cooler is an assembly point for conversations, but a friend at any desk is just as convenient. The coffee "break" is casual and not tightly scheduled as tea is in many British factories. On the "line" in American factories the coffee break rarely exists even today, and in many cases to take a smoke one has to feign urgent physiological need. In offices the scene changes: machines are not pacing machines, except when one is taking a placement test on the typewriter or the like; punch clocks are not in evidence. Office personnel can usually smoke at will. Theirs is not the same freedom the executive has, though, in receiving visitors, or going off at any moment on an entirely plausible business call somewhere.

But the executive class is few in number. Moreover, the increase in clerical and kindred workers since 1900 has gone principally to the women. At the moment we are chiefly interested in male full-time workers. Among them the greatest increase since 1850 is in the category of operators and kindred shopworkers. This category handles machinery, not paper. If there is any gearing to be done, the paper-shufflers will gear themselves — however loosely — to the machine-workers. More males work full time in this category than in any other.

What time weight can we assign to the factor of regularizing the work pace throughout the work day? The task seems hopeless. Theoretically there should be some effect on the organism, but if so it is not clearly visible. Perhaps as a result the worker needs more rest or he is more nervous or tense or his amusements rely more on relaxation. Evidence does exist to indicate that mass-production workers, at least, have a higher rate of absenteeism and quitting the job than other workers, that they seek promotion or transfer not so frequently for higher pay or status as to get a job that is not harnessed to an iron monster, a job that permits some talking and sociability and a break in routine every now and then, without having to signal for a relief man. The poorest weaver of palm baskets in Sardinia working from dawn to sunset on the stoop of her house can eat, drink, laugh, and talk, watch the passers-by, stretch and keep an eye on the children.

The newness in work I have spoken of as work concentration or intensity or pacing is best described as the time stress imposed by machine operations. In typical cases the operators are compelled to keep up with a machine or conveyor line and to complete each cycle of operation within a fixed time; failure to maintain the pace leads to breaks in the system; there are no pauses in the work. Actually, besides the operators, there are many other occupations that work with a new time stress. The assembly line has become the model of production. It affects all business and sets the standards for efficiency even outside the business world. More concretely, machines are all geared to clocks, and many kinds of work — train dispatching, advertising, airports, television — have about them the tenseness of the fast-moving minute hand. A later chapter will go into the subject more thoroughly.

We could go on with our accounting by assuming that the operator is paced so steadily at his job that at the end of his work day he needs one hour or two back in more relaxation than he would have needed with a 7- to 8-hour day, 5 days a week at the pace of the 1850s, when such a day and week would have been considered part-time employment. But our rough calculations would now become sheer guesswork. What is more important than a numerical guess is to point out that we cannot assume that either a job or an hour on one are the same in 1950 as in 1850. We know what assembly lines mean in terms of the pacing of work. There are machines, such as an automobile or a sewing machine, which give the individual a sense of freedom and power. He feels more powerful and more skillful when he is operating them, and when he does not want them any more he can shut off the motor, flip the switch. There are others, such as a milling machine or automatic lathe, to whose tempo you must pace yourself, and they only turn off and on with an impersonal someone else's flick of the switch or on a job-time sequence. Pacing machines are the kind that give the industrial system its character. We call our world an industrial age rather than a commercial age because of the dominance of such machines. After eight hours with them, or the synchronized kind of life they impose on the rest of the workaday world, a man's fatigue is different from that after the same hours of work time in a nonindustrial age. Because of these eight hours, modern man needs more of his twenty-four for rest, or recreation of a not too taxing sort. Exactly how much more, we cannot tell.

Whether the remaining 8.5 hours we have come down to are free of work or not as compared to the 1850s can be decided by anyone interested in protracting the kind of time accounting we have used in this chapter. The greatly increased migratory mobility of Americans also steals away time. Each year, one of every five families moves to take up new residence. Americans living in the house of their birth are almost all children. The reason for moving is typically a new job, so that this, too, is part of work, of what the economists call the mobility of labor. On the higher echelons "executive mobility" and "personnel circulation to provide across-the-board work experience" are familiar phrases of the business language. A medium echelon of nonexecutive engineers and technicians moves by the thousands between New England, the deep South, Southwest, Far West, Northwest, and Midwest, largely in the field of electronics, aviation and general defense work. On the lower echelons we can see two major currents of migration, leaving aside that of "Westward, Ho!" One current moves large numbers of whites and Negroes from South to North. The other shifts masses of countrymen from rural to urban areas. All movements seek opportunity. Migrants going in one direction cross other migrants in the night going the other way but seeking the same gold. What the migration involves in terms of time and effort for all parties concerned we have not ventured to estimate, but certainly a heavy loss of time goes with getting settled, and husband and family's becoming adapted to the new locale, similar though it may be to the previous one. In single occupational categories also one could find encroachments on time, some so subtle that the employee is not aware of them. The executive's lunch on the expense account is a good example. At lunch he eats into his free time at a lower rate of remuneration than he gets for his work time. Instead of sitting in the park or going to the zoo, he works for his lunch money. The office employee too, though not on an expense account, often talks over business while eating the "Businessman's Special" luncheon. But such examples are peculiar to one or another group.

So much for factors broad enough to influence the whole

United States pattern of work time and free time. If added up, all the elements that did not exist in the pattern of 1850 but do exist today (the machine pacing of work, migration, the journey to work, moonlighting, women working) — all factors that take away from time off the job and yet are related to the job — the difference between 1850 and 1960 comes down to a few hours. To go beyond this would be making the mistake of treating imprecise matters with a precision they do not have. Perhaps after this exercise of ours, others might like to develop new measures to reach a closer approximation. We wish them all the accuracy with which the ancients measured the circumference of the world.

A TALE OF THE TIMES

The great and touted gains in free time since the 1850s, then, are largely myth. We could have approached the problem at the other end, by questioning the figure of a 70-hour work week in the 1850s. The compilers of that figure, when they published it, were careful to state its problematical aspects. It has been a popular figure; no one has raised a doubt about it, not even those the authors themselves raised. Besides clutching to our bosom the pretty statistic, we have made other mistakes. I have pointed out that we calculate free time by the decline in the work week. This is a strange way to keep books. It is like counting each year that medical science snatches from death not just as another year of life, but as a year of happiness. Death is so much feared that the mere sparing of life is regarded as beatitude. And work, it seems, is so oppressive that any time saved from it is regarded as freedom. The figures here, too, work out comfortably for those who wish to see or portray the United States as a lush playground.

Why should free time be calculated this way? Instead of considering it the opposite of time on the job why not first decide what it is and then add it up? Had we done so, we would not have needed a shaky figure for 1850. When Americans are asked why they would like a few hours, a half day, a day more of free time, they answer typically that they could then get the shopping done, or take the children to the dentist, or replace that worn-out weather stripping on the back door. They mention such unfree things because they assume "free" means "off-the-job." The word leisure has turned into the phrase free time, and the two are now almost interchangeable. We have slipped backward to the level of ancient Greece before Plato, when *scholē,* too, meant either leisure, time or free time. It was through the efforts of the philosophers that leisure found its identity. Today the benefit of their thinking is largely lost to us.

Why should this confusion in terminology continue to exist? Does anyone benefit from it? In a way everyone benefits from it. The confusion helps us to think of our life as the best of existing or possible worlds. Industrialization gives us not only work and many other good things; it gives us the gift of leisure, that is, free time, more free time than ever this hitherto backward old world has seen. It is the signal for a new era, a new way of life, a tribute to freedom and democracy and the fruits they have borne us. Only industrialism and democracy could ever have produced such a marvel. If people somehow feel that this leisure is not passing their way, it is easy to show them how wrong they are. Cite the facts, in leisure hours gained; compare today's leisure with 1850 or 1900. They can go on thinking they have lots of free time and wondering why they do not. Perhaps this makes each person feel petulantly virtuous; he believes all his fellow Americans are having a gay old snap of it while he works like a dog and never has a moment's free time.

We have seen where most of these hours have gone. Free time can perhaps be converted into leisure, but this is only a chance, though an important chance. We should also have pointed out that the country or century or group used for comparison with today's free time makes a lot of difference.

Steelworkers a hundred years ago worked a 12-hour shift, 7

days a week; miners rarely saw the sun in winter. So far we have made our chief comparisons with this one earlier setting. The time was 1850, the place the United States. It was a point from which we had some statistics to go by. Marking a century's distance, it also lent an ample perspective. Moreover, since we were not citing Greece or Rome or some other foreign country, we did not have a patriotic bias to contend with. The only bias we might have had was a progressive one: we might have wanted to show how much progress has taken place since then in these United States. Having skirted that danger, we can now choose other times and places for comparison.

Instead of ancient Greece, let us consider modern Greece for a change, a country not yet fully industrialized. Most of the population is agrarian, living in villages. The intense work of cultivating and harvesting takes only a few weeks. Outside of these periods Greek farmers have an evening with ample spare time. They pass it sitting in the village *cafeneion,* reading papers, talking politics, gossiping, playing backgammon, and just leaning back watching the passers go by and the evening close in on the square. By custom the women cannot hang around the *cafeneia,* though they can stop in to buy something to take out. Their time of talk and gossip is while drawing water from the fountain, while working in the village laundering pool, while marketing, and in and around church. Except at the market, the men are conspicuously absent from these feminine gatherings. They usually do not go to church unless it is a holiday.

In the more populated towns the schedule is not much different. People rise with the sun, the streets bustle with women buying food and men on their way to work. As the morning goes on, the streets empty. In early afternoon, there is a briefer flurry; then the shops close, everyone goes home to eat and sleep. Another brief flurry in late afternoon. Some of those who went to work in the morning return to their labors; some do not; the government offices close in the early afternoon. Between seven and eight o'clock in the evening the streets and squares repopulate themselves. The cool of the day or the relaxation of twilight brings everyone out. The promenade is on. Crowds move through the town, from one end to the other and back and back again, walking, talking, stopping, in motion once more. Children play, boys and girls divide off, tease and flirt. By nine-thirty or ten the lights go out, everyone is back home, and the town drifts to sleep until the light of rosy-fingered aurora touches on house walls. As in the villages, the coffee houses are numerous and well-frequented. No business presses on the men who sit there. Those who cannot afford the tariff sit on curbs, benches, and monuments. A few cents for coffee rents a table at least for half a day.

Do we have such leisureliness here? Some may say we do, that one can find, specially in the rural South, the kind of front-porch life we all once had fifty or one hundred years ago. Undoubtedly, today one could find places in the United States where life still moves at a pace similar to that of the 1850s, but they are isolated instances of something that was once general.

If instead of to the 1850s we go farther back into the Middle Ages, a long period of ten varied centuries, what do we find? The amount of free time would be even more difficult to estimate than that of a century ago, were it not for the fact that the years typically went by according to a calendar of holidays. It varied from place to place. The number of holidays during the year seems commonly to have been about 115, to which the inviolable 52 Sundays had to be added, making a total of 167 days. Even serfs and slaves had many of the same holidays. One hundred and sixty-seven days a year amounts to over three days a week. Converted to a week with work days 12 hours long, longer even than in the frontier days of 1850, the hours come to 45.6 a week — worked at a tempo closer to that of the 1850s than to the present. The average does not include market days, which usually were also days of no work. Not bad for dark medieval times. And we are talking about peasants, not just about nobles, kings, and patrons.

In Rome working and nonworking days went in the ratio of

about 2 to 1. Much depended on the number of public games. At the end of the republican period, there were seven sets of games occupying 65 days. In Greece at about the same time, the late first century B.C., according to Strabo the geographer, the Greek calendar had developed into a complicated catalogue whose fêtes and holidays exceeded its working days. Rome's own calendar within a century or two began to resemble the Greek. By the middle of the second century A.D., Roman games took 135 days, and by the middle of the fourth century as many as 175 days. In republican times the games lasted only part of the day; they gradually began to take up the whole day from early morning onward. At the later period they went on into the night in many cases, requiring artificial illumination.

Apart from exceptional periods of brutal transition, each community weaves its work and nonwork fabric together. Comparisons in our favor are delusive. Since 1850 free time has not appreciably increased. It is greater when compared with the days of Manchesterism or of the sweatshops of New York. Put alongside modern rural Greece or ancient Greece, though, or medieval Europe and ancient Rome, free time today suffers by comparison, and leisure even more.

Free Time and
Its Uses

COMPARISONS with the past put aside, what can we say about
the present? We no longer need ask where did those thirty-odd
hours of new free time go. Still, we should like to know how people spend what free time they do have. The problem left suspended at the beginning of the preceding chapter warrants some
attention now. Is there only work time and free time, and perhaps
sleep-and-eat time, or is there something else, too?

We have already noted that certain activities like visiting
relatives or going to church had a sense of obligation about them.
Though they were not work, neither were they free. We have
three choices. We can in arbitrary fashion squeeze such activities
into one or another category; we can lump anything that is not
one or the other into a nondescript catchall category; or we can
add new distinctions to those we already have. For reasons that
will be obvious later, the practice I shall follow will be to divide
the 24 hours of the day into four categories. *Work* and *work-
related time* we considered in the previous chapter along with
free time. *Subsistence time* will include the minimums of sleeping, eating, and related activities like cooking and shopping. To

fit proverbial requirements subsistence time should include provision for shelter in addition to food and sleep. Unfortunately most of the data we have either does not include such activities, or else contains them in a category like "miscellaneous work in the house" or "home operation and improvement" or "home furnishings and equipment," where the repair element is mixed with the ameliorative or esthetic. Time spent in medical care and in lying in bed sick would clearly fall into the subsistence category, had we good information on the average amount of time they take. In classifying expenditures instead of activities, medical costs would certainly be listed under subsistence expenditures, although even here at times the esthetic element enters in the form of plastic surgery or the removal of undesired protuberances or hair. The provision of clothing, too, though apparently subsistence activity when one thinks of warmth or dryness, includes a host of other motives as well.

Even the maintenance of cleanliness is not so easily classified under subsistence. Cleanliness of body alone has great variations. Within these variations the effect on health seems negligible. The use by female office workers of body deodorizers in the form of soaps, liquids, or unguents is not as much a function of hygiene as of work: they work boxed up in offices, not in the open air of the fields. Shopping for food seems clear enough, but what of taking more time to find exotic foods or to pick deodorizers, or to find that dress with the right touch of seductiveness, or to choose a good pocketbook for the night's ride home?

The difficulty is partly that we are dealing with activities that are not wholly visible to an observer. A man "reading a newspaper" for instance may be reading to inform himself about his city, or to learn what is playing on television tonight; yet within the TV log he may be looking not for the wrestling matches but the governor's monthly report to the public. Or he may not be reading at all but gazing at the page while thinking about what he's going to tell the foreman about the new enamel they are using in trimming at the shop. Whatever activity one chooses can fall into a number of categories. There is no such thing as a leisure or free-time activity in itself. We are here back to the difficulty we at first thought had been resolved in the change from the term "leisure" to "free time." Evidently as long as the word "free" is there it will make trouble. Normally parents do not feel free, nor are they free by law, to let their children go cold and hungry while they themselves are fat and warm. Does work have a greater obligation about it that it should be classified as a consumer of unfree time, while the care of children consumes free time? As long as "free" is attached to "time" there will be the problem of deciding what is meant by free, unless we want to assume that work is the only thing unfree in the modern world, and anything unrelated to it is free. The fact that a polarity of "work" and "free" exists is interesting in itself. It reflects perhaps not so much the domination of work over all other values as that, whereas other things with a sense of obligation may also be felt as enjoyable (for example again, the care of children), the job offers, or once did offer, such a prospect less often.

Motives, then, are apparently unavoidable when we treat of free time. Where shall we put flirting, the raising of children, serving on the local zoning committee, going to church on Easter? As happens with child care, which usually falls into a "housekeeping" or "housework" category, the time spent on such activities is not normally found in the available studies, and when it is, they are apparently so elusive, or take up such small quantities of time, that they are thrown into some such category as "social activities" or "visiting" or "miscellaneous." In the so-called subsistence category there is still another difficulty: though we call it subsistence we are not treating of minimum levels (below which death follows) but the low levels of customary decency. How much warmth do people need in their shelter, how much light? Does it matter if water is inside the house or outside, whether it runs or is drawn up, and how much need there be? Similarly for clothing or footwear.

The zone of what is necessary to the organism becomes even

hazier as one leaves food, clothing, shelter, to move over into the area of sex. A sexual appetite exists but its variability and muta-bility in and among human beings are so great that its extent cannot be measured with any accuracy. The significance of these remarks is that one cannot confidently say for example that food of type Y, if eaten in more than X quantity, is consumed for mo-tives other than nourishment. Or is the housewife who drives miles to a particular bakery for fresh bread going above the sim-ple subsistence level when she could have got the same carbohy-drates in a cellophane-wrapped loaf bought at a nearby store, thus saving 15 minutes of subsistence time? Should this excess quarter-hour be charged to free time instead of subsistence? It is also possible to keep alive, as some ascetics do, on what by United States standards would be almost no food. Does anything above the ascetic level properly go to a category other than subsistence, and if so, into which category?

Further problems appear in the multiple character of human activities. A man can eat, listen to a phonograph, read a novel or newspaper, and beat his foot to music, all at the same time. The organism is one, but by convention we have divided its senses into five, each of which can be conceived of as receiving, translat-ing, and acting upon different parts of the environment at once. We can be aware, or totally unaware, of the multiple character of activity and thought. One way out of the difficulty, seemingly, is to classify the activity as the doer would himself. But unless you use his exact word (in which case, though, if you continue the practice, you get a category for every word he uses), you risk dis-torting his purpose. For instance if he says he's shaving, you may classify that as care of self. But he may be thinking, while he is shaving, that he had better give himself a close shave today since he has to see the vice-president this morning for a special assign-ment, or because he is to see a girl this evening whose voice over the phone twanged a bow somewhere. Perhaps the category should be work time (special "good appearance" effort for ad-vancement purposes). Yet if you asked the man himself, the doer, he would reply with the conventional activity term — "action" meaning the most visible activity — "I'm shaving." The mental activity goes unrecognized because it is not commonly supposed to be an answer to the question, "What are you doing?"

Children, after a hard day's play outside, if asked what they did, characteristically reply, "Nothing." They simply haven't learned what it is that adults expect them to report. After a while they learn that by and large they should report their most visible activity and its prime motive . . . if acceptable. Among adults, we are not likely to find many reports of "nothing," for in most cases today "nothing" is an unacceptable answer. Nor will we find many reports of "thinking," for that is next to nothing, and not worth reporting if some more obvious or violent body movement was occurring at the same time. If a man is thinking and smoking, he will be described as a man smoking. So in our data we will find the visibly active movements predominant. We should realize that they do not always give us a full or accurate picture.

Although it would seem a simple matter to find out how much free time a person has and what he does with it, problems crop up at every turn. Indeed a study giving us a complete account of a person's activities would be impossible. We shall have to rest content with the descriptions we do get, realizing, however, that they represent what we or someone else was interested in seeing and recording about still another person's activities, who in turn had his own interests about what to report.

The categories we have chosen thus far change only slightly the slogan of the old fighters for the short work week. Their work is our work time; their sleep is our subsistence time; their "all the rest" we too shall call *all the rest* at least temporarily, putting in it the endlessly minute time devoted to activities concerned with church, love affairs, or the Red Cross; and then we add free time, a category they did not name. We now have four major categories. In the following estimates all the reservations we have just made apply, and not only to the subsistence category but to the work category as well, for one can have free time while at work just as one can work while off the job. Work time, if we use the calculations made earlier, takes up an average of 10 hours and 40 minutes a day (job about 8 hours, journey to work 1½ hours, sphere of woman's work in housekeeping allocated for man, about 20 minutes, do-it-yourself work, about 40 minutes, moonlighting, 10 minutes). Subsistence time takes up an average of 10½ hours (sleep 8½, dressing, eating, cooking and shopping, nearly 2 hours) (Table 3). For all the rest, including prayer, getting the car fixed, going to barber, dentist, shoemaker, or laundry — items which are usually overlooked — we can make a low guess of 20 minutes per day. This makes a total of about 21½, leaving 2½ hours a day of free time. A 2½-hour evening of free time, I should guess, is not unusually large for most of the world's stable communities. There are variations in customs, of course, that would call for a different set of categories. Obviously, in countries with long and convivial eating hours, not all the two or three hours spent at table should be classified as subsistence time. The calculation we have just made for this country assumed a 6-day week. Most men have a 5-day official week but many of them work overtime in the evenings or on Saturday morning. If, in order to give the worker the benefit of the weekend, we calculate on the basis of a 5-day week, we shall have to say that the job alone takes an average of nearly 9½ hours a day. On work days he would have not 2½ hours of time free but only about one hour. Two and a half hours or one, what are they free for? That question is now the order of the day, and this chapter will try to piece together a quantitative picture of the way free time is spent in the United States.

THE THINGS BOUGHT

Obviously the amounts of money people spend for certain goods and services can tell us something about their activities. A recent study done for commercial purposes estimated that of the average household's expenditures the per cent spent on recreation and recreation equipment is 5 per cent (Table 5). This is not far from an estimate obtained from government statistics (Table 4). In 1959 recreation accounted for 5.2 per cent of consumer expenditures. Neither estimate included the amounts per household given to the government in taxes and spent by the government, federal, state, or local, for recreation purposes. For 1960 the figure was $894 million, which, divided by the 52.6 million households in the United States, gives us an additional expenditure of $17 or so per household, an almost negligible item in an annual household budget of over $4,000.

This average of 5 per cent or $215 (Table 5) (+ $17 of taxes) is spent on recreation and recreation equipment. Included under this wide heading are admissions paid by spectators to motion pictures, cultural and sports events, exhibits and museums; bowling, golf and other fees paid for sports participation as well as fees for amusement rides and dancing; expenditures for all kinds of sporting goods such as boats, camping and fishing equipment, arms and ammunition, golf, tennis, bowling, baseball, and other sport equipment; for games and toys, including playing cards and bicycles; for optical goods such as sunglasses, binoculars and microscopes; for photographic, musical, and electronic instruments and equipment (including radios, TV sets, phonograph records, and sheet music); for pets, pet equipment and services and packaged pet foods; for all kinds of reading materials — books, magazines, newspapers, comic books, programs, pamphlets, and journals; for luggage and trunks, for rental and storage of recreation equipment, recreation dues, and repair of recreation equipment.

The $17 per household spent by the various governments in the United States on recreation includes amounts spent for capital equipment and for operation of facilities by federal, state, and local governmental units, but not the full amounts. The federal portion represents expenditures of only the National Park Service; state outlays represent estimated total state expenditures for forestry and parks; outlays by local units include expenditures for parks and other types of recreation by municipalities, counties, park districts, and other local units.

Taking the average not of all households but of various classes — income ($2,000, $3,000, etc.), education (grade school, high school, etc.), occupation, age, geographic location (Northeast, Central, etc.) — we find that the relative expenditure for recreation varies hardly at all, remaining constantly at 5 or 6 per cent (Table 6). The only groups to go above or below are the persons over 65, who spend 4 per cent, and those under 40 without children, who spend 7 per cent of their household income on recreation.

How can one account for this peculiar hovering around the 5 to 6 per cent point? Is there perhaps a recreation need which, no matter how much a man earns or how old he is, takes that much out of his total effort as measured by the money he makes? This is not likely. There are other more plausible explanations. One is that each person finds himself in an income, age, school, work environment where there are implicit standards set on how much should be spent for various kinds of things. Somewhere in the United States there may be the machine operator earning $4,000 a year who has bought himself a Mercedes-Benz, who lives on potatoes, cabbage, and beans in a two-room cold water flat without a TV set, doesn't touch alcohol, and lets his wife take in laundry. If there is one such person, ordinary comments, criticism, laughter, recriminations, ridicule, advice, raised eyebrows, and significant pointings to the head have brought enough pressure to bear so that in the country over there are doubtless not two.

A man so thirsting after a Mercedes may appear to be a caricature rather than an example. Such a man should exist, except that we expect to find a certain uniformity in any guess. And not only within a category but also among categories. For there are not only local or class or family means of expenditure but national norms too. The variations in clothing and accessories

between the poorest and the richest households is that between
11 per cent and 14 per cent of their respective incomes, and
amounts to the difference between $223 for the poorest and
$1,083 for the richest, about five times as much. Similarly the
difference between the same poor household's 5 per cent on recreation expenditures and the rich one's 6 per cent is about
$400. These differences may appear great to some, but only the
livery worn by Trimalchio's household servants would have gone
far beyond the horizon of either the rich or the poor economic
household, while Trimalchio's food costs would have knocked
all others to the ground in quick order. One name for the radical
democrat or the extreme advocate of equality is leveler. That in
a democracy expenditures, especially conspicuous ones like
clothes, jewelry, and automobiles, are influenced by the leveling
frame of mind is not surprising.

The influence of friends and relatives, neighbors and fellow
citizens, works to iron out differences in these figures. Some are
flatter than others, however. Expenditure for medical and personal care is as constant a figure among the various groups mentioned as money spent for recreation. One can detect here perhaps the leveling influence also of medical insurance programs.
Another leveling factor in these figures is that they are themselves averages built upon other averages, a fact that cuts down
extremes — as in the case of a man who drowned while fording a
river with an average depth of 2½ feet. Furthermore, expressing
the averages in percentages rather than dollars also helps give a
sense of equality and at times even of an inverse linear relation
where a correlation is to be expected. In food, beverages, and tobacco, the poor consume 36 per cent and the rich only 24 per
cent. Most of the expected correlations do appear once the figures
are put in dollars.

The widest range of difference appears in this category of food,
drink, and tobacco. We tend to think of this group as relatively
inelastic; it is also one in which heavy spending is conspicuous
within a category — let's say in home entertaining — but not

among categories, exception being made for the cigar which, in recent history at least, has been a symbol of the capitalist. The percentages here can be deceptive in that it is high on the side of households with lowest income. Food, drink, and tobacco make up over a third of their budget; it is only a quarter of that of the most prosperous householders. In dollars the difference would be reversed, in that the low-income group spends $689, while the high one spends $1,913. This is the most we find in the way of average difference. Hardly Lucullan. Other categories with notable though lesser fluctuations in range are expenditures on automobiles and in home operation and improvement, which includes rent, maintenance, etc. All these differences put together can in no way be called Gargantuan, yet they are greater than those in the area of recreation.

It is possible that the variation in food and drink costs reflects also the difference in price between beer and hard liquor, or else that drink is no longer the curse of the working classes. It is possible, too, that at the points of variation in the automobile and home categories we are face to face with two areas where a display of prosperity is possible among groups. Having an expensive car or a home in a certain neighborhood is well-controlled within groups: until a man is a vice-president or senior executive in a corporation, he usually does not move to a particular suburb, or have a particular make of car, without sanction from other inhabitants of the suburb or owners of the same brand of car who are his superiors. Only when he is their peer is he invited to take his seat among them. But outside this particular peerage there may be groups where bizarre spending, or no spending at all, for cars is a possible course of action — as among teen-agers, or college professors. Or, as in the case of the farmer, a heavy-duty car or truck may be necessary for his work, and therefore his automotive expenses will be greater than the factory worker's.

This last observation leads us to another, and to what may be the most important possibility. Recreation expenditures, the category whose constancy in percentages I have taken pains to explain, may not be the proper vehicle for free-time expenses, but merely for certain residual expenses. In the household budgets we have been discussing, there does appear a residual category of expenditure, labeled as such: expenditures for "other goods and services." It has about the same constancy as the recreation category, oscillating between 5 and 9 per cent.

The recreation and recreation equipment category, which fluctuates between 4 and 7 per cent, includes, as we have noted, many things. Both a bow and arrow and a motorboat would be recorded here. But these items are not the only recreation expenditures, and indeed on the whole may not be major ones. Is not drinking a free-time activity? Alcoholic drinking on the job is banned almost everywhere in the United States. Drinking wine with meals is rare. Milk and coffee are the most common drinks at meals. Alcoholic drinking thus appears during the hours after work and after dinner, the hours of free time if ever there are any. A substantial part of the food and drink category should go to free-time expenditures. But so should a substantial part of every other category. "Clothing and accessories" includes sport coats, a suit to wear at parties, a hunting cap. "Medical and personal care" includes removing warts and getting hair curled or straightened. "Home operation and improvement" can include a swimming pool or a den, a terrace or a recreation room, and "home furnishings and equipment" will furnish both of them, and equip the gardener as well as the amateur bartender. Of "automotive" expenditures, it is worth remembering that one goes by car to the cinema as well as to work, and that the most practical way of seeing some of the national forests for which the average taxpayer contributes his $17 a year is by automobile.

We therefore cannot accept the figure of 5 per cent as the average amount of income American households spend on recreation or free-time activities. If we could subtract the right amount from each of the other categories, we would have a more accurate allocation to free-time expenditures than that contained in the leftover category of recreation and recreation equipment.

I consider it worth while to take the reader through the maze of these difficulties rather than lead him out quickly by the hand. Quantities and figures are used in many fields today. Free time or leisure is no exception. Since we shall be confronted again and again with "the figures" in this chapter, too, it will help to know the problems involved in interpreting them. Yet this is not the only reason I have chosen the tortuous route. By going this way we are more likely to run into some of the shadier nooks and the subtler puzzles. Once out of the maze, the avenue may appear the wider for it. We have just seen again that no activity can on its surface be classified as one of work, subsistence, or free time. How the individual feels about it must be taken into consideration, too. If, then, we go on to use classifications made in such a way, it is always with this reservation in mind, and only because we have no better data at the moment.

Such is the case with the figures we have gathered on actual consumer expenditures for recreational goods and services over the years 1909 to 1959 (Table 7a). These are not based on personal reports of expenditures, as were those just discussed, but on actual sales of tickets or goods. Expenditures here are grouped under specific headings like theater, motion pictures, spectator sports, clubs, commercial participant amusements, pari-mutuel receipts, reading, gardening, radio and television and their repair, records, musical instruments, durable and nondurable toys, and sports equipment. As we pointed out earlier, these figures all together add up to approximately 5 per cent (5.2) of total consumer expenditures in the United States (Table 4).

By putting the separate dollar figures into percentages we find that slightly over a quarter of the money Americans spent on all such things in 1959 went into the radio-TV area; about the same proportion went into toys and sports equipment; less than one tenth was spent on reading; 8 per cent on motion pictures; 6 per cent on gardening; 5 per cent on billiards, bowling, dancing, etc., in commercial places; 5 per cent on clubs; 2 per cent on the theater and opera; and less than 2 per cent on attending baseball and football games, horse races, and other spectator sports. These then are many of the activities Americans engage in during their free time. Most of them seem to have little to do with work or with subsistence time.

The list, here as before, however, suffers from a lack of complete estimates of the free-time activity or expenditures involved — in clothes, automobiles, cosmetics, eating and drinking, and so on. (For instance entertainment as an expenditure or drinking in a tavern do not appear here.) Furthermore, though a man may buy golf clubs — seemingly a clearly free-time expenditure — he may have bought them to be able to play at a country club with a group of businessmen who have the power to increase his income by purchases, promotion, or better job offers. Golf clubs in this case would constitute a business or work purchase. He may also buy them for pure free-time motives, and yet after playing nine holes once or twice, may, for lack of skill or sustained interest (or for lack of free time!), leave them stored in the attic. Expenditures can reflect an intention to spend free time but not necessarily its actual spending. Thus the mountainous totals spent each year on "leisure equipment" cannot be taken at face value. On one hand, they are too small, since they do not include the more mixed categories like eating and drinking. On the other hand, they exaggerate, in that a purchase of an article designed for free-time use may not be so used, or even used at all.

The government's expenditures for recreation must be considered from a separate angle. Each taxpayer pays for government parks and forests, and hundreds of million visits are recorded annually. There are fewer persons involved than the number of visits discloses: those who make more than one visit are tallied over again. Those who do repeat visits are hardly the same ones who on the basis of the progressive income tax spend a larger sum for governmental recreation expenditures. We cannot even say of taxes that they show an intention to spend free time in the way the government spent the money. They show simply that Congress voted to spend tax receipts in this way. Congress evidently doesn't know how people want their taxes spent. Not long ago it charged a special body, the Outdoor Recreation Resources Review Commission, to find out what their needs and preferences may be.

THE THINGS DONE

The second kind of data I propose to examine is a more direct index to activities. It consists of the results of interviews about what people do in their free time. One national survey asked a sample of the United States population over 15 years old what leisure activities they had engaged in "yesterday." The interviewer handed out cards on which a list of activities was printed, and instructed his subjects to indicate those they had done. Of each 100 persons 57 had engaged in watching television, 38 in visiting with friends or relatives, 33 in working around the yard and garden, 27 in reading newspapers, 18 in reading books, 17 in going pleasure driving, 14 in listening to records, 11 in going to meetings or other organizational activities, 10 in special hobbies like woodworking and knitting, 8 in going out to dinner. These were the ten most frequent activities. The second ten were: participating in sports; playing cards, checkers, etc.; "none of the activities listed"; spending time at drugstore; singing or playing a musical instrument; movies; sports events; dances; play or concert; attending technical or adult school (Table 8).

This list not only gives us an indication of the frequency with which such activities were engaged in; it also confirms our supposition that the previous lists built on expenditures excluded important free-time activities. Perhaps this is the moment to list all the activities that have come to our attention so far. We can then say that at present the American's use of free time includes watching television; listening to the radio; listening to records; reading newspapers, magazines, books; working around yard or in garden; pleasure driving; going to meetings or organizational activities; attending lectures or adult school; visiting; going out to dinner; going to the theater, concerts, opera, movies; participating in sports (bowling, riding, skating, fishing, swimming, golf); sight-seeing; singing; playing musical instruments; dancing; going to government parks and amusement parks; attending sports events; placing pari-mutuel bets; spending time at the drugstore; playing cards; engaging in special hobbies (photography, stamp collecting); keeping pets; and playing slot machines.

If we want, however, to know something of how much of each day Americans spend on activities like these, we shall have to turn to the third kind of data at our disposal — studies of time budgeting. The diary study that gave good service in the previous chapter (Table 3) contained a category "leisure activity" that included games and sports, as a spectator or participant, going to church, as well as other activity at home that was not work, like playing cards, listening to the radio, watching television, talking on the telephone, visiting with guests.

Note that "talking on the telephone" is considered a leisure activity. In the list of activities previously made, it did not appear. On second thought, telephone conversation, like visiting, can certainly be a free-time activity. The housewife's talking over the phone is supposed to have supplanted her talking over the back fence. The teen-age youngster today has the reputation of hanging on to the phone, too, for half-hours at a time. What, though, about a father's ringing up a friend to arrange a ride to work in the morning or mother's calling the plumber or either one's phoning the doctor about the said youngster's fever of 101°? Similarly, "at restaurant, tavern, barber, etc." was not classified as leisure here, yet in the previous list, going out to dinner was held to be a free-time activity. By long tradition, at least, the tavern, too, has been considered a hangout for men in their free time. We should certainly add going there to our list of activities. As for the barber, it might first be thought that time spent there should be put into another category in the study, per- haps "dressing, bathing, etc.," since that seems to be the "per- sonal care" category. Anyone who remembers, however, the lei- sureliness of going to the barber for a shave and trim might well classify it as leisure. But in the cities, at least, those days are gone.

Once more we are faced with the same difficulty: whether to count a given activity in the free-time category. "Going to church" is another heading we do not feel right about. In the diary survey mentioned it falls under leisure. We would take it out of there; yet we have not ourselves decided where we should put it. This problem is somewhat different from that of going to the barber or going shopping, for none of the categories estab- lished — work time, free time, subsistence time — fits going to church. The barber, we would probably agree, goes either into free time or subsistence time (personal care), although in the lat- ter case the question of cosmetics raises its pretty head to remind us that we still haven't found a conventional category for flirting, love-making or courtship either. They remain in "all the rest" time.

Shopping, on the other hand, can easily be put in subsistence time, it would seem. The average shopping time we have for women is about 20 minutes a day. Men shop too, spending about one fourth as much time at it as the women (Table 3), and this time is not what they spend shopping for neckties or shoes, but at the grocery or supermarket, at the "dime store" or druggist's. At each of these places, men seem to shop as often as women, but take less time. Perhaps they are speedier, or do merely supple- mentary shopping, buying whatever the wife forgot to buy. The median for men as well as women for going to the grocery or su- permarket is 8 times a month, to the druggist's, 4 times a month, and the same for the department store, and "dime store." The preferred shopping days for both men and women are Friday and

Saturday. But women shop more in the morning and afternoon, while men prefer evenings (Tables 9, 10). Shopping on coming home from work seems to be one of the American male's prime functions.

This last information we have from another survey which focused on drugstores (Table 10). Surveys, however, cannot help us to decide how much of shopping is a mixed pleasure. Undoubtedly some is pleasant and done therefore only in free time. Window shopping is a good example. The effect on a woman's morale of shopping for a new hat is reputedly phenomenal. Whether this is true or not, no one can deny that there are other motives for shopping than those at the subsistence level. Dining-room tables in ordinary life do not spread themselves. Those who spread them can do so plainly or tastily, with boiled potatoes or *pommes soufflées*. And the pleasures of the board that is not only well-laden, but savory — into which category shall they go? In America the palate seems to have been recently rediscovered. The market for exotic foods is a new one. Perhaps it owes part of its existence to the man's share of the shopping, or perhaps to the extra money that his wife brings in; in which case he remains the breadwinner and she the sugar-and-spice-and-everything-nice. The new foods have not yet brought about any remarkable change in American cuisine, but in shopping patterns many things are new. The shopping of teen-agers, for example.

Advertisers today are often apt to grow lyrical over teen-agers. There are so many of them — and they have so much money burning holes in their pockets. The sight they offer is one of kids at a fair. They're impressionable — advertising-impressionable, promotion-impressionable and brand-impressionable. Receptive to new ideas, they're not hoarders, they're spenders. They are not set in their ways but they want to be on their way — to the counter of commodities. What they hear, read, or learn about, they "need" or "must have," or "can't live without," or "die" if they can't have. The girls deserve particular notice. They must try everything new — lipstick colors, synthetic fabrics, packaged foods, *ad hoc* appliances. They eat tons of snacks, hot dogs, hamburgers, drink gallons of Cokes, smoke cartons of cigarettes. They love to entertain after school, before and after the big game, a few friends or a big gang. They love to get gifts and to give them and to talk over the phone; to shop with goggling eyes and loose purse strings; to decorate their rooms and redecorate themselves — their hands and feet, heads and face; to go off to college — with transistor radios, portable typewriter, a set of matched luggage, stereophonic phonograph and disks, cameras, wrist watches, new clothes. And/or they want to get engaged (seventeen is the median age) and (from fifteen on) prepare for marriage (one half of all blushing brides are in their teens) with a dowry of silver, sheets and towels, glasses, dishes, and electric blankets. And they are rich, these 8½ million girls, having over $4 billion of their own each year, plus other billions of their families' over which they each exert the influence of a small Svengali. And they multiply rapidly. Each year the class increases by half a million.

These youngsters are not shopping for food, clothing, and shelter. Does their activity go under the head of leisure? Whether youngsters have leisure is a question we have not yet made up our mind about. The excitement the automobile causes among many of them, specially the males, is another facet of their use of time. The pensioner may go along slowly; he reads the morning paper, writes some letters, shops for groceries, patches up the house a bit or gardens before lunch, then a little nap perhaps, or a walk in the park or to the library, picking up the evening paper, cooking dinner with his wife or a crony, going bowling or to play billiards or to a meeting or movie, or watching television, and then to bed. A car might help in shopping or going to the movies but it doesn't have the fascination it has for the American young. For most youth, it is much more important to arrive at driver's license age than at voting age. The car is technology in their hands, a machine to command, power at the touch of the toe, danger, skill, privacy from family, courtship. They are the true pleasure drivers. They can drive around for hours, never bored or tired. When they return home and parents ask what they did their answer is like the child's. Instead of "Nothing," they reply, "Oh, just drove around with the boys."

Let us look at the automobile and travel more broadly. According to our time-diary study, daily travel takes about an hour and one half of the man's time and about one half hour of the woman's time (Table 3). We need help from other surveys, however, for the diaries were not given to persons in process of travel, in vacation resorts or foreign countries.

To those unfamiliar with the streets of the ancient parts of the world, streets so narrow we would call them alleys, built for the horse, cart, and wagon, the long, straight wide stretch of an American street or road warrants no special notice. The American has become a species whose locomotion is based less on two legs than four wheels. He travels an estimated 5,000 to 10,000 miles a year. Walking, he would hesitate to try it. By horse, he might do it if he spent most of the year in the saddle. Where does he go in these many miles which each year would take him across several continents? Well, there is work, which takes in about 10 miles per trip 200 to 400 times a year. There is shopping, which takes 6 miles or so once a week or more. Travel by salesmen or truck drivers we are not counting. Then of course there is visiting, going to the movies, to the bowling alley, trips on holidays and weekends and annual vacation. Three out of four American families have one or more cars.

During the depression it was found that families one step away from relief were buying a secondhand car. Like the cigarettes that some persons then on relief would buy with their money in preference to food, in the United States the car was already a necessity, as it is even more so today. In fact the Bureau of Labor Statistics lists the car along with food, clothing, and shelter. Even in a bicycle-sized town life, work, schools, and shopping are all distributed differently from what they were in the days of the horse. The automobile has stretched out the town's radius. Grocery stores once dotted a city. There was usually one within two or three blocks of each customer. Today the super-markets are grouped together in shopping centers on town perim-eters reachable only after passing through miles of residential zones. Rarely is the main shopping within a mile of the house. For life in present-day America the car is hard to do without.

Not only have work and education and shopping moved farther away, so have all kinds of out-of-the-house entertainment and recreation. What is called "pleasure driving," going out in the car merely to drive along, to see things on the way, perhaps to stop somewhere for a few minutes, anywhere, then to return, has already been mentioned as a form of free-time activity. In the evening the car is often used in the time that once was spent on the front porch; the American simply set his porch on wheels. A study of a suburb in 1934 put at about one hour and 45 minutes a week the amount of pleasure driving each person indulged in. There were no drive-in movies in 1934, nor were there half as many cars as there are today. The storm of traffic has reduced pleasure driving, it seems; most people are not enthusiastic about it. The young are the ones who enjoy it most. Other developments, however, like refrigeration and TV, have come to center the evening more definitely in the house, bring-ing the front porch off its wheels this time and into the living room, at least for the present.

Another estimate of automobile use, made in 1942, calculated how many of the miles run each year by the average car were not devoted to business, shopping, taking the children to school, or seeing the doctor. The amount came out to one half of all driv-ing. A more recent estimate (1958) reports that travel connected with work or business accounts for not quite one half of all auto-mobile trips a day, the rest being connected with social, recrea-tional, shopping, and other purposes. Accordingly, one third to one half of the purchase price and upkeep expenditure of all the cars we see on the road in a year can be put down in the cost ac-counts as a free-time element. So common as not to attract notice are cars loaded with fishing tackle, boats, skis, golf bags, or fresh-killed game; cars jammed into lots outside ball parks and bowling alleys; and cars filled with the family in their Sunday best. If the automobile is a work and subsistence necessity, it is also a free-time necessity.

In outdoor recreation, the days are past when a family would pack a basket and take a streetcar to go out in the country for a picnic. Almost half a billion visits are recorded each year to national and state parks, forests, wildlife refuges and reserves. The hunter or fisherman will carry gun or rod; the pilgrim to battlefields and birthplaces may carry a camera; but almost every visitor rides up in an automobile and seldom wanders far from it. In visiting the Grand Canyon the vacationer, as one of a group of three or more, now travels on the average over 4,000 miles, to Glacier over 3,500, and to Yosemite nearly 2,000. He was on a trip of more than twenty-two days when he visited the Grand Canyon, yet he stayed in the park not quite a day and a half. Whether he came primarily to see the park, or whether his visit formed only a part of other ventures, he typically stayed there only a short time. But he almost invariably came by auto, and what is known of his habits indicates that he was a sight-seer limited by time to the sights he could see from the places he could reach by car.

Without the car, there is but one main place for outdoor recreation — the municipal park. In or near the cities of the United States, specially the larger ones, there are 20,000 to 30,000 parks or related areas. For each million Americans in towns or cities there are 200 or more parks, yielding about 7/10 of an acre per 100 persons. This acreage, substantially below the standard often adopted of one acre for every 100 persons, is even smaller than it seems. The average is brought up by high acreage in several regions — notably the mountain states — where there are several large, rather undeveloped county parks. Furthermore, to get to county parks often requires the auto again. Though they are often crowded and may not have some one facility you most want, county and municipal parks do include bathing beaches and swimming pools, ballfields, summer camps, golf courses, tennis and horseshoe courts, play and coasting streets, picnic areas, and, among fairly new developments, band shells and dance pavilions, arboretums, bridle paths and nature trails, bowling greens, gardens and zoos, boathouses, ice-skating rinks, and even mobile units to transport recreation to those who lack the mobility to go to it.

Another way of spending free time without an automobile is to travel to places where the automobile can't — across water, for example. Once there, a car may be bought or hired, it is true, but at least a good part of the journey was by boat or plane. Not all travel to other countries requires leaving the car behind (Canada or Mexico), but most foreign lands are not attached to North or even South America. Since World War II, travel abroad has increased sixfold. "Year after year," says the form letter from the President of the United States enclosed with each passport, "increasing numbers of our citizens travel to foreign countries." The number of passports issued or renewed in recent years is over half a million. The most frequent travelers abroad today seem to be housewives. About one quarter of all passports go to them. Overseas travelers ranging from 10 to 20 per cent each as a group are students, sales clerks, skilled technical workers, and the self-employed (Table 11). Nothing is fixed about these proportions. In a few years, the rankings may shift places up and down, depending on grants, loans, ship and air fares, changing school terms, international conditions, and so on.

The fact remains that four out of every five Americans do not go on vacation where the family car won't take them. With any kind of vacation travel, though, free-time activities change simply because surroundings and atmosphere change. But perhaps not excessively, now that all hotels, motels, and boardinghouses can boast central heating, electric lights, clean towels, hot and cold running water, indoor toilets and bath — and that ultimate comfort, the television set. The hunter or boy scout may still huddle round the fire swapping stories, but the portable radio and television have supplanted many a fire and storyteller. How many we do not know.

Storytelling at home is also a lost art. Still reeling from the blow of radio, it finds in television an even more powerful foe. That rather conspicuous and ungainly box in the corner of millions of living rooms dominates the American evening. On the record (Table 8) it appears more often than anything else among the things people said they did "yesterday." As an expenditure television does not reach the proportions of a car, but in repairs alone it amounts to about three quarters of a billion dollars, almost as much as is spent on gardening; almost twice that spent on pari-mutuel betting; about that spent on all commercial parks, bowling, golf, and riding; or on all clubs and fraternal organizations; thrice that spent on all spectator sports, including the two "great national sports" of baseball and football; and over twice that spent on all opera and the legitimate theater (Table 7a). In the United States the television set is more pervasive than the automobile or the bathtub. Everybody (nine out of ten households) owns one or more sets. One would presume that TV viewing makes up a large part of the "leisure at home other than reading" category.

There seems, though, to be some discrepancy in available figures. The diary study indicates that the time devoted to this category (including playing cards, conversing with visitors, talking on the phone, etc.) in the weekday hours between 6 P.M. and 11 P.M. is slightly over 2 hours for men and about a half hour more for women (Table 3). These figures are averages, of course, yet according to another survey more than 90 per cent of all TV sets are turned on every weekday evening; the average set is going 4½ hours each night. Another study estimates family use of TV at over 5 hours a day. The hours for TV alone add up to one hour more than that for the whole leisure-at-home category above. One reason for these differences may be that in the latter surveys a national sample was used, whereas in the former one a single "typical" town was selected for intensive research. Another may be that while the one study relied on diaries, other surveys used personal interviews or phone calls, or recording devices attached to TV sets. People may want to seem less dependent on TV, and so report it less, whereas the clock of a recording device moves on inexorably. On the other hand the clock keeps track of electrical impulses, not what people are paying attention to.

The TV set may be on without drawing more than an occasional glance from a group of bridge players. Perhaps only the children take in the 6–8:30 shows until the moment when father and mother, having done the dishes and cleared the deck, look around for the kids to shoo them to bed. Afterwards the parents take over for a few hours of TV programs, thenceforth designed for exclusively adult interest. This was the case with the radio, and now so it is with television: as the hours grow late the programs become more grown-up, for grown-ups need no one's permission to stay up late. Another point to remember is that the questions, "Is your TV set on now?" and, "What program are you listening to?" do not follow with, "What are you and the other members of the household doing at this moment?" Some may be giving full attention to the screen; others may be in a different room; still others may be watching TV, all right, but at the same time knitting, or fixing the wiring on a lamp, or polishing silver. What then is the activity? In the time-diary, the person is supposed to record his principal activity. In the silver polisher's instance, the choice is not easy. Neither the recording device nor the short-question telephone call even permits a choice; each simply lays everything at the TV set's knob — turned right or left.

Whether the hours are 2 or 3 or 4 a day, per person or per family, other studies too seem to confirm a high score for TV watching in the evening hours. Indeed the television seems to have the evening licked into shape. Even by the lowest estimates, no other form of recreation comes close in time devoted.

PARCELS OF TIME

Evening has always been one of the most faithful friends of free time. Before gas and electric lighting came into being, the hours of work could hardly be longer than from dawn to dusk. Down deep in the memory of the species sundown must deliciously remain as the hour of nothing to do. It has always been the time of relaxation and sociality, of food and drink, games, dances, song and story, and for some *l'heure bleue,* the hour of transcendence, the moment for dreams and longing, *l'ora che volge il desio.*

Other islands of free time rest upon meals. Take lunch, for example. In the middle of the day, in the heat of the sun, in many if not most parts of the agrarian world, labor ceases, shelter is sought, food and people come together, time out is called, to eat and digest. The American lunch differs somewhat. Ranging from twenty minutes to one hour, the interval is supposed to be not for rest but for the ingestion of food. In Aesop's fable of the sun and the wind, the sun was stronger; it took a man's clothes right off his back. But the sun at noon beats on the heads of relatively few Americans; it has no power to make the others stop work. Digestion is the only natural force opposed to working on, but the American at lunch foils it by eating lightly — "lunch" comes from "lump," as a lump of bread (lunch and the job go well together etymologically, too, a lump and a piece) — avoiding soporific alcohol (until off the job) and filling himself up with sleep-chasing coffee. That business is often discussed in this lunchtime is well known, but as a practice it occurs mainly in the professional or executive classes. An office or factory worker would need a certificate from a physician to take a rest or a nap after lunch. Among American farmers a nap seems still to be part of an acceptable pattern, on Sundays even more than on weekdays, and on any day more prevalent among men than among their wives.

Breakfast does not seem to offer much free time anywhere. In fact it only grows more frenzied with all members of the family trying to meet different schedules — bus, train, school, shopping, work. The days when the *paterfamilias* read those portions of the morning newspaper fit to read to the family assembled at breakfast seem to be past.

Almost all Americans who work have a vacation, another larger island of time. Nearly half of all workers have two weeks a year, and nearly another half three weeks. Here too we have parallels in other parts of the world. The seasonal character of agricultural labor grants months of free time, or, as more typically put, enforces months of idleness. The American vacation originally took its cue from another kind of ceasework — the summer exodus of the workless European well-to-do classes. They went more to the mountains than to the sea; they didn't stay two or three weeks but three or four months; they fled the city's heat for a change of element, but rest and recuperation were also attractions. The feudal pattern had been that aristocrats left court and city to go in the months from June to September to supervise the harvest and its partition. After Rousseau and the French Revolution the bourgeoisie in emulation took to going to a summer place. But they had no tasks to do there, as the aristocrats had, and so the modern vacation got its start. In northern climes — where coal exists, and steam, they say, is something like an Englishman — the summers are hot and humid. With the spread of air-conditioning perhaps their debilitating effect on the city workingman can be reduced even further than by the simple expedient of brick roofs or tile. Up to now, summer remains the favorite vacation period, with fall the second choice. The spring season is almost as low as winter, suggesting that in the United States, March, April, and May are not to be counted on for good weather.

Signs are, though, that times and weather are changing. In number of vacations, autumn, winter, and spring together now surpass summer. With air travel pushing the range farther away, the choice of climates becomes wider; taking off in February is not so bad if one can find sunshine somewhere. But finding cool air in August is even better, because it's still easier to stay warm at home in February than cool in August. For this reason jockeying and pressure along the rail goes on among employees when time comes to decide who is going on vacation when. As a compromise, vacation time is often taken in two batches of two weeks each by those so fortunate as to have a total of four; or else the compromise may be between summer and winter; one hates to give up refuge from the August heat, and yet the gray winter months are so many. . . . Happily, with staggered vacations the factory machines need not slow down, and for the tourist business any smoothing out of seasonal humps is an advantage.

"Taking a vacation" is so obviously part of free time that it did not appear as an activity in the list previously given. Of course, it is more than one activity: it embraces many — pleasure driving, fatiguing driving, swimming, canoeing, and so on. On any average given day about one million and a half American workers are on vacation (Table 12). We have some notion of what families with an income of $5,000 and over do in this time. About two thirds of them take a vacation trip, remaining three or more days away from home. One of the two thirds actually take two or more such trips. All told these vacationers go by car for a distance of over a thousand miles round trip, have over twenty days a year available to them, take two vacation trips, over 90 per cent of them in the United States, averaging about ten days each, mainly in the summer, about a quarter in the fall, and the others divided equally between winter and spring. Evidently, the more people make, the more they spend while on vacation, and the above families spend a lot of money. The poorer families seem hardly to go on vacation from home, and when they do they spend little. The estimates that have been made of how people spend their money on vacation trips give at least a vague idea of what they do in this time. Lodgings take 43 cents of the dollar, restaurants 14, entertainment (movies, boat trips, summer theaters, rides, golf, shooting galleries, games, and so on) takes 11, transportation in the vacation area another 7, and taverns 6. The remaining 19 cents go for items like groceries, barber shops, appliances, gifts and souvenirs, and laundry.

The American is cheered by other shorter respites too. He has his weekend of Saturday and Sunday. It is not the long weekend of English renown, not even the two full, free days we once thought it was, but, facilitated by the automobile, the weekend often takes him outside the city. Sunday seems to be the day for the outing or the pleasure drive. Saturday differs from the ordinary work day, the time-diaries reveal (Table 3), in that some men don't go to work. Traveling takes up about the same amount of time as on weekdays but more of it is used for weekend food shopping (this takes twice as long per person on Saturday). More time, too, is spent visiting friends and relatives, watching or playing games or sports outdoors, going dancing. There is a barely perceptible rise in the category of "at restaurant, tavern, barber, etc.," which may reflect more eating out on Saturday night, as well as the popular custom of going to the tavern. Indoors one spends more time in watching television or playing cards, having guests over, and so on; more miscellaneous work is done around the house, probably the home repairs, or the do-it-yourself of the home-from-work male; slightly more time is spent preparing and eating food, possibly because the children and males are at home for lunch. And sleep is caught up on.

Occasionally a day or two of holidays is added to the weekend. These three or four days then become jolly times with a general letdown in pace, more loafing about, sometimes a trip somewhere for a few days, more dropping in on others and vice versa. Labor Day and sometimes Christmas and New Year's Day make double holidays; the usual single ones are Thanksgiving, Washington's Birthday, Memorial Day, and the Fourth of July. In some places Lincoln's Birthday is made a day without work; in others Veterans' Day is commemorated. The way holidays are made in the modern world would make an interesting inquiry. Compared to ancient or medieval times, as we have already pointed out, the number of our holidays is minuscule. Did we ever have more? If so, what happened to them? The Colonies before, and the United States after, the brief brightness of the eighteenth century were molded by the ideas of the Reformation. By pulling so many saints down from heaven, generations of Protestants sheared the calendar of holidays. Once there were no saints, who was there to celebrate on these days? At the time of the French Revolution, during Robespierre's period, the Republic substituted a tenth day (*décadi*) for the seventh day of the Sabbath. This cut the annual days of rest down to 36. In the *ancien régime* the church had guaranteed the worker 52 Sundays, 90 rest days, and 38 holidays. The new regime, having deprived the saints of their halo, enthroned new ones, in lesser number but with ringing names: the Supreme Being and Nature, the Human Race, the French people, the Benefactors of Mankind, Freedom and Equality, the Martyrs of Freedom, the Republic, the Freedom of the World, Patriotism, Hatred of Tyrants and Traitors, Truth, Justice, Modesty, Fame and Immortality, Friendship, Temperance, Fidelity, Unselfishness, Stoicism, Love, Conjugal Fidelity, Filial Affection, Childhood, Youth, Manhood, Old Age, Misfortune, Agriculture, Industry, the Forefathers, Posterity and Felicity. This virtuous and highly political calendar cut holidays by more than one half, but was never fully put in use. As it fell into oblivion, the Christian calendar came back into its own. However, it had lost its firmament, so rich in restful saints. The result was an even clearer gain for the long work year than had the political calendar been kept with its some thirty deities.

In many countries over the world today where technology is the leaders' great hope for salvation and progress, the number of feasts and holidays makes a sore issue. Festivities often last for weeks at a time. We in the United States never had such celebrations. Without New Orleans we wouldn't know what *Carnevale* was. Today most American workers and employees get from six to eight paid holidays a year, depending on local law and employer generosity. There are no national legal holidays in the United States. The holidays celebrated in every state, the District of Columbia, and all United States territories and possessions number five only, of one day's duration each. Of these few days, one alone is a holy day in the sense of being completely religious — Christmas. Since Easter falls on Sunday it is not counted as a real holiday. The following day, Easter Monday, is rarely given as a holiday as are the main five. One other day is partly religious, partly patriotic — Thanksgiving. One is purely patriotic or political — the Fourth of July. New Year's Day is a curious feast day for the United States — primitive in its celebrating a mythical death and birth, pagan in its Bacchanalian echoes, Christian in its commemorating the beginning of the Gregorian calendar year. Labor Day is a novelty, too, in that it is neither political nor religious. It was first celebrated in 1882 in New York. Two years later the *New York Herald* commented that it was a day above all others, the one "in honor of the greatest of saints — St. Labor."

Hardly considered a holiday any more, so well established is it, the one holiday that the pressures of business or even of a nation at war can rarely dislodge is Sunday, the specially sacred day. In the United States it is a common-law holiday, unlike the others, which are fixed by statute or executive proclamation. On this day men abstain from work (Table 3). If there is work they have to do, they don't like to do it. They may not be able to say why — specially if they are offered higher pay — but they just aren't Sabbathbreakers. Sabbathbreaking is one of the taboos of modern life. Christians and Jews have so persisted in observing their Sabbath that even those who do not consider themselves religious observe it faithfully. The rules of the Scribes enumerated thirty-nine main kinds of work forbidden on that day. The ideal they aimed at was absolute rest on the Sabbath from everything that could be called work. Even travel is not to be embarked on, whence the phrase, Sabbath-day's journey, for an easy one. Some believe that the Sabbath is not for enjoyment. Perhaps they have forgotten that the positive duties of its observance are to wear your best clothes, eat, drink and be glad.

The American's Sunday practice conforms quite well to Sunday theory. Without a doubt he gets more rest: he sleeps at least one hour longer on Sunday. Very few of his friends work on that day. Of course, there are thousands in any big city who must work the "swing shift" at night and on the Sabbath to keep services going on in hospitals, power plants, newspaper offices, on police patrol, food and fuel shipments, and transportation systems. Their free time comes when others are at work. Their afterwork hours typically begin at dawn when all the usual commercial amusements and sports are closed. Unless they can find others in the same fix who are willing to go on picnics and play softball at 6:00 A.M., their free-time endowment loses in value. Religion, however, does not discountenance those who must work on the holiday, for their work by and large does not violate the Commandment to observe the Sabbath. Traveling does not decline on Sunday as compared with other days of the week. It remains about the same, if anything increasing a bit. Since few shop on that day, the traveling is probably done in going to church and to Sunday school, visiting friends and relatives, going to the movies, or pleasure driving. At home perceptibly more time is spent at the television set, on guests, and in reading, while household chores decrease and do-it-yourself or repair work is kept to a minimum.

Those who don't go to church on Sunday, and even some who do, play or watch sports and games more than on weekdays, and go to the movies, theater, and concerts more. According to some views, these activities break the Sabbath. Many nineteenth-century English and American writings railed against the workingman's Sunday habits. The vast body of church members in the United States today seems to have little objection to playing on Sunday, as long as it doesn't dissolve into licentiousness. Drink used to be the curse of the working class, but the moralists seem somewhat less worried by it than a century or so ago. Today the majority of Americans have a 1½ or 2-day weekend free of work (Table 3); thus, as far as the job is concerned, they can celebrate the Jewish Sabbath and the Christian Sunday, or either.

In symmetry with one holy day in seven, the Israelites used to have a Sabbatical year in which they were to let their fields lie fallow. The ones who chiefly profit from this idea today are the professors, the possessors — but by no means all of them — of one of the rarest blocks of free time in modern life, the sabbatical year. It amounts to a year of leave with either full or somewhat reduced salary, without obligation to teach, and the liberty to rest, travel, or study at will. Some colleges and universities still grant it. It appears nowhere in the industrial world.

CATEGORIES OF PERSONS

The persistence in the universities of this relic of ancient times, the sabbatical year, reminds us that a college education may make a difference in the way people spend their free time. Many small surveys exist, which alumni societies have conducted on and for the enlightenment of their own alumni. In most cases they offer us small opportunity of comparing college men with others, since the others did not fall within the survey's purview.

One national survey done in 1956 did attack the problem directly by questioning both college and noncollege women (Table 13). First of all, we see, over half of all college women work compared to a third of noncollege women. A higher proportion of college women work full time, and an even higher percentage work part time. Fewer college women marry. Slightly more of them own their homes. These classes of women show little difference in their musical preferences in the religious sphere — almost all of them say they like it — but from there on in all other types of music the college women show a greater liking until hillbilly music is reached; then the tables turn. As subjects of conversation school problems, theater, music, art and books, politics and foreign affairs, absorb college women more than their counterparts, who prefer more personal chitchat about mutual friends or clothes, and talk about homemaking (food, cooking and home decorating) and movies, TV, sports and games. College women participate more in sports, and many of them in more than one.

Bowling and fishing or boating are the two sports in which the noncollege women are more active, but even then by only a narrow margin. A higher percentage of college women belong to the PTA, to the major book clubs, and, with a somewhat lesser difference, to the League of Women Voters. They have also traveled more outside the United States and one tenth of them have been to Europe or the Mediterranean, which only 4 per cent of the noncollege women have reached. Vacations are longer for the college women, and on their vacations they tour more and stay put less.

Obviously some of the things college women do more than the others is partly due to the better paid and greater number of jobs they or their husbands hold, their larger receipts from dividends, interest, and allowances, the greater number of cars they own, the lesser number that are married, and the longer vacations they have. But their liking of music, active sports, and certain kinds of conversation over others seems to show real differences in taste. Whether these should be related solely to their education is another question, not to be entered upon here. We merely note that in several ways college women seem to spend their free time differently from those who never entered the precincts of higher learning — and we specify these ways. They undoubtedly differ also, and probably more importantly, in other ways as well, but we are limited here as in other places by the fact that the survey we use is done with an eye to marketing consumer products with special appeals. We are nevertheless grateful for such surveys, for without them we would have even less data than we do. However, we must periodically warn ourselves that the facts brought to light by a survey might by their very interest lead us to assume that the important aspects of a subject — in this case the free-time interests of two orders of women — have been covered.

If we turn to another kind of study we shall see immediately that different kinds of activities and categories are thought of. Several universities (mostly state universities interested in helping out the farmer) have made studies of the use of time in rural families. One rather thorough study in 1954 (it went so far as to count the time spent filling out forms), a survey mainly of dairy farmers, persisted in a classification of all activities, recorded by time-diaries as work, leisure, or combinations of the two. The combinations were divided into work-leisure and leisure-leisure. There was no work-work combination, possibly because no such combination was thought to be frequent or steady. It is true that one can visualize queer possibilities, but there are also genuine examples. Instead of a man pumping with one hand and throwing feed to the turkeys with the other, one can think of sewing and watching the baby sleep, or stirring a pot while listening for mistakes in Johnny's oral rendition of a composition for his English class.

Perhaps it was because of this omission of a work-work combination that child care as a time consumer came out so low in this study. It appeared mainly in the hours between 7:30 and 8:30 A.M. when mother was most actively trying to get Johnny and Susie cleaned up, dressed, and off to school. But if she sews in the evening, or goes over the accounts, while they are working on their homework or already asleep in their beds, is she not doing two jobs? If one of the children were sick, there would be no time for sewing; or if one kept uncovering himself at all hours, a trip every now and then to cover him would take time and steps. Or, put in another light, can parents leave children to go to a movie? If they cannot without enlisting a baby sitter, the time spent, whether paid or not, becomes clearly calculable. And even when the children themselves go out, their mother may not be free to leave, for they may have to know there is someone at home to return to. Though the reasons may lie elsewhere, these farmers did not go to the movies. Out of 2,617 recorded diary days, on only 9 was a movie ever attended, an average of less than once a year.

Anyway, the other combinations were listed as eating-reading, eating-TV, visiting-TV, visiting-eating, sewing-radio, sewing-

TV, and so on. The diaries revealed that on the whole men watched TV from 1½ to 2 hours a day and women from 2 to 3 hours. They also indicated that men spent from 1 to 1½ hours and women 1 to 2 hours a day listening to the radio. The first reaction to this information might be that it was rather strange that the radio should be used so much with TV in full swing. It could have been that some people owned TV sets, but others still had only radios, and so the averages worked out to show each person split in a TV versus radio allegiance. But no, almost all had radios (96 per cent) and not enough were without TV (14 per cent) to account for the difference. Many farmers, indeed over half, had more than one radio.

Now, the dairy farmer's day starts early, even in winter, which is when the diaries of this study were kept. Up between 5:00 and 6:50, off to barn chores before breakfast, then breakfast, off to field work, shop work, more barn chores, or what have you. Yet the peak hours for his radio listening were in early morning, at noontime, and in early evening. As it turned out, most of the extra radios farmers had were in the barn. In fact a few who had only one set kept it in the barn, not the house. It follows: in winter most dairy farm work is barn chores; in the barn the farmer or his wife can listen to the radio while milking the cows. The cows can listen too. Without the possibility of double-classification, this starting the day off with work-leisure, with cows and music, or the voice of the county agent, might have escaped us under the weight of all-work barn chores. The combination of barn chores-radio also appeared in early evening, and eating-radio appeared at noon. All three radio peaks were present and accounted for.

The more important gain from these diaries is a realization of how often these double activities occur, and how infrequent is a single classification. Radio plus chores (barn or house) and eating plus reading are two favorite combinations. Also familiar are radio plus reading and radio plus eating. Triple combinations are possible (eating plus radio plus newspaper) and even quad-

126 Of Time, Work, and Leisure

ruple or more (just add child care, one point for each child), but the survey did not go into these refinements.

If the radio associates with almost any activity, TV is highly exclusive. The men did nothing else to speak of while watching it. Since the smallest intervals to be recorded in the diary were 15 minutes each, activities taking a shorter time, like going to get a can of beer from the icebox, did not appear. The women watched TV longer every day in the week, although in the men's case the picture tube as well as the radio speaker was somehow worked into their daily chores. In general, though, watching television exclusively was the thing to do in the evening, particularly between eight and ten. The favorite time for reading was not in the evening but during or right after lunch, from 12:30 to 1:00. Two thirds of it was newspaper reading; the rest was mainly looking at magazines.

The farmers in this study worked on weekdays an average of 10.5 hours; on Saturdays work took almost the same number (10 hours), and even on Sunday the average hours worked were not negligible — 6. The result is a 68.7-hour, seven-day work week. This is wintertime, when farm work is supposed to be, and is in fact, lighter than in summer. The time-diaries were distributed in winter because that was when it was thought the farmer had more time free. In general the free-time blocks we singled out earlier were taken up as follows: lunch — reading, listening to the radio; evening — television; Saturday — about the same as weekdays except for more time taken later in the evening (at 10:00 P.M. on weekdays most farmers were in bed; at 11:30 P.M. on Saturday more than one fourth were still up and around), dating, dancing or card playing; Sunday — church in the morning (as much as 35 per cent, women slightly more than men), visiting in the afternoon or evening (as much as 40 per cent, or 2 hours average per person), card playing (over a half-hour average for both men and women), and some pleasure driving; television watching and radio listening dropped off, while reading went up, probably pushed by the big Sunday papers.

The inevitability of chores makes a work day even of Sunday for the dairy farmer. The livestock must be tended. He evidently tries to cut down these chores on Sunday and succeeds in reducing them by about half an hour, and lets the other work go. One would have to say the farmer does try to respect the Sabbath.

The men on a weekday evening, from eight on, were usually free of work. The women trailed behind, having household and child-care activities still to do. The idea that woman's work is never done must be a masculine one. This study seemed to show that whenever the men were about, women were working, whether the same could be said of the men or not. The men rarely report doing housework. They sit longer at the table than the women. On Sunday when the men are in the house more and with their wives more, the women sleep less than the men. On weekdays and Saturdays, however, they sleep more than the men on the average, and in the afternoons, too, women clearly have more free time than men. They spend it visiting and in other pursuits. Perhaps this information lends weight (but not very much) to the reports mentioned earlier that some married women think an extra day off for their husbands would just keep them in their way.

Actually, in terms of the work week, farm women were just about the peers of men. If the men worked 68.7 hours, the women put in 67.5. The difference is hardly worth mentioning. About a third of women's work was outside the house, usually taken up in barn chores. Indoors, housework took the longest share of time, followed by food preparation, and, thirdly, child care.

Visiting is an important activity among these families. Roughly as much time was spent visiting as in reading. On Sunday the radio and television sets get a chance to cool off. They owe this chance to the visiting that moves farm families from one house to another and, in any case, to places other than home. But it isn't visiting that breaks the isolation of today's farm. For every hour spent visiting, four more were spent on television, at least three on radio, and over one in reading. In disposing of his time, the dairy farmer seems to give about one minute a day to visiting for each eight he gives to the media of mass communication. Whether a farm locality was near an urban center, or surrounded by urban influences such as industry or retail trade, did not make much difference. Television and radio still fenced in a wide area of free time.

None of these daily farm habits are to be regarded as immutable. Since 1958, when the study was reported, they may already have changed. If not, they may change in the next six months or six years. In any case the South Dakota cash grain farmer might have altogether different free-time habits from the Illinois feed and cattle operator, some related to the exigencies of his particular work, some to his education, others to his traditions, and so on. We don't know, for example, how much visiting the Wisconsin dairy farmer did before the advent of television. Other studies indicate that having television in the house cuts down visiting and entertaining.

Jumping now in one leap from the rural to the urban and from the agricultural to the industrial, let us take a look at the manual worker. What are his main hobbies and recreations? This was the substance of questions asked in 1956 of a sample of steelworkers and other manual workers in the same cities as the steelworkers, and of manual workers throughout the country (Table 14). One of the first things to catch attention is the number of these workers involved in sports and games — a good third in hunting, fishing, boating, camping, and rowing, and slightly fewer in watching matches and races of all sorts. Participating in games like softball or bowling wins the vote of about one fifth, while sports that are not games — for example, swimming, hiking, horseback riding, ice skating — interest somewhat under one tenth of these workers. Television, radio, theater, and movies all together also draw, it would seem, about one tenth or slightly more. Other things, like craft hobbies, gardening, picnics, reading, music, playing cards, and traveling, gain the interest of 5 per cent or less.

Are we to judge from this that steelworkers and other manual workers are less attracted to television than farmers? This would be difficult to conclude since television, we know, is turned on during much of the day's free time. The question that was put to manual workers was what their "main" hobbies and recreations were. Television is so much a part of their everyday life that they may not even have bothered to mention it, or they may have thought that something out of the house was what the interviewer had in mind. As a matter of fact, they may have been encouraged in this last view by the preamble to the question, which said, "Considering all seasons of the year, what are your main . . . ?" "Seasons" suggests the outdoors.

Whatever they understood by "hobbies," the same question was not asked of the Wisconsin dairy farmer. Perhaps they would have mentioned television infrequently, too. On the other hand when would farmers have had time to do the things that manual workers say they like to do? After eight in the evening they were free, but most of them were in bed by ten. On Sunday their day was taken up with barn chores, visiting and television. Furthermore, would they have done these things after eight in the evening had they had the energy? Hunting and fishing might be available, but the right time is not at 8 P.M.

As for the commercial spectator matches, games and races which take first place with the workers, there is little facility for this kind of sport on farms or in the towns near farms. A city with a mass of people is needed to support them. The farmers at any rate didn't mention any such activities in their diary. The authors of the study would have lumped them into the "miscellaneous leisure" category at least, had they occurred with any frequency. Card playing was the mainstay of this category. Something called "group sports," composed of attending or participating in such sports, did appear, but was said to have taken up only a small space, as did dancing and dating, in the "miscellaneous leisure" pigeonhole.

One thing lacking in the farmer study was an indication of how holidays were spent and whether there existed any period comparable to the worker's vacation. Certainly for other kinds of farmers, those less tied to livestock, there are slack periods. With all of today's mechanization of the farm and scientific planning of crops for tillers of the soil, there still must be a harvest time. The worker, we know, has a vacation period, but manual workers do not seem to leave home in that period as much as college women, or women in general, or people with an income over $5,000 a year. Only about a third of the manual workers took a vacation away from home lasting one week or more in the previous year. Another 20 per cent or so had taken such a vacation in the previous five years, all right, but this left almost half of them who hadn't been away from home in 5 years or more. Those who did take a vacation almost invariably took their car, and usually one to three other members of the family. Most of them traveled to another state, going 300 to 1,000 miles or more away, and spending between $100 and $300. Manual workers throughout the United States on vacations away from home took the more economical course. They earn less than the steelworkers, so they spent less. They must be better at bargaining, for with this less money they took longer and more vacations, traveled more miles and more often to another state, and took along as many members of the family. But here, as with trips overseas, the picture can change considerably from one year to the next.

Most of the workers said they belonged to no social, recreational, political, or athletic clubs or groups. About one out of every five wives belonged to the PTA (which tallies with the figure arrived at in the previous survey of women). For themselves the Masons is the favorite organization, embracing about 5 per cent. Others are spread out thinly among Knights of Columbus, Eagles, Elks, Moose, and others. Hardly any belong to the Lions' Club, the Exchange Club, or Rotary; the most popular here is the Kiwanis, which obtained 1 per cent of the steelworkers.

A group within a group that might be interesting if we knew more about it is the one which, among steelworkers, other manual workers in the same cities, and manual workers generally,

scored exactly 13 per cent. That group was composed of those
who when asked about hobbies or recreations said, "I don't have
any." Perhaps among the farmers they would have found a similar brotherhood, possibly larger. The latest census figures show
farmers working an average week of about 12 hours more than
machine operators (Table 15). The farmers might have added,
with the country's sneer for the corruption of the city, that they
don't have time for such things. These city workers, who
aren't permitted cows and radio in the morning, could say the
same thing. Note that among the farmers' time-diaries there were
no entries for the journey to work, nor was there unaccounted-
for moonlighting, nor any working mothers. Note also that the
men neither did housework nor took care of children, and that
their pace was set not by machines but, if anything, by animals
long appreciated for their placid disposition; also note that the
farmer does not have to signal for a relief man when he has to go
to the toilet, that he has his radio to keep him contented on his
chores, and when driving to town in the open hunting season, he
keeps his rifle or shotgun in the car: a man can't tell when a deer
may cross his path, or vice versa. The manual worker, whose
shorter work week does not include these benefits, can justly
maintain that his job does not leave him as much time as it
seems. After all, his evening too begins not much before 8:00
P.M.; his Saturday is taken up with shopping and work around
the house and yard, and on Sunday his rest is as necessary as the
next man's.

It is time to take several steps up the industrial hierarchy for a
look at the workers' or the employees' bosses. Nowadays, though
the owner or proprietor may have disappeared from sight, still a
boss remains. He is called an executive. One of the first things to
note in dealing with this class of person is that, as part of the class
of managers, owners, and officials, he works longer hours than
anyone else (Table 15). He doesn't say so, but these longer hours
are a form of moonlighting. Or worse yet, to use a labor-union
phrase and way of looking at things, these hours amount to a

form of scabbing. The executive has an official work week of 40 hours, and no matter how much he gets paid for those 40 hours, he works overtime for nothing. Most of this overtime is done in the evenings at home. Two thirds of all executives, it seems, more or less regularly bring home work to do at night, or over the weekend. A few return to the office to work at night. A few more say in effect: "Work outside the office? Never." Certainly they can leave the brief case at the office; whether, once through the revolving door, they can shut their minds off is another matter.

At any rate, the above findings are the results of recent surveys of the supplementary work hours of executives. Office hours in terms of the executive's physical presence run from between 8:00 and 9:00 A.M. to between 5:00 and 6:00 P.M. On arrival home, he eats and drinks or drinks and eats and then is ready for an evening's work in his branch office — his home, equipped with telephone and sometimes dictating machine, almost always a typewriter and plenty of paper. But the typewriter isn't needed much. What is needed is to get papers read, reports annotated, perhaps a speech outlined or drafted, some checking by phone — in short, all work thrown into the brief case before leaving the office because the regular day is so much taken up with committees, conferences, meetings, talking, and seeing people. Individual businessmen note that their serious thinking is most often done at home. The office evidently provides a poor setting for work requiring sustained concentration; neither is it adapted to reading. Home is a good place to work, because, like the office in the hour before 9:00 A.M., and on Saturday, there is nobody around in the late hours to bother a man except the wife, and she is soon off to bed rather than stay up with an uncompanionable husband. Other nights may be different, however. One night some business entertaining, another night a conference to go to, a third perhaps spent at the office with a secretary to tidy things up and get the backlog of letters out.

Civic work these executives see as part of the job, something, to be sure, they don't particularly care for, but to be done out of a sense of duty. Duty to the company, be it clear, not specially to the civic body. Businessmen reveal slight interest in civics. Perhaps they feel uneasy in this area; perhaps they fear becoming involved in some controversial cause which might hurt their chances of success. In any case, they give only about a couple of hours a week to activities which are connected with the general government of their communities.

The idea, however, does not quite seem to have been put from mind. A considerable number — almost one third — report that after retirement they would like to take up volunteer civic or political work. Then the pressures will be off. Perhaps also some executives dream of finishing their careers with a last, bold fling in the public forum. It may be they recall Cicero's defense of old age on the grounds that, after all, one could always sit in the Senate.

As for charitable undertakings, there are many suggestions in the replies that the word "voluntary" hardly applies to them. "It's a duty I owe the community," stated the director of labor relations for a large company. "However, I loathe volunteer charity work." Several others comment on having once undertaken some major community assignment — "but never again!"

Something less than one third think of these activities as being related to their work — perhaps indirectly related, but nevertheless viewed as improving their own chances for advancement or serving the public relations of their companies. Roughly another third think of them as being leisure activities, while the largest percentage, though by a small margin, classifies them rather interestingly as being "a job of a different kind."

In other words, this large section of executives seem consciously to see their lives as divided into two spheres of obligation: a major share to go to gaining a livelihood, and a necessarily much smaller share to the community. As for the family, executives feel that they are neglecting their family and have an uneasy conscience about it. Hobbies, few; books, few. For there are books that are not books, and books that are. Books about business are not books. We are still talking about time that is alleged to be free. Music? Art? There seems reason to doubt whether the free time of the executive class in the United States can be called the soil for a flowering of literature or the arts. About 5 hours per week go to activities in this area. A few permit themselves the luxury of a dozen hours or more — an amount of time that would allow some solid reading, plus one evening (but hardly two) at the theater or opera. One does find an individual businessman who not only gives time to serving on the board of the local opera or orchestra but actually enjoys attending, and he is even rarer.

A recent picture of the executive, pieced together by a brief survey, reveals that the average time he spends at the office each week is about 43 hours. The pattern is evidently set by the standard hours of the employees, with the businessman having relatively little freedom to alter it. The average office building becomes a dreary place after the working force has left. A law partner can stay to dictate a brief but the secretary to take it down has left. Through the window of today's glass skyscraper one can see an occasional individual bent over his desk. For the most part, however, emptiness and quiet have replaced the bustle of the working day, broken only by the onsweep of the cleaning forces. The man who wants to work longer hours must find another scene for his labors. So it appears that an additional 7 hours a week are spent at home doing paper work, business reading, and so forth. Then, there is the inevitable business entertaining, carried on both within the home and outside it. Another 5 hours or so go in this way.

The sum of these working hours — office, home, entertaining — comes to a total of 55 hours a week. This does not include time spent in traveling to and from the office, averaging a bit over 5 hours per week. Nor does it include business travel, which, for some executives, can run as high as 30 hours a week in itself.

However one assigns travel time, such a work week is very long for mid-century America.

One cannot but ask whether there are not some factors that mitigate the excessively long hours of work which such figures as the above seem to imply. The president of one of the country's largest companies, when asked whether he thought that executives worked inordinately long hours, smiled and answered that they like to tell you they work too much. Whether they actually do or not, he added, depends on how you define work and where you say that it stops.

The question is complicated by the nature of the executive's work. It obviously must require a type of thinking which cannot be measured by any poll. To shape policy, determine goals, and create programs is not a function to be performed at stated hours of the day or while a man is seated in any particular spot. If the executive tends to picture himself as being constantly at work it may be in part because he feels under some pressure to give a tangible proof of his contribution. So much of what he does is not capable of being readily evaluated; it does not lend itself to being seen and immediately appraised by his associates. Hours of work thus become one vivid sign — an outward and discernible mark — of the extent of his labors.

The main reason, however, why the executive works long hours — and is understandably convinced he works long hours — is that his way of life permits no clear-cut distinction between work and free time. As we have seen, the executive has a job with a social side, and furthermore he enjoys his work. What he may not realize quite so clearly is the degree to which his work is penetrated by qualities which one would ordinarily associate with voluntary, carefree, and social pursuits.

The picture as a whole (which, incidentally, does not differ much from that of the government executive, either) shows what has already been anticipated: that the job of the executive, despite its obvious pressures and responsibilities, has within it many of the things like friendship, challenge, and entertainment that make work agreeable. The net result of the executive's attitude toward work is summed up in the answers to a question as to whether, if they had an independent income assuring them their present standard of living, they would continue to work. Not surprisingly, close to 90 per cent said they would.

In this chapter we wished to learn something of how Americans spend their free time. Now activity is both difficult and costly to observe systematically. The problems are similar to those of making a documentary film — getting and keeping the photographic eye there where it is needed. Most studies, getting around difficulties by using some form of the interview, ask people how much time they have spent and for what, for example, or to recall what they did on a given day, or to keep a record of hourly activities. They are subject to all the weaknesses of the interview, and inasmuch as they ask for recall to errors of memory. The case study, too, is based on interviews, as in social work or psychotherapy, but its greater length and intensity put it almost into another class. By fullness of exchange alone it eliminates some of the most unsatisfactory features of the survey interview. It loses ground of course in the areas of representativeness and statistical comparison; not that the case study cannot move into these areas, but, as in direct observation, the cost rises prohibitively. Studies using participants or spectators as observers are rare. Fiction so-called also describes the way people spend their time, making use of observation, imagination, and sympathy. Introspection, however, is not highly regarded in social-science circles these days, so literature is little used in research. These remarks are but a reminder of the problems involved in trying to find out how people spend their time.

Among the various ways of observing how time is spent there were three, we discovered, that lend themselves easily to measurement. One method is to see what people spend their money for. Presumably they are in some sort of interaction — and all inter-

action takes time — with whatever it is they buy. Another way is
to rank their activities by the frequency with which they engage
in them or by the importance they assign to them. A third
method ranks activities not by frequency but by length of time
devoted to them. When time intervals are divided in fair detail
within a day, for example by half-hours, the procedure usually
goes by the name of time-budgets or time-diaries, thus differ-
entiating it from the first two methods mentioned, namely expenditures and activity-ranking. For the most part we used these
three kinds of quantitative studies for our purpose. Furthermore
we chose, whenever possible, studies that used a sample of the
whole American population. Many quantitative studies of free
time exist but treat of such small communities — a suburb, a
plant, a neighborhood — that to generalize from them for the
country as a whole would be inadvisable.

From the surveys we used we made lists of activities people
engage in during their off-work hours — movies, sports, gardening, etc. — and got some idea of the time they consumed. We
soon found, though at the cost of lengthy analysis, that the surveys always stood in need of scrutiny, qualification, and reinter-
pretation. Things were seldom what they seemed. The effort to
appraise them was worth while, perhaps; one should be able to
judge for oneself how much and how little such studies convey.
The main thing was not to be misled by them. Whether they told
us something we didn't know or whether they merely reminded
us of things we had learned elsewhere, doesn't matter. In
both cases they serve a useful purpose.

We saw something of the lives of men and women and teen-
agers, the variety of activities they engage in. Some, like TV,
driving, and multiple activities, we considered at greater length
than others. We saw something of where people went or stayed
(indoors, outdoors, in parks, forests, or abroad) and the way in
which their time took the form of units (evening, meals, vacations, holidays, Saturdays, Sundays) or of cycles and phases
(work days and weekends, work day and evening, school, work-

ing life and retirement, the single, married, and with offspring).
In addition to see how patterns of activity can vary from a national norm we looked at some groups more closely — college women, dairy farmers, manual workers, and lastly the executive.

A hard worker, the executive. The kind of play he seems to enjoy is something after hours where business is involved — cocktails, the golf game, the clubhouse, the conversation at the night club, at lunch. The executive may not be able to tell work from play; nonetheless, he has little free time, perhaps the least of all categories of persons we have here examined. The class that is able to wrest the highest monetary rewards out of the economic system and close to the highest rewards in prestige cannot or doesn't want to have the most free time. When in the nineteenth century England led the world in trade and finance, London executives took 4-day weekends. If executives are so powerful a force in America, as they indubitably are, why don't they get more of that free time which everybody else, it seems, holds to be so precious? Strange.

In Pursuit of Time

IN THE workingman's world there is something called an "overtime hog." The name, a union epithet, refers to the worker who is forever trying to put in overtime. Among the biggest of all the headaches shop stewards have is the question of who is going to put in overtime and get its premium pay. These days, it seems, there is not enough overtime to go around. The average in manufacturing industries reaches two to three hours a week or about half an hour a day per worker. So it raises all the dangers of favoritism.

That someone can favor a friend by seeing that he gets overtime work may sound at first like a teacher's keeping the good boys after school to write on the blackboard one hundred times, "I have been a good boy." We do not know how many workers push for overtime. There may be only a small noisy group of the same persons, who hover about the shop steward's head like gnats. Or they may not be the same persons but a somewhat changing group in need of more money for special reasons — an accident or illness in the family, for example. Nonetheless the term "overtime hog" raises the suspicion that perhaps business executives are not the only ones greedy for work. Perhaps there is even a general desire for less free time, though it somehow rings false. We said that the case of the business executive seemed strange because here he was, free and powerful, yet electing to work longer hours. He says he wants more free time but since he takes more work instead, we judge he wants something else more. The ordinary worker is not free in this sense, we suppose, and therefore cannot choose more free time if he wants it. That he or some of his group can and do choose more overtime, though, gives us pause. What evidence do we have, solid evidence, that people want more free time?

Well, what kind of evidence would we accept? The opinion polls give a cloudy answer. What they seem to tell us is, depending on who asks the question, you can get an answer either way. Polls of workers both conducted and reported by their unions speak of 80 to 90 per cent of members of the United Auto Workers, for example, as being in favor of a shorter work week. The Gallup and Roper polls give different results. In one Gallup survey manual workers opposed a 4-day week of 8 hours a day by 55 per cent to 39 per cent, the other categories of workers by even more, and the general population by three to two. One of Roper's polls was put this way: "There's a lot of talk about the possibility of a 4-day work week in the future, or maybe even a 3-day work week. Which one of these statements do you think comes closest to expressing the general over-all effect it would have on people?" The answers were as follows:

1. People would get soft and lazy with all that leisure time   20%
2. People would simply get bored having too little to do   20%
3. People would find things to do so that they would be just as busy as they are now   32%
4. People would enjoy the extra time, relax more, and be happier   24%
5. Don't know   6%

(The percentages add to more than 100 because some people gave more than one answer.) Now perhaps some of the people who chose No. 3 gave a choice also for No. 4, but as it stands No. 3 is not a choice clearly favorable to leisure. It seems to be almost the contrary since it says people will be no less busy. Yet the report of this study said, "The 'ayes' clearly have it. An extra day or so off each week would be warmly welcomed by a majority of 56 per cent." It arrives at this 56 per cent obviously by taking No. 4 and adding to it the dubious No. 3.

This is but one example of the perhaps few dozen polls in existence bearing on the subject of whether Americans want more free time. Without doubt they all have their points of interest. That 40 per cent say people would get soft and lazy or bored with more time may cause a flicker of curiosity. We may be too lazy and the reader too bored to let ourselves be drawn once more through the maze of objections that can be raised to this kind of survey. One more query only and we shall move on: Does anyone think that had the same question been asked and then the person allowed to answer in his own way, the results would have been the same? Or (we cannot resist another query) suppose Nos. 1 and 2 were omitted and another substituted like, "People would take on part-time and overtime work to make more money." How would that change the picture? And so on into the night.

What about being realistic, as some people would say, tough-minded and hardheaded? Why not find out what people spend their money for? After all, this is a choice just as much as or more than merely picking an answer in a poll. Those economists who often fall into thinking that all choices are reflected in the market would probably be more in favor of this approach to the problem. What kind of expenditure, then, would clearly reflect a desire for more leisure? A motor boat? No, if anything, this indicates an estimate that present free time is enough to use the boat in. Moreover, we have already spoken at length of the difficulty of separating the boat or the golf clubs or the swimming pool from business pursuits. Whatever is bought, there is no sure way of knowing from the purchase itself what the motive is for buying it. What about products, then, that are sold as timesavers?

Product X will save lots of running upstairs, or miles of steps per day, or so much elbow grease, or two hours and seventeen minutes of bending over the kitchen stove, or three trips to the stores per week. Undeniably many things are sold with such a pitch, but how many, exactly, or even roughly, we don't know. There has been no comprehensive study of selling appeals that would enable us to estimate not only what the advertising intends to say but why the buyers bought what they did buy. Nor is there any way to distinguish the timesaving from the laborsaving or the hygienic, nor the esthetic from the nutritional motive, not to mention certain other reasons for buying which so-called depth analysts have come up with, such as the variants of mother love, homosexual urges, virginal purity, phallic envy, and others of the psychoanalytic family.

In recent decades personnel has gone increasingly into the occupational category of services (Table 16). Now may we not say that the money being spent on services in recent years indicates that more and more people want to avoid doing the work themselves, and therefore wish to be waited on or served personally? Unfortunately this cannot be sustained. One reason is the peculiar lumping together of occupations in this one category, including the oddities of the do-it-yourself market; another is that the time saved by using commercial services — such as a laundry — may be time saved for work purposes, for example, so a wife can take a job which will keep her from being able to do the wash at home any more. The purchase of services or timesaving equipment may indicate that time is being sought — and this is important of course — but regrettably it does not tell us to what use the time saved, if any, is to be put.

There is at least one kind of expenditure which it may seem safe to classify as not a leisure expenditure — life insurance. Since its benefits appear only after the spender is dead, one cannot say he is spending this money on leisure. Even here we have a similar objection. As any insurance salesman knows, a good selling argument is that a policy brings peace of mind. The prospective buyer can thereafter go into the bush on his hunting trip confident that his family will be taken care of in case someone mistakes his head for a pigeon. Only one not prey to this worry would deny that his free time is freer.

On the whole we would have to say that résumés of expenditures are not informative for the present purpose. One could indeed take the total of individual spending and maintain that the higher it is, the less free time on the average is there likely to be. Somewhat in this way a few students of income and expenditures have come to the conclusion that the American has taken gains in productivity partly in cash and partly in free time. Proceeding from the fact that productivity has gone up while the work week has gone down, they have simply calculated what income workers could have earned had they not chosen to take a reduction in work hours, and come to the conclusion that American labor has taken its gains at the rate of two thirds increased pay and one third increased free time. We do not find fault with the calculation. We simply cannot accept as fact that the work week has gone down as much as is claimed, and therefore that the worker has elected to accept part of his pay in free time. The time involved in activities off the plant premises but work-related nonetheless — activities like the journey to work, do-it-yourself chores, housework, geographical work mobility, overtime, and moonlighting — this time is not less than it was at the turn of the twentieth century. Such being the case, the American is actually working as hard as ever, and in his drive for shorter hours he is, if anything, trying to keep his head above water to find time for shopping, repairs, family, receding rivers, snows, and forests, etc. — on all of which the job had made subtle inroads. Ask workers what they would do with more leisure time if they had it. Nearly to a man they will answer "Work around the house," or, in slightly lesser measure, "Spend more time with the family." It is the worker, not the employer, who pays for time spent in traveling to work and back, just as it is the worker who pays for the toll of factory smoke on health and hygiene of home and person. We would maintain, therefore, that what has deceived those students into thinking the American has taken part of these productivity gains in free time instead of cash, has been the *seeming* decline of the work week. The hours in the standard or official work week may constitute an important part of the American's work but not his work *in toto*.

If anything, the American has taken his gains in productivity in cash. He may spend the cash for articles related to his free time, but of time he has taken no more that we can see.

INDUSTRIAL ESCAPE

Neither money nor time units, then, give us any surety that people in the United States want free time. There are other things that might prove to be indications. For instance, are there large numbers of persons who by their way of life can be considered to protest against work's domination of time in American culture? We brought up in an earlier chapter the difficulties that await anyone who tries to lead a life without a regular place in the world of work. The force of law and opinion is against such persons. Nor do they find sympathy through peregrination. And not only the wandering kind find it hard to get along without work, but even those in the big city, who in the shadows and intestines of its anonymity hope to live with as little work as possible, find out what is often true for thieves — that for the rewards involved the work is greater than had the effort been applied to a legitimate job. Hoboes used to have various cabalistic signs which they wrote on fences and walls to communicate with one another in their wanderings. The ones that most typically represent the feeling toward nonworkers in the United States perhaps are ▦ police unfriendly, ☫ jail is a workhouse, and ✳ town is hostile.

The tramp or hobo, the Bohemian, and many nomadic and sporadic workers may be held to be protesting not only against the lack of free time but against other things too, like the regularity of the working world. Within the working world itself, though, other kinds of protest are possible. Some students of industrial relations sometimes refer to them as acts of "job resistance," and take their incidence to indicate a low state of work morale. All involve leaving off the job: absences, disciplinary layoffs, quits, transfer requests, dispensary visits, work stoppages, and grievances. Other more subtle indications may be used. Lack of participation in "voluntary" fringe benefits or insurance plans of the company may indicate a desire to leave it.

Take the entity, nonclinical, called the common cold. Could anything be better designed to obtain free time? Its etiology is such that it can happen to anyone, at any time ("summer colds are the worst ones"), at any place, any number of times, through no fault of one's own. It is supposed to be contagious, too, so even if one wanted to be a hero and drag himself to office or plant, no one there would approve of it — medically speaking. It can also develop into something more serious if one doesn't take care of himself. While a cold is serious enough to warrant staying away from work, it is so easily diagnosed that a physician is not really needed; moreover, it reacts so poorly to medication that the physician cannot do much more good than the pharmacist. It is generally most uncomfortable for about three days; its full course is thought to be two weeks. The organism can gauge its own range depending on how much rest it needs. The body has its own work, and often works in marvelously mysterious ways.

But in this approach too, though the point may be credible, the data collected are not accurate, extensive, or comparative enough to let us say with confidence that there is clear evidence people generally want more free time. Certainly the persons who often exhibit such behavior, whether quits, non-participations, or frequent colds, are shying away from their jobs. But whether they reflect an increased tendency, whether there are only a few of them who are always the same and always have been the same ones, or whether they are the signs of a more general current —

these are all things we cannot at present tell. The same applies to other factors one could think of, notably alcoholism, gambling, and a host of other phenomena usually considered social problems. They have often been interpreted as flights from family or sexual difficulty, rarely as escape from work. There is no evidence that it may be the first rather than the second. One can only say that escape from the regularity, monotony, and domination of work is not as often looked into as a motive as are the other things.

A more positive approach may be to ask what kinds of occupations workers aspire to. Do they want those with more free time on and off the job, with less intensity, with less dedication demanded? Or jobs where the pattern is strictly work — you put in your hours, keep your nose to the grindstone, mind your own business, and get more money or reputation? Not much information on such preference is now available. To separate the money, prestige, and free-time factors becomes highly complicated once one gets into it. As yet no study has been done that tries to individuate these elements.

There is more to be said about the styles of life aspired to. In the last decade or so people have been moving to the suburbs at an average rate of over a million a year. This most intense migration in the nation's history has sent about 50 million Americans, nearly one third of the population, into suburbia. Obviously there was something they didn't like about life in the city. Obviously also, the suburb did promise them time and space, two things the city has in short supply. The happy land of homes and gardens, of pure air, greenery and shade trees, of time for children and friends, picnics and clubs, does smell of a desire for an unhurried life — as it was supposed to be in the old agrarian days of sleepy tree-shaded towns and wide-awake intimate government. This may be what people expected to find in the suburbs; what they got is another matter. Time has become an implacable master putting the commuter, the nursery school child and youth, the mothers who can't be mothers, all of them on relentless schedules. We can guess they wanted a life with less hurry. We are probably right, though we may be reading something into the story and leaving something out.

Putting together what we know of the suburbs with all other evidence, if we were asked who precisely are those who want more free time, for what uses they want it, and with what intensity, we would have to say we don't know. And we would have to give the same answer to the kindred questions of whether they would prefer more money or more prestige with the neighbors, or more status at the shop or in their family, or to be in a position of command, or whether they simply want more free time. We *can* say, however, that people seem harried and rushed (especially married working women with children under eighteen, their spouses, and also urban and suburban dwellers generally), that often when asked why they would like more time they say "to catch up with the housework" or "to get the shopping done" or "to get the basement windows to open again" or "to spend some time with my family." Yet these people have been told by learned journals, daily newspapers, and weekly magazines that nowadays everybody has more time; they have had the figures cited to them; still, somehow, they themselves are pressed for time. Their own lack of it doesn't so much make them doubt that others have it (though there is some doubt of what they read in print all right) as feel that somehow — only temporarily, as they suppose — they are stuck. A not incidental point is that when people find out you are engaged in studying leisure, they may plead in the jocular tone often adopted in talking about the subject — a tone that has significance in itself — that if you discover where to find it, please let them know. For them so far leisure has been a mirage.

Large numbers of persons, it seems, earnestly desire or need more free time, although we may not be able to say whether they would not, if given a choice, prefer something else. Most interview studies tells us about the present moment, and while it interests us, we are also interested in other things. The man whose family is starving will not be much preoccupied with leisure. Lack of food or money is his worry. Restored by food and drink, he begins to think of other things in life. Similarly labor-union leaders may on one day say that the shorter work week will be labor's major battle over the next five years, but six months later, with the onset of a business recession or an inflation, the subject is dropped from the program. Still, if we leave to one side short-run fluctuations like recessions, or the ups and downs of bargaining about the work week, there is the longer-run change that is spanned by at least a generation. Since the turn of the century Americans have pursued time.

One major reason for this change has already been discussed. We have seen that the bonanza of free time that was supposed to be at the American's disposal is legendary. The false image grew out of a punch-clock accounting system. The only entries were time in and time out. Time out was called free time. The economists described the system as one characterized by the free organization of labor, and the phrase free time came into common usage to mean time off the job, as though the company's entrances were not doors to opportunity but the gates of a prison. Perhaps the usage began when work was more unpleasant than it is today, or perhaps, as is more likely, it was picked up by factory workers and pushed by them into the currency it holds today.

No one seems to have noticed this contradiction but it had an important effect on all workers. It allowed a false accounting system to grow up. Instead of counting free time by first figuring out what was free about it and then adding up, the process began upside down: whatever is not time on the job is free. To calculate how much free time you have, take the job's official hours and subtract them from 24; or, to be more exact, take 8 out for sleeping, and subtract the job hours from 16; or another way is to take the work week ten or twenty years ago and from it subtract today's. That also should give a clear gain. In the meantime other processes began insinuating themselves into the worker's life so that he was bearing the cost of added hours without knowing it. If he lived first in one of those concentric circles of the big city characteristic of the early part of the century, his house was fairly near the factory. If the factory moved out to the periphery because of cheaper land or labor, he had to follow it or another factory, or, if not he, his sidekick had to move out there. The factory did not assume the cost of the longer time it might now take him to get to work. And, to make the point, no one counted the loss of time anywhere as part of work time. This is one example of how the American finds himself with fewer on-the-job hours and less free time.

Similarly insidious events took away other hours: the rise of work-pacing, of moonlighting, of women's ranks to become one sixth of the labor force, and so on. It would be wrong to say that American workers have had something put over on them. The same ignorance afflicts office workers and executives as well. They too count their free time by subtracting their work time from something bigger. And then there are days in which they puzzle about where their time has gone.

But is this all? Is the American's chase after time due to this, that he sought to cut down work in only one of its guises, and as it appeared with other faces he did not recognize it? Is free time valued so highly today only because no one has it?

The desire for time we have just considered seems really to be a need for time in which to rest or to get done the many tasks or duties that fall to one's lot after 4:30 or 5:00 or 5:30 P.M. There is more than this alone, it would seem. How else would we explain the important change in our vocabulary over the last fifty or one hundred years, a change in which the "idleness problem" has been supplanted by the "leisure problem," and though idleness was excoriated and leisure is lauded, the problem is still the same — the problem of free time. We have seen there is not so much free time as has been believed and this ought to lessen the fears of those remaining in the anti-idleness class. It is something like saying that, really, workers don't have as much time as we think to get drunk; they are hard at work at numerous chores involving shopping, transportation, housework, repairs, and children. The anti-idleness people might reply that the workers have always had enough free time and have more than enough today. If they didn't waste so much of it in frivolous or inane things like TV, they would have time to spare for children and housework. But many people will be disappointed to hear that there is less free time than they had thought. Even were there enough to get all the chores done, they would not be satisfied.

Just as, for some, idleness and leisure like an hourglass have been turned upside down, but remain the same problem of time, so for others, work and leisure have been turned topsy-turvy. For us of the twentieth century the hymns to work are dim memories of infancy. To look for one today is like looking for the dodo. Not even corporation presidents go all out in favor of work. A paean to leisure, though, can be found in almost any magazine one picks up nowadays. Leisure is in the air. Governments now have to promise it, or, better yet, write it into the constitution. In Russia after the death of Stalin, his successors reportedly gained favor by reducing working hours. The official work week there is now supposed to be 45 hours. The latest plans for the next seven years call for a reduction to 40 hours, and then a resolute advance on a 32-hour goal. Leisure is one of the fundamental rights of citizens guaranteed by Articles 119 and 122 of the Constitution of the Union of Soviet Socialist Republics (December 5, 1936). The pattern by now seems world wide. In some parts of the globe new regimes, though they have hardly yet managed to build more than two factories with foreign aid, immediately show further signs of their progressive modernity by promising future factory workers that their hours, already hypothetically at 40, will soon stand (hypothetically) at 35.

All this I would call no more than a change in vocabulary. But a change in vocabulary, though subtle, is an event in human history. This change is an important one, for, by turning things upside down, it reveals itself as a revolution. The linguistic evidence is the strongest we have that a change in attitude has taken place, stronger certainly than the data we brought to bear in the beginning of this chapter. Linguistically it is also important that the word leisure has now become a full adjective. It indicates that the word is getting extraordinarily heavy usage. We now have leisure time, leisure rooms, leisure trips to leisure lakes, leisure clothes, leisure equipment, leisure spending on leisure items. This is too great a change, I think, to be explained simply by the fact that the amount of free time the American is supposed to have is more fiction than fact. As in the very phrase free time, there seems lurking here some hostility to the idea of work. Since in American life, work stands high, and since leisure is thought to be the opposite of work, just the pursuit of leisure implies slowing down on the race track of work.

In Chapter III we had already asked the question, has the work ethic broken down? Our contention there was that among workmen the work ethic never existed, and that if it had gravely affected anyone it was the white collar worker whose ears were more attuned to the preaching of the business classes. Among these clerical and professional groups, that strange phenomenon, the fear of free time, strikes more often. The so-called Sunday neurosis that psychiatrists observe in patients is one manifestation: the panic of Sunday without work at the office to guide one's activities along proper channels.

Related to these victims are those who feel their free time must lead to some worthy purpose, be filled with constructive activity of the kind that leads to better work or success. Reading, for example, is a favorite of these people, so long as it means reading for some end, reading something constructive, informative, self-improving, educational, worth while. Going to lectures at night school, for example, is also constructive, informative, self-improving, educational, worth while. We shall return to these kinds of worthy people in Chapter VII. One would guess that they do not suffer great hardships, since the free time available is only apparently available. But for them the worry is not simply that they have more or less free time than before; they also feel their own ideals being sapped. The calm, inky waters of free time are lapping at their foundations. They feel themselves succumbing, and succumbing they are indeed. Here where the foundations of the work ethic did and do exist, they begin to be eaten away.

An imposing counterweight is the mass of people who don't know what it means to put in a good day's work, who do everything sloppily and wastefully, who take time off from work whenever they can. The recent coinage "goofing off" fits perfectly. The ones who goof off are not the old experienced workers but the young ones, those who still live with their parents and so are not yet regular workers in the sense that their bread and butter depends on their job. The young usually pass through a period of adaptation to work in the industrial world. Although they get some training in punctuality and regularity at school, the kind of application and taking of orders that work requires proves often to be difficult to support at first. Then, too, World Wars I and II have affected the young in similar ways. They bred disillusion with existing ideals — and work is an American ideal. They also discouraged any way of living that entailed putting off present pleasure for an uncertain future — and until World War I, saving and thrift were American ideals.

The fact that the population of the United States is young, and has been for some time, increases the influence of youth's attitude. This influence does not deeply penetrate into the older generations, however. It colors many activities with youth and sportiveness, drawing on the history of America as the New World, the unexplored continent, and a young country. An ill-defined but appreciable tension seems to exist between the young and the old, who are, and for about the next ten years will be, on the increase. Before long one may see the veneer of youthfulness thin down and more attention paid to the qualities of age. Youth on its part is confronted with the spectacle of elders who never seem to die. One may well thank medicine for the strides taken to extend longevity, specially when it applies to a beloved parent, uncle, or aunt, but when all the posts to which one aspires seem to be held by vigorous octogenarians, the importance of watching the positions of youth and age becomes clear. It is also clear in unions where leaders are caught between the pressure of the senior workers to push the retirement age further away, and that of the young who already think it too high.

Once youth is married, its period of rebelliousness is about over. Getting a job, leaving the paternal home early, marrying early, having children and a temporary, mortgaged house early, the American soon enters on a docile period where the grievance is no longer how to put up with a job, but how to get a job that makes both ends meet.

I should identify part of the quest for free time in youth, then, in the role of rebelliousness it must fill in a country that encourages going higher in the social and economic scale than one's father, but that at the same time does not guarantee against sinking lower than one's father by not even being able to get or hold down a job. There have also been other irritants to the tranquillity of youth in the twentieth century — war, depression, and the longevity of the preceding generation. The length of time devoted to school has grown longer, a factor we have not yet mentioned. The popularity of a college education nowadays, no matter what kind, has the effect (1) of postponing one's entrance into a work environment and (2) of putting one in a position of having to have money without the sole legitimate means of getting it, namely, a job. Still it is not only that they are older and unhappily without their own source of income. There seem to be special attractions today for youth's spending money in one way or another. With neither work nor a family to feed, clothe, and shelter, the things they want to spend money on can only be, in terms of the usual classifications of expenditures, leisure goods.

Youth of high school age has ample time. School lets out at 3:00 or 4:00; homework makes few demands except on the serious students; the law makes part-time and weekend jobs less available to youngsters both by its age restrictions and its bureaucratic requirements for even the most temporary of helpers.

Once at work or in college the amount of time at loose ends diminishes. So the position we find youth in is the odd one of having enough time for itself but by its pressure for leisure goods giving the impression that it and the rest of the country is pushing for more time.

MIGRATORY TRAILS

Other changes, in population or elsewhere, may help give us the answers we seek. Certainly, the change in religious strains after the initial Anglo-Saxon settlements is notable. By now the vast immigration of Continental Europeans, largely Catholic, must have had some effect on American attitudes toward work. Whether Catholics or Protestants make the better workers is not a question to interest us, even could we answer it. We wish merely to note that by the nineteenth century the position of work in Protestantism and Catholicism (both Roman and Orthodox) was different. In the former it commanded a key post through which other — though not necessarily all — values could be attained. Catholicism, instead, continued to give an explicitly relative construction to the place of work in the hierarchy of values. I do not want to become stalemated here in an argument that has gone on for many decades concerning the relation of religion to work. Nor do I intend to base a whole claim on religious differences.

The arrival of large numbers of immigrants from Mediterranean areas — Italians, Austro-Hungarians, Jews, Greeks — brought cultural elements not entirely derived from the official religion of each, but elements going back into paganism, climate, and history. The importation of Negroes from Africa also brought about an influence beyond that of religion. The nineteenth century's industrial force had not yet been felt by these immigrants. At first it seemed that the influence of the new land was all one way. The haste to get everyone melted down into something resembling the Anglo-Saxon (the post-puritan, not the Elizabethan, Anglo-Saxon, that is) was so great that by and large the ones to be melted down threw themselves into the pot with fervor. They came out speaking a different language and wearing new clothes. This was not all. Their head shape changed, so did the outline of their mouth, and their way of walking. With these and other changes they began to be able to pass as pure melted-down products of the melting pot. Observers have noted how quickly immigrants took on a new coloration. In World War II it was difficult to find speakers of a foreign language among their descendants. Their religions also took on American hues. Nathaniel Hawthorne had noted with a mixture of horror and fascination that Catholicism in Rome was quite different from Puritanism in New England. Had he later contrasted Catholicism in America instead, he might have been less horrified and less fascinated, too, for the differences were less.

Assuredly all qualities and traditions were not dissolved. Some stubborn lumps must have remained in the pot unmelted. European mixtures have often sought out the kind of work where one does not merely *do* something but also *is* something — the self-employed, the professions, the arts. Many have grown with and helped develop the activities that once went by the name of "the entertainment industry." The phrase is a good example of how much the activities in question — the theater, movies, radio, music, variety, TV — needed a fine word like "industry" to bolster their performers' morale. Today, to keep pace with changing fashion, the name could well be changed to the "leisure industry." People of European extraction have also grown up with advertising, a business that got started later than banking and manufacturing, though from a rather prosaic beginning, which the next chapter will trace. It changed its course by hitching onto the lively arts, and swung into Manhattan. Even the American Indian who refused to jump into the melting pot — or his history alone, if nothing else — has had an effect on the graphic arts and specially literature. And the Negroes for their contribution to jazz, and even for the ridiculed role they sustained in symbolizing laziness and resistance to organized work, deserve a chapter to themselves. The two roles are not unrelated.

Jazz today is the symbol of American youthfulness to any part of the world that can be reached by radio or record players. Undoubtedly in the world outside it is considered a symbol of American freedom, uninhibitedness, and impatience with the old. It is of course a manifestation of American life, but perhaps more the kind that is a direct reaction than a spontaneous outburst. Jazz through all its stages and in all its variants, except the tamed varieties, has always offered a violent contrast to traits prized by industrial society. To calculation, rationality, control, discipline, and moderation, it opposes trance, the physical, release, abandon, ecstasy. Only by fixing legal hours for closing early before work days and by limiting the number of holidays can the insistent, releasing beat of jazz be kept from running through the night, every night, and developing into the kind of festivities that in other times ran on for days and weeks.

Much that we have been saying here has to be taken for what it is. There is little available information on occupations by national, religious, or racial origin. Our suggestion, however, is not extreme. The people who came to North America either before the sixteenth century or after the late nineteenth century were not the same as those who came to conquer, to settle and prosper in the centuries intervening. Their language habits, talents, and traditions were different and, though in some cases rather thoroughly rectified, they were not extirpated. Call it atavism, if you will, that which prevented them from easily fitting the work patterns of manufacture. In the next chapter we shall see whether the original patterns came more smoothly to the head and hands of Englishmen. Perhaps the sharp contrast between North and South America is most definitive of the importance of religious and national origins. Nor should we forget that climate alone cannot explain either Latin America or our own South — nor in this latter case is race even the main explanation.

The aristocratic pattern there outlasted that in the North by many years, and helped form an attitude toward work that to this day does not easily adjust to the new factories coming down from the North. But more on that too in a following chapter.

The later flow of population in the United States, then, contained elements that might have contributed to the rise of a different attitude toward work, not at all one of laziness — for almost all of the new immigrant masses had been used to a life of toil. They were for the most part from agricultural stock. The Negroes who came North were also used to laboring in the fields, as many of their early blues songs remind us. Up here or over there, work was different in kind. These people could never quite appreciate the importance given to it as a beacon in life. Since World War II, hundreds of thousands of Americans have traveled to foreign countries. The war itself brought many more to other lands, and while for most the horrors of destruction and misery made a poor setting for learning what other countries had to offer, many soldiers, male and female, found themselves stationed during or immediately after the war in peaceful posts, friendly, allied or subdued. As with those who travel to these places today, some appreciated what they found that was different, while others were repelled. The travelers stand a better chance than did the soldiers of coming to know a culture intimately and less with the scorn that conquerors have for the defeated. The war and its aftermath did bring cultural contacts, favorable or not, and the present finds the United States in a vast effort, military, governmental, and even civilian, to understand foreign cultures. Recently a college girl living abroad for a year told a journalist that what most impressed her was to find that it was possible for America to be criticized. At home she had never heard of such an idea. Apart from Canada, Germany, Holland, Scandinavia, and perhaps England and Switzerland, wherever the American goes — Mexico, Central or South America, Indo-China, Malaya or the South Seas — the attitude toward work is different from his. Europe, where most Americans originated a generation or more ago, is where most of them now go on trans-oceanic voyages. Since the war the majority of them have gone to France, Italy, Spain, and Greece — all countries less affected by the nineteenth century's doctrines than, say, England or Germany. So on these travels, too, we would have to admit that unfamiliar conceptions of time, work, and leisure could well be stimulated to circulate farther and faster.

IDEAS AND DISBELIEF

To continue in the realm of ideas, we cannot say that our educational system has, over more recent years, planted in us the seeds of dissension. In England it is sometimes asserted that the slackening off there of the will to work may be due to liberal education's spread to ever larger groups. This may be true for England, but in the United States the proportion of scientific, technical, and business courses to general studies has not changed lately. We do not propose to examine school curricula in detail at this point. The liberal arts — taken to be, in the modern version, history, literature, Greek and Latin, music and other arts — remain in their low status in the educational hierarchy. This remark, though, applies essentially to the elementary and high schools. To college and universities it applies in lesser measure, though their number in the agricultural and technological category is high when compared with the English or Continental situation. The business school as part of a university, for example, is not known elsewhere. Some businessmen at present seem to be interested in the liberal arts to the point of supporting school programs wherein executives can be taken off the job and given courses in cultural subjects. So far, however, they are a small portion of the business world, and have not made enough of an impact to be considered either a tendency or an influence. Yet they are exceptional enough to be worth bringing up again later.

A more plausible possibility is that with a decline in political and religious dedication comes an increased demand for free time. The demand seems to get louder in periods when large or important groups of people begin to doubt the trueness of their political system and their gods. They then begin to feel the performance of duties and ceremonies as burdens, and to wish to have time free of them. Previously they may not even have thought of them as matters they either wanted to avoid, or ever could with impunity. If a man feels going to church on Sunday to be a chore, it is no longer free time for him. Before he musters the courage to think of quitting, however, he wants other time in which to be free to do what he wants. Many will deny that the United States has undergone a decline in faith. But there is some truth to this. One important indication is the rise and spread of the doctrine that no one organization or component of society, not even the church or state, has a greater moral claim on the individual than any other. In many fields — labor, the professions, business, even the churches themselves — the doctrine keeps a tight hold on the thinking of leading men, although few are acquainted with its name: pluralism. It is pertinent also because from this doctrine it follows that neither church or state has a greater obligation than any other groups or individuals for guiding free time or leisure. The field is thus left open to all comers, granting, as we shall see later, a special avenue to commercial interests.

As part of a decline in religious and political belief — probably the very first part — one generally meets with widespread skepticism about an afterlife. One of the best known couplets of Lorenzo the Magnificent was

> *Chi vuol esser lieto, sia:*
> *di doman non c'è certezza.*

This sentiment won over many of the Renaissance's leading lights. Today it may be less poetically but no less exactly expressed, "You might as well enjoy yourself while you can; who knows what tomorrow will bring?" This *quién sabe* attitude is a common one. It follows that one should get the most out of life while still alive, without worrying about acts that might debit or credit his account in heaven. One pursues time, therefore, not to accomplish something but to enjoy oneself, have fun, be happy. The more free time there is the greater the chance to try the many wide-open avenues and so the greater the chance of happiness. In this life happiness is possible. (No religion says this.) In the next life, oblivion.

No doubt the disbelief in an afterlife is so significant as to warrant consideration later. What increases its power is the American's conception of his country as a land of infinite natural resources. The very word resources conjures up in his mind something that lies waiting to be used. The wealth of the United States he has been taught in school lies in the natural resources that for the most part are underground — coal, iron, and oil. Once dug up and put through the process of refining, they are transformed into products to delight the most jaded spirit. He never thinks of the country's resources in terms of art, manners, the beauty of cities, music or poetry. And since either the hereafter doesn't exist, or if it does, the resources there will be ample for providing heat at the very least, the word resources in the American's mind has lost its meaning of a reserve, or, even more precisely, of something that once drawn upon surges forth again — like art, music, flowers, but not the output of mines which leaves empty holes and ghost towns.

Resources are to be enjoyed in the present — if not in this moment, then in the next generation's moment, which is perhaps the limit of the hereafter. One raises children and sees grandchildren whom one would like to have a happy life. In this sense there is an afterlife with which the American is greatly concerned. He spends much of his money on insuring that those who live immediately after him have money. But that is almost as far as his practical vision extends.

As far as a personal afterlife goes, he is not apt to have one. America, however, will live on forever, always discovering new resources through science. This is the most recent version of the resources credo. Life in the present is not like a cornucopia whose fruits pour out in effortless profusion. Our mines are not a buried, inverted cornucopia. We exhaust our mines? We wrest new secrets from nature by which to extract from her new resources. With a wave of industry's wand resources turn into products. The world is one big colorful fair. All one needs is money to buy things. That's easy: America is rich. Money and what else? Time, time in which to enjoy these things.

So it is possible that the American, convinced of the wealth and resources of his country, in full sight of its bulging shop windows and counters, feels that he could acquire the means to get lots of the attractive things about him, if only he had the time. Without much chance of a hereafter, there's no time like the present.

Some might prefer less far-reaching explanations of the American's pursuit of time. Why seek cosmological guesses when it is easy to see that men have always looked on the machine as a promissory note for more free time? Haven't we seen that as far back as Aristotle this hope existed? With automation coming in, men now believe the moment has arrived to call in their note.

First of all, in answer, the machine has never been considered with a single attitude but with many. At some times it was thought a toy, at others a mystery best not carried too far, at still others a simple device or trick like a lever or a backstage pulley. The more frequent hope has not been that time would be saved so much as backbreaking labor. This as we have seen has already happened in the United States where machines have taken many of the aches and pains out of labor and turned toil into work. Even in the not so backbreaking manual occupations, like dishwasher or glasscutter, if the worker has to bring his hands into contact with dish or glass, he feels his job is degrading and his employer behind the times in not providing him with some sort of motor to plug in. This brings us back to an earlier distinction.

Machines that can be pedalled or plugged in, that are self-starting and stopping — lathes for example — are of a friendly species. The operator gets attached to them. Yet except in this affectionate sense, they retain their original purpose as a means or expedient to something the operator wishes to make. Our word machine comes from the Greek *mēchanē,* a device, which comes from *mēchos,* a way out or a solution. But machines that start and stop at the word of someone other than the operator himself, machines that he must adapt himself to, pacing machines, are unfriendly. Workers have never been persuaded that good could come from such machines. The machine, in this the most applicable sense for discussing the industrial present, the worker has always regarded with suspicion. Even today labor's views on the shorter work week spring from the fear that the machine, if left to itself, will throw men out onto the breadline. The argument that the pace is set by somebody, and this somebody can be controlled, is not too persuasive. When the worker thinks of the machine, above all the automated machine, he thinks of it as an impersonal force. He cannot be shown to his satisfaction who it is that made it, that sets its pace, what his name is, what his face looks like.

The worker in driving for the shorter work week thus is not calling up a note payable on demand. Rather he is trying to soften the demands of machine work. He hopes to lessen work's domination of production through individual competition and to reach a collective, guildlike protection by taking the machine's saving of hours and spreading them among all workers. As such his attempt falls into the modern pursuit of time only by accident. The effort is like plowing under corn to raise the price — the objective is more money, not more corn. Except, in this case, if one plows time under to win work security, there is a salvage value to the buried time: it becomes free time. The value is a result of calculating free time upside down, as we said before, by counting how many fewer work hours there are, rather than how many more free hours there might be.

Even were the demand for time like the demand for a note,

there would still be the question, why should the note be payable in time rather than money? Or, as we mentioned earlier, why not in work less laborious? In this coin the machine has paid off well.

HUMAN NATURE VERSUS WORK

Another seemingly simple explanation is that, at bottom, human nature doesn't like work. Of course, one cannot spell out all the qualifications needed for generalizing about human nature. What the body needs for exercise, what happens to it even because of a simple thing like the sedentariness of modern work, are questions involving so many details that a monograph on physiology would not be enough in answer. There is something to be said for the idea, even though the statement is broad and bland. The body, we gather, finds restraint and regularity disagreeable. As long as work confines muscles, and only a few of them, to but a few movements, men will try to avoid it.

A term like restraint or constraint carries its own measure. A sprinter who has just finished a hundred-yard dash would not ordinarily feel constrained if he were then ordered to plump himself down in a deck chair. Furthermore in making his dash he has the crown of laurel in mind, but if a passer-by asked him to run a hundred yards just to see how fast he could do it, no doubt he would refuse. Perhaps if it were a young boy who were asked, he might do it for an ice cream cone. The man of twenty-five for such a reward more likely would not. He would want the pot sweetened, and the man of forty-five would want it even sweeter. Similarly in work the rewards would have to be commensurate with age and training. The younger worker is less averse to physical activity, but by the same physiology more prone to feel constrained by a job that requires him to sit or stand still. It may not be enough that his hands are moving with speed. The rest of him may feel as pinned down as the ten-year-old scholar for whom the teacher feels it is enough that his brain be exercised. In Pinocchio's country, instead of there being no school on Saturday as with us, there was none on Thursday. Pinocchio, who couldn't sit still — though made of wood — sought a school week of one Sunday and six Thursdays.

At times, and here we have another hypothesis, the rewards of work are changed without a change in real wages or salary. In Chapter III we spoke of the pleasant nonwork elements of the job, how they varied with the job and usually deteriorated in machine-paced work. If such elements increase or decrease, the rewards of the job of course change accordingly. The rise of industry brought with it a new respect for work generally. Though we cannot see that the work ethic ever won over the mind of workers, that it had an impact is certain. It increased nonmonetary rewards of work like esteem and prestige, and for some workers became a path of virtue and salvation. The self-employed, too, of course basked in new glory. In like manner a war or invasion would so increase the feeling of national solidarity that everybody, including women, working in the national defense would be accorded greater respect. The first case raised the rank of work ideologically; the second case related work more crucially to the national emergency.

A recession, to take another instance, brings on the threat of unemployment. That in itself changes the job from one of comfortable to questionable security. Since many workers have no job, not even a shaky one, work suddenly becomes a rarer and more precious thing. Labor becomes more punctual, obedient, careful, disciplined, respectful. Its productivity goes up. As depression becomes the enemy with starvation lurking behind it, the rewards of a job shoot sky-high. And yet all the while the money part of it may be going down in both real and current terms. To decrease the monetary value of a job all one needs is prosperity. The shortage or high cost of labor makes it easy to get another job if one loses the present one. Jobs are easy to find and therefore not so important. During this phase one can hear it said most frequently, "After all, it's against human nature to work."

Legislation on unemployed workmen's compensation in this country exemplifies the way in which changing rewards affect thinking about the relation of human nature and work. During the dark days of '33 the advocates of compensation proposed taking steps on the ground that men wanted to work but there just was no work to be had. The possibility that men would not wish to work but to shirk by living off their unemployment money, was not accepted generally. With the coming of the war and the going of the depression, the arguments passed to the other side. Opponents took the offensive with the now more plausible thesis that it is human nature not to like work. Even the advocates now had to set to work to block loopholes in the legislation, just so "the few" who don't like to work would not spoil things for the "vast majority" who are hardworking men and women. On the basis of the one fact — that unemployment compensation today numbers strong opponents who insist that workers resort to it just to get out of working — we might have nodded assent: it is human nature not to like work and to seek free time. The appearance of things would have favored such an interpretation. The changing rewards of work in these different periods, though, make it impossible for us to use the changed attitudes toward unemployment compensation as evidence either that people don't want to work or that more and more of them want more free time.

So we should watch out lest our conclusion about the demand for free time be one that reflects not human nature but the rewards of work as things stand today. We should agree with part of the human-nature position if it were put thus: work requires persons to be physically present at certain times and places and consists in certain physical and mental movements. The less the time, place, and movements can be chosen by the worker himself, the more likely he will be to seek relief by avoiding work. We shall meet the worker in this aspect again in a later chapter and see more of how he and the machine and human nature get along together.

Since work implies some constraint in return for some reward, the worker (from the time of Adam's fall) likes to take it easy when he can. In our day, then, how do we explain that workers work nearly a 48-hour week and moonlight and watch their wives and daughters go off to work? This is the question we posed at the beginning of the chapter. We agreed that the American is on the trail after time. We also suggested that some of the causes for his being so are the seeming decline in the work week, the effects of war on large numbers of youth, the presence of wives and mothers in the labor force, the influence of foreign populations and travel, the sparkle of resources and products, the decline in religious and political dedication along with the rise of pluralism, and a natural dislike for any exertion considered constraining. Still, while inclined to view some other factors like the influence of liberal education or the hope placed in the machine as important, we are not satisfied with the picture as it has developed.

If union leadership asks members to strike for shorter hours, they will do so, but they do it not so much out of dislike for work as for fear of no work, or to have a higher pay rate start after fewer hours, or in obedience to the authority of their leaders. The difficulty we have yet to resolve hovers around these points. In the conflict, unionists choose this word leisure as the battle cry. Why not simply say, "We are striking because we want shorter hours so that we can spread the work week the machine is reducing"? Perhaps they consider such a confession would be weak in economic theory. But what kind of theory do they have in using the word leisure? No one says why workers need leisure, nor need anyone say why, evidently. More free time is accepted as inherently good. Union heads can line up the ranks for battle with the cry, "Leisure!" just as advertisers can peddle their wares by it. Yet it wasn't always considered virtuous to be at leisure.

Spending money on one's leisure was thought to be bad too — spendthrift.

The change in meaning in the word leisure, we said earlier, provides the firmest evidence to be found that people want more time. The things this chapter brought to light explain the desire only in part. They fail, I feel, to explain the greatness of the change or the conduct of persons apparently infected with the idea. If the American likes more free time so much, why does he work the hours he does? Why not say, "I'll take a day off this week, or next, and take life easy"? We did ask this question of the executive, and started to ask it of the worker, but stopped by accepting the idea that he wasn't free in the same sense. To take it up again though, why isn't the worker free too? Isn't our economic system based on the free organization of work? A man can elect to work or not, or just as much as he sees fit. Certainly the American earns more than he needs for subsistence, else why all the talk about having the highest standard of living in the world? What does the newly-popular concept of "discretionary income" mean if not the amount left over in the sugar bowl after food, clothing, shelter, and taxes are already taken out?

The American today is supposed to have a large discretionary spending power. He is reported to have more money than he needs to spend on the necessities — about $1,100 more per capita, and about four times more than he had to spend discretionally in 1940. So he could if he wished make the choice for more time. But he doesn't. He pursues time, but not very far. He soon runs out of wind.

Shapers of Choice

We can see, at least in part, why a demand for time presses on the mid-twentieth century, and why for the American the word leisure comes in for so much praise. What we have is lip-service: on one hand, "Isn't leisure a wonderful thing!" On the other, business-as-usual, or more than usual. There has never been such a high proportion of the population at work. This conflict does not sound like the American, agreed. When he wants something and knows what he wants, he bulldozes toward it. Perhaps he is not as free as he thinks. But let us put such disquieting thoughts aside for the moment to pose a related question. It will eventually lead us back to the puzzle.

In the last chapter we asked what reasons there could be for the desire for more time. We never asked what would account for the way people use the time they do have. Obviously whatever affects how a man wants to pass his free time may also affect how much of it he wants. In this chapter as we seek to discover what shapes a man's activity when away from work, we shall often be dealing with the quantity of time a man wants more or less of. He can't very well desire more time unless he has an idea of what he wants to do with it.

Where does he get his ideas? He is not born with them. In seeking an explanation it may be a help every now and then to try to figure out why we do not do as we did once, or as others do

today. We need every aid imaginable; the task is a slippery one.
It is only slightly less than asking why do we do what we do, ever,
in time free or unfree or anything else. The free part, to be so,
should be free of the unfree part. But is this possible or even desirable?

To start, we can take some of the kinds of influences in nature
and man that have been known or believed to give his way of life
a particular turn. Take topography or landscape. Mountain
sports are one thing, valley sports another. A river in the valley
permits rafting, a mountain stream presents a trail, both offer
fishing. Seas and shores, coves and bays, hold out their own possibilities. Wide-open spaces give one kind of vista, rolling hills
frame another. Some physicians consider a height from which
one sees long expanses as the most reposing of landscapes. Topography may fit the pattern of free time by controlling the pattern
of labor. Logrollers in Burma cannot roll teak logs unless the
rain comes down in torrents. When the dry season is on, the work
day lasts from sunup to sundown. When the season is wrong for
men, elephants, and teak, the weeks go by in idleness. The Nile's
inundations impose their own pattern. As soon as the mud flats
can support a man's weight, sowing begins; the growing season is
but a week or two off. By April and May the crops are harvested,
the land is black hard mud-soil, and the inside-the-house season
begins. The heat outside is too great; the Nile goes down to a
ditch of red slimy water. Then comes the water to cover the land
again; the rats scurry to the dikes, men and beasts half walk, half
swim from one village-island to another. The High Nile festival
used to come in late August, and until November little work
could be done: feeding cattle, repairing tools, etc. Free time was
as great a sea as the Nile. The kings of Egypt used it to build the
pyramids, while the priesthood profited from the clear night
skies of the desert to make a leisurely study of the stars.

Climate certainly makes a difference. One can go ice skating
on the Zuider Zee but not on the Tiber. Torrid climes permit no

toiling in the sun; temperate zones are more flexible. The beverages one can squeeze out of the desert are not at all like those that can be pressed from grapes. There also seems to be a general debilitating effect in hotter, more humid areas. One must take care though not to blame climate for everything. The South American's siesta does not show he lacks energy. In the Philippines, it has been said, the Spaniards turned an active, enterprising infidel into a lazy indolent Christian. The Romans, who were paragons of constructive activity, still take the afternoon stretched out in the shade. Generalization about climate should beware, too, of shifting sands and streams: the mysterious movements of the Gulf Stream and their effect on the climate of Europe in past centuries, make interesting pages.

Diet, it is clear, can bring changes in bodily energy and thence in forms of recreation. The fermented juice of the grape has had an exalted rank in the intellectual and artistic life of the West. Coffee, too, has won an indisputable place. In Paris alone there were the Café Régence (where Diderot, an inveterate café-goer, used to appear regularly to converse and play chess), the Café du Caveau a few doors away, the Mille Colonnes (where Madame Romain, *la belle limonadière*, held sway until she got religion and entered a convent), the Café Lamblin and the Café de Foy. Stimulants like coffee and tea have a place in the history of leisure and free time. Drugs and dope do too — the Chinese's pipe of opium, the Peruvian's chew of *coca*, the Arab's *narghile*, the Turk's hashish, the Indian's *peyote*, the East Indian's betel nut. Specialists studying the different effects of diets rich in flesh or fats or starch have come to many conclusions, such as what to eat for the day's three meals. The first two, the American breakfast and lunch, are the work meals (except on days off), and the third is the free-time meal. Dieticians seem unanimous that the last should be the big meal of the day. It is thought to be the only time of day when sleepiness would not hinder important activity. That meals should be three instead of two or five, and that there should be particular hours at which food is taken, both relate to the day's work and play. Midnight suppers and chocolates for breakfast are not part of the industrial schedule.

There are many other things of course that affect the health and energy of a population. The air people breathe may be malarial or black with coal dust or poisoned with chemical fumes or teeming with water drops. There is not much chance of free time without health of mind and body. Time may be free from work, but not from pain and anxiety. Related to health is a group of factors that might be called physiological. The age of the population, for example, will influence both its will to work and its desire for play or for the more active sports. Glancing generally over the age groups in a study used in a previous chapter, one cannot help noting that television takes first place in all age groups (Table 8). Less expected perhaps is the popularity of visiting, which takes second rank until forty years of age and moves over to third place afterward. After forty years the top five activities are television, working around the yard and garden, visiting, and reading books and magazines. Participation in sports, on the other hand, ranks in the top five only during the teens. The activities that persons sixty and over seem to relinquish most frequently are going to the movies, listening to records, driving for pleasure, hanging around the drugstore, going to dances, and participating in sports or going to sports events. Other studies confirm that with age a gradual decline takes place in all outdoor activities. In this century the population of the United States has been aging, but before long, perhaps in ten years, it will be getting younger, which means that the free-time activities associated with youth may become more conspicuous still. Another factor, the proportion of one sex to another — although the difference between them is usually described not as physiological but as anatomical — may affect their pattern of association, and whether they spend leisure together or separately or in the presence of a chaperon. The reported gallantry of the settlers of the American West is usually explained by the scarcity of females then and there. Other factors typically included in the study of physical anthropology — racial differences in length of arm and leg, in quantity of skin pigment, and so on — may play a part, too.

It is a short step from a consideration of physical composition of populations to one of population density. The mere bringing together of crowds of persons creates problems of health. The problem of refuse and excretion alone takes on gigantic proportions. Unsolved it can mean rats and plagues. A broken water supply can bring on typhus. Apart from disease, a heavy density of persons can cause problems of food supply which in turn can lead to uprisings within a country and war without. Dense population also invariably raises the money cost of free-time activities. Sociologists sometimes make the mistake of equating free-time expenditures with free-time opportunities or activities. Thus in surveying a country they conclude that in leisure facilities the rural zones are underdeveloped areas. They do not offer the opportunities of the city with its parks and playgrounds, bowling alleys, and shooting galleries. But having the woods and fields usually within eyeshot, the country dweller has no need of parks or playgrounds. If he wants to bowl, he can bowl on the green, and as for shooting, he can hunt either in or out of season without making special arrangements for dogs and a guide.

Most of the traditional games and sports of the world require time and space. This the country has, not the city. Several hundred children jammed in a small school yard produce a more crowded stage than Pieter Brueghel did when he painted them playing all their games in a frenzy in one town square. A game like craps suits the tenements. Cost of equipment is negligible; any number can play; strangers can join in; a shooter can stay for one roll of the dice, for twenty minutes or two hours; it is quiet and needs little space for movement; a doorway or hallway where the police pass infrequently is enough. Pitchpenny, played with coins or bottle tops, and jacks for girls also require little space. As soon as people begin to move in, space goes at a premium.

Our country dweller has to be like the legendary Daniel Boone who pulled up stakes whenever he but caught in the air the whiff of another human. If not, unless he wants to shoot craps, the cost of his free-time pleasures soon goes up.

What has happened to Walden Pond makes a sad but instructive tale. It has special interest because it deals with the land of Thoreau, one of the few American figures worthy of mention in the history of leisure. The four families who once owned the land around the famous pond deeded the tract to Massachusetts "to preserve the Walden of Emerson and Thoreau, its shores and woodlands." Every year many Americans and foreign visitors journey there as to a memorial. Not long ago the Ambassador of India came, paying homage to a man to whose writings Mahatma Gandhi had acknowledged a debt. But Walden Pond has clear cool water and a pleasant beach. The county commissioners in charge of the property, sensing the general need for swimming in the hot summer days, established at the south end of the pond a public bathing area. Then just outside the property on the other side of the boundary road up sprang trailer camps and hot-dog stands. What has happened to the solitude now? The opportunity to commune with nature is negligible. One wonders how Thoreau ever managed it. More recently the commissioners began to enlarge the swimming area. Protests poured in; the *Times* of London carried an editorial, a "Save Walden" committee petitioned the courts, and the Superior Court of Massachusetts issued a temporary injunction stopping the bulldozers after they had ripped up only an acre or two of trees and shoved but a part of a hillside into the pond.

There are areas of Yellowstone Park now where so many lodges have been built, roads put through, and parking spaces cleared that it would take but little to feel oneself in an amusement park or back in the jammed city. In almost all public woods and forests the wild flowers and undergrowth are trampled by too many feet. The bulldozed earth washes away with the rains. The roots of trees rise up in agony to die before their time.

Once a high forest goes, it will not return in a man's lifetime, nor in his son's nor his son's sons'. The forced feeding of wildernesses has not progressed very much. The Romans in order to sail against the Carthaginians took to wooden ships. After them came Amalfi, Venice, Genoa, and Pisa, all republics with an urge for naval warfare. The result was that Sicily and Calabria were deforested, and still today their topsoil washes out to sea. A resource is no resource if it cannot resurge. But even if one is being used up fast, while it lasts it has an effect on leisure and free time. If a country has a lot of coal and iron, and steel has come of age, they lie there inviting exploitation.

I went into the relation of resources to free time in the last chapter, without pointing out, however, another sense in which natural wealth may be important. With reason it is said that leisure cannot exist without a surplus, without the possibility of producing more than is needed to survive. Once a reserve exists, a group of persons can be taken from production to live off the surplus, or else the surplus can be divided up among all so that each has less work, or, as we would say today, a shorter work week. There is a modern economic bias in the hypothesis, which we should like to take up later. By and large, it seems to make sense. The greater the surplus, the bigger the class that can sit around doing nothing, or the shorter the general work week can be. The chair, it has been said, symbolizes the life of leisure. Chairs are comfortable, upholstered, part of everyone's life, and the time in them is of leisure not of labor or the struggle for existence. Whether or not true, the promise of leisure in resources and surplus is so firmly believed in that it deserved mention at this point.

Closely related to resources but independent of them in some ways is toolmaking and technology. Petroleum was always around, but the methods for extracting, processing, and consuming it were not. Some would go so far as to say that scientific hypotheses, too, were always around but that it took technological advances, the work of engineers and inventors, to select the right ones and carry them forward. At any rate, before the wheel was invented no one went roller skating; before Prometheus brought a flame down to mankind, there was no telling of stories around a campfire; before shoemaking, one had to dance barefoot. The technological level in other realms of life like work and transport usually infiltrates the activities of free time too.

With technology one clearly enters the sphere of man-made factors. The same is true of shelter and architecture. Their influence as a shaper of how man spends free time is enormous. Thus, if houses for an office worker's income are built with two bedrooms, there will only be sleeping space for the parents and two children. The family can crowd up if other children come along, but there is certainly no room for the grandparents. Somewhat as among the Trobriand Islanders, where when a commoner gets old he leaves his house and goes to one of the small huts specially built for old people, the elderly today seek small apartments. The repercussions of an apparently small change like this are intricate and not easy to follow through. In the big old American frame houses of the end of the nineteenth century there was not as we would say today "room for the grandparents," but "room for the grandchildren." The perspective was from the top downward, not from the middle downward and then secondarily upward. Without grandparents in the house, the free-time activity of parents remains confined to that house or to the few hours a week they can afford a baby sitter. And then, it is not worth the cost just to go visiting friends. For longer trips away from the children, the baby sitter cannot stay, or parents wouldn't have the money to pay for one — nor feel safe about it anyway. Without the time, patience, and experience of grandparents, who's to tell children stories? All children and adults yearn for stories. Houses built nowadays often have a special room for TV, so the set plus comic books at least takes care of tales for children, and fills many of the parents' free-time hours as well. These are perhaps some of the unexpected influences of architectural change.

The city itself is an architectural conglomeration. Since the

American has moved farther from work, the slowing down of city traffic that we noted in Chapter IV has cut deeply into the American's time. Moreover, whole areas are restricted by zoning regulations to residential structures with prescriptions as to height, distance from one another, and so forth, often with the result that taking a walk through the place becomes a dull affair. Gone are the interest and charm that lie in the variety of shops and services, of shoe shiners, delicatessens, candy and magazine stores. Leveling all land before building — an engineering tactic favored partly because of the existence of laborsaving machinery — takes away the play of perspective and light. The streets become tedious corridors. Without squares for people to gather in, a city increases the pressure to meet within houses, cuts down the range of contacts, raises the cost of a part of free-time activity by requiring it to go on in commercial, roofed-in buildings, and increases the dependence of public opinion on centralized, house-penetrating means like the radio and TV.

The type of work a population does is another factor shaping the kinds of play it prefers. The housewife who is cut off from all contacts during the day — except with children and the sound and visual images of print, radio, telephone, and television — may look forward for recreation to the return of her husband (for all his faults still a live presence). He, of course, spends his day in close contact with his energetic peers and may look forward to something less exhilarating than company.

It is dangerous, however, to think of the effect of work on free time as only an opposing reaction. The busman's holiday reminds us that the pleasure of doing a respected activity well may be greater than the promise of any other activity. If the busman takes his girl for a drive, he is in an area where his skill calls forth admiration, and even if he takes his family instead his capacity is not in doubt. The coordination of muscles alone in any skilled task often provides a satisfaction that, if carried over into play, increases the pleasure of play. Just watch the laborer at an amusement park head for the sledge-hammer game. Though most Americans spend the greater part of their work time in sitting, their free time is not therefore spent standing. Some muscles may become developed at the expense of others, so that after a while sitting a long time is less tiring than standing two short minutes. The American, even after subtracting the hours he lies down for sleep, spends most of his twenty-four hours on his rump. Work may be so exhausting mentally or physically that it leaves free time heir to passivity. On the other hand it may be in so well-cooled or well-heated an environment that one will shirk free time outdoors just because of heat or cold.

The variations in effect any activity can have on free-time doings are numerous. Merely from the examples already cited activity can be classified into a series of polar types — active/passive, participant/spectator, solitary/social, indoor/outdoor, in-the-home/outside-the-home, sedentary/on-the-feet. Some of the criticisms of the way leisure is spent in America revolve about these poles. However, the information available does not inspire enough confidence to say with any exactness how much free-time activity is, for instance, sedentary versus on-the-feet. One would expect farm families to spend less time indoors than town families, and that is what one gathers from a survey of how much time each type spent at home rather than outside. In both kinds of families mothers were inside the house more than twice as much as fathers: farm mothers about twelve hours a day, not counting sleep, and town mothers about an hour and a half more. For farm fathers on weekdays the time passed at home was not quite four hours, for town fathers about five hours. Even on Sundays, fathers, of farm and town alike, were out of the house more than mothers.

During the depression the activities of a group (predominantly female, white, single, and of long residence in or around Boston) were studied along the lines of a number of our categories here. Saturday and Sunday, it was learned, were less solitary than weekdays. Solitary activities took the largest share of time, with two-person activities appearing next in line. But the majority of cases were unmarried persons, and the definition of solitude broadly admitted one's being among the congregation at church, as long as one came to church unaccompanied. The farm/town research also examined a category, shared/non-shared activities, that is related to solitary/social activities. It looked at only inside-the-home activities, and, of these, none but those involving family members. Also even though others may have been present, an activity was considered "non-shared" if the others were not doing the same thing. And the survey mentioned earlier of dairy farmers covered several related categories, such as visiting at home and visiting elsewhere. There seems to have been more of the latter, and women evidently visit more than men.

Obviously there are difficulties in generalizing for the United States as a whole from surveys of farm and town (3,500–7,000 inhabitants) families in three counties of southern Michigan, Boston females (mainly single) during the depression, and dairy farmers in Wisconsin. Though such researches may be done with care and in some cases, as that of the Boston study, with imagination, a wider and more typical picture is needed. For this reason, with literally hundreds of small surveys available on agricultural experimental areas, home economics, alumni and consumer markets, our attention has concentrated on studies with a national breadth, principally those used in Chapters IV and V. Unfortunately they must slight many of the finer distinctions that smaller or more intensive studies can focus on. Thus the national diary study shows that on the average American men are out of the house about ten hours a day and women only about four hours, but it tells us little of whether their activities were social or solitary, in the open, or as participant or spectator. It does turn up a different facet, though, to wit, that free-time hours are almost all spent at home, indoors, on all days including the weekend (Table 3 and Chart A).

It is possible to approach these questions in other ways, however. We know that more men than women leave the home to go to work. We know that housework and child rearing still are woman's lot. So, for the category in-the-home versus out, men are more out than women. After work we have an idea of how much time is spent before the TV set. Hence, we can say that most free time on weekdays is spent in the home. We know what proportion of the population is married and how many have children; as a result we can say that men and women are rarely alone in their free time, and mothers with children under six practically never. If they are in the home, they are mostly indoors. Furthermore, the open-air market, like open-air work, is disappearing. No more to be seen are the huge piles of radishes, carrots, lettuce, turnips, artichokes, onions, and spinach rising architectonically from bins and carts. The main outdoor activities, except on vacation, take place during transportation, also well-heated, in going from one place to another during lunch, and in certain sports during the summer months. Even the Sunday automobile ride in winter is closed in and heated. Outdoor cafés don't exist. Walking, it seems, as something to do during free time, has gone the way of the left leg muscles we used to use for the clutch. Not since the depression has walking been a pastime. So the bulk of the American's free time (as well as work time) is spent indoors.

Almost all office workers sit. What proportion of other workers stand on their feet on the job is not known, but the number is surely diminishing. Streetcar conductors used to stand most of the time; bus drivers now sit. Diggers used to stand; the excavator in his cab sits. In the service trades, waiters and waitresses stand at one's table, eventually; judging, however, from the service, we may at least suspect they have disappeared to sit behind the swinging doors. Cafeteria lines have increased, thereby standing customers upright while waiters find a job easier on the feet. For work time it may be hard to determine the ratio of seat time to feet time; for free time it is simpler. Taking the grand list of activities in Chapter IV, we can see that the exclusively sedentary activities are found among those most frequent and time-consuming — TV watching, reading, motoring, meetings and lectures, visiting, dining out, going to the theater, concerts, operas, movies, and playing cards.

One should not confuse sedentariness with passivity or indolence, of course. The American's frequent drive across country seated in a car is a feat of pure endurance. Yet, put the same man to work in the rice paddies, and his legs will buckle before the noon sun hits his back. Nor should one confuse the sedentariness of most of the population with the inability of youth to sit still, or children to sit at all, when other kinds of bodily contortions are possible. The advertising phrase of "the new active leisure" at most applies to a small proportion of the population who, like the young, are supposed to enjoy all those money-costing sports like boating, skiing, traveling, deep-sea fishing, and so forth. Vacant-lot softball, craps, and mushroom picking are not on the list.

Now, sitting and standing, in spite of in-between states like slouching, are positions clearly defined anatomically. Thanks to this, we can agree on whether the nation stands or sits most of the time. When we come to other categories such as participant/spectator or active/passive, the line of demarcation is vaguer; it is not so simple to figure out where to put a given activity. In horse racing, most would agree, the jockey is nearly as much a participant as the horse. What about the owner or trainer or stableboys? What about the gentleman who goes to Ascot in ascot and binoculars? What about the bookmaker? At the end of the line, what about the man who never sees the track or the horses or the race but who through a bookie puts $2 on Susy Virgin's nose to win? Who of all of them is participating most, and who least, and who, if anyone, not at all? How can getting up to go out to the race track be measured with telephoning to place a bet? True, there is a participation of both money and physical movement; there are other kinds too, that lead on to triumph with the winner or despair with the loser. Any siding with one of the contrasting teams in a sport brings more than mere spectatorship. To a Chicagoan, a game between the Red Sox and the Yankees is only of relative interest. To a Northsider in Chicago even what the White Sox are doing is of small concern, as is the performance of the Cubs to a Southsider. Let one or the other win the pennant, and the taking of sides by part of town gives over to city pride — then all Chicagoans become rooters.

Is there nothing to be said then for the distinction participant versus spectator? Only in the sense of physical exercise. The spectator, though he crosses the city by crowded subway, fights his way to a seat in the stands on the 10-yard line, and then stamps, swears, and shouts himself hoarse, nevertheless consumes fewer calories than the men running, throwing, stumbling, and knocking one another down on the gridiron.

Similarly with the distinction of passive versus active leisure. Some define passivity almost as submissiveness, making its contrast aggressiveness. Others make the basis of the difference the intensity of the experience, thus changing the opposing pole to something like relaxation. There are other definitions, too, but in common usage *active* refers to visible movements and not to what may be going on underneath the skin or within head, stomach, or heart. A television show may be absorbing for the viewer or dull; in terms of physical movement there is little activity to sitting in a darkened room, even for the eyeballs, except when our viewer gets up to get his can of beer from the refrigerator. The emphasis, unless it is on visible physical motions, is misplaced, and even then must include both work and free-time activities. Some of those who criticize the way free time is spent in the United States are partly to blame. They start by wanting to show how sedentary and motionless we have become; they end by trying to extend their criticism to passivity of mind or to unresponsiveness. These are important criticisms but cannot be measured or evaluated by the typical active/passive yardstick.

We have taken a long sidetrack to show that it is not simple to estimate the effect of work or other activities on those of free time, and vice versa. A person may also react in work, of course, to the way he spends his free time. Being tired at work in the morning from indulgence the night before is one clear example. Not only that; some of the pigeonholes for classifying reactions have to be cleaned out and rebilleted. With this done it is clear that American free-time activities are for the most part done sitting, in company, indoors, and at home. Work for the majority is also sedentary and done indoors. In these categories, then, the reaction of free time to work or vice versa, if there is one, is not opposite but similar, along the same line, except that work, in contrast to free time, is done away from home. Should this last suggest that the at-homeness of Americans is due in part to their leaving home abruptly and completely for the better part of the day? Perhaps. But when farmers, tradesmen, or artisans in a European village repair to their evening meal, they do not necessarily stay at home afterward. Invariably there is an *osteria* nearby where many of them go for a glass and a game of cards. Perhaps there is more to be laid at the door of technology than of work, yet the effect of the American rush hour is of tiredness, of being spent, and always of a frantic hurry to get home.

Nowhere else in the civilized world is this homing urgency found. The usual sight is a dilly-dallying along the way to a late dinner. Perhaps the net separation of ten hours without a return home for lunch accounts for it. In countries with the siesta there is enough time for lunch and a nap at home only because the journey to work does not take much time. In cities that are growing outward, like Rome today, the distance to work is so great that before long the workers themselves exert pressure for a shortened lunch period. Since they don't have time to go home anyway, they can eat lunch at work and at least leave for home earlier. As a result they are away from home all day and the habit of stopping in after work at a café for an hour or two with an apéritif begins to weaken.

But in America the forces working toward at-homeness are greater. The technology necessary to make the home a self-contained unit with telephone and refrigerator, the custom of everybody's getting married so that he has wife and children waiting for him in the house *avec tous les conforts,* and also the virtual isolation of the woman in the autarchic household so that she makes life disagreeable for the husband if he comes home at the decent hour of eight o'clock — all these and other things too are of undoubted importance. Yet work and the tiresome journey to and fro play their role in the at-homeness of the American. At 6:00 P.M. of any weekday nearly three fourths of the male population from 20 to 59 years of age has arrived safely home and doesn't leave the hearthside for the rest of the evening (Chart A).

In part this nesting activity goes back to an earlier evolution. The net separation of home and work, just mentioned, and the growth of cities into sprawling, black, transportation maps are two factors that help make the home a refuge against the impersonality outside. The trend seems to have begun in the reign of Victoria. Massive, comfortable chairs and sofas appeared in solidly appointed houses. By now the home as a sanctuary has legal and constitutional support in both England and the United States. On the Continent there is no separate word to distinguish home from house, and an out-of-the-house life for men still exists in the café and *bistro* where they can eat, drink, write letters or poetry, discuss women, and argue about politics and literature. In America and England in recent decades this homing instinct has become more prominent. Men used to go to clubs, union meetings, pubs, the movies, and even to church affairs. Attendance at such institutions has dropped off. When making evening calls, social workers have noticed this and been surprised and puzzled to find so often that the man of the house is at home. Rarely any more do they hear the wifely complaint, "He's out night after night." Without a doubt the new media penetrating the household account for the change. Radio put the salesman's talking pitch inside the American's house; television put his feet up on the living-room coffee table. And to keep the American in the living room, a song and dance had to be added to the sales patter.

Together, indoor work and indoor at-homeness may make the

American timorous of outdoor temperatures below 60° or above 85°F. Certainly his ingenuity at the technology of central and individual unit heating makes it difficult to feel cold in America without deliberately going ice skating, or being foolhardy enough to take a walk instead of a ride on a wintry Sunday. He is somewhat better at withstanding heat and humidity than cold, but with the coupled heating and cooling systems now appearing, it won't be long before he feels suffocated on the un-air-conditioned summer street.

In considering the effect of work on free time, there is probably good reason to distinguish the activities of the weekday from the weekend. Since the weekend, for some at least, offers two full work-free days, it provides the occasion for those activities that take more than just an hour or two — trips that take the family farther from home, the 18-hole golf game, the overnight visit or fishing trip. In these couple of days the reaction to too much indoor life sets off the dash for the outdoors (packing the highway bumper to bumper, and poisoning the air with carbon monoxide) on the way to trees, wild flowers, lakes, beaches, fish, deer, and duck. Would we be sun-worshipers today, were we still farmers? The same two-day span is also the occasion for those activities in town that are the reverse of the work pattern — irregularity in hours, overindulgence in food and drink, lack of sleep, and the unconfined physical motions, the violence, symbolized by dragged-out Friday drinking, late Saturday night parties, drunken brawls and speeding. This is the explosive kind of reaction to work. Its favorite moment is the weekend. Sunday is used to get over Saturday.

A catch-all phrase in sociology — made popular by William Graham Sumner — is *customs and mores*. It refers to all the ways and moral stances of a people, such as their kinds of family relationship and ways of educating youth. A number of customs, like early marriage, have already been seen to shape the spending of free time. Division of labor between the sexes with almost all of the males going out to work and, as yet, most of the females staying in the house (Table 3) is another custom that continues to affect the uses of free time. From some of the points touched on previously one gathers why a serious problem of matrimony today — often not recognized in its essence as one of free time — is that the husband and wife each want to do different things: he often prefers to be or go off by himself; she would rather spend her free time with him. Some biologists might argue that there is a truly sexual difference here in that the male — not being subject to pregnancies — is freer to move about and scatter seed wherever it may bear fruit. If so, the housewife's isolation during the day, often from other women too, may be too trying even for the maternal instinct.

Perhaps the best way to illustrate the effect of customs and mores on the shaping of choice is to ask ourselves why certain activities no longer appear to be considered leisure. Baudelaire asserted, unequivocally, that the natural occupation of the leisured was love. Without leisure he would say, love could only be a plebeian orgy or the fulfillment of a conjugal duty; instead of a fiery caprice, it becomes an act of loathsome utility, nothing else. The word he used for the man of leisure was *dandy,* a crossbreed combining the restraint of the English gentleman with the artistic bent and manners of the Renaissance *signore* or courtier. Ovid's advice in the *Art of Love* is, "Take your time, walk slow." Conversely in the *Remedies for Love* he says, "Point one — shun all leisure. Throw away your leisure and you've broken Cupid's arrow." Catullus, in an earlier age, sides with Aristotle's diagnosis of the cause of Sparta's fall when he blames his Lesbia's licentiousness on her leisure, on the idle hours she fills with legions of paramours.

Less civilized peoples too sometimes present a Boccaccian state of affairs: among the remote Baluchi of western Pakistan the penalty for adultery is death. If it were enforced, there would be few Baluchi left alive. The rule is served only enough to supply a dash of danger. Hence, in this group of migratory shepherds the major spare-time activity is reckless and moderately risky adultery. The men go off to watch the herds, but even when husbands are at home, women can still play at the game by embroidering caps and tobacco pouches with silk thread their lovers have given them. Such activity as a category for leisure has not appeared in any available study. Does it mean that love affairs have disappeared? Highly unlikely. Love affairs have gone underground. They were also underground in nineteenth-century France, or, better, under covers, with just the amount of danger to spice the affair into an adventure. Until World War I, actually up to World War II, Paris, Rome, and Vienna accepted Baudelaire's dictum.

In twentieth-century America, even mid-twentieth-century America, the love affair is not yet thought of as an occupation of leisure. The phrase itself is rarely heard, and what would once have been called love affairs today often go by the name of sexual promiscuity. Such language comes from the many psychiatrists, counselors, and social workers who condemn the free-time activity as neurotic. The usage becomes absurd as soon as one juxtaposes the neurotic behavior of a factory worker or office employee with the love affairs of an Austrian officer. Freud for all his moralizing would never have been so provincial. He would have worried about the case only if the officer was in love not with countesses or servant maids but with the luster of his orderly's polished boots.

The leisure of the Trobriand Islander, said a noted anthropologist, suffered once the colonial government took away his spare-time wars. The idea that people could respond to the question, "What's there to do?" with the answer, "Let's have a war," is far from our thinking. In this spirit, though, young Spartans used to make excursions against Helots, and Yale boys conducted pitched battles with "townies." Today in large industrial cities like New York, London, and Milan, youth bands of one neighborhood war against those of another. We don't think of them as free-time activities. Yet youth has time on its hands, time to kill. The violent rivalry of the various quarters of town was well known as a pastime in the Italian city-states. There are bridges in Venice that still bear the scars of recurrent battles in their names — *Il Ponte dei Pugni, Il Ponte della Guerra*. Gradually these frays were sublimated into yearly contests, of which living examples still exist in the *Palio* of Siena and the *Calcio* of Florence. In America only in collegiate sports does one find battling so well channelized; in intercity commercial baseball to some extent, in commercial football hardly at all.

It is perhaps also valid to include in the display of free-time violence all the bursts of fist and other kinds of fighting with which the policeman and medic are familiar on Saturday night, as well as the weekendly slaughter by car with which the policeman and medic are likewise familiar. A remarkable thing about the highway slaughter is that it is a complacent slaughter. Few people get as wrought up in denouncing it as they do in the case of war. It is well known by now that more Americans have been killed by automobiles than in battle. The fact may be a credit to our foreign and military policy but hardly to our concern for peacetime life.

Our interest in these phenomena is in their effect on free-time activities. We want to know what shapes choice; to know it we should be sure we know what is chosen, and also what is rejected. I did not say that love affairs or warring have disappeared. I merely point out that hardly a soul thinks of them as leisure activities, the reason being that on both these points one enters a moral zone where the activity under certain conditions is publicly disapproved. Some activities can hardly be mentioned to oneself, much less to someone who comes around asking questions about what you do in your leisure time. As a general rule, then, an activity cannot violate the mores and yet be considered a free-time activity.

Our repeated warnings about the dangers of putting too much trust in questionnaires and interviews in this area come again to the fore. A single question like, "Would you prefer to have quitting time on your job set an hour earlier?" is an invitation to fancy. It almost implies that there is no objection to it other than the worker's desire, and that for economic or political purposes those five hours less a week are unimportant. If the question were prefaced by something like, "Considering the world situation, would you rather . . ." or more directly, "Considering recent Russian economic gains, would you, etc. . . .," the answers would add up to a much different total. The respondent does not now get the impression that the only thing that matters is his own wish; it may be that national defense, a moral issue, is involved.

Another area of "leisure activities" in which a responsive answer is unlikely is politics or political affairs. "I study politics," "I engage in politics," or "I interest myself in politics" is an answer the Greek citizen might easily have given. An older English tradition had it that a citizen was to keep himself informed about politics, but in America, although one still finds the moral in civics textbooks, the notion that politics is a dirty business has overwhelmed it. The amount of time the American devotes to keeping politically informed seems negligible. Politics for him seems uninteresting. The parts of the newspaper or TV program that attract his attention are not the political parts. The majority yawns, even in the final heat of a campaign. Some clubwomen volunteer to work for one of the two political parties, of course, and numerous businessmen sit on committees as long as the activities are the kind that "benefit the community," to wit, politically nonpartisan. At best today we find the Puritan idea of learning and self-improvement making it a duty to be informed about politics. But like many other things preached by Puritanism, the pleasure went out with the obligation. Politics is no fun, so why should it be part of free time? Thus if an activity bears a shade too much of either a negative or a positive moral tone — having love affairs or keeping informed about politics, respectively — it falls outside the boundaries of free time.

Customs and mores include the law. The law is a political concept. It often backs up existing morality, as one can see in the case of love affairs; whereas the psychiatrist talks of sexual promiscuity, the law books refer to fornication and adultery. The phrase customs and mores found favor with sociologists partly because it avoided both political and religious overtones. It is a secular phrase. Yet religion's role in morality cannot be swept under the carpet. The case of love affairs or wars again makes a good example. We will say more about this, and politics, too, later in a more appropriate context.

Getting along now to the other factors shaping choice, I should like to leave the national plane and descend (or rise) to the group or individual level. For example, if a guild or union formed to protect the workers' wage and employment, acquires a meeting place, the space can be used for both a headquarters and a recreational center. Facility for free-time use appears as a by-product. Church grounds have often been used in the history of Christianity as a place for play and dancing. Groups can sometimes influence the quantity or quality of free-time activities of other groups. English churchmen in the nineteenth century preached fire and brimstone against drinking; employers held the same opinion; the preaching of both groups must have had some effect on the employed classes. The heads and owners of establishments generally find business a more exciting and personally rewarding game than do their employees. The one hardly notices the hours fly by while the other watches time ride past on a snail. The variation is great from one establishment or even part of an establishment to another, depending on many factors, some of which we have already considered, and illustrates that the factors that define a given group often forecast its taste for free time. Groups with money, or an eminent family history, or of certain age or sex, or intellectual attainments, or at neighboring workbenches, often have particular ways of passing free time both because of the special access or tendency their money or history or mechanical skill gives them, and because of their desire to distinguish themselves from other groups. The professor's love of books may take him beyond his field into reading in others, and into the collection of special editions, or beyond, into the testing of persons he meets by allusions to recent or ancient writings.

Within these groups there sometimes exists an individual who because of special qualities stands at the front of, or even transcends, the group. When cowboys headed for town, their foreman and top riders rode lead. About the middle of the nineteenth century in England someone in the group that was interested in making money (or perhaps in the group interested in doing good) initiated the first lending library. It revolutionized reading habits, and thus affected free-time activities. Three-volume Walter Scott novels cost a guinea and a half. Only the rich could buy them. The not quite so rich bought fiction serialized in monthly parts at a shilling apiece, or, later, in magazines like *All the Year Round, London Journal, Argosy,* and *Leisure Hour.*

As an example of a more outstanding individual take the beautiful Madame Tallien. The universal queen of society, "Notre Dame de Thermidor," made and broke one fashion after another. Paris at the time of the Directory was agog at the antics of an odd assortment of profiteers and newly rich with their own way of speaking and dressing. The heights were reached by the *Incroyables* and the *Merveilleuses.* Men's breeches became tight pantaloons, their coats were hunched up in the back with high collars and cut away over the hips. Women stared at their rivals — and much there was to stare at — through lorgnettes. They wore lightly girdled gowns cut low, baring breast and shoulder, skirt slit nearly to the waist, flashing ring-encircled legs. The *Merveilleuse* went to the Opéra-Comique, the galanty show, dancing and promenading, on the roller coaster in summer and the ice pond in winter. She devoured the novels of the Marquis de Sade. Her time became "precious." La Tallien, with the *Merveilleuses* and the gross women of the parvenus on her trail, went from antique to Turkish to English, from black hair to blond.

At the same time David the painter, another extraordinary

figure, was stamping his idea of what a beautiful woman should look like on the females of the day, including Madame Tallien, and also for the females of posterity. His ladies show the long loose robe, high waist and breast, and small head. Madame Récamier's portrait recalls the style. The furniture of the time bore his imprint too, becoming in the hands of master cabinet-makers straighter and stiffer and decorated with palm leaves and dolphins. As we have noted once or twice, a seat and free time are related.

Among poets who as individuals shaped the spending of free time, we can mention Byron, and more recently d'Annunzio, both of whom set the pattern in dress, posture, speech, reading and writing, tears and deeds, sports and pastimes, including those praised by Baudelaire. Perhaps the style setters are no longer poets, and as Ovid spoke of his times, we can speak of ours: Poems, we are sorry to say, aren't worth so much in this town. Instead of poets and poems, let us take some of the factors like population, shelter, and forms of work to see where they fit in the history of leisure. Let us go back not quite to the point where contemplation and meditation were held to be activities of the highest order, yet sometime a little before Baudelaire spoke of the gentleman's true pursuits.

WORKERS OUT OF VILLAGERS

"The leisure problem," as it is called today, has existed ever since the beginning of Europe's transition from an agricultural and village world to an industrial society. Any uprooting of people will change things so much that time disappears in the flurry of reorientation to a strange world. Rather than explain everything, though, with an airy wave of the hand and a bored repetition of "The Industrial Revolution, of course," I propose to examine the reorientation more closely. In England its stages are clear. England's experience is valuable not simply because it was the first along the path, but also because that experience is close to ours. We share language and ancestors; in both of us the making of farmers and villagers into workers and the lack of an urban tradition have affected the case. For a half-century we followed this experience closely, tagging behind at times, stepping ahead at others. Since the turn of the present century the roles have been reversed. We now step ahead more than we tag behind.

The point at which we can begin is at the start of the fight over shorter hours. The movement took place between 1830 and 1850. From the time the Ten Hour Bill was enacted in 1847, free time instead of spare time can be said to have come fully to life in our age, and the modern problem of leisure was born with it. But the terms free time and leisure were not yet in great use. Idleness and drink were their precursors. The Ten Hour struggle was on the face of it a struggle for shorter hours, but as sometimes happens the face of it was not the heart of it. Often, as we shall mention again, the campaign of labor unions for a shorter work week seems to be a tactic to distribute available jobs. The machines are ever doing the work of more men. If the work isn't spread, some or many men will be out of a job. The aim is protection rather than more free time. The same motive, it is clear, started the ball rolling for the first campaign for shorter hours in modern times, over a hundred years ago.

On the surface the workers, primarily in the textile industries, were battling for shorter hours for women and children. Since over half the employees in textile factories were women, with adult men making up only a quarter and children the rest, it was unavoidable that if women and children had to be put on shorter hours, then everyone had to be put on shorter time. Otherwise, and this was the objective, only men could be employed — if machines with increasing horsepower could keep running long hours. If the surplus of adult male labor were drawn in, wage rates would also go up. From various sources it is clear, too, that the interest in children and women was sec-

ondary: at one bargaining stage the adult workers were willing
to extend children's hours from 9 to 10 provided they could have
a 10-hour day themselves. It need not be supposed the workers
were deliberately concealing their motives. An early resolution
of theirs minced no words: it was to equalize and extend labor
by bringing into employment the many adult males who, though
willing and ready to work, were obliged to spend their time in
idleness, while females and children were compelled to labor 10
to 16 hours a day. The last part of the statement was taken up by
persons outside of the working class and added to the list of
brute facts about child labor in unhealthy and cruel surroundings. It thus became part of the humanitarian revolt that began
to have an impact on Parliament. Before long, in about ten or
fifteen years, the workingmen's reasons for continuing this struggle had changed. Child labor receded farther into the background, young persons and women became the humane objective, but the shorter working day began to interest the workers
in itself. Just before mid-century 70 per cent of the men interviewed by the factory inspector were in favor of the 10-hour day.
Even many of those working 12 hours a day said they would prefer 10 hours at less wages. The story begins to have more interest
for us at this point.

Why does more time mean so much to them at this juncture,
actually just when the final Ten Hour Bill was being drafted?
Conditions were good, for one thing. The cost of living was going down, trade was active, piece rates had risen, new machines
gave them more money in shorter time. A family at work was
earning what it needed in much less time than the 11½-hour day.
Now what do I mean when I say a family earned enough for
what was needed? I refer here to what the families themselves
thought they needed. For instance the bricklayers of those days
set their wage rates themselves in each district by calculating the
prices of food, house rent, and other things necessary for their
subsistence. They appeared contented, said the secretary of
their Society, with wages that pay for "the cost of living and a

little more." A cotton-mill worker reported cheerfully that with 10 instead of 12 hours a man could do with one less meal a day and so save the money lost. The remark recalls the attitude of the Afghans; they have refused to work for the higher wages of industry because it means they will have to eat more. If the basic diet is oatmeal, herring, and potatoes, or bread, bacon, and tea, why not improve the diet? Certainly the Englishman or American today would consider the diet below not only the decent level but the nutrition level. Why choose time rather than food or other things?

To answer we have to go further back for a moment to see in the first place how the workers got to where they were, to wit, in the factories. England of the 1830s was on the verge of a transformation. It had already appeared in the textile industry but even there hand-loom weavers still competed with power-driven machinery. The country was standing on the edge between agrarianism and industry. The past still had a strong grip. Indeed it was the past, the then not so distant past, that was calling them back out of the factories. They or their children had at the end of the previous century just been uprooted by the enclosure movement and driven off the land. The hamlet no longer had a place for them, yet not until driven out would they leave. As far back as Elizabethan days, to supply the labor needed for industries newly expanded into the large-scale class — metallurgy, refineries, shipbuilding — skilled workmen had to be imported from other countries, while unskilled English hands could be got only from forced labor, or by impressing rogues and rascally vagabonds, or by conditionally pardoning criminals and war prisoners.

Great forces held back the movement of labor. Workers had first to be removed, and gradually removed they were. When monastic lands were thrown on the market, sold or presented to supporters by the king, the final owners in the last speculation that followed paid prices too high for any rent obtainable from tenants. To get a return on capital many owners laid down arable fields to grass for sheep, since wool was the backbone of the export trade. Tenant farmers, not being sheep, could not graze or yield wool. They were turned out and sheep brought in. The evicted had either to find new land in the waste marshes, moors, or forests, or go into service. In either case it meant a deserted hamlet and an uprooted people roaming the countryside. Vagrancy did not appeal to the Crown because it signified discontent and problems of law and order. It did not appeal to the farming landowners either, since it meant a shortage of seasonal labor. Lastly the towns with their guild hierarchies did not like the arrival of strangers in any number who might in the end, as in fact they did, disturb the balance of things. In the seventeenth century the Act of Settlement still tried to control vagrancy by impeding movement, thus contravening the desires of employers who cried a labor shortage.

The opening of the nineteenth century saw a phenomenal increase in population (about 18 per cent from 1810 to 1820) due largely to the decrease in the death rate. From 1700 to 1750 the growth was 400,000; from 1750 to 1800 about 2½ million; after that, the rate of population increase rose even higher. This might appear to have been no problem to a modern employer seeking a labor supply; here it is a godsend. But it was like pulling a molar barehanded to get the villager out of his home. The spread of the enclosure system in the second half of the eighteenth century put an end to pioneering the wasteland; the frontier was now closed. Still the villager refused to submit. If he moved to find work, it was often to the nearest village, where if anything happened to him back he went to his parish, his last refuge. If he went too far out and stayed away he might lose the chance of the poorhouse. Even when a model employer or factory appeared on the scene to offer help to villagers near starvation, as rarely occurred, they chose their customary state. They might go with all their children to the factory with higher wages and steadier employment and get installed in the comfortable quarters provided them, but after a few weeks the going was too much.

Though they might be weavers and the factory a spinning mill, the new work habits required of them went against the grain. They returned to their bit of land, rented or owned, which they worked long in the summer, short in the winter. From their land they would move over to the stocking frames in their houses, then back to the land, and over to the frames again, with women and children doing their share. Here there was no having to stay with the unfeeling machine until someone shut off the power. The life they knew was unpunctual and chatty. A shoemaker got up in the morning when he liked and began work when he liked. If anything of interest happened, out he went from his stool to take a look himself. If he spent too much time at the alehouse drinking and gossiping one day, he made up for it by working till midnight the next. Like the Lapons or the Trobriand Islanders he worked by enthusiastic spurts and spent long periods without toil, which among nonindustrial communities is a way of working more common than is generally supposed. He made up his work with a willingness born of the fact that the backlog was of his own doing.

Then came the new Poor Law (1826) and Amendment (1834) and finally the Union Chargeability Act (1865). The parish was pulled from under a man. If the parish could not help him keep his children from starving, a man was driven to work or to let his children out to industry. As factory workers these early employees left much for the employer to desire. The rural mentality was always with them. Up into the eighteenth century, mill owners had turned the men out to do field work whenever business was slack. Others had closed the mills in harvest and haymaking seasons and put their workers in the fields. Once the worker had earned enough, he quit. In the factory where piece rates were in effect, at the precise inch of cloth he stopped; in the mines, at the necessary pound of coal. A manufacturer trying to increase output, or merely count on regular production — it was enough to make him tear his hair. What he might have predicted was the worker's willingness to earn enough to buy his rock-bottom oatmeal, herring, and potatoes. Even this hunger was not absolute. Without any knowledge of calories, the worker knew that if he worked less, he earned less, sure, but he ate less too.

The new entrepreneurs, as they themselves wailed, seemed destined for bankruptcy. Laments over idleness perhaps hit their highest note in the first half of the nineteenth century. In the textile mills work had got more and more disagreeable because the new machines required the worker's unflagging punctuality and attention. First the four-, then the six-loom weaver made its bow to workers. Machines in the meantime had speeded up. The average number of picks woven per minute climbed steadily from 90 to 112 to 130. These and other improvements in but a few decades raised the earnings of the piece-rate workers, who, after all, comprised four fifths of the industry. Of course this simply meant that they knocked off or wanted to knock off earlier. In areas, too, where mechanization was not notable the workers stopped working when enough was enough. The stonemasons of Newcastle, 422 strong in 1867, struck for shorter hours. Employers offered a pay raise if they would stay at work for the old hours. Four hundred and one of the men voted for the shorter hours and only 21 for the 30 shillings a week. When the voting results were announced to the membership, a "loud and prolonged cheering" broke forth. We have caught up with the later stage of the Ten Hour Movement. The workers want more time off even at the expense of more money.

What was in the back of their mind was recapturing a bit of their old independence. The rapidly growing towns were as yet no more than overgrown villages. In them the worker kept his country mentality. He earned with the intention to spend on the subsistence level and to play as though his town were the old village. Only by a stretch of the modern meaning would we call him a worker. Driven from house and land, faced with starvation, he moved from his village to the nearest larger one; his children went from there to a town; their more numerous children from town to an industrial center. He, the original villager, never became a real factory worker. His armor was impermeable. He never succumbed. In his children, though, he had an Achilles' heel. Had it not been for child labor the eighteenth-century industrialists would not have taken the strides they did.

In an agricultural economy children had always been workers. For them were reserved the light tasks — chasing the crows, feeding the pigs, bringing home the cows. In trade and handicrafts too they were employed, and at long hours, but with all the slowness and irregularity of preindustrial working habits. In fact, income then was not individual but family income. The family was considered at work all together, and their earnings made an indivisible pool. In a domestic industry like weaving everybody in the family worked. Whenever they thought of their income, it was as a unit, so that if they made more than enough all together, they never thought of removing children or wives from the work and letting the man carry it alone. Rather would they all take shorter hours together. With the appearance of the oversized workshops that served as the first factories, it was not at all contrary to family morality to put children to work too. The capitalist did not tear children from their mothers' laps; mothers sent their children to him. For a time, specially wherever the whole family worked in the same place, abuses did not appear. With the splitting up of the family, control went from the parents to the owners.

Parents should have known better, perhaps, than to separate themselves from the children. They did it not so much because they were starving, or because their senses were blunted by the miserable life they led — though both these possibilities held true to some extent. It was also that, coming from the village as they did, the possibility of exploitation of children by grown men was not immediately suspected. However, it soon became clear that no compassion like that of parents for children ruled the heart of the factory owner. Whereas the adult could not be broken to factory work easily, the child's habits had not yet been firmly formed. He could be trained — by force if necessary — to heed the machine. After a time children became more valuable than adults. The first advantage was their cheapness, the second their adaptability to factory discipline. So they went from cotton mills to mines to potteries to the matchmaker's. Eventually Parliament rescued them. Eventually, but by then industry had found its labor force, and the next generation had been trained in proper work habits.

The Ten Hour Movement did do one thing. It crystallized the work day and in so doing crystallized free time too. At the time it was stirring up textile workers, the less developed industries worked longer hours, some of them, but in the old style. The working day, a jellylike substance, could hardly be called a notion, much less a concept. Without much machinery, the workshops then would seem to a present-day observer like a hangout for pieceworkers. A carpet factory or a pinworks took off a half-day on Saturday. A tobacco works had no hours except those the workers made. A pipe factory would be open from 6 in the morning to 8 in the evening; the workers came and left when they pleased; the place was usually empty at 7:00 P.M. What time the workers had in which to do nothing must have been like the spare time of nonindustrial days. When work is not fixed by machines, unoccupied time appears every now and then, somewhat as a surprise, but as a surprise one expects occasionally without knowing just when it will come.

The idea of a pastime fits spare time well — some little thing to do when what you had to do didn't take as long as you thought. To pass spare time people also knew of longer-range things to do that could be picked up and dropped at will — knitting an undershirt, for example. Many a housewife, having finished her tasks earlier than expected — perhaps because a rain prevented her from hanging the wash — used to sit down to knit, and, given like good fortune for a neighbor, to chat. Our shoemaker had shoes to make or repair. When he was playing cards at the alehouse he wasn't making shoes, but neither was he spending free time. Time in the modern sense had no part of the scheme. He had shoes to make, ale to drink, and cards to play, all of which he did without need of the words work and leisure. What the 10-hour workman now had, though, was free time, a lump of concentrated nothingness he never had before. Work time and free time are now split, to remain so till this day.

All during the sixteenth to eighteenth centuries, riots to restore the commons took place in England. The spirit of enclosure, however, was rampant. In 1786 an observer predicted that in half a century more an open field or undivided common would be a rarity. The countryman-worker in his quest for free time wanted to retain some of his old life. At first, his nostalgia could be relieved, at least in part. In the old villages there had been cockfighting, badger baiting, whippet racing, coursing, hunting, fishing, and bowling, fighting matches, football, quoits, and dancing in the streets. The worker's hopes for a return to these pleasures were soon dimmed. His troubles had begun when he lost his space, the ground he thought he and his family had a right to, his native ground, his place in the world. He got back neither that space nor a new one to measure up to it.

As the town grew and spread out, the worker kept losing space. Though he never fully realized it, by losing space he lost money and time. The open spaces in the towns were soon replaced by enclosures. After the sons of sons of the villagers piled into the big towns, after numerous, dispersed workshops came to be concentrated into a few central factories, there was little left but dirty streets. Unlike France and Italy, with whom ancient Rome left an urban tradition, and where, in some of their cities, one still drinks the same clear water piped in by Roman engineers, England knew nothing of city management. With squalor all about, said a student of this period, it was no wonder that, when they woke up to the fact, the English thought "soap was civilization." In the era before railroads the densest population in the cities huddled around rivers, canals, or ports, and in its middle rose the center of industry. By the 1850s, with hordes encamped in wooden shacks on either side of former cart tracks, where was the worker to enjoy the free time he had won from the Ten Hour Act? The boating of those who lived on Thames-side was cut down by river traffic. Bowling on the roads stepped aside for wheeled traffic. Gambling was almost unknown, testified London's Commissioner of Police. As to gambling houses, "I know of none," he said, tongue-in-cheek, "except the Stock Exchange may be so considered."

All the things the villager used to do for sports and recreation required space. A millwright who had once been on the Continent complained that there was nothing in Manchester a man could do on Sunday but go to the public house, and go with the intention of getting drunk, sitting and drinking glass after glass; in France and Switzerland, where he had worked, people went to dances and had games and different recreations at the places they went to, and cheerfully enjoyed themselves, he said, drinking but little. There were no games in Manchester, and no open spaces.

By this time Sunday had become the deadest day of the week. "Sunday is our great difficulty," said one witness testifying on public houses, "we cannot get over Sunday." The Reformation had seen to making the day a dismal bore, and enterprising businessmen thought that the move was in the right direction. One of the first steps in the right direction was Luther's assertion that the only holiday to be observed was Sunday. The medieval calendar would never have suited a business calendar — there were too many holidays. Lowering the saints down to mortality was another step in the direction of improving the calendar. If Christian martyrs never made sainthood, their day was no different from anyone else's. But back to Sunday. In 1856 Sunday band concerts began in the London parks. The Archbishop of Canterbury objected and they were stopped. (At that time the resident of many a small town in Sicily could hear over a hundred band concerts a year in the main square.) In the same year the Commons rejected overwhelmingly a proposal to open the British

Museum and the National Gallery after Sunday morning services. This was a day to be spent in silence and meditation, not in having mass first and then enjoying oneself by singing, dancing, talking, drinking, or doing whatever the day offered. The word *holiday* in its origin implies dancing.

With all the joy gone out of the Lord's day, it might as well not have existed. To take all joy out, one must say, seems too often to have been precisely the purpose. The thought seems to have been that if there were nothing but work for a man to do, he would no longer see any point to stopping work once he had earned the exact number of pennies he needed. In fact in some areas Sunday did not exist. According to Andrew Carnegie, by 1866 every ton of pig iron made in the world, except in two establishments, was made by men working in double shifts of 12 hours each, having neither Sunday nor holiday the year round. Thus one of the earliest shorter-work-week laws on record was violated, that of Moses. The strategy of the gloomy holiday in many cases did succeed in being perpetuated for over a century. Many more workers turned to drink. Slow suicide seemed to be the answer.

Fortunately there were those who were not so blind as to miss the chance of profit. The period roughly from 1850 to 1900 reveals a *volte-face* by an increasing number of businessmen and investors. The original idea of the early manufacturers and bankers had been that the best way to get a good day's work out of hands was to encourage thriftiness, abstemiousness, and seriousness. A new group appeared on the scene now, whose pockets would fill more quickly if the worker, once the day's work was done, became a spender, an imbiber, and frivolous. A state of affairs that enabled this group to earn honest money deserved a better name than idleness. From this time on, with opportunity knocking, the word idleness crawls out of its ugly cocoon to turn into a beautiful butterfly — leisure.

The possibilities in commercial sports were not perceived immediately. What first attracted attention may have been the crowds of thousands that flocked to amateur games, whereas only hundreds had come before. Those games, like horse racing, essentially spectator sports to begin with, attracted villagers to the commons in crowd proportions. The profit in refreshment stands may have touched off the thought — in someone with money — of hiring or, better, buying tracks, and so on. Persons began to organize games that had existed as country or aristocratic sports. Football, once the game of former public-school boys, horse racing, the sport of princes, boxing — recall that the rules were established by the Marquis of Queensberry — golf, a game played by Scottish kings — these all became, as the saying goes, moneymaking propositions. And to them the workers turned, abandoning their quoits, bowls, and rabbit coursing and the host of other games they had played for nothing or for the beer with their skittles. They had to go farther and farther away to enjoy them too. Most of the small race tracks had gone under. The big ones took their stand where the railroad could bring out the crowds. The worker was now making more money and had his free time in one chunk each day. His own space was gone; even the space he could afford to rent to stand or sit on for a few hours was taking him a long time to get to. He was beginning to lose time and money along with his space.

With the new diversions came new publications, magazines and dailies like *Sporting Life* and the *Sportsman*. Neither producing nor paying for things like games and magazines fell within the old notions of production as something having to do with agriculture or industry. If these last two categories be considered as phases in an economic evolution, then the third phase, devoted to giving such services as sports and sports magazines, sometimes called the tertiary stage by economists, came to prominence in the twentieth century in the production and purchasing of travel, recreation, art, literature, science, philosophy, personal and government services.

Before we get ahead of ourselves, we had better recall that the worker, deprived of his customary space, yearned for the pleasures he used to get from it. He was willing to spend part of his good money for them too — both by taking time off from work and by paying for his sports on the barrelhead. But, rural man that he was, he was not ready to let loose of his purse strings. Yet by the end of the nineteenth century he began buying more food and drink and clothes. Not only did his intake of food increase, but he got his calories through more exotic and costly imports like bananas, oranges and lemons, cocoa, and others. Variety, too, appears in all categories. More than one kind of dog biscuit turns up on the market, thus making possible the rarefied choice of dog biscuits. The number of persons employed in the preparation and distribution of foodstuffs went up far beyond anything ever seen before. At the same time all sorts of inventions and schemes for goods or services began to be patented or to seek investment, from the preserving of lobster to the hiring out of toboggans or the promoting of musical comedies. Many had their start as limited liability companies, only to fall by the wayside, but others survived and when they did, prospered so as to encourage newcomers to ignore the cadavers strewn about. Something must have happened to break the habit of oatmeal, herring, and potatoes. Changes were going on indeed.

The improvement in roads and rails made it practical for a businessman to extend the range of his products. More important were causes stemming from urban concentration. One would guess that the purse of the second-generation city dweller had little more chance of being parted from its owner than it had from the owner's father. It was not enough, though it did help, to be able to flash new things before his eyes. But if to get a house to live in he had to commit himself to a high rent, there was not much to do except open the purse.

The squalor of the city camps led to plague and disease. The municipalities finally had to provide sewerage, lighting, and pavement. Newly arrived hordes of immigrants stayed in the outskirts. They had to find ways to get to the factory. The problem of the time and expense of the journey to work wheeled into sight. The bicycle appeared not long before this time. Originally an article of luxury, like the automobile later, it soon became a necessity for workers. Housing also began to make further incursions on the budget. Cottages were torn down to make way for factory and office buildings. Tenements were built. They seemed to have advantages over the cottages — running water perhaps — but required a higher rent.

The use of the word *tenement* for the new big housing buildings is ironically appropriate. The word comes from Old French, meaning a holding or a fief. Its special connection with land emphasizes that the new space allotted for a rent to the second-generation townsman was nothing like the old holding. The cost and rent of land in the industrial centers kept going up with the entrance of each immigrant. Stories began to be piled one on the other. A "flat" meant a story. Then flats began to get smaller so that there could be more than one on a single flat. *Apartment* was a word signifying an even smaller piece. The process whereby the ceiling descended and the walls closed in was beginning. Today we would think that compared to ours the space in those flats, apartments, and rooms was enormous.

It was no use crying for the cheaper and roomier living of the cottages. The cottages weren't there any more. So the working man had to open his purse wider for diversion, rent, health, and a bicycle. Businessmen began to discover that with a higher cost of living the workman sticks to his loom. His family as a result was seemingly better housed, for instance. The secret of this improvement of the worker's lot, though, was that he could not choose to be housed as he was before, neither better nor worse. The kind of shelter he once had no longer existed. Nor, given the lack of a city tradition in England, were large squares set up where people could gather to talk and children could run around in play. The hardness of England's lack of sunshine probably helped remove this solution from the mind, but, sun or no sun, squares could have been used by adults at least half the year and by children all year round.

Not only were goods and men moving faster and farther because of improved communications, but machinery was moving faster too. The standardization of screws and parts speeded the mechanization of industry. It also made the machinery run faster. All industries turned to machinery. The old-fashioned workshops died on their feet. The new products like the bicycle which came to life in the hands of artisans passed quickly into the maw of machinery. Thus more and more workers were pulled in and introduced to the regular discipline of factory life. Work everywhere became more intense, free time more completely cut off from work and space, and it, too, more intense.

NEW GUIDES FOR NEW TIMES

The villager had no problem of free time. He knew what to do with whatever amount he had. But no one, least of all himself, quite knew what to do with the worker's free time, primarily because no one grasped what he had become. That he was until recently a rustic, everyone knew. The first attempts to get his money used the games of the past on a larger, commercial scale. But they were not enough. He was less of a player in these new sports. Moreover he himself had changed. The new work had made him a man of different habits and necessities. It had reduced the worker's habitat and that, too, brought changes in him. The significance of some of these changes was better seen at that time than it is now. At least the problems were discussed in public. There were other important changes. In 1870 the Education Act insured the worker against illiteracy. From then on learning how to read and write was part of the program for everybody. The program itself was what was known as democracy. It had suffered a slight setback in England nearly a hundred years before because of the excesses, real and imagined, of the French Revolution. The aristocratic fear of the Jacobins could not hold out long against the commercial cry for equality. The opportunity to learn to read was one of the first equalities sought, and though the opportunity later could be better described as compulsory, everyone learned to read, at least to read a newspaper. As it happened, this was enough, and also important. Its results were less clearly foreseen. The man had money in his pocket. He was learning to spend it for things like bicycles, football games and rent. Besides the bread and meat to keep his family going, what else would he buy? This was a difficult question and remains so today.

Perplexity of this kind troubled the men who were out to make money with the money or credit they already had at the bank. They had seen the success of some shots in the dark, but they had seen more fiascos. Obviously this kind of market was capricious. It was different from cloth or shoes. As population had grown thicker, businessmen had experimented tentatively with advertising by handbilling or posting simple notifications of the existence of certain goods and services. Their efforts fit the etymology of the word *advertising:* to draw attention to or inform. Once the tax on advertising in newspapers was lifted in the 1850s, there were some efforts in that medium as well, for things like insurance, watches, wines and spirits, commodities then of interest to persons of more wealth than workers. In fact the newspaper reader at that time was of the educated classes. As reading spread and the halfpenny paper arrived, advertising perked up. By the turn of the century its era had begun. It had already begun in America.

In the United States no "taxes on knowledge" like the advertising or stamp taxes held back the progress of industry. The British got rid of them only in 1861. England can lay claim to have taken the first steps in modern advertising, but America soon afterward set the pace. As early as the first decade of the 1900s American newspapers loaded half their space with advertising. The English today are still shocked to see a whole-page newspaper ad.

Machinery, too, in America took a more audacious stride.

There was more free land to be had in America than in England, to be sure, and this indeed held back the progress of labor unions. Given the availability of land and the shortage of labor, the first known strike in America, at Philadelphia in the building trades, was set off by a demand for a shorter day's work — from six in the morning to six at night — plus (and here we come again to a familiar pattern) a demand for extra pay for overtime. So as early as 1791 the question of shorter hours appears. A quarter of a century later the journeymen millwright and machine workers of Philadelphia met at a tavern and passed a resolution that ten hours of labor were enough for one day. Their ten hours though, went again from 6 A.M. to 6 P.M., allowing "an hour for breakfast and one for dinner." In Philadelphia, New York, Boston, and elsewhere such strikes and protests went on sporadically, and before the middle of the nineteenth century one could speak of a ten-hour movement in the eastern United States.

As long as the open West existed, little could be done on a national scale. It was not until the end of the century that the 10-hour day established itself in a majority of industries. Many pockets of resistance held out in industries like steel, cotton, baking, lumber, and the railroads. With land to the west and a labor shortage, manufacturers were ever on the lookout for labor-saving machinery. Given a vast population without a parish system to sustain it, an uprooted population that had gone from emigration to the United States into migration within it, the adaption of men to machines went somewhat easier than in England. To men, time, and machines nearly a whole chapter will be devoted later on. It is advertising on which we now should turn our gaze.

Advertising in its original sense does this: it informs that goods are accessible. It is a stentorian peddler whose voice must ring not across mere village lanes at 8:30 in the morning but day and night over the din of the city and the breadth of the land. One manufacturer with machinery could now supply a whole nation with his products. He would be rich if they but knew of his wares (an easy task given literacy and the cheap newspaper), and wanted them (not nearly so easy). Advertising became a success. It made people buy at a rate that more than paid for the advertising, and this was what counted for the businessman.

To make people buy it is not enough to put goods in front of them. How to account for advertising success, then? We have seen that farmers and villagers were ejected from their land and hearth, and sought sustenance in growing industrial centers. Their work grew concentrated, their free time blocked off and set in a constricted space. The first wedge into their purse, fattened on the job, was driven by commercial diversions and an ineluctable higher standard of living. They would buy diversions, then, but which diversions? With bread and coal one knew how much people had bought last year and had a fair idea of how much they would eat this year or heat the house next winter, but how many if any, would buy an article just invented called roller skates? Though the market for diversions had tempting possibilities, it was too risky. If only a way could be found to make it less capricious. Advertising was the answer. It had merely to wave the diverting quality of its wares in front of readers to find buyers galore.

Here advertising goes beyond saying merely that a certain good exists and can be had; it also points out what the good is good for — as the free-time possibilities of a car, a perfume, a book, a radio, a horse race, a cigar, and even lectures. A peddler would do this in trying to seduce an onlooker into buying from his cart.

Advertising had another appeal to make, it was soon learned. In the new world of cities there was danger of being lost as a person, as someone whom others knew something about and respected. Whatever shortcomings the villager suffered from, anonymity was not one of them. Aristocracy, where one's status is fairly well known at a glance, had no such trouble either. These were worlds of position. In them one *is* somebody. What one is, or stands for, can be told not solely by house, field, shop, or clothes but also by language, manners, and antecedents. Findings themselves in the city, farmers and villagers had no field or shop, nor clothes or antecedents that made sense to neighbors themselves uprooted and from strange regions. Not even their games were the same. It is like having a group of people together who after a few drinks feel like singing but don't know the same songs — one or two start singing a tune; the others don't know it and remain silent and frustrated until the song peters out. Another few begin a new song. It meets the same fate. After a while everyone gives up. The advertiser is he who in such circumstances says, "Look here, I have a printed songbook with new songs; it costs only a dime, and, think of it, now you can all sing together." If for the last line he substitutes a picture of rich people singing from the new songbook — or drinking a whisky, or standing alongside a car — he is changing his tactic to one of snobbery. This last aspect of advertising could and did become important only because of the anonymity of the city, where no one knew another and also, and more fundamental, because antecedents and land, the marks of the aristocracy, had given way to new insignia — production and money. In a society where equality of birth was the order of the day, where long-established patterns of meeting and dealing with people were gone, money became the coin of status.

Money can be spent on many things — a fur coat, flowers, a mistress, a do-it-yourself kit, an automobile. Which of these reflect prestige, which are the mark of the worthies? Equality of birth had nothing to do with remaining equal. The prizes in life went to those who succeeded in moving upward on a ladder runged with money and prestige. Those who won success were supposed also to have won happiness and perhaps even the favor of God. With mobility rather than station the secret of life's treasures, movement pressed upward. If it could not go upward much or at all, or went down, at least by working hard and skimping on some things one could *pretend* a distinction to oneself and to others by purchasing some of the signs of success. Not many had contact with the elect. The contact in itself was a sign. The advertisers seemed to have many contacts among the worthies. Products began to be placed in a snobbish setting; the purchaser felt the comfort of believing that their exhibition (a fur coat or costly carpet) or use (a high-rent house, a witticism from a fashionable comedy) put one closer to those one needed to associate with in order to be judged successful.

A third pertinent need that advertising exploited was the saving of time. Proponents of industry had tried to soften the impact of machinery on men by praising its labor-saving assets. Machinery that saves men's labor, they also argued, usually saves their time. We have seen that one of the oldest fears of workers is that the machine may save too much time and thus throw nearly everyone into unemployment. The wave of enthusiasm for individual devices evidently brought no such danger and if they appeared to save both labor and time they rode in on the great wave of mechanical enthusiasm. The automobile obviously saved time because it got you to work and back home and to and from shopping faster. Household appliances also comprised a notable group. The refrigerator saved daily traffic with the iceman as well as daily shopping at the stores; the carpet sweeper saved the time and muscle used in beating the rug; automatic furnaces spared the back and the time spent in stoking; hot running water saved time lost by heating it in a kettle. Timesaving was a successful pitch because it had the prestige of industry and science, and, not to be forgotten, because the worker in his mobile state had always less time than his official job time made believe.

The appeals of advertising are limited only by man's ingenuity and conscience. No advertiser openly recommended spending money on a mistress one can boast about. Not that mistresses in any age have the reputation of being stingy with their protector's money. Indeed they rival the modern consumer. Though at first a related kind of personal advertisement did prosper, advertisers could not encourage this kind of conduct among those who bought a halfpenny paper. It would be immoral, and besides, the whole system would topple. The most the advertiser will do in these days is to suggest buying things for a lovely female whose relation to the male is left vague. The hawker at a fair, now, he will gladly propose such a purpose for his brilliants to a man who looks like the right type. The hawker can make his pitch to the individual, the advertiser cannot, but both carry big bags of tricks. My selecting three of their appeals here was to show how advertising succeeded in getting people to buy many things in a way their forefathers would have condemned as damned foolishness.

In advertising, the producer of goods and services had an instrument that helped him take some of the freakishness out of the market. For a time the advertiser had chiefly the newspaper to puff his wares. Then along with improvements in printing came the radio and after that TV. As for television, the advertisers themselves pushed and subsidized its invention; they helped bring it into the world, having seen in radio a preview of home-penetrating power. The film, too, has been their ally in a telling manner. Almost without exception the makers of feature films have not been subsidized by advertisers, yet so urgent has the need been to prove one's success in life through the buying of goods that film makers have unwittingly catered to the public. They have put heroes and heroines in so costly a context that at times it would be impossible to find any person or group living at that level of expenditures . . . except in the movies. Since these films are exported, great masses of nonindustrialized peoples have got the impression that all of northern Europe and North America lives in that high style. We ourselves have had it so much with us from the childhood of our cinema days that it escapes us completely.

All of which conveys that people would stop, look, and listen at advertisements even if, as with the films, there were nothing to sell. In fact much effort and money today goes into so-called institutional or good-will advertising. A steel or chemical company may advertise not to sell its wares — of which they sell enough — but to build up the corporate image, as they say, to keep the public (for the moment not a consumer) from forgetting the service the company performs to the nation or to national defense or to humanity, science and progress. And sometimes a company advertises on this scale because the owner or his wife wants the personal satisfaction of being nationally recognized or simply thought more of by their friends at the country club. All these efforts go into the dollar totals for advertising, but a better name for them is publicity.

Another twentieth-century ally of the advertiser has been the installment plan. Through it or other schemes of deferred payment, the worker commits his future money and time. Title to the goods may come in the future too, but he feels, and, more important, looks to others, as if he were the owner in the present. In any case, wear and tear begins with his signature.

Of the one hundred or more most important inventions exploited commercially in the twentieth century, about one third were labor-saving and about one half were in the field of consumer goods — the phonograph, rayon, nylon, the radio and TV. At the same time the occupations that have seen the greatest increase in personnel have been the so-called service industries (Table 16). This reflects not only a greater demand for games, toys, entertainments, sports, motors, cameras, and government social services, but also the rising importance of an in-between class of persons who live on salaries, keep their hands free of grease and grit, and experience less of the work pacing that mechanized jobs impose on workers. This category, not too precise in its limits, has been variously called the *petit bourgeoisie,* the *salariat,* the lower middle class, or the white-collar worker. When we have talked about workers in general, we have usually included this group of them that came to prominence in the 1900s.

Because of their position as straddlers between upper and

lower classes they feel it necessary to distinguish themselves by all moral and legitimate means from the workers. Unlike the proletariat, but like the aristocracy, the *salariat* has a fixed income; like the proletariat's and unlike the aristocracy's it comes from a boss, however impersonal. The aristocrat's income came from the rent rolls. In money the salaried sometimes earn more, sometimes less, than the wage earner. Their means of distinction lies in their cleaner hands, the relation of their job to literacy and the ancient scribe, their different work clothes, and a careful selection of the insignia money can buy — education, flowers, house, furnishings and neighborhood — and to be able to point out to a stranger that the man he is looking at or talking to works but is not a worker.

Paradoxically the ethic of work made more progress with this group, concerned as it was to adopt the opinions of those who stood at the top of the new hierarchy — the producers and the moneyed. Vulnerability to the snobbery in advertising is greatest in this class of persons. Their conduct has given rise to the concept of the nation as a group of consumers. The concept exaggerates in implying that everyone acts as a member of the class.

Everyone may be a consumer, but those who consume most consumer goods are the salaried, not the wage earners or the professional classes, although these others have also been led down the spending path by one or more vulnerabilities to advertising. The working class in England still clings to the doctrine of enough money to live on and a little for the frills; the professional classes still hold to values they put above buying things with money. The class we have been describing, too, does not consider money its highest aim, otherwise at times it would turn to the higher pay of the worker. What it needs is a clarification of position, and its chief method is to buy and exhibit the goods and services proclaimed by advertising to be those of the on-high.

Wherever one talks of category or class, large or small, one is bound to ignore the exceptions and make everything sound too simple. That a physician can cater to rich widows, or a worker indulge in silk pajamas and Havana cigars, or a foreman or office manager give in to oatmeal, may not be novel, but is still exceptional. By their earning power many classes of workers soon left behind their brethren who remained in comparative poverty. The affluent worker's resistance to spending crumbles at the advertiser's approach, but less easily to the snobbery appeal than to the other two we have identified — recreation and timesaving.

More or less the same kinds of goods are advertised today as were at the birth of the halfpenny newspaper. In the United States, the most heavily advertised products — each representing at least $10 million a year of advertising billing — are soap, drugs and cosmetics, foods, soft drinks, automobiles, home appliances, alcoholic beverages, and tobacco. In England at the century's turn the *Evening News* and *Daily Mail* advertised Vinolia soap, Bovril, Vi cocoa, bicycles, tricycles, and sewing machines on installment-plan terms. (In 1892, the *Evening News* added a new service for the readers — a Saturday football supplement.)

From the very beginning in the United States, solid manufacturers and bankers were suspicious of advertising. Today, in durable goods, where men from production, engineering, and finance rule the roost, the advertiser is looked on with disdain. In soaps and cigarettes he is treated with respect. Consumer goods still describes the area where advertising makes its heaviest sales contribution.

As there is a continuity in kind of goods sold, so is there in tactics. We still see advertising using the same three charms it acquired soon after birth in the industrial era. Things to buy to use in free time (current examples: awnings on the patio, gracious living, travel in the style of the new active leisure, the thrill of an outboard motor), things that mark the buyer as a person to be looked up to (brand of soap, cigarettes, consumers' guides, books, perfume, house furnishings, cars), and things that save time (the automatic dishwasher, the electric saw, the deep freezer). These appeals have variations. For instance, a patent medicine offers to pep people up, stirring them to buy through the fear that tiredness is abnormal and makes one a failure at the energetic work and play so much a part of success. All in all they have done much of the job of turning the American into a spender. If you ask the American why he works when he could have time off, the answer is that there is something or other he needs. At one time he may have needed extra work to pay the medical bills for an accident or to set something aside for a rainy day or for his children's schooling. This argument has been weakened by unemployment compensation, pensions, social security, public schooling, insurance of all kinds borne and advocated by government, industry, the church, and the family. While not eliminating the need for emergency money, these provisions have had a reassuring effect on fears of emergencies. The part they have played in opening up the American's wallet has not been well recognized. They too, along with the cinema and the installment plan, have been allies of the advertiser. Without rainy days ahead, the old kind when it could pour for years at a time, the American need not fear opening his wallet wider. No, money for medical bills or even a nest egg is not likely to be his answer. He works because there's something he needs, or, he might simply say, because he needs money. And what does he need money for? To buy things, of course.

Certainly there are activities that don't require money. Mushroom collecting, for instance, a favorite sport of the Russians. Loafing is another inexpensive activity. The advertisers don't recommend it except as the reward for buying a plane ticket to some place where people are said to sleep under sombreros all the while the sun's up, the kind of place that for some reason is thought to be particularly restful or at least picturesque to American tourists. In the United States, where loafing would cost nothing, it is not considered good form. Time is money, if for no other reason than that if you loaf you don't earn money.

Can't the American buy free time with the money he earns? By working shorter hours and taking less pay, it would be as though he paid a substitute to go to work for him part-time. The

American doesn't need all the money he makes just to live, does he? We are back to the question with which the last chapter closed. In the U.S.S.R. to earn a loaf of bread the Russian must work much longer than the American for his loaf. Without quibbling over the relative nourishment in the two loaves, the difference should mean that the American can take his free time much sooner than the Russian, for he earns his daily bread in less time. Yet he does not take a work week shorter than the Russian. Evidently the American has not bought much free time, or he buys only what he can get at a bargain rate, or solely when he can't get something else like employment security or higher wages in exchange. There's not likely to be the cheers the masons of Newcastle shouted out on hearing that their week was to be shorter, even though their pay envelope was to be lighter. If you loaf you can't buy things advertising dangles before your eyes, things you need to have, even if you must skimp on lunches to buy them.

Of the three major reasons we have given for the success of advertising in helping turn the American into a consumer, the first and third — suggesting something to do in one's empty hours, and ways of saving other hours lost in the city's concentration of space and work — are clearly related to free time. The remaining reason, the appeal to snobbery, seems at first unrelated. Actually it is but one step removed. Its relation is to work. If one works, one has less time off work. Some union officials today say that one reason their men take on second jobs is that they have bought "major items" on the installment plan and are anxious to pay off. As a Spanish proverb puts it, *el hombre que trabaja pierde su tiempo*. The man who works loses his time. Consumption eats money, money costs work, work loses time. It's as simple as a nursery-rhyme chain of causes.

Women's role in the world of work exemplifies the pattern nicely. In the United States about one quarter of all widows and unmarried divorcees have always taken jobs for their subsistence. The "high cost of living," that friend of the employer, however, pulls other women into the labor force in order to supplement the family income. Firms look about for cheaper sources of labor, for help they can pay less than men. If all men are working, which is practically the case, business can look only to those persons whom moral reasons have kept out of the labor force. The sick and the infirm offer little. The aged? Perhaps a bit more experimenting with moratoria on retirement or the encouraging of stories in the press on how much the older person suffers without a job will help, but not much. Less than 10 per cent of the retired over sixty-five years old seem willing and able to return to work. What about children? Indignation is still too strong to cope with, although much of assembly-line work could be handled by twelve-year-olds — or chimpanzees, for that matter.

On reflection, the only ones left in large number are the women. They can be persuaded to work in the lower-paying brackets of the lowest-paid occupations. And over half of them are not working. This makes an excellent labor pool to draw from. Well, how shall we need them, in full-time work or part-time? Each firm decides for itself. The part-time supply is greater than the full-time, but perhaps something can be done to increase even the latter. The woman is in a changeable position because the community has left her worse off than Buridan's ass — equidistant between two bales of hay. At times one seems to move a little closer or the other to recede.

Women go to work at an early age. Before marriage there are almost as many of them working as there are single men at work. A fact of importance. In the concentration of population that industry fostered, the former ways for young women to meet men were largely lost. Neighborhoods were slowly built up, but with a constant flow of people to the cities and the rapid moving from city to city in the United States, the one stable and respectable place for ordinary girls to meet groups of marriageable men is at work. We have already encountered the social aspects of the job. Wherever in the chain of contacts girls meet their future spouse, they marry him early (median age about twenty)

and have children early. The number of children to have is
also fairly fixed by custom — at present, two or three. Before
long the children are off to school and themselves married young
so that mother has an empty house, and less work and interest in
it than she had before. She could have more children but this
goes against the prejudice for having children at an early age
(median age of mothers at birth of last child, twenty-six years).
What then to do with her free time? She goes back to work, if
there's work to be had. Some women do not, of course. (What
they do with their time would take a special story.) But many
others do. At the age of thirty, the low point, about one third
of them have jobs; the percentage then climbs steeply until age
40, and still climbs up to age 50 when it begins gradually to go
down. Almost two fifths of the women at work are over 45 years
of age. To get a substantial number now out of the house and
into the labor force requires further incursions on married
women with children of school age.

These women may be bored at home but they certainly have
work to do. When a child is born, the mother (an American
mother, namely one without domestic help) should get it
through her head that she'll be tired for five years. Let a man try
holding in his arms a weight of 15 to 25 pounds, lifting it up and
putting it down all day long. After less than a month of it he'll
complain of his back. Ironing is more tiring work than building
a brick wall. Cleaning windows eats up 3 to 7 calories a minute.
Driving a taxi in city traffic takes only 2.8 calories. What could
make mothers leave this work undone at home to go out to a
job, only to return to do the work they left undone? Usually the
need for commodities is enough. Does this mean that the typical American adult male cannot earn enough on a full-time job
to support his small family? On the average the working married
woman added $1,363 to the family income. Did the husband
need it to make both ends meet? Are we back, then, to the concept of the family income of the Middle Ages or of the 1800s
in New England cotton mills? If so, we shall soon be dipping into

child-labor resources, too. They might be better than mothers as a resource, but to have both mothers and children working, and separated from each other . . . that would only bring on problems similar to those we saw at the beginning of the Ten Hour Movement. If mothers claim they have to work to contribute to living expenses, how do we propose to answer except by saying that in a time of prosperity the average American father cannot earn enough to support his family?

Perhaps before saying this we ought to ask about other possible reasons for working. The wife's desire to improve her standing by buying the luxuries other women have has been called a distinguishing feature of women's employment. Today more than half the families in which both spouses work have incomes of $5,000 or over. If a family has an income between $6,000 and $10,000 the chances are one out of four that both spouses hold jobs. Or perhaps we should ask whether "living expenses" covers more than mere living, however we want to define it. If a mother says she works for the money to help build or buy the home, or to finance their children's education, is she working for living expenses? What about the one who takes a job just long enough to buy the sofa or fur coat she needs? Or the one who works for the down payment on a lakeside cottage, and then for the boat for the lake, and for the motor for the boat, and for the dock and the boathouse and the gasoline and the repairs for the motor? Stick beat dog, dog bite cow, all over again.

Getting back to the employer who needs labor power and has decided that for the kind of jobs he has, part-time work would not be economical. His problem will be to recruit mothers, many of whom have already risen to the demand for part-time work. Now, if a woman is to leave children at home all day, all year long, or even in a nursery, or with a neighbor, at the very least she has to have the idea that raising children is a task that either does not require her presence or is not as important as working and making money to buy things. Once convinced of one or all of these ideas, raising children loses its interest, subtlety, excitement. If the same arguments persuade the opposite sex, as well, the child rearer loses her interest, subtlety, and excitement in the eyes of men, too. Every now and then we see articles and advertising praising woman's place in the home. Motherhood then becomes an art, a daily adventure, a drama with variety, love, and esteem. There may then be a recession in the offing or layoffs in the wind. But when the career woman has her day, the magazines and articles talk about the charms of the woman who works, her smartness, fascination, and ability to be all things to all men — wife, lover, mother, scientist, tennis partner, breadwinner, household engineer.

This shifting back and forth of values is not the temporary shift that occurs in emergencies like the last war when women were brought into production to take the place of men, and where no change of belief is involved. Everyone knows, despite what they may hope, that this kind of situation is a temporary one, and that jobs are a male prerogative. In the real struggle between wife-mother and career woman each side has its violent advocates. What few suspect is that the fluctuation back and forth serves a purpose. It creates a labor reservoir ready to man the pumps at home or in the factory, depending on the economic barometer. Only the advertiser treats woman with unfailing respect. Whether she is working inside the house or out, she buys the goods he sells.

Some could maintain with stout reason that there is madness in the method. It leaves both kinds of women with a permanent disability. Neither the one nor the other has much respect for itself or can feel the wholehearted respect of men. For the men, finding it difficult to figure out what a woman is or what they seek in her, are victims, too. The blurring of male-female outlines came up before. Our problem is not here, however. What we should like to ask is why is it women don't take things easy at age 35? With a husband at work, with children in school or married, with forty clear years ahead of her, why is the only choice between that of housewife and career woman? Why is the alternative either work or work? Isn't free time the time to think of leisure?

This chapter began with the question, Why does the American do what he does with his free time? After looking at the play of many factors that shape choice — like population, customs, diet, age, and technology — it came down to asking, Why does he consume so much? Today both men and women in their disgusted moments may describe the situation they are in as a treadmill, the dog-eat-dog, the rat race, as crabs in a bucket, or a vicious circle. It hardly sounds free. More like a trap. The Indians sold Manhattan for a few trinkets. It would seem they were not the only ones to be taken in by a handful of beads. Dazzled by the jugglers, the individual sold his time for shiny objects. We have seen him fall prey to advertising and turn into a consumer. The things he now wants cost money, money costs work, work costs time.

I have nothing against the cycle. But while it is spinning around, to hope for leisure is useless. Consumption gobbles time up alive.

The Fate of
an Ideal

THE individual seems free: he can get information, vote for whomever he wants, buy whatever he likes. But he seems buffeted by advertising, as dazed by winking lights and bright colors as a rustic. The more he spends to save time and buy status the more he must work to have the money to save time. To find his way out he seems to know no better than to bounce from one purchase to another like balls in a pinball machine, lighting up the lights, ringing the bells, and totaling things in the millions. What these things may be hardly matters so long as they can be counted with three, six, twelve zeroes. He seems unduly suggestible to advertising. At least those who don't like the way he spends his free time might say that.

Yet advertising has failed in an original task. It was supposed to sell particular and capricious goods. It did sell them but not as well as hoped. This is why businessmen are never quite sure about advertising's worth to them. "I know half the money I spend on advertising is wasted," one of them once said, "but I can never find out which half." The reason he cannot find out about the other half is that advertising can only partly influence a person to buy a given article. Much of the rest of its influence goes on to move the person to buy not necessarily a particular commodity but just to buy in general. The result has been to turn the American into a spender, a person who cannot be relied on 100 per cent to buy a given item but who can be counted on to buy something that is advertised. Thus advertisers are only half rivals. In their other half they belong to a fraternity whose collective product is the by-product of individual members and their clients.

In our view the collective product is the more important, for it has had consequences that reach into economic theory, government policy, production programs and the business of science and research. Some persons may puzzle over the fact that businessmen continue to doubt the effectiveness of advertising and at the slightest dip in the market threaten to cut the advertising budget down or off, while at the same time other critics, like the educators, fear advertising for its malignant power. Actually there is no real paradox. The one group fears for the one-half, failure to deliver sales increases for a particular toothpaste; the other group fears for the second half, the power to standardize people's taste.

We are at the moment considering the more general consequence of the second half — the turning of the American into a buyer. Since he has to buy often, he gives the impression of being a consumer, for the goods advertising can sell best are nondurable things to eat, to wear out, to let fall apart or become "obsolete." Economic thinkers early realized that a general propensity to buy would make for brisk trading. They foresaw that once the lowest classes began to yearn for "comforts" or the "blessings of civilization" the material as well as the moral progress of the country was assured. Today marketing is a subject taught in universities, and consumption economics is a robust offspring of economic theory. The change-over in government policy came officially with the acceptance of the spending doctrines of Keynes, perhaps in England before the United States. "We shall," he said in 1937, "be absolutely dependent for the maintenance of prosperity and civil peace on the politics of increasing consumption." From then on, the unbalanced budget, the manipulation of bank and consumer credits to stimulate buying, the democratization of credit by easing loans and installment plans for individuals, the leveling of incomes by taxation — all became part of the daily life of the Treasury, the Federal Reserve System, the Department of Commerce and the Bureau of the Budget and Congress. For those whose years reach back to the turn of the century, it sounds more than dissonant to hear the President of the United States ask all citizens, whenever the curves on economic charts begin to nose-dive, please to spend more money.

Production characteristics, too, have changed. The durability of goods is decreasing. A manufacturer, to keep his head above water in the heavy seas of buying, must float a new series of products as often as possible. What is now called obsolescence in certain once rather durable goods is often simply the use of less durable materials and the ballyhooing of small stylistic changes. The producer is less a producer than a seller; the consumer is less a consumer than a buyer. The goods he buys are made to consume themselves faster; it is not that the ordinary American has suddenly grown more destructive. Destructive he may be, in his use of materials, but the tendency has been long in coming and is merely accentuated or evoked, not created by the cheapness of present-day goods, which in themselves arouse contempt. The producer, for his part, now produces only what he can sell. What people want seems to be a mystery. He only knows what people can be made to buy. This he can learn from research.

Research in advertising has taken great strides in the last three decades. It took its first steps forward with the hope that it might discover why the *other half* of advertising money was wasted. Today thousands upon thousands of people are interviewed or scored periodically, store and factory inventories run into more thousands, millions of punched cards fall through automatic sorters — all just to fatten charts and graphs for advertisers, market analysts, and sales managers. They still have not found out about the other half.

But they, the research agencies, have often helped support the advertiser's claims to his clients. What is more to our point, they suggest product innovations — changing the color of a shaving cream, an ingredient in a laxative, the packaging of a toothpaste, the front bumper of a car, a new switch on a toaster, a portable TV set. In this they work hand in glove with chemists, engineers, and physicians, all the more respected kind of technicians and scientists. Industries set up research laboratories to invent new products or discover new elements in old ones, and give money to universities for related purposes. The universities worry less and less about stooping to such folly. After all, the by-products — they think — will pay off in the training of young scientists and the paying of the salary of university administrators. Of course, all this adds the luster of science to the advertiser's claim.

Industries, moreover, begin to diversify, to take on more and more products, until their list of offerings is as long as a used-book-store's catalogue. A chemical company that may have started off with munitions, an electric company that may have begun with lamp bulbs, a food company with a breakfast cereal or a soap company with only one kind of soap bar, an automobile company with one make of car — to keep selling and selling all now find it advisable to take on one new product after another, and end with long lists of just barely related items: from cars to refrigerators to hi-fi amplifiers, from soaps to peanut butter to hair curlers, from lamp bulbs to toasters to air conditioners, from toothpaste to room deodorants to people deodorants, from flour to breakfast cereals to super-miniaturized transistors, from gunpowder to fertilizers to synthetic fabrics, from radios to deep freezers to TV sets. Much of the research that goes into these products might be called find-a-pitch research. A new feature must be found, added, or made, so that a new selling argument can be used. Why should a well-established toothpaste company spend millions of dollars advertising its product to increase its share of the market by 1½ per cent when by setting up a "new" product with a new name (of the same parent company) and by spending the same millions, it may capture 20 per cent of the market for the new item?

Here is the picture then of the advertiser and his client. They have realized that a change has taken place. They have seen that though they can't make the American buy one brand of each soap or cigarette or synthetic fabric or packaged food, they can get him to buy and try one thing after another. And it is true that the American doesn't believe any single advertisement, and may openly treat it with guffaws or contempt, but he fights against a pounding sea and in the end is to be found rolling *with* it. The old ideology of parsimony and thrift, parodied in the I.W.W. song as "Work and pray, live on hay" has now changed to "Work and spend, to the end." The advertisers now have many hats at hand and put on one after another.

PEDDLERS OF DYNAMISM

Innovation is the keystone of the new ideology. It finds support in the circumstances of American history, the vast territory to explore, the westward-ho, the migrations from Europe to the east coast, then to the west coast, the lack of guiding example, and other things as well. Modern science with its belief that to-morrow's discovery will show today's proof to be an illusion; progress with its notion that history moves toward perfection; and now industry with the claim that all product change is im-provement, labor-saving, timesaving, scientific, progressive, and democratic. Kept afloat by the installment plan, the liberalizing of credit, the raising of lower income levels, everybody can afford to breast the stream of new products. And since their dollar is like a vote, they really voted for the product. It's what they wanted, have been wanting all along, really needed, as a matter of fact.

The innovation argument is almost entirely a business product. Paid advertisements carry it. It is more than an argument, more than propaganda. By now it has become an institution, a characteristic of the market, as I have said, and as such another ally of advertising. This powerful ally has long gone unrecognized. Without it, advertising would have less force, and with it unrecognized, advertising gets credit for greater power than it has. The ally is that process whereby an old product upon the appearance of a new one rapidly disappears from the market, chased out as bad money drives out good. A detailed analysis of the reasons for the market's behaving this way goes beyond our scope, but the trait must be obvious to anyone familiar with the distributive results of mass producing, mass selling, and mass buying.

Many of the disappearing products fall in the category of food, clothing, and shelter. If you want bread made with unrefined or unbleached flour, or the flour itself, you will find it hard to buy in the United States. The market for refined flour has driven out the market for the unrefined. Do you remember the taste of unrefrigerated butter? If you do and would like to buy some, you will search far and wide before you find it. The price of new homes runs so high largely because they are mere shells housing costly pipes and wiring. If you wanted to go without electricity and to light your house by candlelight alone, you would have difficulty finding the right candles, they would be more expensive than they were a hundred years ago, and you would undoubtedly get in trouble with the fire department. If, on another score, you wished to make your house more fireproof and more spacious by saving on plumbing costs and investing the savings in brick or stone, and if anyway you didn't like the idea of putting a toilet in the same room with your bath but preferred it outdoors, you would get into innumerable difficulties with the authorities. If you want to save the cost of piping in running water, you no longer have wells or fountains nearby. If you want to save by not buying a car, you will soon learn that for the cheapest shopping you have to drive out, for the doctor you have to drive out, for the cinema you have to drive out, for your children to visit friends you have to drive out, and to be picked up at the commuter's station, your wife has to drive out. You calculate distances nowadays by car, not by legs.

Fashion's changes have long interested men and women and fascinated an elite, but the phenomenon we are dealing with is not fashion. The items mentioned above fall in categories of the essential. If you want to shop for vegetables daily so as to have them fresh, you have to own a car to go to the shopping center, and there you will find many frozen and canned varieties but a poor selection of the fresh. You can't be old-fashioned, you can't go backward, you can't have fresh vegetables — except perhaps at luxury prices. If you want to do without a refrigerator, who is to stop others from refrigerating your food before they sell it to you? Once refrigerated, it deteriorates fast unless put back on ice. Refrigeration, first in transport, then in the house, changed the handling of meat, fruit, and vegetables, and their taste as well. Rapid changeover has this effect: it forces buying new products as the market distribution of the old goes to pieces.

We first met this whole phenomenon in English history when workers had to pay higher rents for supposedly better housing, though they may not have wanted it. There was no poor housing to be found. By the same token now, sooner or later we have to buy the stuff because the inconvenience of resisting turns into discomfort and, before long, impossibility. Nowadays advertising helps the process along by stimulating early buying of new products and also (a matter I shall refer to again in the next few pages) by building up an ideology of innovation, and linking it to progress, science, and democracy. The actual power of forcing purchase, however, belongs not to advertising but to the subsequent disappearance of the old product from the market. We simply have no choice but to buy the new, because the old does not exist, or cannot be found, or has become too expensive, or turned illegal. Accordingly, we must buy more, earn more, work more, and seek (but not find) more free time.

Thus the advertiser profits from an ally. In return he nurtures it continuously with blurbs about progress and innovation. A clear case of sympathetic symbiosis. To overestimate the power of the advertiser as many current critics have done is easy if his allies are overlooked. These allies put money in the citizen's pocket and then take it out again.

The marketing characteristic we have just looked at works particularly well. And therein lies its utility: it works specially on those who do not succumb to the advertiser's verbal or visual lures. The one who sees through the advertisements, who contents himself with the old, who is not so ambitious to move up the social or income ladder, who is confident enough of his own standing not to need the new trappings that advertisers offer in exchange for time-money — whether there are a few or many such souls, in the end they must capitulate. They may be the last to lay the old aside, but lay it aside they must.

In the end, the advertiser, like the propagandist, begins to believe his own advertising. He begins to talk as though increases in consumer purchases — 5 or 10 or 15 per cent — are all that would be required to redress the government's balance, reduce taxes, double the military budget, and leave a surplus. Religious and welfare activities he classifies and measures as consumer expenditures. He notes that more and more people have more dollars than they had ten years ago, that they are climbing up the income ladder, as he likes to put it. And yet there is something regrettable about the picture. Their pace up the income ladder does not immediately reflect itself in a similar pace up the consumption ladder. He would wish people to climb up both ladders at the same time, perhaps one foot on each. As families go up these ladders, their consumption foot, it seems to the advertiser, is always one rung beneath the income foot. If only they would take on at once the buying habits of those whom they find already on the new step of the ladder, the market would show increases for foods and drinks and lots of services. But they can't, evidently because their previous training was grounded on a different concept of how to live. The millions of people moving up and up do not immediately take on the food-consuming traits of those who were up there five or ten years before them. It goes without saying that to get better diet for the health of Americans there should be a higher consumption of foods loaded with nutritional power and money value — meats, dairy and poultry products, fruits and vegetables, high quality cereal products (not just cereals), and the entire array of improved and packaged products that save so much time and labor for the working American household and add so much to the nourishment and savoriness of its meals.

The only way to get around the previous training Americans have had in learning how to live is for advertising and selling to change it. Doubtless it is a major job to make people aware of how much discretionary spending power they have. People are slow to change their lifelong old-fashioned and worn-out habits. With all the purchasing power that increased productivity generates, the consumer must be educated to change his patterns of life if production and consumption are ever going to meet in the higher, ever higher standard of living Americans are entitled to. As things stand, the American standard of living is where it is largely because of the efficiency of American industry and advertising in stimulating new desires and wants in people. Thanks to this economic progress, clearly measured by both ladders, income and expenditures, the American consumer is on his way with a large head start to being the greatest, the grandest, the best.

There is no exaggeration here. These are the arguments that the advertiser uses both in offense (when persuading businessmen or the public of his importance) and in defense (when answering the criticism of intellectual detractors). The problem of making the customer change his habits and buy, buy, buy, is about a hundred years old in the recent history of the West. It reminds us of several things — first, that advertising seems unable to change the habits of large parts of the population rapidly; second, that it seems unable to get customers to concentrate on a single line of merchandise; and third, that evidently for these reasons the buyers of advertising often consider it to be in whole or in part a failure. It is important to remember the failure as well as the success. There are things that advertising can do well. It can give notice of the availability of goods for sale. In the original sense of the word, it turns attention to something. Advertising as opposed to salesmanship simply turns attention on a mass scale, nationally or internationally. It can also give goods a slant. Critics go further to say that advertising can create a need for goods. Some students of advertising in analyzing its power distinguish between real and created needs. The distinction is a difficult one to make, however, for the simple fact that once beyond subsistence or food and shelter, the so-called needs are confounded by convention.

To illustrate: do men need milk, meat, or eggs in their diet? The advertiser points out certain qualities in milk, real or false, and people, taught to think of diet as part of their health, follow the pitch attentively. But their consumption of milk does not reflect a need created by advertising or misguided dieticians. One can better speak of a person's having acquired a taste for the stuff. The advertiser merely points out that milk undoubtedly acts beneficially on one's health. The fact is also true of water, and in countries where there are privately owned sources of water containing different varieties of minerals, water is advertised too. All for the sake of one's health. Or take the advertising of jewelry or a mink stole. The advertiser can surround a bejeweled and mink-wrapped girl with a host of suitors. Is the need for male admirers real or created? Even if created, was it the advertiser who created it, or was it already created by the kind of world women live in? The mink stole could also be set against a background of magnificent villas, spanking motors, or paintings of the masters. This would give a different slant, the snob slant mentioned earlier. The moral here becomes: if you wear this stole your good breeding or the success of your husband will be taken for granted. Perhaps the prospective buyer had never thought that mink would open such doors.

The advertiser thus adds a new dimension to the article. In all this he is doing little more than the pieman Simple Simon met. Wouldn't a peddler selling trinkets at the same fair point out to the girls how the boys would all turn around to gawk at them if they wore the earrings he waves before their glistening eyes? A less spendthrift age would not say these needs were created. It probably wouldn't even use the word, but speak, instead, of temptations. *Needs* is a backward-looking, secular concept, a favorite of deterministic thinking. Temptation connotes too accidental or religious a world. By what and by whom is one tempted and kept from temptation?

The peddler is not so important in noncommercial cultures. He finds people with pennies, but they have something of the Simple Simon about them. The peddler becomes important where selling is important. Whenever he walks into a commercial world and learns to use new hawking devices like the press, radio, the film, television, he transforms himself into the advertiser. In ancient Rome the spectacles in the Coliseum were often financed in one way or another by great merchants and landholders. They advertised, in some cases, the merchant's line of goods and in other cases his good will. This last would today be called institutional advertising. There are great differences between a crowd medium like an amphitheater and a mass medium like the radio. One of their similarities, though, is the prestige or authority they confer on their user. By their cost alone they confer prestige, since in a commercial world the possession of money, legally acquired, denotes success. Whoever uses these media, then, must be part of the world of the successful.

Hawking instruments are never merely that. They belong also to the state. So they are also political, and usually used by the political for urgent communication. People can be assembled in the arenas or city squares for warnings of danger or declarations of war, and thus can be reached by press or television to warn of a polluted water supply, the coming of a hurricane or of an invasion from Mars. Besides an emergency use, these same media serve an informational or instructional function, offering items usually called news or education. In these several ways, the advertiser picks up reflections of importance from the political use of his hawking devices.

The market in a European village could be, and often still is, held in the square where the communal palace stands, and the authorities, in allowing sellers to hold it there, showed they approved of it as a matter of public convenience, tradition, and the exigencies of food supplies. The more capricious items at fairs, though, often had to obtain permission to be sold. Their dependence on the decision of the authorities was absolute. Modern times are closer to the Roman arena where a show could be financed directly or indirectly by either state or private interests and signs publicizing it could be painted on walls. Today in the United States the arena takes the shape of a press or TV station owned by private interests and not the government, and this lends the financier of both medium and advertisement the luster of political authority.

In Europe's past, frequenting the market place and the central church or municipal square was an essential way of putting oneself in touch with the community. The press and TV today serve the same function. When one looks at them or hears or reads them, one knows that millions of other Americans are doing the same thing. Both plaza and mass medium give access to the sense of community. In the mass medium, however, there is no chance of exchange, and the reading, listening and viewing are done if not in solitude, then in a family, not in a political setting. We are again dealing with the American's homeliness. The spread of the mass media have helped take his life out of the public or political realm and put it within the private walls of home. This is significant for several reasons. It puts his idea of freedom in the home: the home is where he really is free. It limits his free time largely to time spent with his family. It characterizes free time spent elsewhere as not quite proper. Free time spent outside the family generally has to be put in the guise of business. The man who leaves the suburb by himself on Saturday to go into the city for a good time pleads a committee meeting or an important client. The worker in order to get to the local tavern on that night must take his wife with him.

The inability to exchange views with the advertising medium — one could always dispute with the peddler and sneer at his claims — adds to the power of the advertiser. There is no talking back. This is not an important factor for the selling of products. It is critical for another matter — the development of art and literature. As for products, the advertiser says he has ways of finding out what the customer thinks. He does have a variety of measures, none of them satisfactory in practice. At the best he has a yes-or-no, thumbs up–thumbs down verdict — the "hard fact of sales." He tries to get more information from his customers but somehow has rarely come up with their desire to have a car that will last for twenty-five years or a house made of seasoned wood. In the United States houses that are built not for speculation but to last indefinitely, are exceptional. The householder today counts himself lucky if his new house lasts until the last mortgage payments. Suburbia's jerry-building soon turns into a rural slum.

The advertiser is not a free agent. His idea of workmanship counts little: he is not an artisan. The goods he must move off the shelf are not his: he is not a peddler. Someone else owns the goods he sells, the megaphone he shouts through. Someone else produces the utility and beauty of the product, or lack thereof. Within these limits the advertiser has great force but he can only move in one direction — aggravation of the problem of free time in an industrial world.

Advertising fails because it cannot get out of its rut. It cannot give what it seems to promise: remedies for the loss of time, space, and status. Nor was there a way of avoiding the rut. The organization of work into the factory system didn't save time. It simply took work and spare time out of a homogenized state and separated them into chunks. Neither gadgets nor commercial amusements could bring time back, because their purchase, use, and upkeep cost money, and money for most people is bought by time at work. The peddler never had this problem, for he wasn't selling time or space. Nor was he selling status. He didn't have it to sell. Neither does the advertiser, but he pretends he does. Status in the United States is not yet to be found in purchase, use, or exhibition. It still resides in what a man does. Essentially it is his job. The rest is but minor manipulations. A new car evidently brings some satisfaction to the purchaser, but to keep his fancied gain in status he must buy a new one each year. In the end it isn't status he has but the trappings of a status which everybody who knows what his job is knows he has not. The job gives an American his fundamental base in the community. From that base the strugglers for status, if they wish to go upward, have much to learn, not only about what constitutes real status but even of what the true signs of it are.

In a mobile society each group changes its passwords constantly. Each stratum changes in size, appearing through time like a span of rock levels found under different pressures. The peddler had no open sesame to the strata that existed in his day. He could only be an acute observer of the customs of the times. The same is true of the advertiser. He cannot sell admittance to any class. He can only offer his own half-fulfilled, and therefore unfulfilled, suburban dream to his audience. And not even this can the audience reach by buying his product. For he is bound to offer not what he himself buys but what his client wants him to sell. In no indirect way the advertiser is lying when he hawks his wares and then buys others for himself. He has to lie, for despite his fine democratic phrases he cannot see himself as similar to the people he sells to, the Coney Island people. But this is of small import; the peddler was no stickler for truth, either. If the advertiser's customers all bought the very brands he uses of cigarettes, soaps, toothpastes, and deodorants, they still would neither have reached nor descended to the advertiser's level.

Time and space mark a man's position; position presupposes a stability of intercourse which we call a community; that stability expresses a way of life, and an idea of what life is worth living for. If leisure is the answer, or even part of it, then we must know what leisure is before we can tell anyone how to make life worth living. The advertiser has no free time, loses hours of it daily to win a little space, has money but an uncertain status, and in his harried existence must leave truth aside for untruth. He lands in the same trap with everyone else. Though he sings Brand X while swizzling Brand Z, he too is a consumer and can offer no other but the consumer's way of life. Advertising can play on the things that men miss in their lives, but, being itself within the system, it cannot give them back time and space. It cannot suggest a way of life, even if it knows of one, that goes against the system. It has to offer money-costing ideas for free time and all else because that's the only way it can live. Therefore it can only play an aggravating part.

Geographical mobility in the United States today makes an instructive example. The American has ever been a man on the move. It was that way from the start. No matter what his national origins, Chinese, Greek, or Irish, his ancestors had to pick up and cross a long stretch of water to get here. Unlike many of today's immigrants, he had little intention and little possibility of returning. He was of tough fiber; he had to be. Almost all the early observers of the American's habits, Tocqueville chief among them, noticed this urge to hop from one place to another. True enough but possibly exaggerated. Just as mass production, though inferior to other production methods in number of employees, dominates all production as an ideal, so the ever-restless searcher and sometime finder dominated as an ideal the settling-down tendency in the promised land. The true adventurers and explorers were the Spaniards and French. Together they covered both continents of the Western Hemisphere, the French pushing all over North America, the Spaniards spreading throughout Central and South America. They alone were not *fleeing* something in the Old World. They were the seekers; the others were the fugitives from persecution or hunger, the colonizers.

The New Englanders did not get far west, where they would have found better soil. What adventuring they did, they took on the high seas. The Southern states fell into plantation life without difficulty. The later immigrants, most of them, searched till they found something and then bunked down. The majority had come from the most rooted of all worlds, the agricultural community. Undoubtedly many of their ties had been shaken loose so that some — who could not before — now found they could play the speculative game of buying and selling property. Most of them did not win their money in speculation, however, but by working hard and living in rural parsimony. Their acquisition of property was due to their savings, their struggle against all odds in order not to find themselves with no ground to stand on nor a roof over their heads, worse off than they were before. They had no nose for property values. Eventually, the land, theirs included, grew in value with urban expansion. Many of them then sold this property but bought other to live on and hold. For they thought land and buildings were most solid. This hopping around from one house to another has a different background from that seen by Tocqueville when open land to the west did give the itch to young feet. But its frontiers closed, the West discovered barbed wire, the railroads from east and west kissed each other — good-bye to adventure.

By the nineteenth century's end a new force for movement had stirred itself. Industry needed a mobile labor supply, not one rooted down. Jostling the pick-up-and-sadly-go-spirit of the immigrant, using whatever allies it could find in the ever-upward doctrines of religion, science, and progress, linking democracy to them and to unending change, the business world has by now succeeded in creating an ideology of stir and movement. There is nothing in the American Republic as a political institution to say that change in itself is good. The Founders permitted change but made it pretty hard to accomplish. Existing religions have rarely looked kindly on unsettledness: it is typical terrain of messiahs. Science rarely has questioned its doctrine that the more one studies and experiments the more one learns; it just goes on doing it in the happy faith that what it is doing will be absurd in twenty years. In this sense it is antiprogressive, for no matter what progress it makes now, tomorrow will set it back. Nor is there any assurance that all errors together will help raise up a genius to great scientific discoveries. In absolute terms science cannot predict progress. It can merely know things and, as it itself admits, the more science knows, the more it knows less about. It might predict better bridges and bombs, which after all are really not part of science, nor necessarily part of progress. Thus government, science, and religion are not by themselves supporters of the doctrine of mobility and change. Chiefly in advertising and in civics books (as the doctrine of progress) do we come face to face with the real backers. Progress itself is a newcomer whose lineage goes back but tenuously beyond the nineteenth century.

Like the Indian following the buffalo, the American follows his job. In no other country does the whole population on the average change houses every five years. People move to a better job or because the company moves them to another location. In no other country does the wife understand so well her husband's need to move at the beck of the job. She may protest, and does, at having to change Johnny and Bessie's school, at having to give up her perennials and to leave the house she has tried to make a home over the last five years, but if he has to go, she does too.

In no other country than the United States is so much spent on roads before what the roads lead to is worth looking at or living in. If the roads all lead to places that seem no different one from the other, all to the good, for then the moving is not such a shock. In the city where the new job is, the cars are the same, the stores are the same, the food is the same, the same schools, the same PTA, movies and TV are the same, the same first-name calling, two- to three-bedroom frame houses and furniture, the same liquor, the same amusements. Not surprising that the people are the same too. The same friendly smile and community spirit. Let us hope the happy countenance is not that of the actor (masterfully drawn in Marcel Marceau's tragic pantomime) whose comic mask got stuck and would not come off his face.

So extensive is mobility in America that much of what makes its citizens seem all alike is necessary. The American hesitates to take a post in a foreign land. Indeed, he creates a problem for the government's work abroad. He fears the shock of difference. To move around with seeming aplomb the American must know that he is not stepping into a dark unknown. We are like gypsies, except that they move in whole communities. We don't, but we see to it that all communities are so alike that leaving any one community behind is not so traumatic. We are gypsies constantly moving among other gypsies.

Already called by his first name by his new friends, brushing his teeth with the same toothpaste, in a home with the same refrigeration and heat, with Johnny and Bessie in school, and their mother in the PTA, finding the same supermarket and drugstore, the same movies coming out of Hollywood, and the same baby sitter or her twin to sit in front of the TV while baby is sleeping, all the migrating American workingman needs is a few vines growing in pots to make him feel he has taken root. In English village life a man who lives in a community for forty years can be as eccentric as the others have known him to be. In America, most people have not been where they are very long. They want to show the others how much like them they are.

Advertising again plays an aggravating part. As the servant of industry it encourages the movement mentality: change and innovation, houses and consumer goods, progress and science, move and buy, buy and move. We have already seen that it is often more profitable to advertise a new product rather than an old one. Newness and difference are held to be good in themselves, yet as a result the American has had to cast himself in the role of a standardized nut that fits standardized bolts scattered anywhere the country over. The importance of the innovation ideology I brought up earlier in the chapter is that it supports and sustains the rapid changeovers in basic consumption categories. If people protest that the American kitchen of the '90s, to judge from Currier's old photographs, was much to be preferred to today's or tomorrow's, they are looked on as anachronisms, medievalists, opponents of progress, about ready to be locked up. The innovation ideology sees to it that the constant, unimportant changes made in materials, textiles, and foods — costing everyone time-money — are not questioned but backed up vigorously and made to seem the spine of progress.

No one is opposed to progress, but let it be clear that it is progress we are getting. If people seek happiness in the new, there is nothing wrong in their doing so. John Locke talked of the pursuit of happiness, of a true and solid happiness, and of its constant and careful pursuit. Men will seek variety, seek it variously and in it sometimes find happiness, but their liberty depends on their not mistaking imaginary for real happiness. Locke thought that men could suspend judgment until they tried out the new and different, and could discriminate thereafter among their desires. The innovation ideology allows neither a suspended nor a revised judgment. You have to buy whether you like the new or not. Locke was speaking of men of discrimination to begin with, and not about people in general (a point to reappear later). People in general are notorious for not suspending judgment, for prejudging, for prejudice. The one-dollar-one-vote doctrine (to be discussed later also) forces people to change the market at the suggestion of advertisers and takes the opportunity to suspend judgment away from everyone. In Locke's theory at least the better elements could suspend judgment, and others might follow their example.

I do not want to harp on advertising. Since for ready reference we have needed a term that included its allies and all its colleagues — the marketing and communication specialists, the applied research and public relations experts — and the whole commercial spirit that advertising represents, we may indeed seem to have returned to the subject too often. Advertising, really but one sector of business, has drawn popular attention to itself mainly because it bombards people inside the home and out, and tries to sell not only goods but also its own efficiency and virtue, as well as that of its clients. In truth it is simply business's loudest voice. People often endow it with a separate life, much as children believe the clouds are alive because they move. Stripped of this animistic aura, of its peddling function, and of all its allies and cohorts, advertising appears in the sharpest light — the mouthpiece of the commercial spirit. And if commercial and democratic societies are often found together, and if Plato was right in holding that democracies have a passion to spend rather than save, to enjoy rather than possess, for luxury rather than moderation, then spending and consuming would follow on the commercial and democratic spirit, with or without the advertisers.

Advertising, being what it is, cannot suggest suspending judgment. Advertising cannot say what we have just said about change and innovation. It cannot suggest taking a stroll with a friend at leisure unless it pockets fares for the path they take. It cannot tell people how to live their lives because it has a master other than the people. It cannot suggest that as long as there is mobility (geographical), people will lose free time moving house and home around the country; that as long as there is striving for mobility (social) the strivers will lose free time trying to increase their consumption and status. Leisure in the hands of the advertiser thus remains a costly, empty word.

Perhaps we should hold him to free time and leave leisure to the philosophers. Since the leisure of others is not the advertiser's to dispose of, though, how can their free time be his? No, he cannot escape the philosophers so easily. Once on free time, once through with work, is a man's time his own? What about his family, his church, his community — have they no claim on it? What if he stays home and watches TV with his family, is this a free-time activity or a family activity? Suppose he goes instead to the local saloon, leaving wife and children in the company of the TV set. The wife may not consider such comportment worthy of a family man, yet both the husband's activities fall within free time. We have already pointed out difficulties of classification for worship and immoral or illegal acts. Murder outside the factory, for example, cannot be an activity of free time just because it occurs off the job. Murder is not in the interest of church or state or family. When it is, it goes by different names — assassination, vendetta, or feud. Free time, then, may not all be the individual's, to be hugged to his own separate self. If some belongs to his family, some to the state, some to the gods, what is there left free for himself?

In the way we have now been discussing leisure it may be clear that the more the individual claims time for himself, the less he is, feels, or wants to be part of the community. A cry for more of this kind of free time then signifies a loosening of the communal texture. The fact has theoretical importance. If that cry were raised today we would have to say that the United States was suffering a spiritual decline. The possibility cannot be excluded. There are too many signs pointing in that direction. We prefer to hold off discussing it until later. At this moment the proposition cannot gain headway because of the ambiguity of free time. As we noted before, many Americans want "free" time in order to do apparently "unfree" things like fixing the house and getting the shopping done before dinner. The idea of wanting this time for their exclusive use — I almost said "selfish" use — seems far from their mind. The word "selfish" raises the doubt that perhaps they did not mention selfish ends for their free time because to do so might seem reprehensible to the interviewer. Nonetheless, one is left with the impression that these persons are short on time, any kind of time, not just free time. It is this that cautions us to be wary of the proposition wherein the quest for more free time in itself signifies the weakening of the sense of community. On the contrary, they seem to want time to do things for home and family, certainly parts of the community.

Since *free time* as a substitute term for *leisure* has its own difficulties, perhaps the moment is right to redefine the terms we have dealt with thus far in this study. In the earliest chapters we found leisure as an idea fully explored by the Greeks. Though it had many meanings in common speech, the one that gave it its long life was this: *leisure* is the state of being free of everyday necessity. The man in that state is at leisure and whatever he does is done leisurely. *Play* is what children do, frolic and sport, the lively spraying of wind with water. Adults play too, though their games are less muscular and more intricate. Play has a special relation to leisure. Men may play games in recreation, indeed except for men who work, play is a form of recreation. As far as leisure is concerned, Aristotle had said that we neither work nor play at it. Though this does not describe the exact state of things, play and leisure do have a special relation which we shall want to examine in greater detail later. *Recreation* is activity that rests men from work, often by giving them a change (distraction, diversion), and restores (re-creates) them for work. When adults play — as they do, of course, with persons, things, and symbols — they play for recreation. Like the Romans', our own conception of leisure is mainly recreative. *Work* can be taken in its modern sense as effort or exertion done typically to make a living or keep a house. The activities engaged in while at work all must fall within moral and legal limits, however broadly defined. A man, though a traitor and a spy, may exert himself to earn a living, but he does not work except perhaps in his own eyes or those of his hirer (note that *employer* is not the right word here).

Chapter IV distinguished *work time,* that spent in work or on the job, from *work-related time,* that spent in order to appear at work presentably (time spent in journeying to work or in grooming oneself for work) or in doing things that one would not ordinarily do were it not for work, like the husband's doing a share of his working wife's housework. *Free time* we accepted as time off the job that was neither work-related nor *subsistence time.* The last we named after activities like eating, sleeping, keeping out of the cold and rain, going to the doctor when ill, all presumably performed to maintain the state of a healthy organism, regardless of whether that organism is put to work or leisure.

We did not use any name to designate those activities of free time engaged in because of the influence of the kind of work done, the busman's holiday kind of activity. Obviously activities in recreation may resemble or contrast with work. And recreation may react in the same fashion to family life or religious devotion. Likewise work may be affected by recreative pursuits, drunkenness being the historic example, along with gambling, romance, and adventure. (Were we interested in coining words, the constant and complex flux of relationships, the lack of pertinent physiological knowledge, and the shifting positions of work, free time, subsistence, the family, recreation, and play would enable us to fill a treasury.) The central idea is easy to grasp and accept, however: work and recreation can be affected by each other as well as by other activities, such as taking care of a brood of children. And for this idea a phrase like work-affected recreation or recreation-affected work is not much of a help, being only one syllable shorter than "work affected by recreation."

Leisure, it should be clear, remains unaffected by either work or recreation. It is outside their everyday world. We further would not call work those lifelong pursuits whose scope is not clearly or primarily earning a living. For the clergy, the career ranks of the military and government, the artist and man of letters, the physician, the professor — for all of these we prefer the word *calling.* They don't work, they have a vocation, something they are called to by nature, inclination, God, taste, or the Muses. One will find such persons among the upper ranks of business, also, where the end often is (and often denied to be) not making money but doing good works in the religious or community spirit.

Free time relies on the negative sense of freedom, freedom from something, in this case freedom from the job. I pointed out earlier how it differed from spare time and pastime. Free time, as defined, while reflecting a poor opinion of work, did help in making it seem that the modern world was progressing toward more free time. It left us, however, with serious difficulties. One was deciding whether free time was free from anything else but work. Taking the negative sense in which the idea originated, can it be said that the meaning now has got to the point, or ought to get to the point, where freedom from other things is sought? For instance, every now and then we have had to ask ourselves, what about family pleasures and responsibilities — does free time mean freedom from them too? If so, the man watching TV at home in the midst of his family is not enjoying free time until he picks up his hat and goes out the door. And then, if he wants to be on free time, he should go neither to local party headquarters to lick envelopes for the coming campaign, nor to the church for evening services, nor to the committee meeting on charity. Does free time mean freedom from all these, too? If not, then it is obvious that the pleasures of free time are laced with duties and responsibilities, thereby clouding the whole idea in paradox. Thus even the negative conception of free time is by no means clear.

TRACES OF THE TRADITION

It may seem that free time is confused and leisure an empty word. We said earlier that the advertiser was impotent before the problems of time and space, status and community, that people landed in his net because they were groping for a station in life, that they had not all been caught because the advertiser's lures could never make good. They might take the bait but then spit it out with the hook, though often tearing a gill in doing so. Before, there had been traditional ways of passing time. With the coming of the world of industry something happened to the tradition that enabled men to fill their work-free hours with unerring sense. Perhaps in the United States the tradition was never planted, or, once planted, never grew. This is the next question to examine. With the rupture of the old in the United States a different pattern came to the fore. Man the spender. Yet not man the spender on others in philanthropic generosity or in the flamboyant Western liberality of "Gents, it's on us" or "Gimme a bottle of beer and $50 worth of ham and eggs for the lady." Instead, before us appears man the spender on himself and on the homestead or, at most, a man who spends to proclaim who he is to others. This last, in personal spending, is the height of his altruism. The soil, free time, resembles a graveyard of obsolete gadgets rather than the garden of leisure. So, perhaps, man the consumer is a more faithful portrait.

Is this the conception we have of him? Lincoln said that not all of the people could be fooled all of the time. The advertiser denies they need to be fooled; they evidently fool themselves. Naturally, the prosperous seller has this idea of the prosperous buyer. There must be others though, with a less partial view of man and his time, work, and leisure.

Since America was taken over from the Indians only a few hundred years ago, one need not delve deep into history to see what happened there to the idea of leisure. The Indians, from what we know of them, cannot be said to have had it as ideal, but firsthand observers described them as having an air of gentlemanly laziness. The Plains Indian seemed satisfied with little. If he didn't get it, *pazienza*. He could stand the pinch of indolent hunger. Labor he abhorred, but hunting buffalo or fighting the enemy, red or white, in rain, cold, and hunger, would never tire him out. In peace he lounged in the grass about the village, sunning himself, for hours watching the children play or dropping in at the various lodges to hear what if anything was new, all with little thought for yesterday and a noble contempt for the morrow. There were many Indian tribes in America. The Mayas and the Plains Indians didn't have the same habits, but whatever their notions of free time or leisure, the invading newcomers were in no mood to pay them heed.

The first English settlers had a hard enough time keeping the wolf and the Indian from the door. Neither the soil nor the Indians were friendly. Surprisingly, one finds that, before long, even under such excusing circumstances, a note of apology appears here and there, that nothing new and extraordinary in literature from this part of the world was to be expected. By the eighteenth century, with the growth of Boston, New York, Philadelphia, Annapolis, Williamsburg, and Charleston, at least a few people began to look forward to a time when the ax and gun, the hoe and saw, would make fewer demands on their lives. Benjamin Franklin in his *Pennsylvania Gazette* in 1749 made a plea for a college for Philadelphia. In the settling of new countries, he wrote, people's first care must be to secure the necessaries of life. It engrosses their attention and affords them little time to think of anything further. Agriculture and mechanic arts were therefore of the most immediate importance. "The culture of minds by the finer arts and sciences was necessarily postponed to times of more wealth and leisure." A proposal for establishing an academy in the province, he thought, would not be deemed unreasonable, since now, "these times are come."

So Franklin thought, or at least wrote, that leisure's time had arrived. Thus it might have seemed in the refined East with its cities, colleges, churches, its gazettes, music, and theaters. The eighteenth century was an age that promised to be golden. A hundred years after Franklin had written his plea, leisure was further away than before. In his day it was about to flower, but didn't. The Revolution of 1776 in itself couldn't have done more than delay its day. But once the Revolution was over, and before a quarter of the new century had gone by, men's minds were no longer what they had been. The sense of a new country and its growth gripped them. The colonials, as Franklin implied, had thought themselves ready for culture, not expansion. The push westward, with ax and gun again, gave much of the land the wilderness atmosphere of the sixteenth and seventeenth centuries, and brought a frontier disregard for all but tools and useful facts. Still later the rise of industry took the path that Chapter VI described for England. Leisure by this time had been forgotten. Stepping in to take its place, as in England, was the shorter work week. Leisure, when it next comes to prominence, makes a false appearance. Thorstein Veblen in the early twentieth century uses it to attack the way of life of the parvenus, the rich families of industrialists. In a manner redolent of Saint-Simon's attack on the monarchy, Veblen castigates the industrialists for using their money to show how much free time they owned.

There was the bright flurry of the eighteenth century, a flurry along the Atlantic coast barely touching the Piedmont and Appalachian valleys. Except for this, America up to the twentieth century, had been in constant motion for three hundred years, expanding, struggling, growing, in process, from the east northward, westward, and southward. As soon as one new community was wrested from the wilderness, one new secret torn from nature, new minds pushed forward to set up another wrestling match with the environment. Even so, the collapse of the eighteenth century's ideals seems too abrupt somehow. Not only did they go out fast, but they had arrived slowly. The Spaniards in Mexico and Peru, for all their destruction of ancient civilizations and cruel subjugation of peoples, implanted a culture that was not only religious but scientific, literary, and artistic. If the studies in geography, mathematics, and astronomy, poetry and drama, and the work of painting, sculpture, music, and architecture in New Spain did not give it a civilization almost as resplendent as that of the Mayas, Aztecs, and Incas, or of the mother country, they at least gave it a comparable luster. Some Indians were taught Latin; one of the few valuable Latin epics written in modern times celebrates the beauty of Mexico. Mexican art has now a three-hundred-year history. If more credit for this goes to the Indians than the Spaniards, the fact remains that *norteamericanos* have no history of art whatever. At the time that Ann Bradstreet, considered the great poet of the Puritans, was setting her daily prayers to limping verse, Sor Juana Inés de la Cruz of Mexico was composing her lyrics, plays, *redondillas*, and delicate spirituals, a poet by a poet's standards.

The idea of leisure was born in Greece and migrated to Rome. At Rome's fall and even before, it took to the monasteries in modified form as the ideal of contemplation, and went both east and west. Its western passage, in which we are presently interested, took it northward with the civilizing monks as far as Britain. In New Spain, as in all of Europe, the Jesuits had an important influence, and in both New and Old England's antipathy for monks and monkish ideas, especially those of the Jesuits, there may lie a clue. The leisure ideal was bound up with classical studies and the knowledge of either Greek or Latin. Without access to these languages in the times under discussion there was little access to the ideas they embodied. Few works were translated.

The first Englishmen to settle, though, were not ignorant men. William Bradford, both first Governor of Plymouth and first to write the story of those hard early years, compared their joy at landing to Seneca's after he once sailed a few miles off the coast of Italy and returned to terra firma with fervent gratitude. John Smith in his memoirs declared that he had always carried with him a book — Machiavelli's *Art of War*. Of the immigrants landing in New England between 1630 and 1645, 140 had received a higher education, 100 at Cambridge, 32 at Oxford, and the rest at Edinburgh and Dublin. The whole colony at this time numbered only about 15,000, so the percentage of educated men must have been high. It is an exaggeration that usually goes unchallenged to say that America is a new country. The men who first came over were already well-dipped in the culture of the Old World.

Circumstance changed those who came here but it couldn't transform them into newborn men, and often the changes that did take place in them merely emphasized traits already there. Like the later immigrants who tried to be 200 per cent Americans, so our Puritans tried to be 200 per cent Puritan. And they succeeded, because their brethren in England at least were surrounded by secular and doubting elements with whom they had to come to terms. In New England the Puritans had a free field. The majority of the educated were churchmen — 90 of the above 140 men. Steeped in Augustine's view of human nature, made more pessimistic still by Calvin, these men generally considered literature and the arts as a dangerous and sinful distraction. Religious service was held without altars, candles, or draperies; the church was a square and bare hall without images, and with no processions, sacraments, or festive celebrations. The Puritans typically considered beauty and religion as antagonists. The church tunes in use in the colony could make no claim to beauty, yet people accused them of "bewitching the mind with syrenes sound." The scruple against using music books during service caused musical notation to be forgotten through almost all of New England in the seventeenth century.

Everything was concentrated on the sermon and the pastor's theological teachings. Yet having studied at Cambridge and Oxford, the pastors, for the sake of dark theology, could subordinate but not smother their love of classical studies. They had hardly arrived when they set up the first secondary institution of learning, the "Latin School." Then in 1636, just six years after the founding of the Boston colony, came the ambitious plan to establish something like the university colleges of Cambridge and Oxford, a design that soon became Harvard University. We could go into the four hundred volumes the minister John Harvard left in his will to find works of theology, Biblical exegesis, Latin classics, patristic and humanistic writings. Our interest should not linger here, however; we know that Latin was important for the early English settlers: it was useful in sermons. Few present Harvard graduates would have been graduated in the Harvard of the seventeenth century if only because they would not have known enough Latin, not to mention Greek.

One should not overstress the influence of the Latin schools. The idea for them came from the wave of Latin schools established in Elizabeth's time. By shutting off the monasteries, Henry VIII had suppressed the higher learning of the times, such as it was. Lay teachers had to be found, and they were few and bad. The attempt to speak in Latin was never quite successful in England and it failed utterly in America, even in Harvard College. The shortage of Latin teachers in the colonies was of course much greater than in England.

It so happened that when New England was settled education was at a low ebb in old England too. When the future founders of Harvard studied at Cambridge there were no great masters to compare with those of that period in France, Italy, or Holland. The great creativeness of Elizabethan times was in drama, literature, and music, arts that had no connection with the universities. The emigrants had not been touched by Ben Jonson or Shakespeare, Bacon, or even the Puritan Milton. For the whole preceding century, English academic life had been absorbed in the bitter battle between Catholicism and Protestantism, Arminianism and Calvinism, to which all else took second place. So English education on the lower rungs in this period was primitive and on the higher was dedicated to theological polemics.

The new yet old settlers could look nowhere save to England for their education. In New England, though the influence of the established church was weakest in comparison with Virginia, Maryland, or South Carolina, there was still nowhere else to turn. Spain was a rival, France was a rival, Italy after its great popularity in Elizabethan England became the target of religious prejudice, identified along with Spain and France as a spawner of Jesuits and the home grounds of that "prostitute of Babylon," the Roman church. In New England, Robert Child, a learned and independent man, was deported to the mother country for having tried to make an appeal to Parliament to reform the colony. The Puritans blocked the appeal, suspecting him of being a Jesuit because he had been in Italy and visited Rome. By comparison, in old England, a learned and independent man, who freely drew inspiration from Italy, was Milton.

On this shore, there was always a small number of rebels. Worth recalling is the controversial case of Merry Mount, the settlement that the Cavalier Thomas Morton with a group of companions started in Massachusetts. Among other things he contended that the Indians descended from the Trojans; he claimed to have noticed in their vocabulary many words of Greek and Latin origin. At any rate his little group admitted Indian men and women and was not Puritan but pagan in inspiration. On May Day they brewed a "barrell of excellent beare" and put up an 80-foot pine pole with a pair of buckshorns nailed at the top. Their May Day song re-echoes the mounts of Olympus and Fiesole:

> Drinke and be merry, merry, merry boyes,
> Let all your delight be in Hymen's joyes.

The Pilgrims gave him and his lads and lasses no chance to prove that such a way of life suited the rigors of Massachusetts. A troop led by Myles Standish descended on Merry Mount, surprised the gay company, tied up and later dispersed them, and shipped their leader back to England by the first boat. Morton later wrote a book narrating the incident and making fun of Captain Shrimp (Standish) and his worthy company. This was in the first half of the 1600s, and, still, no two historians tell the story the same way.

Toward the century's end in Massachusetts there were signs of rebellion against the theocratic oligarchy, but at this time too the Puritan inquisition had its day of merciless penalties, punishment of small children and half-insane women, the ferocious pursuit of the weak and defenseless. If Cotton had had his way in

1641 all criticism of God's appointed would have been choked off by the hangman's noose. Between 1688 and 1693 occurred the witch trials that terrorized all of New England. But in the twentieth century, who are we to damn others?

It was more than a theocracy could do, though, to keep out classical learning and ideals. The rise of an energetic mercantile class in the cities, the growth of populations to the west, the love of the Puritans themselves for books and classical and humanistic learning, soon snapped the tightest bonds. By the beginnings of the eighteenth century, Puritanism in New England was on the decline. The model still was England, however, for the other colonies, too.

The grammar school in England was really a Latin school. The rudiments of English were taught, and sometimes some Greek and Hebrew; otherwise instruction was wholly in Latin. It thus happened that lads of fifteen or more leaving grammar school read their mother tongue with a stammer, wrote it with even more difficulty and ignored the existence of the multiplication table. In a situation where trade is rising to importance few fail to recognize that the three R's are of primary importance for money-making. The Latin school was invaluable for the clergyman's fight with the devil but for the ordinary clerk's serving of Mammon another kind of school was necessary. The common schools, often called the trivial or inferior schools, took on the task of training future money-makers in reading plain English, writing a clean hand, and keeping accounts straight.

Highly valued in England and Scotland in the fifteenth and sixteenth centuries for producing clergymen and statesmen, the Latin school was the only kind to get private endowment. In America in later centuries it found a varying reception. In New England it was welcomed, naturally, for the education of preachers and later of public men; in Virginia, with fewer towns and less need for ministers, it was less warmly received, and some schools taught numbers along with Latin and Greek. The rich in Virginia turned to the Old World for their education; the rustic settlers didn't need Latin. With time, New England, too, began to feel the pressure for English. Frontiersmen learned to take bearings, shoot straight, wield the ax true and lay a puncheon floor, but English, which was supposed to be taught at mother's knees, not at the Latin school, suffered mutilation. When one of the three R's appeared as "refmetik" in a school contract and when the Boston clerk in 1652 wrote of the "pore scollars of Hervert College," the situation was bad, even by the loose standards of the time. By slow degrees the study of English came to the free school, driving out its rival "latting." The outskirt schools, so-called, had no Latin teachers, were closer to the remoter townsmen and supported by them. They gradually became the district schools, sustained by public funds, and devoted to the useful R's.

Higher education at the end of the seventeenth century was worthy of the name only in Massachusetts, Connecticut, and Virginia. New York had too many tongues and too many ships to think about, Maryland and Rhode Island were torn by religious strife, and Pennsylvania and the Carolinas were just newly on the scene. Tobacco, codfish, and skins needed reckoning in pine-tree shillings and pieces of eight. Yet higher education held on against contemptuous remarks like that made to the founder of William and Mary: "Damn your souls! Make tobacco!" and in holding on and winning out for a *studium generale,* kept the tradition of leisure from disappearing. The call was close, though, like that of musical notation among the Puritans in the century before.

The eighteenth century saw many changes that produced a cosmopolitan outlook especially among the seaboard colonies. Until the Revolutionary War the gaze of the rich was on England. The planters went themselves or sent their sons; the marine merchants, fattening on trade in salt fish, oil, candles, whales, fur, rum, ore, tobacco, rice, and molasses, looked outward across the sea to the mother country. The theologians of New England combined their studies of English theology and humanism. Only the minorities — the Moravians, Huguenots, Jews, and Roman Catholics — looked elsewhere and contributed greatly to the cosmopolitan spirit. England still remained the pattern for imitation in intellectual endeavors, in amusements and manners, in dress and architecture. The great houses of Virginia built in the Palladian style were copied from England, not from the Veneto. Reading tastes in the social libraries of the north were for solid, serious English books (and in the private libraries, too) but sometime between 1790 and 1800 in the shade of *The British Classics* in 38 volumes, Aristotle's *Ethics* and *Politics* stole in unobtrusively.

The Revolution changed matters drastically. Feeling against England ran high. France became the new model for imitation. French officers helping the colonists and expecting to find noble savages, bears and buffalo, women of virtue and the successors to Republican Rome, were amused and pleased to see delightful houses, pretty and intelligent ladies, wealth, politeness, and good things to eat at hand. Accustomed to a farming frugality, they were astonished and some even shocked by American worldly liberality. The gallant French fitted into this life with little difficulty and gave a Gallic tone to embryonic salons in the cities everywhere. French politics, war, society, science, and revolution all played a part. French affairs in this period were closest to Americans. With the French alliance, the break with England, the reciprocal travel — to France, Franklin, Jefferson, Jay, and the Adamses; to America, French officers, volunteers, diplomats and (after the Revolution of 1789 in France and the West Indies) cultured emigrés in droves of thousands. When relations with Britain were resumed, the influence of France did not decline, for at the time British society, too, was under the spell of French taste in fashions, amusements, and entertainments.

Boston held out more than other cities against the prevailing Gallomania. The state dinner was preferred to the "light trivialities" that France introduced. There was mockery too, not so much at the French as at the poor imitation thereof — as when at a ball in Princeton a traveler commented that in dancing a French cotillion the women "sprawled and sprachled." Elsewhere every Republican felt he must dress like a Frenchman and every Federalist like one of King George's subjects. French dress to some became more and more uncomfortable. A man's pants went up to his armpits. To get into them was reported to be a morning's work, to sit down in them was a dangerous risk. Hair was not cut à la Brutus, but brushed from the crown of the head toward the forehead. Around the neck went a linen handkerchief; the skirts of a beau's green coat were cut away to a point behind. Brandy was the favorite drink, while the favorite talk was of the latest French play. The ladies with their fans, laces, and mantuas preferred the dash of Paris to the elegance of London. The theater, the salon, occasionally with great ladies, the arts, cuisine, the dancing school, deism, and the taking of religion with an air of skepticism, Rabelais meeting with Calvin, Catholic allies and Protestant enemies, tolerance and internationalism — does all this sound much like America? At Yale, students called one another Rousseau, Voltaire, d'Alembert, and so forth.

It was not long before the reaction set in. In successive stages — the Reign of Terror, Bonapartism, the Jesuits' slaughter of the Goddess of Reason — France began to drop in American esteem. French emigrants did not put down roots in the United States. Many fled here and, as soon as they could, fled back away from here. For all its copying of French life and manners in the last quarter of the eighteenth and the first of the nineteenth centuries, America was not France. The repatriation of French emigrants was so extensive the quality of French language teaching in America suffered. There was still a lot of wilderness to tame, and the visionary mentality of the French seemed not to be of the right kind. The group that tried to found Demopolis, to cultivate the vine and the olive, resembled no society of Puritans. These people may have needed but would never have understood or submitted to a law like that in the Massachusetts statute of 1633: "No person, hawseholder or other, shall spend his time idely or unproffably, under pain of such punishment as the court shall thinke meet to inflicte."

To repeat, America was not a new country. Each settler brought his homeland with him. If the French failed to plant the olive in Alabama, their culture went deeper than their agriculture. Their influence lasted longer in Mobile, and St. Louis and Charleston as well, not to mention New Orleans. After all, how many false starts did the early English make before the Indians taught them how to plant, and how many did later settlers make, each with their own preconceptions from the old country? The Germans looked for clay loams in wooded areas, the English for light sandy uplands. The former, typically thorough, cleared off everything and plowed deeply. The English girdled trees and farmed among the stumps, scratched the soil, and then, horrified, watched it run away in the rains. The Virginians let stock roam freely; the Germans built their barn before they built the house. But while the Englishman tried out tobacco, the German never budged from wheat, thereby losing the cultural as well as monetary rewards of plantation life. Neither the Germans nor the English brought Roman law with them, and this perhaps more than many other factors put together enabled not a few Americans with easy conscience and provincial simplicity to distinguish the free from the slave by skin color.

The colonies at the start were not modern but medieval. Before it was gripped by industrialism, the Atlantic seacoast seemed an extension of Europe. In Virginia, as in the middle and southern colonies generally, the system combined liege lords, patentees, vast estates, the law of entail, indentured servants, and slaves. Going upward from the Moravian settlements in Georgia, the Carolinas, and Pennsylvania to the English in New England, one could see common lands, handicraft industries, religion and state lying side by side. Each American community was ordered in ranks and classes. The churches may have lacked ornament, but a spectacle of reverence went to judges and governors made up of corteges of gentlemen or sergeants bearing halberds. Seats in New England meetinghouses were formally dignified, that is, their value as a sign of rank was weighed and fixed and their incumbents then chosen. Humble folk were not to dress above their degree. Criminals among them were rogues to be hanged, while gentlemen criminals were cleanly beheaded. This was in Maryland. Massachusetts in its place refused to send any true gentleman to the whipping post, although women of vulgar birth enjoyed no such exemption. In New England by the middle of the seventeenth century only about one man in fourteen was entitled to be called "Mr." The other thirteen were simply "Goodman." Politically, gentlemen received preference over the common people for honors, offices, and positions of command. If gentlemen a-hunting intruded into the poor man's field they were not to be resisted, though their incursions did damage. The virtue of a wife was to turn the shining face of obedience to her husband. Children owed the same reverence to parents and masters. This was only on the littoral, however. The interior felt less like an extension of Europe. The frontier began as soon as the settlers lost sight of the sea, and it kept going westward in waves across the Alleghenies, the Ohio, the Mississippi, the Missouri, the Great Plains, the Rocky Mountains, the Pacific Coast, and upward to Alaska. A lot these people cared for the life of the English gentry, or the latest French play!

Thus, with their gaze set toward the west, they let Europe draw farther away. Now came the real ordeal for classical studies — the nineteenth century. Western settlers needed to buy goods and merchants needed to sell, but battles in the Atlantic, the War of Independence, of 1812, the Napoleonic wars — all these cut down shipping trade. The discovery of raw materials on this side led to American manufactures. A new class, destined to power, was born. The manufacturers were tied to the sea merchants by money and blood, but they were not the same class. In 1812, for instance, the shipowners had sunk capital in manufactures; the government fostered them with tax-exemptions and premiums; and a credit system developed favoring only those who could be counted on to meet their obligations. Credit involves money, reputation, thrift — in short, respectability. The merchant had developed into a man of some taste. Culture, not respectability, had become his concern. The manufacturer, on the other hand, was more like his customers to the west — the small trader, the small farmer, the evangelical brethren. His virtues were the household virtues of home, thrift, prudence, the lessons of Poor Richard, and, of course, work. In economics *laissez-faire,* in philosophy utilitarian, common-sensical, in ethics decent, respectable — these would be the applicable terms. Dancing wastes time, so does novel-reading. The number of hours so wasted were once calculated for the nation. They amounted to many indeed.

The moving frontier and growing industrialism leave little room for dancing and less time for reading. The age of Jefferson makes way for the age of Jackson. Among other crimes, Jefferson is accused of insisting that children should study Greek and Roman history instead of the Bible (in the King James translation, not in the original Hebrew and Greek, of course). Such charges angered him to the point of likening the Presbyterians to the Jesuits for wanting to control all the country's education. Certainly a religious revival was taking place. It came to be called the Great Awakening. Enthusiastic, Protestant, ascetic — in these traits it was like Puritanism. It completely lacked Puritanism's love of books and learning and the intellect. Yet all other religions bowed before it. Having unhorsed Rabelais, Calvin was back in the saddle, hitting his pace with the Methodist circuit riders. Wesley had not won over the colonists earlier, partly because of his stand against the Revolution and slavery. But by now France was both atheist and Catholic, and the West had few slaves. The Baptists along with the Methodists and Presbyterians made up the trio of the Great Revival. So fierce burned their zeal that after a time Catholicism and Judaism came to look something like them.

The South and West were taken by a storm of missionary fire-camp meetings and exhortations. Princeton was the base from which they proceeded to demolish the eighteenth century. The North instead fell to the prudish, dependable, self-helping clock-like virtues of the industrial world, less evangelical, more moralistic, but the two ethics found they could live together.

Frontier religion set up its institutions of "higher learning" too, in freshwater colleges. The minister was missionary and teacher both. Denominational colleges, founded for the purpose, took on the problem of ministerial leadership. On the lower levels, the Latin school went into total eclipse. The academy appeared and took on the Lancasterian system — serious, practical, respectable, moralistic. Out of it grew the high school, sprouting soon after the first few decades of the nineteenth century. It was a public school, unlike the academy, and dispensed with the old Latin curriculum. The libraries too grew more practical. In the eighteenth century, libraries belonged to colleges and universities or were lending libraries. In the nineteenth century the public library came into its own. Each town had its Mechanics or Apprentices or Young Men's Institute library. Books on religion and education predominated.

With the Civil War big industry got a good start. The keeper of society was no longer the theologian, the merchant, or the plantation master. The ages of the machine and the frontier took over step by step in a movement that began with the Revolutionary War, and played against each other, the one producing uniformity in parts and men, the other a raw individualism. In the nineteenth century the two joined forces to steam-roller a lovely country, leaving it for the most part a mess of ugly cities and despoiled wilderness.

The stress on native tongue to the exclusion of classical languages typically encouraged chauvinism and a vainglorious isolationism. The rest of the world little interested the majority of Americans. The incoming migrants were but extra poor hands fleeing hunger and despotism. The less one knew of their countries the better. To know nothing at all were best. America was all one needed to know.

Education added United States history to the three R's, but the latter remained necessary for commerce of the lowest to the highest variety. Reading was important also for knowing what was going on in the country. It kept people informed. Newspaper circulation and numbers grew by leaps and bounds. Education helped one move along in life, improve oneself and better one's position. The public-school system, profiting from the work of Comenius, Pestalozzi, and Horace Mann, became free of charge and national, so that everyone could be well-informed and "get ahead." Technical and vocational public schools grew apace; commercial and business courses became part of high-school courses (as a President of the United States later said, "The business of America is business"); mechanical drawing, "shop," printing, "science," and manual training classes became familiar entries in the curriculum; industry sponsored, supported, and supplied texts and educational materials; business filled the rolls of boards of education and boards of trustees; agricultural and mechanical colleges sprang up alongside less well-defined state colleges and universities.

As Tocqueville had remarked in the early part of the century, democracy was successful. Therefore, education, if it was to work well, had to be democratic. Science was successful, so experiment must be the way to progress. Pragmatism, as the educator John Dewey said, was the extension to all of life of the admittedly successful general method of science. Science experiments, education reproduces experiments in the experience of the student, democracy ensures the shared empirical testing of change in the interest of practice or progress. Education turns practical and remains so. The practical leads to a good life, and the good life it finds is practical, too. There are two ways of spending time, idly or for a worthy purpose. The worthy purposes are work, education, self-improvement, support of family, keeping informed, and the like.

The nineteenth century reversed matters, then, and tried to break off the leisure tradition. The three R's and their utilitarian auxiliaries became the wheels that turned the educational system. Now Latin schools, in whatever nooks they still resisted, became the "trivial" or inferior schools. They still had prestige but only among elements left over from the eighteenth century, and among those who wished to associate themselves with these elements. In the last years of the century, the attempt of the industrial rich to copy the English gentry's way of life once more met with dismal failure. It came at an unfortunate time and at all events was in bad taste. The industrialist found it harder than the marine merchant to live a cultured life. He had spent too many years inside closed horizons. These were the people who made so easy a target for Veblen's *Theory of the Leisure Class.*

The leisure tradition in America did not die out completely. In the good universities, those going back to the eighteenth century and one or two more recent ones, classical and humanistic studies have endured. These chiefly eastern universities of Harvard, Yale, Princeton, King's College (Columbia), William and Mary, were aristocratic in origin. The extent of the useless part of their curricula even today shows it. The courses they offer are the closest to those of European universities. In some quarters, they are still suspected of having aristocratic leanings. To drop off quickly to the minor retainers of the tradition, the preparatory academies for boys and the finishing schools for young ladies play a small but sometimes genuine part. Incidentally, finishing schools were started by the French boarding- and day-school models at New Rochelle, and it was a Huguenot descendant who opened the field to women's colleges — Matthew Vassar.

In the South, where industry has never fully penetrated, you can still today see the remnants of life with a different pace. A town like Clinton, Louisiana, portrays the fondness for the classical in the lines of its court house and Lawyers' Row. Up to the First World War, among educated Virginians a Yankee was a person who didn't understand how to use his time. The organization of the South, until the War between the States, functioned through aristocratic institutions — the estate and plantation, the county seat, the established church. Ownership of the land worked hand in hand with the direction of labor and guidance of culture. With the rise of manufacturing about 1812 the South began to lose influence. The middle and western states were growing more powerful. Old Virginia families suffered hard financial losses. The Southern aristocracy turned to Charleston as its cultural center, and it remains to the present, in architecture and tempo, an echo of antebellum days.

There where England was not the leading ideal — in Charleston (France), in Mobile (Spain and France), and in Louisiana and especially in New Orleans (Spain and France again) — a leisurely pattern left traces still to be seen. New Orleans, first Spanish and then heavily French, did not enter into American affairs until the beginning of the nineteenth century. The creole aristocrat there had designed a plantation world even before one was being lived up South. Their life, except for black slavery, had a Latin atmosphere. Wealthy with sugar and cotton, they kept houses in the city, plantations on the river, drove coaches along the Esplanade, sent their children to French masters for dancing and good form, went to French opera in the evening, gambled, dueled under the oaks, and encouraged cookery to scale the heights. The French quarter today, though jostled by tourists, still offers some of the old architecture, cuisine, coffee, and conversation. Little else remains. The jazz of Bourbon Street belongs to a later epoch.

In the colonial cities, around the old universities, among the old families, the ideal still passes down from generation to generation, though not by any means with its original force. The most it is capable of producing is a few more decades of the genteel tradition, as in Boston and its suburbs, and men like Thoreau and Emerson.

Finally, we must not forget the expatriates, the Americans who chose to live in another country because they could not do their work here as well as there. Many went to Europe; a few, but a good few, not only wooed but won the Muses or fame in Paris, Rome, and even London. Irving, Cooper, Hawthorne, Mark Twain, Henry James, W. W. Story, Whistler, Sargent, Mary Cassatt, Bret Harte, Edith Wharton, and Logan Pearsall Smith, to take examples only up to the First World War. There are many more to add since then — Gertrude Stein, e. e. cummings, Stephen Vincent Benét, Ernest Hemingway, John Dos Passos, F. Scott Fitzgerald, George Antheil, Archibald MacLeish, Alexander Calder, Glenway Westcott, T. S. Eliot, Ezra Pound, Man Ray, Henry Miller. Scorned by the nativist and envied by his stay-at-home colleagues, the expatriate still goes out today sometimes in a simple unconscious search for leisure, sometimes to write or to paint, always bringing back to the United States an idea of places where time and work are looked on differently.

If it seems that the remnants of the leisure tradition pertain mainly to the eighteenth century, the impression is correct. That century is far off, and truly, of its few vestiges, only the universities have life and the chance of future strength. That is why if we look today for active signs of the heritage we must look to our teachers. We do find them in the breach, and as we should expect, especially those from the good universities. They know that leisure is important. But the contemporary rage for research (as opposed to simple study), the projects embarked on (requiring "teamwork" research), the increase in school bureaucracy, of machine and paper work — practices as yet foreign to European universities — insure that leisure sets no foot on campus. So much for the faculty. As for the students and for maintaining the ideal among them, the universities unfortunately, have by and large fallen dupe to the notion that there is only one answer to

the problem — to see that everyone gets a liberal education. And
they lock horns with those who say everyone should have some
other kind of education — usually vocational, technical, or scientific. As a consequence, many proposals crop up: adult education, preparing for leisure courses, hobby training, arts and crafts
for youth, and so on. Another main concern of theirs is with all
the leisure time that is becoming available. What will people do
with it? The two concerns are related. The first should answer
the second. The battle, however, is over the wrong issues and
shows how weak the leisure ideal is, even in its last rampart. The
fact that people will have a lot of free time does not necessarily
mean that they will have anything at all of leisure. The educators
therefore are not offering liberal education as the solution to
leisure as an ideal as much as to the problem of too much free
time badly spent.

There are others besides the educators who foresee a problem
in the future of leisure. The business leader is about the only one
willing to say that workers are getting too much free time. Unlike other leaders he can say this without questioning whether
workers spend it badly or not. He feels he is often paying for
hours off the job, and the thought is not appealing. He worries
about how, with the work week growing shorter, he is to keep
costs low and production high. He maintains that workers want
more money rather than more free time, a statement that seems
to be true for executives like himself as a class, at any rate. Nonetheless executives, again as a group, seem to foresee that employees will have further gains of free time in the future — more
vacations, shorter work weeks, more coffee breaks. For themselves they are not quite so sure: they say they won't have less
free time in the future, yet they are not all sure they will have
more.

As to how employees spend their free time, most business
leaders take a *laissez-faire* stance. Setting up a favorable physical
environment by locating plants in suburbs or the country meets
with approval as not constituting an unwarranted intervention

in employees' lives. Of course, most executives themselves live out in the country or suburbs whether the plant is there or not. On the whole they seem to think that employees make good use of their free time. Many feel it doesn't matter what they themselves think, since people should be their own judges in the matter. Most companies have no program for the free-time activities of their employees, but more and more of them seem to be building facilities — ball fields, swimming pools, archery ranges, bowling alleys. A sly question comes to mind when one notes that company recreation directors try to find figures at which they can point with pride, such as a 3½ per cent drop in absenteeism since the creation of the company's sports program. The question is, Did the sports program bring a gain or loss in free time?

The lists that recreation directors make of their companies' activities are often long. In some cases they go beyond providing space or facilities, unless the notion of facilities includes paying for bowling balls, bags, shoes, and shirts. In other cases they serve to recall how often parts of work life, in particular office life, are given over to recreational get-togethers. The Christmas and summer parties are examples so long-standing that we hardly think of them as recreational activities any more. Is supplying beer and liquor for the Christmas party providing a facility? The lists of activities at any rate include softball, volley ball, tennis, pool, library, playing cards, horseshoes, dominoes, chorus, hi-fi, track, picnics, Easter egg hunts, Halloween parties, family days, roller skating, movies, music instrument groups, concerts, chess and checkers, table tennis, darts, fishing, children's parties, lunchtime activities, boat races, craft and hobby work, camps for employees and children, kite flying, art contests, dances, banquets, rifle shoots, and others. Given the geographical mobility of Americans and the impersonality and commerciality of life in big cities, the associative kind of recreation seems destined for a healthy future. Work will become the center of more frequent social relations.

It is not business alone that facilitates such activities. Labor unions also, of course, and churches too, provide their share. Indeed the same lists could be used to describe the recreation program of a labor union or church. Lists like these may have something to do with the rise in church membership in the last few decades.

Labor-union leaders, too, take a *laissez-faire* attitude. There are exceptions, certainly, like those who worry about all the time members spend in TV viewing. The others ask: Why stick our noses into the members' business? Who are we to judge whether what members do in their free time is good or bad? Live and let live.

The disparity in views is not in how to spend free time — *laissez-faire* is the rule — but in how much to have. Business executives, Chapter IV pointed out in paradox, put in one of the longest work weeks. They are the men who win from the economic system the highest monetary rewards as well as the highest prestige. Free time evidently is not one of the rewards they want urgently. They above all others in this society should be the masters of their time, free to indulge in the luxury of an idle day. Most of them never take an extra day off, something even their lowliest girl secretaries have been known to do in order to give ample time to the trip to Bermuda for which they have saved year-round. A businessman once noted that executives, in the matter of more free time, evidently follow the lead of the working class by inertia. True, the amount of free time they have would seem less a deliberate choice than the following of a pattern spreading up from below. No doubt executives sometimes feel that they are a model for the others. If they advocate and themselves take more free time, the pattern will spread even more quickly, too quickly. More important, though, as we have seen, is the fact that the executive gets his greatest satisfaction from life on the job, not off the job. This cannot be said for employees and workers. The workers clean up, the clerks pack up, and both go home on the dot.

In contrast to employers, labor-union leaders can give reasons for increasing free time. They urge a shorter work week with no decrease in weekly wages as the way to keep technological advance from running into technological unemployment. The interest in free time did not come wholly from below. By no means is it the employees or unions alone who have built up the pressure. A curious ambivalence affects business attitudes.

The production and sales divisions are in one way working at cross purposes. Marketing and advertising men wanted to sell capricious wares, consumer goods, leisure items. Chapter VI gave the history of the affair. One point of origin was on high: the hawking of wares. In the effort to stabilize and widen markets one variety of executives have through advertising encouraged the buying of goods for use in free time. They emphasized the amount of free time available and the coming of more, and announced the advent of the new world of leisure. The notion caught on. Now they themselves and the other varieties of executives are affected by it. The ideal of a society with copious free time in which to buy and use many commodities swings full circle to ensnare the ensnarers. The production executive today doesn't mind having heavy sales but he sees little point in giving workers more time off than they need for rest and shopping; he doesn't want his pay rolls bulging with time off. In his view, free time is not free but bound time; he has to pay more for the same hours on Sundays and holidays, at night or overtime. The sales or advertising executive, in addition to rest and shopping time, has to promise people time in which to use the things they buy.

So today's executive no longer feels that to want more free time for himself is immoral; on the contrary, he feels it is a natural and proper thing to wish for and want more of. However, he has not yet reached the point where he will try to do anything decisive about achieving it. The change in him is mainly verbal. Partly arising from members of his own fraternity, the free-time idea is in the wind. The executive has a new readiness to speak about it, and this speaking of it presages a change in habits — not in *his* habits, perhaps, but certainly in the habits of his children.

So far we have little in the way of an ideal of leisure. Some business leaders have seen a related problem — executive leadership. They have seen their executives come out of school, go to work, rise in the ranks, and then go stale. A number of them believe that what their men lacked was education in the humanities or the liberal arts. For badly spent executive free time, then, the recommendation is, go back to school. In their ideas, unfortunately, they obscure the liberality of leisure and the freedom of the liberal arts. If they could be shown that by taking humanities courses their executives showed greater intellectual curiosity and enthusiasm, they would cheer and say, "Now just let someone try to tell us that as a result they won't be better electric men, or telephone men, or whatever the case may be." Now you and I can tell them that if the curiosity of these men were truly aroused, there's no telling what kind of men they would turn out to be, telephone, electric, or anything else. Another handful of executives sees that great literature and art reflect an order as well as a way of combining the rational, the descriptive, and the evaluative into one harmony, and *that* for them comprises the basic formula for management decision. A similar position holds that business needs broad-gauged men, and the humanities broad-gauges them. Still another one believes that since the executive deals less with materials than with men and ideas, he needs the education of a humanist. This is like justifying one's love for a woman because through it one learns about the female sex. They all overlook that for leisure and the liberal arts the harmony, the broad gauge, and the exercise of the mind, have their ends in themselves, not in business. Once more, for all of them, the problem is how to change too much of a bad thing to the right amount of a good thing, the thing in both guises being free time.

Among the various organizations, competition goes on to corner the citizen's free time. The unions are not greatly interested in free time for itself; they are simply afraid that machines will produce so much more free time that the workers will have "no time" on which to make a claim at the pay window. They want to spread machine-saved time so that, come what may, each worker will have a tidy little claim check to hand in to the payroll clerk each payday. Why then, one asks, do many of them sponsor sports programs and the like? The issue is one of loyalty. If workers get more free time, the unions get it for them; and if workers enjoy the camaraderie of recreation programs, they will credit their unions for it. Similarly for business. Business leaders are not in favor of more free time, but to hold their employees' loyalties they will provide recreation programs. Any given government too will be interested in the voter's loyalty. Out of the tax money of voters, it supplies facilities for outdoor recreation, but it has to be careful not to poach on the private preserves of commercial facilities. The tension here between business and government warrants fuller discussion later, but there are reasons why the government too is not much interested, for the time being at least, in more free time for workers. A backdrop of missiles and interplanetary space colors its view of the good life, about which statesmen have been known occasionally to speak. The view sees the American way of life, a good life in itself, in danger of extinction unless more work time and less free time is taken.

The churches must compete against all comers. Some of them have a long history of recreation, and the kind of recreation they provide is not much different from that of other groups. They too are not specially interested in increasing the amount of free time. In pastoral work they see the result of too much free time in the delinquency of the young and the despair of the old, and in the materialism of the things people spend their lives working for.

A kind of pastoral work is done also by doctors and psychiatrists. They, like the others, see no urgent need for more free time. Like the ministers, they sense the effect of too much time in the hands of young and old alike as time without a purpose to guide it, and consider it a menace to the *mens sana in corpore sano*. On Sundays, holidays, and other days off some persons get nervous, even anxious. Apparently the schedule of the work day, the fact that it has definite things to do, that, as long as one goes to work or to the office the day can be chalked up on the side of virtue — these things reassure many persons of their productiveness, sociability, and place in the community. They need not fear having to evaluate their own activities — and perhaps change and choose others — as long as the routine itself sanctions it. The Sunday neurosis, as it sometimes is called, seems fairly widespread in a milder form as a malady exhibiting a peculiar uneasiness rather than true anxiety on free-time days. The lack of structure to the days opens them up to choice, and choices without a guiding pattern may lead either to temptation or to reflection, which then leads to a feeling of not knowing how to act, of existing without purpose. Work days roll around to the sound of sighs of relief. If the number of characterless free-time days increases, these phenomena should increase too.

The sense of time becomes important in many cases of psychotherapy. The expanses of time that days off and vacations offer seem to bring to some persons the same sort of fear that agoraphobics have of open spaces. Wide-open time, like space, is frightening. In like manner time pressure, a subject undertaken in the next chapter, has its own disease, a claustrophobia in time, wherein the person feels that he is closeted up in time and can't escape. The organic symptoms associated with time pressure have been given more attention by both physicians and psychotherapists. The heart and stomach seem to be the points time pressure favors for boring into the sound body.

Physicians and psychiatrists, it would seem, should interest themselves in the larger problem. When leisure is spoken of in the United States no one, if asked, would say that a person confined to a hospital bed had leisure, although he is off work. If a man is in ill health he is not even considered to be on free time, much less at leisure. In illness one is not free. Like riding the commuters' train, some sicknesses permit the patient to play cards, talk, read, or ambulate, but usually he is not at liberty to do what he chooses. The broader issue concerns not only those patients who are physically or psychotically ill, but also the millions in the United States held to be neurotic. The compulsions and obsessions, anxieties, bodily disorders, the melancholias and seizures, the alcoholics and addicts — whether one takes the estimate for the United States of 1 out of 10 or 1 out of 3, the figure runs into the many millions. Aren't these people unfree, in spite of free political institutions? Tormented as they are, do they have free time? No need to ask whether they have leisure.

The same concentration on the smaller issues describes the churches' interest in leisure. There are some who ask for more beauty in our lives, spaciousness to our cities, ease and liberation to our pauses, time for looking inward and for speculating about the world and its things. Though they are beating their frail wings against plate glass, they keep the connection of truth, beauty, and goodness from dying. More attention, perhaps too much, goes to the socials and other free-time activities mentioned earlier. And no attention at all goes to the one that sums up all the deficiencies of the notion of free time, in that free time is faceless, without purpose, and without gratitude. For it is no holy day. Nor is it a political holiday. To say free time should be spent in praise of the political or economic or labor-union way of life that brought it to us sounds feeble. Not even the French Revolution could carry it off. This being the case, what is there to celebrate? A holiday is a day of celebration.

The advertiser competes for free time too. Your time is his market and he fights all rivals for possession of it. If you buy his wares, he has a share of it. He is the only one of the groups we have been discussing who is unabashedly in favor of more free time, wide open, for everybody. Question: When do people buy and consume? Answer: In their free time. That the advertiser holds up his side of the fence by himself testifies to the strength of his forces. He has only one assistant here, a part-time, ambivalent assistant at that — the educator, sometimes supported by writers on democracy. They ask for time for adult education; they point out its prospective benefits in teaching civics. Furthermore they harry the others, specially the advertisers, by asking about the good life for everyone and whether the commodity mentality marks the only place free time fits into such a life. They too compete for the citizen's time — asking that more of it be spent on education, less on hard bright objects. The irony of all this competing for free time is that there is actually so little. These rivals are not grabbing off handfuls of fat but scrounging around in a scarcity market.

Apart from the thoughts of a few stray persons, all see the "leisure problem" narrowly, as too much, badly spent, time. That everyone equates leisure with free time indicates how weak is the leisure ideal this chapter has been trying to locate and follow. It indicates further that in their determination to make leisure a democratic notion all have forgotten what it is, if ever they knew. The educators, some of them at least, did know. Back we go to the opening question, Where is there a tradition, a pattern to follow, an ideal? If one existed, it would itself influence the spending of free time; it would be a formidable shaper of choice. Since what little tradition of leisure we have is a remnant of the eighteenth century, let's look again at that epoch. After all, at the end of it this country took its bow. Perhaps the Founders had nothing to say about leisure. Even so, they surely must have had some idea of what government among men is for and what the good life consists of.

The first document that was meant to apply to the imminent United States of America was the Declaration of Independence. On July 2, 1776 the bare resolution that the colonies by right ought to be free and independent states was adopted. A cold statement by itself was not enough for the Founders. They insisted on a philosophic declaration for the benefit of mankind. A committee was chosen and Jefferson as we know prepared the official statement, in which these familiar lines rhythmically ring out: "We hold these truths to be self-evident, that all men are created equal, that they are endowed by their Creator with certain unalienable rights, that among these are life, liberty and the pursuit of happiness." The declaration of the First Continental Congress a few years before had not mentioned the pursuit of happiness — property was in its place; nor had previous documents in the Anglo-American history of petitions and bills of rights reposed on happiness either.

The one who first brings it on the stage of American politics is a classical scholar, George Mason. Ten years before he did this, he had written describing himself as a man who spent most of his time in retirement and seldom meddled in public affairs; content with the blessings of a private station, he enjoyed a modest but independent income and disregarded the smiles and favors of the great. The Virginia Declaration of Rights is substantially the work of this man. In it the natural rights of men include the enjoyment of life and liberty, as in the Declaration of Independence, and also "the means of acquiring, and preserving, property, and pursuing and obtaining happiness and safety." This clause passed unchanged over to the Virginia constitution of 1776. Mason had prepared the statement for the Constitution of the United States too; it was left out through a complex series of circumstances. In one form or another, the clause has been incorporated by two thirds of the state constitutions framed up until this century. Some of them actually go so far as to say in the language of the Declaration of Independence that it is the people's right to "alter or abolish" a government that fails to secure happiness for the people.

I noted that Mason's clause was adopted in one form or other. Though various, the form contains a similar string of words. Life, liberty, property, happiness, safety, seem to be those most commonly found. Though to later interpreters these words were not clear, to Mason and Jefferson they were self-evident. If life and liberty are present they can be enjoyed. The way they are enjoyed is in the pursuit of happiness. Safety and property, the two words that revolve about happiness like satellites, have each a separate relation. Safety seems to have meant a guarantee of peace of mind, an insuring against the arbitrary jolts of tyrants or the rebellious shocks of helots. It comprehended the protection of property as well as person. Property was the means to happiness, and in a way so self-evident that if the one was mentioned, the other was implied. The conception was broad: Lockeian in its feeling for persons and their self-extension through the holding of property; mercantilistic in its permitting the acquisition as well as the holding and protecting of wealth. If land is the backbone of wealth, ships and sea trade are its sinews in this age. Not so for manufactures. "Manufactures are founded in poverty," thundered Ben Franklin. "It is the multitude of poor without land in a country, and who must work for others at low wages or starve, that enables undertakers to carry on a manufacture."

With land or ships and land one had property, then, by which to pursue happiness. Why the repeating of "pursuing" in these eighteenth-century documents? It was meant to convey, I believe, that each person should seek after happiness as he pleased. Property opened up many ways to happiness. Liberty allowed him to follow any one of them he chose. Happiness in an ecstatic sense was not thought humanly possible. Running through the Revolutionary generation was a Christian and Stoic resignation to life's ordeals. What men could arrive at was contentment or a kind of bliss or gladness.

One can quarrel with the details of the analysis here briefly presented. Life, for instance, can be considered also a means to happiness, and liberty can, too. Or property can be considered an enjoyment in itself, not a means to the pursuit of happiness. One can rearrange the elements, but the main interpretation remains unaltered. Though the paths of a Jefferson and a Washington and, to take an earlier example, a William Byrd, differed, there was a meeting ground under them, large and solid as a public square. We can find where the pursuit of happiness led them.

The Founding Fathers had their ideal of the good life. It embraced a creator and the belief that life here on earth is not the first nor last; it held that full happiness is for the hereafter, yet man can pursue and find a measure of joy on this earth, too, if he has a small estate, unharassed by tax collectors, on which to enjoy good friends and good wine, a choice library, tranquillity, and the contemplation of the cosmos, the world and its affairs. To be free of necessity and therefore free to do whatever one wants to for itself alone — this to them was the pursuit of happiness. In this they could not have been more classical.

One can object that times have changed, that the kind of agrarian republic the Founders had in mind no longer is possible, that you can't turn the clock back. We shall happen on this last point again, and may come to the conclusion, happy or unhappy as the case may be, that the clock can go counterclockwise. Moreover it can go backward without pointing necessarily to a rural life. In the Founding Fathers we have an example of men who went far back for their inspiration and came forth with the most original thinking the country has ever seen. They didn't go back to the Pilgrims and Puritans who were supposed to have brought liberty with them in their flight. Nor did they embrace the ideas of Whiggism, much less the notion that Teutonic people carried in bags the seeds of democratic institutions which they planted wherever they went, nor did they exaggerate in history the war of the haves versus the have-nots. "A Library, a Garden, a Grove, and a Purling Stream are the Innocent Scenes that divert our Leisure," wrote William Byrd from the banks of the James to a London friend. His library contained 3,500 volumes. "Playing the fool with Mandy" or someone else also diverted him at times. Whether the seventeenth- or eighteenth-century American had his little estate at Monticello or on the banks of the James or Hudson, it was in fact not far from Rome. Horace was his model, Horace who advised leaving clients waiting in the anteroom while you slip out the back door to a comfortable little villa in a little field with a handful of tenant farmers, a view, an ever-bubbling brook, a mild climate, a garden, and a vineyard producing not a Burgundy perhaps, but an uncut wine fused with bright sun. Here among his friends the gods descended for supper.

James Bryce was right in saying that the Founding Fathers had gone back 2,000 years for the source of their ideas. Jefferson had said in 1825 that the Declaration of Independence "was intended to be an expression of the American mind." Intended to be, yes, and American mind, yes, but an American of those times, not these. By today's notions, American Revolutionary leaders were un-American. They were Romans, with a dash of Christianity and the Enlightenment. But they were modern, and no one denies their political sagacity.

The Romans rarely lost sight of the benefits that leisure and contemplation might bring the state. Partly as a result they fell easily into the idea, as we saw in Chapter II, that leisure is a well-deserved rest from political and military activities. The *otium* comes after the *negotium*. This the Romans thought highly of in the form also of retiring from an active life. The idea was that the old retire to rusticate, not to contemplate. Putting the *otium* after the *negotium* is reversing the etymological sequence. Men like Washington, Jefferson, George Mason, and John Adams were more like the Greeks in holding that happiness lay in tranquillity, good company, and cultivating the mind, and not in political affairs. Jefferson would be so disturbed at having to leave Monticello for public matters that his enemies thought he was putting on an act. But there on his land he had "the blessing of being free to say and do what I please." James Otis held that the purpose of the state is to provide for the "security, the quiet, and happy enjoyment of life, liberty, and property." Washington, if we are to take his word, never saddled up to leave Mount Vernon without a sigh. In preference to political duties he would choose "the more rational amusement of cultivating the earth." Franklin in 1782 wrote wishing for leisure to study the works of nature. Adams, before the Revolution started, thought his public life was over and that he was about to be the happiest man in the world, only to find himself ten years later "without much improvement or a possibility of benefiting the world by my studies." Court life made no man happy, was his conclusion. To a man who wanted only to go to his little hut and fifty acres and live on potatoes and seaweed for the rest of his life, money (even though Congress had just reduced his salary) was not the primary consideration. Mason in his will told his sons to prefer the happiness of a private station to the troubles and vexations of public business.

All these men held an idea of political life that forced them, when the country required it, to leave their books, conversation, and music, to put on the toga or the sword. The difference between the Greek and Roman concept lies also in this: Cincinnatus returned not to his books but to his plow. The ideal of leisure that the great Americans held was closer to Plato and Aristotle.

The democrat might raise the objection, This is all very well for the few who possess or acquire property but what of the many more others? Where are their Vergilian bucolics? This question I shall return to in a later chapter. Suffice it now to say that when Locke speaks of "men" or "we," and the Declaration of Independence of "all men," and the Constitution of "We, the People," they do not necessarily intend the adult population or even all adult males. Neither the first nor the second group voted for the delegates to the Constitutional Convention. Nor does Locke have all adult males in mind when he writes that in a careful and constant pursuit of true and solid happiness lies the highest perfection of intellectual nature. The men referred to are those to whom what they say is self-evident, a small body of self-appointed citizens and delegates with the firm intention to write into existence their ideal of the good life. No doubt the gentry and merchants thought they left elbowroom enough for ambitious and talented spirits. Let them seek their happiness where they will was the eighteenth century's attitude. For us we seek and enjoy a life of leisure in which whatever we do is for its own sake.

The nineteenth century was to raise the hue and cry to define

men more precisely than with the vagueness that meant gentlemen. Once the revolutionary generation passes on, clouds of
bewilderment swirl around the pursuit of happiness. Since the
phrase occurs in so many historic documents, the courts are soon
hard put to cut a clean swath. To go into all the variants, or
simply all the main lines of argument pro and con, that the
courts took from the pursuit of happiness would take a full tome,
but the trend is clear enough to be stated briefly. In a first step,
as we have seen, property provides the means through which one
can find one's happiness; next, property and work both are necessary for happiness, and then through work alone can happiness
be found.

The last few decades of the nineteenth century speeded up the
process of decision. Manufacturers, so hated and feared by
Franklin and the others, were having their day in court. During
the Slaughterhouse cases the brief for the plaintiffs held that it
was impossible to sustain life, enjoy liberty, or pursue happiness
if denied the right to work. In the last of the three famous cases
(1869, 1872, 1883) concurring opinion defined the right of men
to pursue happiness, "by which is meant the right to pursue any
lawful business or vocation." Already in the second case by dis-
sent Justice Field, leading up to this opinion, had proclaimed a
new "right of free labor, one of the most sacred and imprescriptible rights of man." Neither Mason nor Jefferson would have
used the word "imprescriptible." Nor would they have admitted
the right of the freedom of labor as "perhaps the most sacred of
all those that are guaranteed by the national and state constitutions." Neither could they have written the opinion that appeared a century after which slights the comparative few "possessed of such means that they will not need to labor." It is not
creditable "for these favored ones, while young and strong, to
idle away their time and live as drones upon the world." The
opinion then lifts the curtain on the teeming millions that the
Founders never saw, and asks "how are the great masses of the
people to acquire property, pursue happiness, and enjoy life and
liberty unless they are permitted to engage in the ordinary

avocations?" Only a student of constitutional law could tell from these few sentences that such reasoning was often used to defend manufacturing interests. The emphasis today has veered much nearer the verbal sense of the opinions; the previous language simply made easier the later passage to the working man.

In Europe a related though not identical development took place. The attitude of the commercial classes had been that those who don't do anything should be put in a workhouse and made to work. This position goes back far enough to be tangled with the early Protestant view of the idle and the paupers. In the French Revolution of 1848, however, it came forth in a different vest, the one we have seen appear later in the United States — the right to work. In a way the change was understandable: if not working is abominable, then men should be protected from the possibility of such indignity; they have a right to work. The Socialists of 1848 demanded and obtained the establishment of national workshops (*Ateliers nationaux*). Thus, what began as the poor man's gaol ended up as the poor man's goal. Now whether a man worked or could not find work or did not want work, he had the same bright prospects — work or the workhouse.

For us the import is this. Only through work, a new fundamental right, can men (all adult males and some females) pursue happiness. The original idea was the reverse: only through not having to work can men pursue happiness. Not surprising, then, that those idlers and drones who lived by this last notion, the gentry who wrote or approved the Virginia Bill of Rights and the Declaration of Independence, never did an honest day's work in their lives.

LIBERALS AND LEVELERS

In the nineteenth century the most influential philosopher of democracy was John Stuart Mill. At the time he was writing American courts were going to Adam Smith, a Scottish philosopher, to find weight for their position that the manufacturer's property is held by a sacred right and that the right of all men to work for the manufacturer is inviolable too. The unions were not to prevent them, is the lesson the courts drew from Book One, Chapter Ten, of *The Wealth of Nations*. The let-alone attitude toward free time which we have seen both business and labor express descends from Smith. His phrase about the trader's activities being led by an invisible hand to promote the common good is often used to refer to the doctrine whereby if you let individuals alone, and if they all seek merely their own advantage, that advantage necessarily will be the one most beneficial to society. The elaboration of this idea in classical economics is well known; its influence in putting taste and culture on the market was mentioned earlier and will be taken up again in a later chapter. Mill was less interested in working out an economic theory. He set out to examine liberty and representative government.

Like Smith, Mill was not an American, hence he cannot be considered the possible bearer of an American tradition. Instead he should be considered as one who might conceivably have developed an ideal of leisure in democracy for the contemporary world. One of Mill's chief worries was the ever-growing pressure that government, industry, and public opinion put on the individual to conform to their requirements. This, the third quarter of the nineteenth century, was a great period in English trade and industry. It must have seemed that machines were here to stay. Mill must have thought there was little to do to liven the deadening routine of factory work, but indirectly one could do a lot. When men were not working they could devote their free time to politics. There they would learn about cooperation, they would sharpen their wits in discussion and begin to feel a sense of local and national responsibility. If men voted or acted as jurymen, or took a local office, their new contacts would stir their intelligence and reawaken their morality. Beyond politics there was the chance of sharing in voluntary associations. For confining oneself entirely to politics and government would lead to too much uniformity; governments everywhere tend to be alike and shun the experiments that individuals and voluntary associations often make. Participating in local committees, industrial and philanthropic institutions, would take men out of the narrow circle of person and family.

To keep men toward these worthy objectives the first step was enlarging the suffrage. This would bring men around to voting, give them a stake and, hence, an interest in politics; after interest would come participation, which in itself was a form of educating the citizen. At present, men's work was a routine, a satisfaction of daily wants, not a labor of love. Neither the product nor the process of their work life lifted their minds above ordinary beings, stimulated them to reach for books, brought them in the circle of persons of culture. Just giving a man something to do for the public would supply almost all his present deficiencies. "The proofs of this," Mill wrote, "are apparent in every page of our great historian of Greece." His model is Athens. Men's leisure should be dedicated to the *polis*. Participating in politics, Mill pointed out, "raised the intellectual standard of an average Athenian citizen far beyond anything of which there is yet an example in any other mass of men, ancient or modern."

But what if the mass of men you have to work with are too ignorant for an elementary part in politics? They will not be able to educate themselves by participating in public affairs. The government then should educate them. Justice demands this. If people to have the vote should be able to read and write, they should receive an education gratuitously, or at a cost the poorest can afford. Our obligatory and free public schools and our greatly enlarged suffrage reflect these ideas of Mill. So do the state's educational efforts embodied in the Government Printing Office, the Federal Communications Commission, the Office of Education and national museums. In Greece there were always schools. Athenian education went far beyond the ABC's.

English education was to be reading, writing, and, Mill prudently adds, simple arithmetic. He would like to add other things like geography and history but foresees too many problems. Enough for him if a man can copy a sentence from an English book and multiply by three.

Today's notions might classify Mill as a liberal rather than a democrat. In his system those who legislate taxes should be elected only by those who pay taxes. He recognizes a class of betters much as did the Founders, who talked of the *aristoi,* those with virtue and talent. "I agree with you that there is a natural aristocracy among men," wrote Jefferson to John Adams in 1813. "The natural aristocracy I consider as the most precious gift of nature, for the instruction, the trusts, and government of society." Mill counts on men of this stamp to take the first steps by enlarging the suffrage and providing simple education. Indeed the first move would have to come from them; how could it come from ignorant workers? He also counts on their staying in power or on others of their caliber.

If Mill does not seem much interested in elaborating a common curriculum, it may have been because he distrusted public education, which he believed to be a device for casting people in one mold, exactly alike. His conception of the voter's function too was not so much intellectual as moral or patriotic. The citizen in politics could have his outlook enlarged, see the relation of things, feel a national responsibility, a strong sense of community. Even if the voter chooses the wrong candidate or issue, he still profits in these ways. He needn't be an expert; he can decide on general principles, complain with urgency whenever he is hurt by legislation. This might be called the shoe-pinch doctrine in democracy. Aristotle made use of the argument too. It isn't the shoemaker (the expert) but rather the wearer (the ordinary citizen) who knows whether the shoe pinches. In Mill's scheme of things there still was to be a class of shoemakers who had the idea in their heads and hands of what constitutes a fine shoe. The shod had only to vote for the cobbler of their choice.

Once the citizens took a more active role in politics, once they had the liberty to vote and speak and be educated, what then? How does this liberty lead to the good life? Liberty for Mill was doing as one pleased, a phrase that seems related to the idea of leisure. And to have as many choices as possible is a good thing because it prevents the routine of work from turning one stale. At the mention of work, though, the resemblance to leisure evaporates. You can only be partially free if you are not free of necessity. The working classes whose heads Mill wished to lift couldn't lift them while they were tending a loom, driving a quill, or selling goods over a counter. Mill did not expect them to give up their job. It was a necessity. They weren't free of it. Mill's thought must have been that if people are caught in one place and can't be freed, perhaps they can be freed in another place — precisely the idea that lies behind calling time off the job "free." A limited notion of freedom, of course. How can you be free to do as you wish if you have to work all day? How will your free time be free if you have to be ready to go back to work on the dot, and if your free time is clocked too, and if in it you are reacting to your work — blowing off steam, making a whole article in your basement workshop, wearily watching TV. Work is still working on you. Your free time is two things: what your work permits and what your reaction to work dictates. The first is a licensed time; the second may be a licentious time; the third is leisure, conspicuous by its absence.

The Greek idea of leisure encouraged participating in politics, but not so much for the benefit of the participants as for that of the state. Participation would be beneficial because the citizens had leisure to think about politics, not merely to be busy in politics. Mill gets this idea twisted. His citizen, it seems, spends free time exclusively in community activities. He once mentions other kinds, to argue that Sabbatarian legislation is a restriction on liberty. A person ought to use his leisure as he sees fit, Mill holds, even on Sunday. While the amusement of some involves work for others, still the pleasure and useful recreation of many is worth the labor of a few.

Amusements on Sunday are all right, then, on this line of reasoning. Otherwise Mill seems to have a puritanical devotion to good works in politics and in the community as the way of spending free time. The Greeks were more liberal, bringing in speculation, music, wining and dining, friends and poetry. Mill's liberty also is highly political. He said in his essay on it that he did not mean liberty of the will, that he wished rather to treat of civil or social liberty. Essentially he wrote about freedom from the state's interference, from work's restriction of outlook, and from public opinion's busybodiness — all in order that a man could make free choices. He admits, however, that, except in monasteries, nowhere is it forbidden to choose freely among cards or chess or rowing or study or music or sports. The importance of this nonpolitical area of life escapes him; he does not elaborate except to explain — again with an insight that should have brought him up short — that such free choice exists because those who like or dislike one or another of these things are too numerous ever to be put down.

Neither of Mill's ideas — how to spend off-work time and what liberty is — fits the conception of leisure. Both have been excessively politicized. The effects of this narrow political construction I shall return to in the last two chapters. Mill suffered from it also in his view of the way persons achieved a sense of community. What of the force of custom and tradition in making a man aware of the community's views and existence? What of the public opinion whose quirks he so passionately and rightly opposed? Yet is it not a force for community, assuring those who follow it of their belonging together and threatening others with alienation? Work itself, acclaimed as it was then, and is now, as a necessity and a boon for the nation — does it not give a sense of purpose, both local and national, to those who work, and exclude from it those who do not? Voting, on the contrary, does not give enough of this sense. It is too numerical, each voter's vote makes too small a ratio to count. If he can be made to believe by 40,000 drums a-thumping that his vote is the one that counts, then perhaps he will feel the mood of community. The much-lamented apathy of the citizen in modern democracy seems to say that he is difficult to convince. The people neither in England nor the United States have depended for their sense of participation on the voting process or the machinery of campaigns and elections.

In Mill's day there were educated men who believed that the working class had become separated from the national community, and, by a dismal factory life, had been put in a bleak world without sky or horizon. No doubt while the migration from village to cities was going on, and for some time afterward, there was danger that vast bodies of persons were becoming a mass, a people without roots, Englishmen who had no feeling for England. Whether or not the danger lasted until Mill's time, the way of averting it he proposed was too much an affair of formal politics. The Crown symbolized the Empire; Parliament's fame reached the humblest hamlet; thought of the Navy quickened countless pulses; the job reached more persons across the country than could fill posts in government offices and national political organizations; and in his free time a game of darts and a pint in the pub brought a man to the bosom of the local community.

Mill, I should point out, must have banked greatly on the political prudence of the better elements, as well as, in the matter of free time, on their standards of taste. These elements harbored a leisure class. Many of them led a leisurely life. Unfortunately Mill worried too little whether the electoral machinery he was advocating might be ill-contrived to keep the higher classes in power. He himself unwittingly added to their difficulties. The equality he fervently espoused in the suffrage outrode the liberty he demanded from concentrated power. The government, which the better elements made up, took the first step to promote the virtue and intelligence of the people, as Mill would have it. Perhaps the government did it not on Mill's voice alone but for other voices or reasons, some less worthy. The passion in Mill's voice, though, gave it distance.

The government having taken the first step, what was the next and the next? Suppose the people are not content merely to judge whether the shoe pinches, or, if it fits, are not content to wear it? If an educated electorate elects a government which then grants the suffrage without discrimination, the question obviously becomes, Will an ignorant electorate elect their betters? Mill did not see the danger that his higher classes might not be able to resist the onslaught. His conception was that of a small body with leisure guiding a large body of workers. To what? Evidently to the level of political education, as he says, of every citizen of Athens. Now, Mill knew that besides the citizens there was a large body of slaves in Athens. Did he really hope ever to bring workers up to the level of the Athenians, or was he seeking some basis by which he could say in his heart that English workers — if they became voters — could never be called slaves?

Mill's position can be called an outlived version of democratic philosophy. The present doctrine in the United States, which can be called radical democracy, is older than Mill's but has lasted longer. England of the eighteenth century was close to her leading men of the nineteenth century; so was the sixteenth century, and the century of Cicero's Rome. America of the nineteenth century repudiated the eighteenth century. Discarded with it (for it was the repository of history) were the Renaissance and ancient times.

The man who for a time managed to straddle the eighteenth and nineteenth centuries was James Fenimore Cooper. His series of brief essays called *The American Democrat,* published in 1838, came shortly after a seven-year stay abroad, shortly, too, after the defeat of the last of the Federalists, John Quincy Adams, by Andrew Jackson. The book's attempt at balance — Cooper first wrote three chapters on the advantages of monarchy, aristocracy, and democracy, and then three others on their disadvantages — reflects the difficulties the author found himself in. Up to this moment there were still men of "great leisure and large fortunes, who had imparted to their children what they had received from their fathers," but the republic of Jefferson was fast becoming the democracy of Jackson. One sentence best sums up Cooper's stand. "He is the purest democrat who best maintains his rights, and no rights can be dearer to a man of cultivation than exemptions from unreasonable invasions on his time by the coarse-minded and ignorant."

Cooper is one of the clearest and perhaps one of the last political thinkers to insist that a country's form of government affects its culture. His dividing of governments follows the classic Aristotelian threefold distinction, and he has good as well as evil to say of all three forms. He hopes for American democracy that its foundation may be so broad it will sustain a high superstructure. But the tendency of democracies is in all things to mediocrity, since the taste, knowledge, and principles of the majority compose the court. While the tendency lifts the lowest to mediocrity, it makes it difficult to find a high standard. In literature, architecture, and the arts, all in America gravitate toward the core of mediocrity, investing it with a value found nowhere else. Of aristocracy he says that the system makes its leaders bold, independent, and manly, and causes them to distinguish themselves from the mass. In an age as advanced as his, he says, the leisure of the higher classes enables them to cultivate their minds and improve their tastes. Aristocracies in particular, therefore, favor knowledge and the arts.

Jacksonian democracy began with assertions about the capacities of man in respect to political office: one man is as good as another. Governing holds no mysteries, requires no special talent. Common sense and integrity are all that is needed. Rotation of office is a healthy thing. The next step in the doctrine could well have led to electing officials from among the population by lot. Instead, over the span of a century, it took the direction of anti-intellectualism and know-nothingism, both of which have been forces so strong as to stifle men of thought and discernment, and to deprive the country of their help. John Stuart Mill in an attack on America, extraordinary and unusually caustic for him, opposed the idea that ignorance is as much entitled to political power as knowledge. Its terms recall Cooper. It is for the citizen's own good, Mill insisted, that he should understand that the better and wiser should have more influence than the others. This truth should be professed by the government and made part of national institutions, since they make a deep impression on national character. American institutions have forcibly imprinted on the American mind a false creed that any one man (with a white skin) is as good as any other. This belief, which the institutions of the United States mischievously sanction, he goes on, is as harmful to moral and intellectual excellence as any government can produce.

Having dominated politics and sterilized intellectual life for a century, the doctrine took a new turn and branched into the area of consumption where the plenitude of products put out by industry had commercialized the pursuit of happiness. In Jacksonianism, the common judgment of the people in taste, politics, and religion was the highest authority on earth. Businessmen and advertisers, with the help of economists, developed their own version of radical democracy. One man's dollar is as good as the next man's. Each dollar spent is a vote cast by the buyer for a particular kind of product. The best sellers are those the people want. Whatever the people want is good, and they should have it.

The doctrine of one-dollar-one-vote has grown out to block the populist doctrine of one-man-one-vote. The idea that government should tell people how to spend their money or their free time meets with great resistance, except in times of national crisis. Freedom of the individual is proclaimed, and America hailed as the freest country in the world. Business and advertising sponsorship pours into any ideological statement that proclaims freedom, their sense being mainly freedom to let their view of events dominate the organs of publicity. The government, in democratic theory supposed to be the only true expression of the people, becomes an enemy of the people, ever encroaching on its liberty. Contrast this with Adam Smith's freedom of the market, where the penny counts and works out fairly and squarely for everybody. Unlike politics, where the vote is influenced by rabble-rousing vote-getters, in the market there is true equality: one dollar — one vote.

The possibility that advertising shapes choice much as a political campaign does (indeed each has taken pages from the other), that in back of both these shapers-of-choice stand those with money to spend on them, that people, though no one puts handcuffs on them, can thus be told how to spend their time and money — this view of things gets a small spread. It isn't the whole story by any means.

There are many influences on choice, the number depending on how minutely one wishes to delve into human motives. Chapter VI discussed some of them at length; Chapter IX will further discuss some of the more disconcerting ones. But to say that the people are in a free market today, and so can choose however they want to spend their time and money, is true only in an ultimate sense — that one is free to do anything, being blessed or cursed by God with free will.

Evidently, freedom and equality are fine for what the people may want to vote for in politics or to buy for their free time. They are not fine in industry, however, where thorough democrats have sometimes proposed to act out the dogma that one man is as good as another by giving each worker, employer, and manager — that is, each man in it — one vote apiece as the way to govern the factory or office. The worlds of industry and government have become too technical for the ordinary man, it seems. Bureaucracy, in the guise of the civil service and management, bears the colors of the day. In American politics the rotation-in-office idea has wound down to a shaky stop. In American business it never got a proper start, except in selling and advertising, where it applies to new and newer commodities, and still spins around briskly.

We are not here concerned with when it is that government lives in tension with business, and whether the tension is good or bad for the body politic. Good or bad, eye-to-eye or at each other's throats, neither one has faced the question of leisure. What they know is solely the problem, or, in the case of the advertiser, the opportunity, of free time. Into free time both will admit activities that by distraction or diversion restore one for work on the morrow. And both disapprove of any that prevent one from appearing on the morrow. Work is highly regarded by both. They join hands in approving of activities in childhood, youth, and adulthood that prepare for future tasks. Games and sports like baseball and football develop the spirit of teamwork as in the factory or army squad; hunting and boxing encourage a competitive or martial air. Patriotism and work, war and fighting, they both see as parts of the probable future. They approve of preserving the skills that result from hobbies. They maintain that no one class should serve as the model for the people's free time and that taste is subjective and relative, one man and his taste is as good as any other. So, add 'em up, boys.

I said earlier that an ideal affects conduct. What we have just passed in review is not an ideal of leisure. Such an ideal no longer exists in the United States. The search for it in this chapter has taken us up many paths in vain. The commercial spirit, in business and government both, has no interest that any such ideal, without spending attached to it, should come to prevail. Instead, an ideal of free time, or of the good life, has taken the field. The good life consists in the people's enjoyment of whatever industry produces, advertisers sell, and government orders. This seems to be what we have, then. Within it, what does the future hold in store?

Time Free of
Machines

F<small>LAUBERT</small> never finished writing *Bouvard et Pécuchet*. But he
did leave an outline of how he intended to end the book. At one
point in it Bouvard and Pécuchet take turns predicting the future of humanity. The latter sees modern man threatened and
turned into a machine; he sees humanity ending up in anarchy,
the impossibility of peace, and everywhere barbarism through
the excesses of individualism and the delirium of science. Ideals,
religion, and morals will disappear. America will have conquered the earth. The future of letters will be killed by a universal vulgarization. Everything will be turned into a vast carnival of workers. Bouvard sees things in a rosier light. Modern man
progresses. Europe will be regenerated by Asia. By historical
law, civilization must pass from the Orient to the Occident,
China will play an important part and the two worlds will finally
be fused. Future inventions will be marvelous, industry will create a literature, Paris will be transformed into a winter garden
with baskets of fruit along the boulevard, the Seine will be fil-
tered and warm, the façades of houses illuminated, their lights
lighting the streets. As need disappears, so will evil; philosophy
will be a religion, all peoples will join in communion and public

festivals. Man will go to the stars, and when the earth is old, humanity will thin itself out by heading for the planets.

As a prophet neither one did badly. To score higher than they did is not easy. Though we look but ten or twenty years ahead, or to the end of the century, we still cannot see clear. War and total destruction may come; the military situation may be eased up or stretched even tauter. Population may increase, but in this short span not yet so much as to put its full geometric weight on our back. These two gigantic problems have been affecting us for a number of years and their influence will continue. If war comes, we shall be either dead or living in a hell underground or underwater; if it does not, perhaps we shall proceed more or less as we are now. Only the last possibility is germane to the present discussion. As for population, its continued growth will put greater pressure on space. Living space has been diminishing since the enclosure movement in England; these next twenty or forty years will not reverse the trend begun then.

To turn to a brighter side, books and magazines bubble with the good life of the future, with stories and articles about helicopters, video tapes, automated highways, gas-turbined automobiles, electronic cookers and purifiers, new foods packaged with heating and cooling units to cook or chill right in the package, new materials, fabrics, and substances, further mechanizing of the house, space flights, ultrasonic appliances. Will these things change the way people spend their time? Undoubtedly. Riding in a helicopter is different from riding in a car. Traveling toward outer space is different from brushing across the face of the earth. When imaginative advertisers get thinking about "the new leisure" they dream of home workshop equipment, do-it-yourself kits on a complicated scale, and home entertainment media through which by turning a dial the four walls (unless the house is a curved plastic structure) will come alive with the images and sounds of things going on all over the world. (Images and sounds selected by someone else's eyes and ears, of course. The armchair wanderer can go only as far as the notches on his dial.) New extensions of installment buying will come into play so that items like TV sets or washing machines will be rented. Obsolescence planned and unplanned will be such that clothes and houseware will be disposable. Into the incinerator with them! A shower stall will be bought to be discarded when outmoded. Naturally, you will have the money to buy another.

There will be changes in the way men work too, which in turn will affect their recreation. Machines have already done away with much of the need for muscle power in work. In the near future it will be even truer than now that to exercise one will have to engage in a sport. It's a rare bird today whose job flexes his wings. Men in the United States do very little lifting and moving. In their work they start and stop things, set, assemble, and repair them. More automatic machinery will take over much of the starting and stopping, and then the setting and assembling operations. The repairing of machines, along with the inventing and designing, will remain as human tasks. Work will thus become less muscular and more sedentary than before. The result may be an even greater seeking of active sports by young workers; the further slackening of muscle tone in older workers may make them more content to sit at home, reposing on the sturdy muscles that serve so well at work. Those same muscles may well be the last to be atrophied, except perhaps those involved in eye and finger movement. Learning to watch processes and being ready to press buttons, workers find, are the stresses of their new jobs on what they call "the automatics." The tender of the automatics may in time have the dull, nerve-racking life of the croupier in the casino. Emaciated, he will watch with alert and lifeless eyes.

The increase in paper shuffling and reading work too will call for greater eye and digital dexterity. In spite of mechanical aids, office personnel seems likely to increase. Since much more work will be done on costly machines, more office workers will be asked to take a second shift. If the practice of renting such machines at high prices continues, many employees will have to take their free time at odd hours. Recreation and amusement industries too will have to add a second shift. These few examples of future changes in work merely serve to illustrate the possible changes in recreation they may bring about.

It is easy to exaggerate their importance. To take the helicopter as an example, today it can skim over the ugly, choked traffic of cities, soar above the smoke and blight, to drop on isolated beaches or to picnic on secluded hillsides. When and if the helicopter develops a mass market, it will itself blacken the sky, litter the clouds, pollute the air, and choke on its own traffic. The secluded spots will be transformed into heliports lined with row upon row of parked 'copters and other flying machines. The difficulty — one that adds to the hazards of prophesying mentioned earlier — is that a given change often sets off a series of steps that turn back to cancel out the benefit of the change, in this case reducing free time gained to what it was or even less. (We shall return to this difficulty later for its theoretical implications.)

Or one may look on the prospect of low-priced video tapes as interesting. Each person will be able to have a library of them as he now has of books. If he feels in the mood to enjoy a favorite play instead of reading a book, he need only put the video tape on his machine. Carrying on this analogy between books and moving pictures (there *are* real points of difference), just as today a few people go to the good films and plays while many others absorb the bad ones, so tomorrow a few will have excellent tape libraries, but the majority will have large miscellaneous collections of whodunits, musicals, soap operas, westerns, and the like, which will cost less because they have a wider market. The kinds of activities may change greatly; the standards guiding them may change not at all.

Yet many persons today feel we stand on the threshold of a new age of leisure. Two centuries ago Benjamin Franklin thought so too, as we have seen, but he did not go so far as to believe that the country was entering upon an age unparalleled in history, an epoch when instead of being limited to kings, aristocrats, patrons, captains of industry, and the rich, leisure was to be available to everyone, rich and poor alike, and in greater measure than these nobles and condottieri had ever dreamed of. Long before Franklin's time, Aristotle had dreamt a similar dream; centuries after his death the refrain reappears in the poet Antiparos in praise of a new water mill. Sleep peacefully, he advises the millers; water nymphs will do the work of slaves and turn the heavy stone. "Let us live the life of our fathers, and rejoice in idleness over the gifts that the goddess grants us." In fact, in every half-century from the time of the industrial revolution on, we have men of wisdom and vision predicting more time to come. One of the things that bids us be cautious about accepting glowing prophecies for the future of free time is that up to now they have all been wrong about it. Why were they wrong? They all reflected the same dream (more free time) but also, giving rise to the dream there was a common stimulus — the machine.

Now, one is on surer ground when talking about the future of the machine than about the future of free time. The more serious books that try to peer into the future cannot avoid the two great threats of war and population. Usually they make population a bridge to the discussion of the past and future progress of medicine. They also typically contain sections on food, energy, and things or materials. There are problems in each of these last areas when considered on a global and century-long scale. In the near future, given no great change in international standing, the United States is not likely to lack either abundance or innovation in any of the three. The books that look ahead also include, usually, in their section on things or materials, or in a special chapter or in one devoted to the progress of science, a discussion of technology. In chorus they predict that technology will remain, will progress, will spread over much of the rest of the world.

A MECHANIZED TOMORROW

If there is to be food for all peoples, it depends on greater industrialization. If industry is to increase, it depends on sources of energy for whose greater exploitation new machines will be developed and built. If different machines are built for energy extraction, for food production, for armaments, and for the many commodities that Americans have grown accustomed to wanting, then more raw materials, mineral and organic, will be thrown into the maw of these machines. The raw materials may eventually be nothing else than sea water, air, rock, and sunlight. The sea industries may be the largest of all. The factories of the future may be built of lighter, more flexible materials looking in clusters like a fairyland of colored bubbles. The commodities advertisers look forward to — the ultrasonic appliances, electronic cookers and purifiers, the windows that open and close automatically when it rains or gets cold — they may be thought up in someone's head and set down on someone's drawing board but when they reach the buyer they are already machine-produced. A discovery in a chemical laboratory will bring a new processed or packaged food or pill, a contraceptive or a fertilizer, but it won't appear on the market until it can be turned out by the hundreds of thousands of pieces or pounds or tons.

Sooner or later these farseeing books, the serious and not-so-serious alike, usually before or after or in some way causally linked to the discussion of technology, predict a new wide-open field to come for leisure. Within the unbreathing world of machines, great change seems in the offing. The spread of the technological complex over the world is a change already mentioned. The one that excites more interest is the prospect of great increases in the development and use of automatic production and control machinery. The possibility leads many persons to be as sanguine about the future of automation as earlier prophets were about the future of the machine. The phrasing is changed by one line: there will be more and more time for more and more people than ever before in history . . . with the arrival of large-scale automation. The unions will see to it that work is distributed evenly so that there will be no unemployment, the week will be cut down to two working days (or to two working hours), and the rest of our time will be spent however we want to. In the future even more than in the past, the increased productivity of these machines will be deliberately taken and enjoyed as additional leisure. There will be more holidays. Vacations will be longer. Weekends too. There will be a mid-week as well. People will enter the labor force later and exit earlier, and in the middle will take years off to improve their education. None of these books speak much of art, philosophy, and music except to say how much leisure we shall have and how much art, philosophy, and music it will bring us. It is clear that time and the machine are linked: the machine saves time, gives us time.

Chapter VI described briefly how advertising made use of the idea that machines, in factory and home, saved precious time. That same chapter discussed many reasons why the machine has not lived up to expectations. It took away space from men who then needed back the things they had got from space. So they want for things — space for recreation, time to make up the distance they lost, and money to buy these two as well as the signs of a place in the world that their position in space formerly gave them. We saw that the grouping of machines leads to factory complexes, so the journey to work lengthens and mobility of labor increases; that work becomes physically easier, of a kind that women can do, so that often both husband and wife can work. Theoretically there is little to stop a man today from cutting down on his working time, but he goes on working. He hogs overtime, he moonlights, he lets his wife go to work — because they "need things." The kind of things they need are things that money can buy.

So rolls the headlong circle of wanting things that cost money that costs work that costs time.

None of this was obvious to those who thought, and still do think, of the machine not only as a labor-saver but as a timesaver too. Least of all did they see the transformation that would be brought about by one fact alone — that machines require synchronization. Its importance is such that it affects all future prophecies of leisure based on the machine.

The early large factory owners saw clearly enough that their machines required synchronization, but as often happens when a society absorbs a change, later generations lose sight of the reasons for it, and we today have to dig back into those times to reconstruct what has happened to us.

Previous ages, commercial ones too, highly civilized ones, and even warlike ones, got along with the hourglass, the sundial, the water clock, or the timing candle or lamp. There was no fixed moment to attach the hourglass's hours to, and none either for the remaining piece of candle or oil in the lamp; on cold nights the water clock froze, and a rainy day liquidated all sundials. Little did it matter. The water and sun clocks of ancient Egypt were used by the temple priests, not by the soldier or civilian, who relied on the pangs of hunger and on the height of the sun to tell him what part of the day it was. The greatest precision in time the ordinary person in those ages could conceivably have needed was in boiling an egg *à la coque,* where no synchronizing of hourglasses was called for.

When Cellini was casting the *Perseus* he synchronized the action of his men to tools and materials directly. "Bring that thing over here! Take this thing over there!," and to spur them on would sometimes give them a boot in the pants. He gave the signals — auditory, visual, tactual — personally. The group was small, the work irregular. His problem was to get the men and materials assembled for the casting, and of course, as we saw earlier, to be there with them himself to call the shots. The earliest factories were run almost as personally as this. Excellent illustrations for the eighteenth century can be found in Diderot's *Encyclopédie.* Machines were small, requiring small numbers of hands, and at times, specially if the factory was powered by water, the workers would quit early in the day to go fishing. Sometimes the workshop would be open from 6:00 A.M. to 8:00 P.M., and within those hours the workers, usually on piece rates, could come and go when they liked. As machines got bigger and more costly, as the number of hands to each machine increased, as power requirements expanded, irregularity could not be tolerated.

Cellini didn't cast a *Perseus* every day. Most of the time his workshop was bent upon tasks on which an hour more or less did not count. A costly machine primed with steam can't wait an hour for the man who drank too much whisky the night before. And one day is much like the next: at 8:00 A.M. the machine is ready to go, every morning, even through the night, if possible. The synchronizing that went on in Cellini's shop was of man to man. The materials had to be ready and right, but each job required different materials, and there was no regularity in the work, so no flow of materials was possible. In the mechanized factory men are synchronized to machines, which in general have more regular habits than men. Materials too have to flow to feed the machines, and thus a synchronization of men, machines, and materials develops, more impersonal and complex than anything before.

THE STORY OF TIME PIECES

Most men today may not be aware that they are geared to machines — even while they are being awakened by the ringing of a bell and gulping down their coffee in a race with the clock. The clock, though, is a real machine, an automatic one, too. The monasteries did not invent the clock (rumor to the contrary), but they did discipline daily living within their walls to a routine of seven periods marked by bells. The thus-many-hours-for-sleep and thus-many-hours-for-prayer was one of the things Erasmus poked fun at. A routinized or ceremonial life for priests and kings and court too, as a matter of fact, appears in history at other times and places. The ancients, moreover, knew that time could be determined astronomically and did so determine it. But to ordinary people the day was divided into 12 hours from sunup to sundown — longer in summer, naturally, than in winter. Similarly, automatic machines had appeared long before among the Greeks and Moslems. The mechanical clock did not appear evidently until the thirteenth century. For a long time it made its way mostly to church towers and public buildings. In monasteries and churches it marked canonical hours or called the faithful to prayer. (*Clock* comes from an Italian word of Celtic origin, *clocca,* meaning bell tower; its historical relation to an auditory signal is significant.) Not until Cellini's time did it attain any reliability, and even then it had only an hour hand to worry about. The development and perfection of mechanical timepieces was carried on by groups of master artisans who were fascinated by this toy and in their fascination created a new metier — watchmaker.

In the beginning, the clock exerted a strange, almost morbid attraction as though it were ticking off life itself. Whereas the motto on a Roman solar quadrant might read *Lex mea sol,* many of the old public clocks in Europe carried sayings like *Mors certa, hora incerta* or *Toutes les heures vous blessent; la dernière vous tue.* But more and more they came to exercise the attraction of an ingenious mechanism. People felt as if they were carrying the brain of a genius in their pocket. Watches became the foibles of rich clients, kings and queens, and great ladies especially. Marie Antoinette received fifty-one watches as engagement gifts. The new watches, all of them encrusted with diamonds, pearls, gold, silver, enamel, and miniature portraits, were indeed remarkable. Centuries had been required to perfect them, but in each century master watchmakers created masterworks that inspired admiration and wonder. The clock, as the first fully automatic machine, remained the first in its perfection for so long because good artisans had spent so much effort and passion on it. It held up high its complicated meshing of gears as the exemplar for other machines.

Not until the nineteenth century did the clock begin to spread. The cheap watch appears in Switzerland in 1865 and in America a few years later, in 1880. Within eight years the Waterbury factory in the United States was producing and selling half a million clocks and watches a year. Switzerland alone by now has exported between twenty and twenty-five millions. Why didn't the clock remain a toy? Why didn't it delight or fascinate a few people, and stop right there, to suffer the fate of the ingenious toys invented by the ancient Greeks and Moslems? Why were the nineteenth and twentieth centuries its day of diffusion? People don't buy a thing just because it is cheap, and in any case watches, though mass-produced, were not *that* cheap. Evidently they were needed.

Though its original contribution as a model was great, the clock's main function became to give frequent signals, auditory and visual, to enable men to start or stop an activity together. Before the clock there was the bell tower which from far off could not only be heard but also be seen for orientation. Then there was, and still is in some places, the factory whistle. But both these devices were limited for work in the big, noisy cities. The clock, first placed in a tower and later hung up wherever work was to be done, provided the means whereby large-scale industry could coordinate the movements of men and materials to the regularity of machines. Over the span of these several centuries, the seventeenth to the nineteenth, a new conception of time developed and spread over the industrial world, going hand in hand with the modern idea of work.

Time today is valuable. The clock's presence everywhere, and its tie to the factory with its relatively unskilled work, soon gave rise to the idea that one was selling time as well as, or rather than, skill. The lightening of toil and simplifying of tastes brought about by machines gave a related impression: that one was selling time rather than labor. The "hourly rate" and the "piece rate" express these notions. So time begins to be money, and, like money, a valuable, tangible commodity, to be saved, spent, earned, and counted. Clock time first governs work time (one sees the same happening today in countries moving toward industrialization), while social life holds to the old pattern. Later the clock's hands sweep over life outside of work too. Chapter VI presented the case in England. Hardly do you find manufacturers fixing hours of work, than you see workers mobilizing for a shorter working week. Free time takes its bow, like work decked out in clock time.

To be bought and sold in this way, time had to be neutralized. Customary ways of spending days had to be deprived of significance so that one day was much like another, and time could thus be spent in one activity as well as another. Days, hours, and minutes become interchangeable like standard parts. It was helpful that in countries that were to become industrial, Protestantism refused to recognize the saints, thus taking away the 100 days assigned to their celebration. Before this, one could not work on such days. Essentially, as the French Revolution made clear, the process was one of secularizing the calendar. When the year has its religious and other celebrations, certain activities are to be done at certain times and in a certain order. They take up time, but no matter how much they take, they must be done. And they are not interchangeable. At a given time one goes to market or to church, to work, to bed, to festivities, to the tavern or back home. One cannot work at a time for feasting or dancing, for church or the siesta. Something remains of this time in the notion of excusable absence from work — if a close member of the family dies, if a new one is born, or perhaps if one gets married — but the time allowed is cut to the bone, leaving nothing like the fat festivities that once were the rule on such occasions. The payment nowadays of time and a half for overtime or double time on Sunday indicates that one is dealing with a kind of time that bears the imprint of an earlier day. In European languages generally one still does not speak of "spending" time but of "passing" it, a usage reminiscent, too, of an earlier epoch.

With time well secularized, the possibilities of choice seem to increase. One has a whole 24 hours a day and can fill them as one pleases. The lone obligation is to give the first and best part of the day to work. After that — freedom. In this way free time came to be called what it is. The calendar has been secularized, however, but not really neutralized. By and large, work takes first place in time, while other activities partake of work's time characteristics. In olden days what one had was "spare" time, not free time, time unexpectedly left over, as might happen if one got help from a neighbor or found working materials unusually pliable, or if things just went right. If this happened one could properly engage in a pastime, perhaps play cards. But unless circumstances were particularly difficult — a storm having wrecked part of the house or the like — one was not supposed to work in this time, was not to engage in what we would call productive activities. In rural parts of the world today, in Burma, for example, one can see the pattern. After a man's tasks for the day are finished, he is not supposed to be busy. He goes to sit and smoke, gossip and drink "rough tea," or he visits. In Greek villages they say about work done after dark, "The day takes a look at it and laughs."

In the cities of the industrial world, once his debt to work is paid, a man is said to be off duty. He can fill his time as he chooses. He has a decision to make, though: which alternatives to choose for each hour or half or quarter thereof: play, work, chores, moonlighting?

He does have some rules as to how that time should be spent. A man should first of all spend it on things that give visible evidence of doing something. He should be busy at something. In some parts of the world, sitting or standing still, whether thinking or not, is considered an activity. In the United States it is not. Secondly he should do things to better himself. "To better" usually means to do something that will improve his own or his property's position, appearance, or money-making qualities. One should keep one's house in good condition (keep up the property) and should also try to increase its value by improvements. One should not just read (an activity still somewhat suspect because the only moving organs involved are the eyes) but should shun trash for books that are instructive, informative, useful. In short, a man off work should (1) do something and (2) do something productive. An American could not have written the lines that follow, because only to him or to the egocentric species to which he belongs could time be so busy and dear.

> Don't waste precious time
> Now, tagging along with me . . .
> Little butterfly.

The Haiku is one of Issa's (1763–1827).

So, all told, time is not neutralized but commercialized, or, better, industrialized. Free time as we know it is a kind developed by the industrial world's clock time. Here again it is clear that recreation is best understood as an ally of work rather than as its opposite or as an activity independent in its own right. Recreational activities are bound on all sides by work time. The activities with which one fills free time cannot be such as to encroach on work time. The worker on the assembly line, if he had a bad night of it, because of drink or wild jazz or a drawn-out battle with his wife, nevertheless has to be at the plant on time. His alarm clock is not misnamed. It really is an alarm for a serious danger — being late to work. If he gets there on time, he may be able to arrange with co-workers, or even the foreman, to get someone to take his place for fifteen minutes of shut-eye in the corner of a little-used stockroom, but barring extraordinary traffic tie-ups or acts of God, should he appear late on more than two or three occasions, well spread out and for only a few minutes apiece, he can go draw his pay. It won't be long before he gets a pink slip.

Since clock time has precise units, it is measurable. Time-keepers measure the ins and outs of employees; they also measure the time that operations and the flow of materials take. There are always new processes being instituted in a large plant, and one has to know how much time they need. References to time in industrial areas are literal. "Be here in half an hour" means in 30 minutes. Precision inside the plant has its effect outside. "Come here this second," says an American mother to her child, using a word a Roman mother could not have, because the word for "second" was not in everyday use. The ancient Egyptians for common use had not even a minute of any measured duration, much less a second.

The American office schedule is tight and sacred, too. "I'll see you at 4:10, then," is a sentence that would have been comprehensible to no other civilization this earth has seen. Violators of the schedule are punished. If you are not on time for appointments you will come to be regarded as an irresponsible person. If a man is kept waiting in the outer office for ten or fifteen minutes, careful apologies are necessary. In some countries, in the Ottoman Empire tradition, a man can be kept waiting without offense for an hour or an hour and a half. Tacitus, in writing of the ancient Germans, said they never assembled at the stated time, but lost two or three days in convening. When they all thought fit they sat down. This still happens among some American Indians and among literate peoples, too. The social schedule follows suit. In Greek villages no time is set for dinner guests. You arrive and after a while dinner appears. Persons who are punctual are rarities, and sometimes dubbed "Englishmen." In parts of Latin America, if you are invited for dinner at 7:00 you can appear then, if you wish, but eat a snack first. Dinner may appear at ten or midnight. On the Continent still today, except for the clockmaking countries, if you arrive on time for social engagements, you're early. In the United States ten minutes late for a dinner begins to look serious.

The clock then with its precise units breaks the day into equal parts that by conscious decision are to be filled with worthy activities. A man may want to loaf his time away, yes, but loafing is wasted time, and time shouldn't be wasted. It is valuable and scarce. One has only 24 hours of it a day.

The scarcity of time may appear puzzling. One has always had 24 hours of it. They should not seem less now than before. Before, however, one did not have 24 hours. There was a sunrise

and a sunset, a noon or a hottest part, and there was night. Above
all one had a day, a day of a certain character according to the
calendar. Then that great space was partitioned into 1,440 tiny
cubicles. By our standards even those engineers, the ancient
Romans, had vague time notions. The Egyptians divided the
days and nights into 12 hours each (the Babylonians were the
first to do this) but paid little attention to the hour of any event.
One lady's baby was reported to be born in the fourth hour of
the night, but she was the wife of a priest. The night was a constant unit, no matter how light some of its twelve hours were in
summertime. A day of 24 hours or 1,440 minutes divided into 5-
or 10- or 20-minute groups survives in popular custom only if the
divisions prove useful. Today they apparently do, at least in the
cities. A dermatologist can schedule patients in his office at 10-
minute intervals. Many people in business and government schedule 10- or 15-minute, sometimes 5-minute, appointments. Trains
and planes go by a schedule in odd minutes — 7:08, 10:43. All appointments must be kept by continual reference to the inexorable clock. If you miss a bus or train, or only fail to make a stop
light when on a schedule, the result is fear and nervousness at being late, or the tension of not getting done all that you were supposed to. The cramming of hours and minutes takes place because of the belief that time's units are interchangeable and
commercially valuable, but it is the clock itself that permits the
constant checking and adjusting of one's actions.

Other commercial societies have had the feeling of urgency
and of many things to do, similar to ours, but ours can be more
tightly scheduled and made almost escapeproof by the ubiqui-
tous clock and the machines geared to it. We have here, it may
be, why our dreamers of free time foresaw the future badly and
why, with abundant free time to dispose of today, there is everywhere the tenseness of haste. The poet Ciro di Pers in the seventeenth century, when clocks first began to make headway, already saw that they make time scarce and life short:

Noble machine with toothed wheels
Lacerates the day and divides it in hours . . .
Speeds on the course of the fleeing century.
And to make it open up,
Knocks every hour at the tomb.

No other nation by now is as precise in its time sense nor so time-conscious as the United States. Americans generally are aware that time runs by steadily and is being used up evenly, minute after minute, hour after hour, day after day — inexorable, impersonal, universal time. In countries without dependence on the clock, there is largely the sense of passage of biological time. In the seasonal rhythm is an age-consciousness: one notices oneself passing through youth, prime, and age, all the stages that Horace and Shakespeare marked with appropriate lines. There is nothing very precise about the units — one season comes late, one day is long, another night is longer, the heart beats faster one morning and respiration slows down the next.

We have almost lost this rhythmical sense of time. We can hardly believe that some not-so-primitive tribes have no word at all for time, or that if a native of a remote rural area is asked how long it takes by foot, mule, or car to get to a certain place, he cannot say, though he can describe every yard in the road all the way to the destination. Can you make it by noon? He doesn't know. You certainly can make it by noon, you would think? Yes, he says, of course. Is it really possible to go that far by noon? Oh no, says he.

It is not unusual for people living without clocks not to know the day of the week except Sunday and even on Sunday not to know the hour of mass. Until the Gregorian reform of the calendar, toward the end of the sixteenth century, Europeans seem to have been little interested to remember just how old they were, if they had ever known in the first place. Modern biographers of that century probably know more about their subjects' chronological age than the subjects cared to know themselves. We can usually distinguish a 5-minute from a 10-minute wait, without the clock, because we have been trained to do so.

The synchronizing of activities by the clock begins early. The child sees his father arise by the clock, treat its facial expression with great respect, come home by it, eat and sleep by it, and catch or miss his entertainment — the movies, a TV show — by it. Also the child at home is explicitly taught time — it is one of the few subjects nowadays in which parents feel fully competent to instruct their children — by example, precept, and books, and taught also in the classroom, where experience is as sharp as at the factory. Alas for the tardy scholar who comes not at 10:00 o'clock or at noon but at 8:40 instead of 8:30.

Getting first-graders to be regular as clockwork, to use a favorite Victorian expression, is not the easiest job in the world. For children of ten or twelve to master the elements of the American time system takes attention from all sides. This done, there is thenceforth less of the feeling of imposition that people have for the clock when introduced to it only at a later age. Many of the latter learn to like to wear watches or have clocks as baroque ornaments for the house. Whether they are running or stopped makes little difference. They like them as a symbol of wealth and modernity, not as a despot to be obeyed.

CLOCKED FREEDOM

In England during the early days of industrialism, workers turned from the straitening embrace of clocked machinery to gin and revivalism. Today, it is believed, time pressure is reflected in certain nervous disturbances, the claustrophobias in time. Cooped up in time a person still seeks, but finds harder to reach, the timeless worlds of gin-sodden slums and nineteenth-century Methodism. In Samuel Butler's *Erewhon* the workers destroyed all machines, as indeed the Luddites tried to do in the early machine age until shot, hanged, and deported into submission. They had acted like bulls, hypnotized not by the flashing red cape but by the whir of machinery. All the while the real enemy, the matador, was there behind, silent, imperturbable, the clock on the wall. Had they destroyed all clocks, the industrial world would have remained at most a lively commercial age.

There are other signs that the clock's imperiousness is resented still. The impersonality of its coordinating action, the fact that face-to-face synchronizing has largely been eliminated, that bigness is possible only at the cost of (as the phrase aggressively puts it) punching a time machine in and out and being clocked by stop watches — all this is one side of the story. The free professionals today are envied because their time is not clocked off like industry's. The newer, salaried professionals, who now outnumber the others by about six to one, are directly linked to the system.

Of its inhabitants clockland also requires regularity in habits. A person can resent regularity not alone in himself but in others too. In recent years concern has grown over the uniformity in American behavior. Writers usually contrast it with the Puritan individualist. Besides the Puritan as nonconformist, there have been other forces for variety in American history. The many breeds of immigrants and mixtures of races, for one, and their pushing into and taming the wilderness, for another. Each kind of people brought widely differing customs. The American Indian himself, obedient to the camp circle, was to the whites a devil of nonconformism. They rarely approved of his bucking against slavery. With the closing of new lands, the shutting up of the Indians on reservations, and the feeding of immigrants to factories, mines, and sweatshops, these forces for variety had to turn back and cast their lot with the machine.

Once the buccaneering of the frontiers and that of industry were spiritually akin. The flare of energy that swept across the West turned back east and for a while made industry, both owners and workers, glow with a rude, ruddy industrialism. Before long, though, the clock had its way. Some of the old industrialism yet exists, chiefly as an ideal to which lip service is handsomely paid, but the verve has been flattened by standardization. When we speak of synchronizing the actions of men by clocks, we are not using a merely fanciful phraseology. The clock, to repeat, is an automatic machine whose product is regular auditory or visual signals. Who lives by it becomes an automaton, a creature of regularity.

In boasting of American individualism (and though many Americans today speak of fearing conformity, yet do they believe no other country is as individualistic as theirs), one should recall that clock time means synchronization, which, applied to men, involves a loss of freedom of action. A man can claim, "I time myself to others for a second that I may be free later." He owns thus to giving up a part of his freedom as much as if he gave up a part of his sovereignty. He can then argue about how much a part he gives up, but he cannot deny that clocks are everywhere in America and time-referrals constant. As the nineteenth century gave the worker a pocket watch, the twentieth century gave him a wrist watch, a distinct improvement since it could be referred to more easily and quickly. Daily over and over again, one time-binds oneself. (This can be empirically verified, if one cares to, by observing the frequency with which people look at clocks and watches.) Note the word "watch" for a pocket or wrist clock. Advertisers are aware of its power to attract glances. They often place their ads in proximity to a clock. Timing by the clock is an expression not of individualism but of collectivism. That millions and millions of persons live inside one tempo as in a giant apartment house or great beehive, is not a belief on which to rear individualists. In the measure of individuality a country without clock dependence starts off with a lead. A further point to keep in mind is that nonconformism does not and cannot mean nonconformism in everything. The American Indian sat securely in the camp circle. The Puritans and Calvinists were the earliest devotees of the clock. At the revoking of the edict of Nantes,

French watchmakers, the majority of them Protestant, preferred leaving the country to conversion. Their exodus to Geneva turned that city into the watchmaker for the world. These watchmakers and others before them had given the clock a minute hand, so that Puritan divines like Richard Baxter could preach that time be used up to each minute. To redeem time, Baxter wrote in his *Christian Directory,* cast none of it away. "Do not waste a single minute" commanded religion of the seventeenth century.

Too often the so-called work ethic of Protestantism has been confused with mere intensity of work, as though men previously had not worked hard. The European farmer and artisan always worked hard, but with a fluctuating rhythm capable of taking wide variations within the beats. Clock or machine rhythm is different. Chapter VI described how English peasants in the eighteenth and nineteenth centuries often preferred home and poverty to the well-paying factory, where there was no quitting until the relief shift came on or the power was shut off. If you watch an assembly line today, in an automobile plant, let's say, you will not necessarily be impressed with its speed. Men may be standing around with tools in their hands, talking if located near enough to each other and if the noise isn't excessive. At times there is a break in the line and then — this one interruption to the flow — there's nothing to do but stand around idly. Moreover the operation may not always be of bovine simplicity but in some jobs complex and delicate.

The impersonal tempo, rather than the simplicity, bores into the worker. He may feel like going much faster that morning, but he cannot, or he may feel like snoozing or talking or making love or going out for a breath of air and a drink or exercising different muscles. A worker may be using certain muscles to the almost total exclusion of others, so that at times for reasons he can't explain he is ready to explode or hates the thought of getting up in the morning.

Time-and-motion study men have gone wrong because they

undervalued a related matter: the capacity of muscles to find the way of doing a physical task that best fits their particular structure. One group, the optimal school of time and motion study, had assumed that every job had one best way of being done and that their studies could show it in terms of the least time and effort. At moments it must have been like an anthropologist trying to teach natives how to save steps in a war dance. A workman who has been working a machine for a long time, like a pianist in fingering certain passages, does it in a way that brings his individual dexterity of hand and mind to the task. It might be shorter for him at a given stage to take a half step backward and cross his left hand over his right to reach for a lever, but the movements may come awkwardly to him, as they do to one who tries to learn rugby, the piano, or a language late in life. Some muscles have to be coordinated early, others have not, depending on the individual's history. Therefore, while one may say to a worker, "Have you ever tried doing it this way?", one may not say, "This is the optimum motion pattern on this job, so do it this way." His own style of movements may take longer but tire him out less. If he has to do it *your* way, the result may be absenteeism, breakage, grievances, and "human nature doesn't like work."

Not the speed, but the regular, methodic, continuous, faceless pace, and, when it occurs, the unnatural adaptation of nerves and muscles, deaden the worker on the line and make him every now and then want to shout until his lungs give out. The worker is one, we should remind ourselves, who must earn his livelihood by applying body and mind to tasks set by others. Yet the body and mind are not always in the same condition, nor did they evolve through millennia to produce an organism designed for these very machines. An organic and a mechanical rhythm, though the first be reared in the shadow of the second, find it hard to mesh the one's cells with the other's gears. Automated machinery, so-called, will not change things greatly if it also requires men to be synchronized with its workings. In their love of music the Greeks had realized that work forces a man to lose his own rhythm. *Scholē* was the most precious thing imaginable because only in leisure could a man keep his particular rhythm and discover how it merged with the pervasive rhythm of nature.

In earlier chapters we distinguished pacing and nonpacing machinery. Obviously we have not been dealing here with machines that are self-paced, like a lathe or automobile or sewing machine. They do not require synchronization, and if some automated machinery can be made to fit the category it will not have the same effects as pacing machines. For all kinds of machines, though, let us recall that it is one thing to work to your own time, and another to work to someone else's time, and yet another to work to clock time.

OTHER PLACES, OTHER TIMES

Regardless of how much the pace of machinery is felt as an imposition, one thing our training has done is make clock time seem real to us. We set up visual and auditory intervals by the invention of the clock. We train ourselves to judge the length of these intervals. Before long we regard them as equidistant and as time itself. Time becomes self-evident. You're considered a fool if you ask what it is, or doubt that it is objective, universal, irreversible, non-projectable, quantitative or set in inelastic, non-compressible units.

What we call time nowadays is but the movement of synchronized clocks. Two persons may have two clocks; if one goes into another room with one of the clocks while the other stays behind, both can meet in the hall when the bells on the clocks ring (auditory signal) or when the hands point to a certain numeral (visual signal). But the simultaneous meeting does not mean that the elapsed time has been equal for both persons. It may have been nothing to the one who went into a different room, and may have been forever to the other. What it does mean is that both can agree to move on a given automatic signal. If the two persons had moved together at the sight of a smoke signal or the sound of a pistol shot, the signal would have been considered personal because set off by a man, whereas we feel the clock is impersonal because it is automatic and tied in with other clocks. No matter what man does, this is *the* time. Not even God can turn it back or forward, or stop it. Our globe, it seems, has a pulse beat that we have set our clocks to perfectly, and they now tick, whir, and vibrate in tune with the beat of the world.

Steady, reliable, punctual though the clock is, we cannot take as serious the notion that it produces or reflects or represents time. We are no better off than Augustine, whose place in the history and philosophy of time ranks high. He knew what time was, as long as no one asked him. If he had to explain it to someone, he no longer knew. One can speak of images of time, though. The one that fits the modern conception is linear. Time does not repeat itself, it ticks off in a straight line, goes from t to t_1 in a continuum, runs in an even flow or in a stream with graduated steel banks, moves like the assembly line or the ticker tape. Essentially it resembles the picture Newton drew of time in his *Principia:* real and mathematical, flowing uniformly, embracing all objects and phenomena but aloof from them, keeping its own independence, indestructible, universal, nothing happening to it yet enveloping all happenings of the universe as space envelops all objects, every indivisible instant of it the same everywhere. Newton, of course, like other thinkers and writers of his day, had been impressed by the new and marvelous clocks.

This was not the first time in history that time had been considered to proceed in a straight line. Whenever an emperor decided that time began with his rule, the linear conception was there: year One began with Alexander, Seleucus, Augustus, and Diocletian. The idea seldom gained popularity outside of the ruling, educated, technical, or priestly classes, however. After the fall of Rome, even before Descartes, time had been thought of as a line. Medieval astronomers represented it as such. Descartes may have been the first, though, to serve the industrial world by plotting time as an abscissa. Yet, without the widespread distribution of water or mechanical clocks, the notion of linearity is not likely to become commonplace. Other ages with such a conception did not divide time so minutely. Only the mechanical clock did that, and only the mass-produced clock and watch have been able to give it currency.

The clock's face is round as the moon and its hands eternally cross themselves in repetition. Its form was devised in a day when the prevailing idea was less linear than it is now. In most parts of the world the wheel is a better symbol of time than the line. The image is based on the sequence and repetition of activities, both social and natural. The days and nights come and go, the moon waxes and wanes, the tide ebbs and the seasons take their turn — seedtime, harvest, the falling leaf and thawing ice, the lambing of ewes. Everything lives, dies, and is born. This time is circular, eternally returning, biological, rather than mechanical, picturing man's place in the world in the ancient saying, history repeats itself. Its units are broad and variable — the day and night, noon, Sunday, the moon a sliver or a big silver coin, the end of winter and the warm breezes of spring. Its purpose is reflected in its acceptance of God's scheme of things and the apportioning of life equally to generations wherein the family lives on. *"E la sua volontate è nostra pace,"* says Dante. In accepting what God wills for us do we find our peace.

One can briefly distinguish a third kind of time sense, which for lack of a good name may be called impressionistic-time. Routine activities or happenings take no time. Only the vivid instant, the exciting period, the important event, leaves the impression of time or duration. All the rest doesn't count, since not experienced as the passing of time. In spatial terms it is like taking a walk on a fine day: one doesn't remember how many steps one took, each approximately equivalent to a yard; one remembers a stretch of tall grass, a house whose annexes make a dynamic whole, the new red sign on the hardware store, and the piling up of pink clouds in the bluing west. For some the pink clouds are the time. "A leaf falls. An instant. A century." So Basho (1644–1694) puts it. For others the only things remembered as time are those that made a gross impression — a drought, a battle, a conquest. An event that happened in our seventy years ago happened in their yesterday: as if handed a deck of cards they were to pick out three and throw the rest away. The thin pile of three is then their past. If we did our schoolbook history in this manner, World War II happened in 1961, the depression in 1960, World War I in 1959, the assassination of Lincoln in 1958, the Civil War in 1957, and so on. The Trukese have a time system like this, apparently, but other civilized people have elements of it in their life also. Many Arabs feel so close to the prophet that it doesn't matter whether they are living in the tenth or twentieth century: the prophet was yesterday. The Hindus, too, it is said, lack a genuine (in our sense) chronology of their past.

There are other kinds of time conceptions. Some communities, I pointed out earlier, lack a time system. They recognize age alone, or, like the Hopi, have expressions for earlier and later, but no word for time nor verbs that indicate time. Then there is a tribe in Guinea that distinguishes only two times, a favorable time and an unfavorable, recalling the Roman *dies fasti* and *dies nefasti;* and the Navaho, who can think only in the present.

Even among us more than one time conception exists. There is temporal polyvalence, today favored by the special theory of relativity. With it a proliferation of times has appeared. Each discipline lives its own time, sometimes more than one, like a watch whose parts age at different rates. We now have a pluralism of times — physical, of relativity and of quanta, physiological, biological, historic, artistic, social, psychological, individual, and mathematical. Dethroned is Newton's absolute and catholic monarch. Every galaxy has its characteristic time and so has every man and molecule. Now we have writers who, like Locke before them, try to convince people they should abandon their so-called natural, intuitive, or *a priori* ideas of time so that they can conceive of time as it really is. There is nothing more difficult, they complain, than persuading people of this. Actually what they are trying to do is undo Locke and Newton.

These time systems are never found in a pure state but always as a mixture whose composition enables us to call them one or the other. A holiday in our system, and our history, too, when taught as dates-to-remember, exemplify impressionistic-time; the passing of the old year and the celebrating of the new are clear examples of the cyclical time mentality. When Augustine thrust a stick in the spokes of time's wheel, stopping it to allow for the *novum* of Christ, he located the measuring of time in memory. One measures time as one recalls the interval between two succeeding notes sounding in the ear. Augustine's ideas thus partake of impression time though his role in the history of time concepts usually places him on the linear side. For purposes of orientation, others, like Goethe, Nietzsche, and Spengler — with their defense of cyclical time — should be mentioned; and Bergson, whose *temps-durée* has in it the psychological element in both cyclical and impressionistic-time. By and large, though, the modern industrial world runs on linear time, a time linked to space, for all time is in space, and — a point we have not yet noted — marching by on a track that slants upward toward the sky.

TIME ON AN UPWARD PLANE

Were linear time to begin in limbo and end in limbo, its world would lose all sense of purpose. This has never happened. We mentioned a few pages earlier that some emperors simplified things and celebrated their rule by dating time from their regime, looking on everything before it as more or less prehistoric. Linear time does have a beginning. Augustine argued his point eloquently, for it was he who broke the circle into which time had fallen along with the Roman Empire, and, unlike Herodotus, who spoke of the cycle of human events, he cast aside "false circles" and proposed the straight line of history. Though it was not until about the eighteenth century that the *Anno Domini* chronology became definitive, we now date our history from Jesus Christ and we need not go into the problem over which Augustine was challenged: What did God do before he created heaven and earth? For the Christian, primordial time began with God and *christiana tempora* led to eternity, final time, a union with God, a time of no time. *"Là ove s'appunta ogni Ubi ed ogni Quando"* is Paradise for Dante, there where every Where and every When converge.

At a point in the history of Christendom a particular confusion appears. Political and religious ideas, time on earth and timelessness in heaven, merge and blur into each other. The Calvinists helped mightily to put living on a slanted plane if not to cast it out in a vertical thrust. Their version of the Kingdom of God was of one that must be built into the New Jerusalem by man's efforts here on earth. They thus excel in temporal striving toward atemporality. Also for the atheist and the agnostic (and the Christian in misguided moments) a paradise of final time will come when time will no longer be significant or exist as a problem. The ultimate goal will have been reached. For the democrat it will be perfect democracy, for the anarchist the absence of government, for the communist the classless society, for the scientist the discovery of truth after countless errors that seemed like truth — all the while giving hope to each of them is progress, that vague strong dogma that no matter how stumbling the step and full of briers the path, mankind is constantly on its way upward, bettering itself and constantly trying in its delight to be engaged to History. As the belief in the hereafter suffers attrition, all the more important becomes the belief in a future temporal paradise where all time will have a stop.

Time on an upward plane embodies the layman's drive for the millennium. Linear history is going somewhere unique, is never at rest. Bent on reshaping man and machine, it permits no free time unless the activities in it reach upward for the same goal. All else is worse than vacant time; it is lost time, never to be found again. Or else it is the indicted "time wasted." In the American panorama of motion and commotion lies the vision that through man's dragooning of man and of nature, a shining world will rise to redound to the greater glory of God (once) and to the glory of the lesser god Progress (now). In the circular time mentality no matter how excited a nation becomes in thinking that its turn to be top dog on history's cycle is arriving, the thought that the top dog inevitably revolves to be bottom dog acts as a cynical damper of enthusiasm. Nietzschean and Spenglerean theories of history seem rather to have predicted Nazism than to have given rise to it. When it came to be, it was literally millenarian — the Thousand Year Reich.

In this conception it seems the elements of religious as compared to political faith cannot be disentangled. Nonetheless the idea of a final time, a time of no time, is religious. For this the words "sacred" and "spiritual" have as opposites "secular" and "temporal," the first referring to matters that pertain to mere centuries, and the other to whatever exists at all in time. The time of no time, final time, or paradise, is not to be expected in the centuries to come, nor to be obtained through the efforts of lords temporal. It refers to a world spiritual.

So clocks do not tell any time, nor do they measure any except clock time. They divide a day, no particular day, an abstracted or average day, into beats, and mark the divisions by synchronized signals. The Babylonians who gave the day 12 hours, to fit the year's 12 months, could have fixed another number, say 10 or 15. In the French Revolution, the day was divided by fiat into 10 hours. This would have had the handiness of fitting the metric system. But each hour was more than double the old hours, habits were too strong, all watch faces had to be changed; Napoleon reestablished the old system. The Hebrews had given the week seven days. The First Republic, again, tried to change it to 10 days. It met with the same difficulties and the same Napoleon.

Today's day usually is based on the sun's cyclical rising and setting, typically conceived as the turning of the earth on its axis. Linear time, whether it rests on a sidereal, solar, median, or legal base, has a natural, circular foundation, but once the day, a shaky unit of precision, is divided into 1/86,400, it loses its claim to naturalness.

Whether seconds are beat out by mechanical, ammonia, electrical, quartz, or cesium clocks, and whether they lose but one second every thousand years, has an effect on the time of only those warm-blooded beings (which we are said to be) who have been clock-trained in childhood: "First put in the 12, the 3, the 6 and the 9," says the teacher to the children who have just cut out their paper clock faces. The relation of man to clock time can be grasped if we go to the trouble of, or merely visualize, putting any kind of clock, the oldest or the newest variety, before a man who has never seen one before, who has lived without it, as did most of the world before the industrial age came to life. Our inner clocks may tell us no more than that the night is for sleeping or allow us to navigate skywise like bees and crabs, or they may be more subtle than we can foretell — if fish once walked on land and men shall walk on stars — but to these outer clocks they have no relation except the one we choose or have been trained to give.

Outer clocks have mainly an industrial and more recently an engineering and military use. Once outside of these spheres, the conception of time, as composed of linear, objective and equal units, often becomes impractical. There is one problem of free time that illustrates this clearly. Retirement in business today is the period in a man's life when he is separated from the industrial world's work. The prospect should be a pleasant one, a period of well-earned rest, of a happy release from cares. Many of those who like to call attention to the benefits of the industrial system point with pride to the added years of free time that early retirement brings. Yet it has another face. A frightening image of drying up into inactivity seems to pass through many minds.

Large numbers of executives and workers don't want to retire earlier; some want never to retire. We can take away declining income as an element in this picture, and also the loss of productive status; we are still left with the fact that the free time of ten years in youth and of ten years in senility are two different decades. What do ten or fifteen or a thousand units of free time mean to someone in the state that Strindberg described of his old wife. "My wife is getting blind; on the whole she is glad of it. There is nothing worth seeing. She says she hopes she will also become deaf; for there is nothing worth hearing. The best thing about being old is that you are near the goal." And yet the tranquil pleasures of a green old age may be enjoyed a thousandfold over the youth's hectic scratching around for fun.

Locke did his best to try to give people the idea of Newtonian time. We cannot know duration except through the succession of our thoughts, he wrote in his *Essay Concerning Human Understanding*. We are not aware immediately of the duration of our own thinking being. We must apply our own individual duration to all that which is outside ourselves and imagine thus a measure, common and commensurable, one instant behind the other in the duration of everything that exists. But this, which in Locke's time was so hard to conceive, comes naturally to us who have lived with linear time and clocks for over a century. Now what we find difficult to believe, and why this chapter had to go in some detail into exotic time systems, is that there can be other kinds, no less true, no less satisfying, than this.

To conclude this enigmatic subject: Technology, it seems, is no friend of leisure. The machine, the hero of a dream, the bestower of free time to men, brings a neutralized idea of time that makes it seem free, and then chains it to another machine, the clock. If we but say "free clocked time," the illusion vanishes. Clocked time cannot be free. The phrase connotes, and justly so, that the "clockedness" has a purpose and a collectivity that is at odds with freeness and individuality. Clocked time requires activities and decisions that must always be referred back to (synchronized with) the machine and its ramifications in an industrial culture.

Thus whatever free time we have is unfree from the start. That we oppose it to work really indicates that we still regard work as the dominant obligation. Any time *after* work is finished is "free," but even *that* time, if work must be clocked, is workbound. The difference is that free time in relation to work is indirect; it is tethered with a longer rope. So, through machines, we are bound to the clock. We can break away only a few fragments of a day or a weekend. Really to go off into something new and different is impossible, for at a precise inexorable hour and minute we must answer again to the clock.

Our kind of work, though freer of toil, requires a time-motion that makes our spare time free time and thereby links it inescapably to work. Aristotle was right about recreation. It is related to work, and given and taken so that work can go on. Thus it is with modern free time. If one had been asked earlier where in a list of expenditures the cost of a watch was to be charged, one would have said "To work, obviously." Now one would have to add "To free time, too." Free time has no independence of its own. The most one can do to escape today's time pressure is to "get away from it all," to take a vacation in any place that has a vaguer time sense than our own. We search, then, for places that are as yet freer of the clock than we are — the remote village or shore, the mountains, the woods, the Mediterranean country, the island. A surer solution is to go mad. Otherwise we cannot truly escape, for by now the industrial and scientific Western time crust covers the globe and will soon grow on other planets. The moon may still be the timeless world it has ever seemed for lovers, but it won't remain so for long.

In the picture of the future I have sketched in this chapter, there was no mention of a change in our ideas of time. There are some straws in the wind that lead me to suspect they will eventually change, perhaps after first losing their space-bound character, but not in the near future we have discussed. That no such prospect is in close sight indicates that clock time, as industrial time, will continue to guide our lives. Machines by now have manipulated everyone, their owners and tenders both, into living by the dictates of the clock. An ignorant visitor from a clock-less land might wonder why we reject the tyranny of men while acquiescing to the tyranny of an idol. As long as our basic time concepts remain unchanged, it is useless to look for relief to time-saving gadgets. The story has been told that after the French Revolution a young man asked an old one what life was like in the *ancien régime*. "People had time," said the old man. "Rich and poor alike." *Se non é vera, é ben trovata.*

We have transformed civilization and our lives to win time and find leisure, but have failed. We are not even back where we began. We have lost ground. Worst of all, we have raised a range of Himalayan institutions and habits that block our way forward or backward.

There is no doubt that Americans have reached a new level of life. Whether it is a good life is another matter. This much is clear: it is a life without leisure. Some may say that the sense of abundant unscheduled time is unnecessary, but while pieces of clock-time may be enough for free time, they are not enough for leisure. For leisure is not hours free of work, or even weekends or months of vacation or years in retirement. It has no bearing on time conceived as a flow of evenly paced equal units of which some are free and some are not, and all are on crusade. Indeed, the contemporary phrase "leisure time" is a contradiction in terms. Leisure has no adjectival relation to time. Leisure is a state of being free of everyday necessity, and the activities of leisure are those one would engage in for their own sake. As fact or ideal it is rarely approached in the industrial world.

We see now that in their life with machines people lost not space alone but time too. More subtle than the changes in space, the changes in time went less noticed. They were of capital importance. Men were given a reformed time, a reformed calendar, and a reformed cosmology. Time nowadays must be pursued. If

pursued, it hides out. It shows itself only when it no longer hears
the baying of the hounds. If you have to pursue time, give up the
idea of leisure. To transform the lead of free time into the gold
of leisure, one must first be free of the clock. And that is just the
start.

Transforming
Free Time

WHAT kind of rule is this? The more timesaving machinery there is, the more pressed a person is for time. Take modern home appliances, an electric beater or whipper, for example. Cuisine has not improved over the last hundred years because of the superiority of one beater over another. A soufflé today is no better than it was a hundred years ago. In fact, the gourmet would argue the contrary: a motorized beater is of no use in making a good soufflé, or even a good mayonnaise. If time is saved, then, it may be at the expense of the culinary art, but is time really saved?

Note that the time counted consists only of those one and a half minutes less it takes to whip the egg whites. The electric beater costs more; whatever costs more has taken somebody's time to earn the money to buy it. This time is not counted. Money is not exchanged for labor and skill alone, but also, as current phraseology might put it, for labor and skill through time. The worker, we mustn't forget, sells his time. Furthermore, of the one and a half minutes saved, how many are depreciated? Once cookbook authors recognized that some things are easy to do, their recipes began to call for beating, whipping, chopping, and mixing without prudent limits. So the same one and a half minutes saved, repeated unnecessarily, are no longer saved but added. How often was the grass cut before the lawnmower (now motorized) was invented? In sight of grass mowed to the quick the American may be happier for his success in keeping nature under control, but he is no healthier, the grounds no cleaner, the landscape no lovelier. Still this is not the point. Rather, how much time does he save as a result of the timesaving lawnmower? Let us hope such tools and appliances save some minutes; if not, who would find time to keep them in repair? Motorized appliances are harder to repair by oneself, so the housewife gets on the telephone — and so on, until she reaches for the time-money it costs the breadwinner to pay the repairman.

Let us move on from the level of the lowly household to the wide plane of diplomatic action. In the Vatican until recently vacations have been brief for the *curia romana*. A hundred years ago, though, it took so long to send a message to Spain, say, and to get an answer back, that the custom was to take off the months from mid-August to mid-October. Or we can use a transportation sequence from the pages of modern history: A man has to walk one hour to work. He doesn't think much about it until he learns that there are ways within his reach to do it in less time. A horse was always too expensive; a bicycle, though, called for but a small capital outlay and an almost negligible upkeep. As yet, neither horse nor bicyle, as means of transport, brings about a time and space revolution, although the bicycle begins to extend the city's limits. Then comes public transportation, followed by automobiles. Though at first a man can get to work in ten minutes instead of his former one hour, it isn't long before he is spending one hour riding or driving to work. Some might point out regretfully that he lacks the healthy exercise of a morning walk. Yes, but usually he can still walk if he wants to. (Most bridges still have pedestrian runways.) From home to the job would take about five hours. Others might point out that the air he breathes in the roar of rush hour traffic is not so pure as it used to be — but you can't have everything.

In big-city rush hours people push and cram into bus and sub-way: they must get to work on time. On the way out it's the same thing: rush. Dinners and families are waiting (why is home on such a strict time schedule?), or a courting is on, which means get home, eat, clean up, change, and back to make the date. Wherever time-saving appliances, communications, and transport abound, time-harried faces appear at every turn.

TODAY'S FREE TIME

To save time through machines is not easy. To transform free time into leisure is not going to be easy either. The modern idea of free time and the classic ideal of leisure revolve about different axes. Off-center to one another, they cannot be called opposites. Were it not for this, they would be poles apart.

Let us consider at some length and afresh the various components of the contemporary idea of free time, often said to be leisure. In the absence of other tradition it lives, as we have seen, in the shadow of work and commerce. Since the world of industry runs on quantitative time, free time runs to the same rhythm. Because of this, free time exists in fragments — off-work hours, weekends, vacations. Sunday, the hoary, ineradicable day snatched from the work week by religion, makes the lone exception. On the other days the job picks free time to pieces. By saying that free time is time off the job, one may forget momentarily that the job comes first, and that unless one has a job he has no free time: he is unemployed. The positive is employment; the negative is formed by the prefix "un-." We have no word for un-leisure like the Greek *ascholia* or the Roman *negotium*.

Work influences the drive for betterment that often appears in free-time activities. To improve one's position and increase one's skill, to be always on the lookout for something better, to pursue happiness, to be ever anxious (as the Puritan saying urged) to "do ye nexte thynge," to let up never — much of this constellation of habits grows out of striving for greater skill and status at work.

Before improving himself, a man must be able physically and mentally to do work. Rest is needed. The uncritical and immobile way free time is spent — at home in the evenings in unthinking or unchallenging activities, chiefly as an armchair spectator — seems related to the pacing and concentration of work, especially in factories, within a span of hours. Of course it also seems related, for all classes of workers, to the tenseness and discomfort of the long ride home, which often tires a man out more than the job. Increasingly free time is being consumed in predominantly ocular activities, and, within that category, in the pictorial variety — picture magazines and film screens — rather than the kind that involves an intermediate step of deciphering, like reading. Cicero once sent a friend at Stabiae a letter touching on the difference. "I don't doubt that you in your lovely bedroom with its lovely loggia overlooking the Gulf are spending the morning hours these days with edifying reading while we unfortunates who had to return to the city are sitting sleepily in the theater."

Unthinking is perhaps a better word than passive to describe these activities. One could apply passive to not getting up to go out of the house, and certainly to that part of the Roman repertoire that was putting Cicero to sleep. If one dozes off before a stage or screen, the activity is passive in the ordinary sense of the word. But there are subtleties that bear watching: the whole question of passivity as characteristic of free time today warrants fuller attention at this point.

A man lies down on a bed and closes his eyes and remains that way breathing regularly for eight hours. If his breathing becomes imperceptible and other signs used to distinguish life from nonlife have vanished, the man is usually judged dead. If we assume he does no more than breathe in this period — a most unreal assumption — is the man active? What he is doing is called sleeping. In fact, we may either say that he is *doing* something ("he's sleeping") or that he *is* something ("he's asleep"). If we admit he can have dreams, then we can picture a veritable turmoil of activity going on in his head and muscles. Actually, we have but to think of his circulatory system to visualize other kinds of incessant activity. Let us imagine the same man in a chair, still breathing, his eyes open or closed. He sits there for an hour. Is there activity going on apart from his breathing and the transformation of cells in his body? We do admit he may be thinking or reflecting or meditating. So there is the possibility that a man is always somehow in action.

Now let us suppose he faces a wall or a screen. Is he more active if he imagines moving figures on the wall, or if moving figures are projected there, or if legitimately alive actors are performing on a stage? The question is not easily answered. We should note that in the second and third instances the representation was made by others, while the first instance was a self-production. The second and third examples interest us most, for the key to the passivity of mind of today's free-time activity lies there. Most critics of the cultural scene hold that sitting before a TV set is passive, whereas going to the theater is not. Clearly they are not objecting to the lack of exercise in sitting before the TV. Nor are they complaining that at the theater the spectators number a relative few, while in TV the viewers constitute a mass audience. Previously, TV critics complained in the same way about the movies, for which one had to go out of the house. What they object to is not so open-and-shut. It is not the caliber of the representation, nor the play — for someday on TV one may find good actors playing Marlowe. The real objection touches all modern mass communication. For the movie or TV screen, the newspaper or magazine, the viewer or reader has no way of making his reactions known directly to the writer, producer, or performer of the story. In conversation one can praise or condemn another's views, and in the theater or opera one can hiss, boo, whistle, stir nervously, or stand and clap for eleven curtain calls. Human beings, except for rare pathological cases, are influenced by other human beings. Such active attention cannot be given to communication systems. One can write or telephone to an office; who knows where the message will go and who, if anyone, will ever look at it? Or else wait to be counted in a rating survey — which will not be likely to ask what you really wanted to say anyway. The rating, like the program itself, allows no backtalk. Nor can you influence the program by buying or not buying the product it advertises. The product has qualities of its own. For this reason, it is misleading to call these systems mass media of communication. The word communicable signifies a common lot, a sharing. These media don't share; they convey or transmit. They could better be called conveyors or transmitters. The older words used for radio — transmit, receive, broadcast — are closer to fact.

These considerations stand apart from another important one: that the possibility of active attention or communication builds up a critical audience which in time raises the level at which artists or communicators present their story or play to the public.

But here I wish to concentrate on the so-called passivity of free-time activities in the United States. The same supineness is part of listening to music on disks. As with books, there is a variety to choose from; the setting for listening, though, is not so rigid as that for reading. In order to read, good light, immobility of the reader, and the absence of need to do any but the most routine tasks are required. Today the setting for music can be ignored. Chamber music can be listened to in the kitchen. The organ's ringing out of *Sleepers Awake* fails to keep anyone from taking a bath, answering the phone, scolding the children, or making a ham sandwich. Music, chosen to suit the mood, has become an accompaniment to other activities and largely a tranquilizer or relaxer, a soother of the tense breast. The musical skill required to play, read, or compose music oneself has given way to the mechanical skill required to assemble excellent turntables, tuners, amplifiers, and speakers. Except for technicalities of reception, listening to the music is uncritical. You can buy better speakers but not clap, boo or shout "bravo" at the end of the composition and hope it reaches the musician's or composer's ears.

A certain refrain recurs when the mass media are criticized: If people don't like what they hear or see, they won't buy the things that are publicized; sales are the best index to popular approval. Sales, to be sure, have always been an indication of how much a product is liked. How good an indication it is, is hard to say. We have seen that a person may be forced to buy something he wants less than something that has vanished from the market. A restaurant may have a menu two feet long but if nothing on it meets your fancy, you have no choice but to eat something you don't want . . . or not eat at all. Moreover, there are many extraneous factors that enter into a purchase. Just what is being approved when a record is bought? Are people buying the music, the performance, the attractive wrapper, the love life of the maestro, the prestige of the orchestra, or the low price put on for the after-Christmas season? Whether sales are heavy or light has little bearing on the main point anyway, which is that the mass media of transmission develop an uncritical audience. This result, I suggest, is causally related to the previous point. An uncritical audience develops because the media *transmit* rather than *communicate*. They offer no chance of real response.

Evidently, the present world has given us a new way of being spectators or listeners. This discussion of passivity is not based on participation on one side and spectatorship on the other. I should not contrast the activeness of the workingman's watching television today with the passivity in which he once used to sit on the porch and brush away flies; nor would I cite the substitution in the clerk's backyard of a badminton set for the old hammock (which, incidentally, still decorates many of Charleston's gardens). Perhaps Americans are indeed participating less in sports, music, and the theater than they did once. Existing figures give no clear answer. Many critics do base their complaints about passivity on this: the lack of participation in activities requiring movement. Defenders in reply utter the words, "the new active leisure," an advertising phrase that exploited the "improvement" bent of Americans and their vulnerability to youth-and-motion ideas of themselves. America's oldest tradition is youth, said that disreputable Englishman, Oscar Wilde. As with kittens and pups, energetic play everywhere characterizes the young. With slight variations the rule must be universal. Full-grown cats and dogs, when they have nothing to do, curl up and go to sleep.

Man is not a beast who just sleeps and feeds. In fact it would be ungenerous to call beasts mere sleepers and feeders. They even have some of man's pleasures — lying in the sun, courting, fighting, maneuvering, striving in concert, playing. Yet man has pleasures beasts don't have. Rarely do animals watch other animals except as direct objects of love, fear, play, rivalry, or help. They are not capable of representation. They know neither the drama nor the story. This alone would distinguish man's free time from the beast's. He has his stories and plays, and beyond them the whole world of imagination and ideas. Only man is so lucky.

Unfortunately, modern devices for recording and projecting sound and images have removed people from direct contact and thus lowered their critical attention to the point where they are almost in the state of the older cats and dogs. What good does it do for a man to yell, "Kill the umpire!" to a TV set? He might as well doze off.

In sum, the charge that free-time activities are passive should be founded on the split in spectatorship, between the old kind, in which any man in the audience could make himself heard on the spot, and the new kind, in which the word "uncritical" or "unthinking" fits better than "passive."

Give the individual worker not just a few evening hours but a few days to play with and he may show another side of himself, and another characteristic of free time today. He needs rest and undemanding distraction or somnifacients, but to bring himself each day to the round of disciplined work and timing he seems also to need periods of letting go of himself in noise, boisterousness, and violence. Other times have recognized a need to let loose by providing a carnival season — to which our New Year's Eve is closest in spirit. Other times also provided for physical contests between various quarters of the city. By comparison, our intercity baseball is a pallid rivalry. Peasant life, too, needs relief from the myopia of the daily backbreak, to get away in the color and alcohol of fiestas.

In part perhaps because there is so little of festive relief; in part also because work's demands are less physically exhausting and yet more confining than they used to be, Friday and specially Saturday night are nights that fill up the volumes of the police blotter. The pleasure in doing what one was unable to do during the work week — stay up late, sleep late, get drunk, fight, whirl away at one's own crazy speed, act the boss, give way to the Dionysian rhythm of the dance, spend like a sailor — this is called fun. Some would call it puerility because it seems as if adults were acting the child, or, as is often the case, the adolescent. It is true: children are notable for play, and the pleasure they get from it they call fun. Adults have fun, too, and without being puerile, their fun comes from play and games less energetic and more refined than the child's. The pleasure of having fun is a recognizable part of spending weekend free time properly. For this reason political and religious activities are not considered free-time activities proper: they are not fun. Nothing serious is free time either, unless it is of the kind that leads to success. Political and religious activities are in neither the fun nor the success category. The fun pattern, for all its orgiastic flare, is well under control. Sunday is a quiet day and the evening ends early. On Monday, back to work.

Similarly with still longer free-time periods. Only the retired don't have to worry about getting back to work. Often that is what worries them most — that they will never go back to work. The others, the younger in years if not in spirit, obey the clock, whether they go off for one free week or four, whether to a lakeside cottage or to Palm Springs.

There is no such thing as prison leisure. By contrast with ordinary life, however, prison may offer the chance for unhurried thinking, reading, writing, and conversation. In his autobiography Trotsky pointed out that prison life developed political thinking and provided, for those who never had it, a kind of general education. In more recent times Adriano Olivetti, the late industrialist and philanthropist, attributed his increased interest in political theory to time spent in political asylum. All this applies principally to political prisoners, and those around them. The list of political and literary figures who have composed works while in prison or exile includes such luminaries as Thucydides, Polybius, Dante, Marco Polo, Machiavelli, Tommaso Campanella, San Juan de la Cruz, André Chénier, Lenin, Louis Aragon.

Recreation, certainly, can be had even in jail. Prisoners have recreation programs and directors; they are given exercise and recreation so that they will stay in their cells more docilely and keep in better health. We would be justified in saying that all the activities mentioned above as common to today's free time are recreation. They are dominated by work because they are either influenced by work scheduling or done to improve skill or status at work; or, also, because they make it possible, through rest, distraction, and release, for men to keep on working.

The commercial and industrial world we live in further affects the modern idea of leisure. First of all free time is spent generally in the company of commodities, sometimes called leisure equipment, facilities, products, or items — a TV set or a juke box. This characteristic is sometimes labeled a part of "American materialism." The term is not common in Europe, except in applying the word to America. The sense possibly takes its origin from socialist language, wherein materialism is directly related to the means of production, referring essentially, in a system based on capital and industry, to factories and mills.

Perhaps, since machines were and still are made principally of iron or steel, and since many early assembly-line products like cars used steel in large quantities, materialism and metals were associated. The result is that today the charge of materialism reflects a shiny steel and chromium culture. In Europe a materialist is generally thought of as a person who thinks chiefly of his carnal appetites, and since this involves flesh, metals can play only a subsidiary role. Metals, however, are as good an indication as any of the commodity-acquiring habit in the United States. The per capita consumption of metals, steel, copper, lead, zinc, aluminum, magnesium, chromium, nickel, and tin is about one ton, easily the highest in the world. We also use up hundreds of pounds of nonmetallic minerals, but, except in stone, sand, and gravel (which we consume in tons again for highways and dams), our margin over the rest of the world is not great.

The commercialization of free time, a development Chapter VI traced historically, insures that free time is spent collectively or uniformly. Whatever free-time accessories are offered to the consumer must be marketable. The work-oriented education and specialized training Americans receive, combined with their lack of a leisure tradition, leaves them open to suggestion from advertising, or, on a local scale, from recreation directors, counselors, or coordinators, however they may be called. Moreover, to be marketable in an industrial world means to be salable to many people, whether they are counted by the busload or by the millions in a TV audience.

True, not in every case does a product have to seek out the lowest common denominator of taste, intelligence, and pocketbook to become marketable. There are markets and submarkets, big ones and little ones. Yet a product needn't be something-for-everybody to be spread widely enough to give the impression of uniformity. American "detached" homes are much alike, cheap little houses. Inside there is the usual assortment of household electrical appliances, radio and TV; outside, the same little lawn and alongside or in front the automobile in shiny colors and

chromium. The department stores sell thousands of identical
ladies' hats, suits, and dresses for each age group, and myriad
perfumes and soaps. The supermarkets bulge with things done
up in series, weighed, packed, wrapped, packaged, and stacked
in rows. From one end of the country to the other we see the
same small towns and bigger towns, the same new products, the
same new cars, the same new houses, and the same new food.
(Other countries like France and Italy may have the same *old*
food, but it is good food and varies from region to region.) Apart
from being rich, there is no escape, and even then it is difficult.
If everything must be marketable on a large scale, as we saw before, things that are no longer marketable — skills like marble
cutting — go out, and can no longer be found at any price.
Hence, the impression of a country filled with nothing but
sameness.

Free time, then, is spent in company with accessories in a
similar manner. People, further, have similar amounts of free
time and expect that they will profit from it as much as the next
fellow. Equality of free time and its activities and benefits seems
to flow naturally from the universality of work in the United
States. Everyone is influenced in free time by the context of work
time. Equality flows, too, from the rapid leveling of income in
the last thirty years, and from the doctrine of equality in general,
not only political but economic — the notion that one dollar is
one vote. Thus, if before the French Revolution rich and poor
alike had time, today they both have free time and they fill it
alike, with more or less the same activities and kinds of products.
The poor man's rowboat is the next one up's sailboat or outboard motor, and the next one's motorboat and for the one who
doesn't have to worry about upkeep, a yacht.

Of the rich men we have (and we still have a few), how many
keep a trio or a string quartet on an annual basis in order to have
good music when they want it? It wouldn't cost much more than
$50,000 a year, and some of it could be charged off to business
entertainment expenses. (You can well imagine the incredulous

look on the tax agent's face.) Like marble cutters and regional handicrafts, good musicians are becoming hard to find — recordings have driven them out into more lucrative and steadier jobs. That is only part of the problem. The much larger part is that the rich man would get no fun out of having a chamber-music quartet around, and neither would the poor man. To get even the former to like such music, you have to organize a program for him somewhere and then get him to attend by hook or crook, generally by stressing its publicity and uplifting aspects.

This is not the place to think of the things people could do if only they were influenced in their free time by something other than this month's advertising campaign. Nor need I spend much time pointing out that the uniformity is not confined to possessions or commodities, but extends to thought, or to a uniform lack of thought in the meditative, reflective, or contemplative sense. Constant low-level attention to the movies, TV, radio, and print prevent a person from ever being alone with himself. Whenever he is giving attention to other persons, he is influenced by them, and within limits this is both natural and desirable, but of course he is not alone with his thoughts then; whenever he is alone and awake, he puts himself into a fireside sleep, absorbed by the screen. As a result he has not heard from himself in a long time. The moment for being inwardly attentive is never allowed to come. Perhaps you can judge the inner health of a land by the capacity of its people to do nothing — to lie abed musing, to amble about aimlessly, to sit having a coffee — because whoever can do nothing, letting his thoughts go where they may, must be at peace with himself. If he isn't, disturbing thoughts cut in and he will run to escape into alcohol or the flurry of activity called work.

Perhaps it's just as well, though some persons think it abominable that everyone walks, talks, hurries, smiles, smokes alike, and is as odorless as a TV image.

We say everyone. This is an exaggeration, and like the others just preceding it, to be taken in the spirit of the French *tout le monde*. It is hardly necessary to remind ourselves that the United States is filled with many kinds of people, that they all have their differences, large and small, that the South and North, East, West and Midwest and north Midwest differ; that tomorrow's Americans are not today's nor yesterday's. Yet there are uniformities among them, some obvious, some unknown to them. If we can recognize some, perhaps even tomorrow's Americans will be more understandable. "Everyone" and "the American," then, refer to many Americans and sometimes to almost all of them, as in the statement, "Everyone in the United States works." Custom, soil, climate, thought, continental position affect us all.

Right now, we are concerned with those uniformities brought by our kind of work and industry and their effect on leisure. Is it polite in the United States to ask someone you have just met what he does for a living? Do men shave in the morning for work or in the evening for their "leisure hours"? Are love affairs tailored to the business pattern — no frills, few flowers, no time wasted in elaborate compliments, verses, and lengthy seductions, no complications and no scenes, please — and do they constitute no excuse for being late to work? Is the country well-known for its "casual dress," — a phrase that could refer to "sloppy dress," one that has been proudly associated with comfort and leisure, but of both the comfort and the leisure time spent in such dress, work (including work around the house) is a clear beneficiary. An American business suit and sport coat are equally loose about the muscles. Baggy pants are useful in any kind of sedentary pursuit, be it on a horse or in a swivel chair. On the distaff side, short skirts and short hair emanate efficiency and visible activity, too. And are the parks and squares filled by anyone except bums and foreigners? Central Park and Washington Square are examples. Perhaps everybody is at work, or people nowadays want more excitement than a stroll in the park, or the advertisements do not recommend stretching the legs, or perhaps people want to avoid the wondering that wandering brings. The promenade used to be part of the American scene from New Orleans to Brooklyn. Now it is disappearing even in Europe.

RESISTANCE TO CHANGE

All these qualities, then, whatever their causes may be, describe the current idea of free time, or leisure. Set off from yet mesmerized by work, it is limited by the clock and available in only small fragments. At times busily active; then at others passive and uncritical; and in most cases uniform or collective. Supposedly beneficial for everyone who has done his work and has a few dollars in his pocket, it appears flanked by commodities and bent on fun. Matters like religion and politics and education it tries to avoid. The modern idea is what it is, today. And tomorrow? It will be the same.

Democracy has not changed the idea much. We are so used to thinking of free time as accompanied with accessories that cost more than a jackknife or a pack of cards or wooden balls to bowl on the green that we conclude the poor and rural people of the past had no free time or had less variety in it. The prejudice affects the questions that are put in free-time questionnaires and interviews, so that if the person doesn't own a radio or TV set, or has no cinema or public library within ten miles, owns no sailboat, saxophone, gramophone, do-it-yourself kits, or power tools — he is, poor chap, out of the swim of things. Indeed he may be. But we noted in a previous chapter that this doesn't mean he has no free time. Has industry changed the characteristics of free time much? Yes, as we saw also in a previous chapter, making things worse by expropriating time and space. Has universal education changed the idea? Everyone reads today, but the bulk of what they read would not stand up literarily to the tales and songs of storytellers and storysingers of preliterary times.

Reading and writing have become an index of educational

progress. Doubtless they help increase the size of the community and enable a man to serve in the factory and army and to know what's on sale today, and what's going on in town tonight. Is this the knowledge that philosophers of democracy were interested in? Socrates was against writing; Plato expressed a similar aversion. Sicilian noblemen for a long time refused to learn to read, holding that, as with numerals, the job is one for servants. Does reading serve as anything today but a bulletin board, a function largely reduced by radio and television, which do not call for reading? At one time a writer wrote a book for readers he knew almost personally and on whom he could count to read the book with care and thought. Today, and a hundred years ago too, a large proportion of Americans read, but few read anything better than the newspaper, that daily letter from the world to which they never write back. At one time poor people read well enough to read the Bible. Today the Bible is read by priests, students in theology and some in archaeology. Other people read books about the Bible (in which they learn that the Bible is great literature), and in overwhelming numbers all the newspapers, books, and magazines that these days come hot off the presses.

Like the other mass media, print today is used at the uncritical low attention level as a kind of drug to kill the dull hours of public transportation or sitting at home with nothing better to do. The more pictures in it, the better. Eighteenth-century America had few readers and few writers, but they were good readers and good writers. The Revolutionary soldier, reputedly a good soldier, could not read or write. The favorite reading matter of the United States Armed Forces today, reputedly a democratic military institution, is comic books. And the most easily digested fare for millions of civilians seems to be the illustrated weeklies. In most cases of comic books and the others sold in drugstores and supermarkets, the author does not matter. He has too many "readers." Only a minuscule percentage of readers ever wishes to talk to or dreams of talking to the author. But he who addresses a prologue to *"Buveurs très illustres"* announces that wondrous things are to come . . . and is a different kind of author.

If democracy, industry, and universal education have not improved the quality of free time, what about the prosperity they have brought? No one can say that this is not the right moment to take stock. It is true that the military budget is large; still we lack nothing. Democracy reigns, industry flourishes, everyone's son and daughter not only know how to read but will soon be college graduated, and pockets are jangling everywhere. Certainly the abundance of things has helped persuade the American that he's on top of the heap, that his way of life is the best in the world, that he has the proof (as long as he can buy appliances and things) that he is enjoying life and giving his family what it needs in order to be happy. The face of a suburban woman who knows she is dressed and made up like an advertisement in the slick fashion magazines — the smugness written on it is a lesson in containment. The New York girl, the high-school senior, is a better sight to see, the one who knows, too, she is made up like the ads (different ones). At least here the smugness is naturally uncontained. Progress is still riding high; American physicists and businessmen are expansive — the first about the universe, the second about the economy. If a new throughway is financed to save workers ten precious minutes, the event is heralded as a triumph for business, government, and foresight. In the next year the ten minutes plus ten more will be lost to increased traffic.

This progress resembles the change from legs to bicycles to cars. Those in favor of technology consider it progress if technology manages to repair some of the damage it has done. The time and space Englishmen had at the coming of industry are lost. Englishmen and Americans pay up for it every day. Yet wherever a park is opened up, it is unblushingly heralded as a triumph of good government or philanthropy, and progress in any case. The partial recovery of lost ground becomes progress.

The common man's free time still has not become what J. S.

Mill hoped. If anything, the cultural efforts of the nineteenth century, the Chautauquas, crude though they were, showed more of a will to learn than anything that can be seen in TV programs and audiences. Although the American's free time has not at all increased in the magnitude broadcast, he could have chosen more time. To Aristotle it seemed childish to work for the sake of fun. Today, with plenty of money in his pocket, the American is not, if he can help it, choosing more free time over more money. He prefers to exert himself so he can buy the leisure equipment, facilities, items, products, commodities, and consumption goods he and his family need — at least need more than they do free time.

Perhaps people won't have a choice. Perhaps with the spread of automatic machinery free time will increase even against their will. The number of jobs should not decrease so long as people continue the circle of buying whatever they and the machines produce. More and more is produced? Then more and more will be bought. There are two possibilities, though, that might change the sequence. The kind of jobs automated machines provide are those only a limited number of persons have the wit to fill. Intelligence is not equally distributed among all men. Secondly, the market may not expand as far as machine production can. The businessman may believe in an eternally expanding economy but he too has the idea that automation can cut down the number of workers on a job. The direction is the same in both cases — toward more free time. There will either be the same number of jobs — but with their hours cut down drastically and legislation to prevent overtime and moonlighting — or, more likely in view of the first possibility, a relative few will work, and the rest will live on Easy Street.

Easy Street might be something like ancient Rome at the time of the rise of the *plebs urbana*. The workers were a dedicated and skilled few — administrators, lawyers, artisans, merchants, inventors, and military officers. The *plebs* were those who had free time and the vote to insure their bread and circuses.

The circuses, like TV, went on at all times of the day. We are the Romans of the modern world, boasted Oliver Wendell Holmes. Today, we can see another Roman side to us moderns. The interesting jobs are held by executives and managers. They comprise the group that works the longest hours. They include the advertisers. The rest like their job not so much for the part that is written up in the job-description but for the social and status elements in it. If they were paid for not working wouldn't they gladly drop the work and, all together with their friends and their votes, raise the cry for bigger and better circuses?

Before I let you formulate your own answer, let me recall one thing. This kind of free time, and that of the *plebs,* is not leisure. Point by point the characteristics of free time today as an idea or an activity differ from the classical ideal, the exact opposite in some places, total irrelevance in others. To start, the measurement of leisure by time is out of the question. Time has its stop in leisure. In free time, it becomes an obsession, leading some writers to define leisure as disposable (uncommitted or unobligated) time. For leisure the idea simply does not apply. Even for free time the notion is as awkward to handle as its economic counterpart, disposable income. If free time were the blocks of time one could dispose at any given moment, and one were to be asked, "Can you spare me ten minutes?" or, "Can you come with me on a three-week trip tomorrow?," the answer might be yes or no or maybe, but none of them necessarily expresses free time. The obligation or commitment or power to dispose merely shifts scenery: The issue becomes, Who is asking and why? How obligatory or committing is the request when asked by one's boss, one's husband or a co-worker? Leisure remains a concept outside of time. Anything framed in time shorter than a lifetime is not leisure. *Hay mas tiempo que vida,* the Mexican saying goes. There is more time than life. And it is true. If you look at life instead of time you will see.

Not being divided up by time, leisure does not suffer the fragmentation that free time does. Any stopping or shrinking of an activity in leisure is intrinsic, done for the doer's own interest. The self-improvement, the always pursuing-something and bettering-oneself aspects of present free time are negative qualities as far as leisure is concerned. Life is not on a vertical incline, nor is truth. It comes not to him who is always on the run after something that tickles his senses. Neither busily active to some end nor supremely uncritical of whatever passes by, the activity of leisure refers chiefly to the activity of the mind.

Free time is opposed to work, is temporary absence from work, but leisure has as little to do with work as with time. If someone has to work it means he has to do something not for its own sake but for money or something else. Therefore it is not leisure. A man of leisure, however, may be intensely engaged in something which an innocent observer might call hard work. The difference is that its end or pursuit was chosen for its own sake.

Fellows, and friends too, are those chosen for their own sake, not for some ulterior end like business or party. In no case can leisure be collective or organized. It does not depend on other people. If one is alone, he can be at leisure by himself. Commodities are irrelevant. A walk outdoors will do. As the *Republic* opens, Socrates goes to the house of a rich old man named Cephalus. It took no show of commodities to get him to make the visit. To lure Socrates all you needed was the promise of conversation. How Cephalus's house looked or was furnished had little importance (although Socrates notes that his host's head bears a festive garland of flowers). In most of antiquity there was little furniture anyway. The Etruscan house, for instance, would have a bed, blankets and bolsters, armchairs and chests. The rooms were illuminated by oil lamps hanging from the ceilings. The classic ideal of leisure was indifferent to what we would call materialism. It was even more indifferent to the idea that leisure was everyone's right and that everyone could benefit from it equally. Only men brought up as free men *should* be brought up could benefit from leisure. For a proper education, as Pindar says, book learning is not enough. Persons who are themselves free of necessity must surround you from birth. Hoi polloi are not free; they are dragged along by any sensation, they itch after things, are prey to fears and anxieties. Book learning will never help them out. Pindar does not swerve from an aristocratic position. Though one considers his views extreme, the Greek philosophers who developed the concept of leisure — Plato, Aristotle, and Epicurus — all held little esteem for hoi polloi. The people would not know what to do with leisure was the consensus.

A man of leisure, according to Aristotle and Plato, was a man who devoted the best of himself to the state, and who believed that cultivating the mind, so important for the state, was the brightest of all activities, the single one in which man was revealed as related to the gods, and in the exercise of which he celebrated the gods. Politics and religion were at the heart of leisure. Fun never dominated the picture. This element, which some writers today maintain is a characteristic of leisure or free time — its mood of the anticipation of pleasure, its having-a-good-time-ness — is not a necessary part of leisure. What a man does when he does not have to do anything he does for its own sake, but he does not think of it as fun or having a good time. It may be difficult or easy, pleasant or unpleasant, and look suspiciously like hard work, but it is something he wants to do. That is all.

So the ideal of leisure differs on every score from today's and tomorrow's free time. In the chapter before last we found that the classic tradition exists in the United States only in attenuated form, and for the most part in the oldest universities. The ideal of leisure, however, has been deformed almost everywhere, even there. Perhaps only among classical scholars can we meet and recognize the pure thing, and by no means in all or even most of them. The point at which the deformation is most obvious is in the idea that leisure is owed everyone and everyone can benefit from it in equal measure. The educators try to say that leisure and democracy were destined for each other. To the Greeks, who were more liberal than we in the matter of bedfellows, these two would still be strange partners. First of all, contemporary educators, like so many others, have confused free time and leisure. Their predecessors in the nineteenth century were unable to resist the model of the German trade schools which made a clean sweep of the country. Possibly to oppose this movement, taking allies wherever possible, the educators have absorbed strong strains of radical democracy and European socialism.

The main ideas of Jacksonian democracy are familiar. The socialist position is also familiar, whether one thinks one knows it or not. As far as this subject goes, there is little noteworthy difference between the two. One has merely to read old socialist writers, or look at the statements of contemporary socialists or communists or at the program of so-called socialistic or communistic governments. They are and have always been in favor of a shorter work week and leisure for the working classes. So familiar are the ideas that I shall not go into them. Whenever anyone talks of "socialist" or "communist" ideas of leisure, all we have to do is substitute "democratic" and the notion is clear to us. But saying "socialist" or "communist" is not the same thing as saying "Marxist," and even less is it the same as saying "Marx's ideas."

Marx, whose ideas influenced the whole Western world more than it thinks or is willing to admit, is one of the rare thinkers who expressly noted a relation between the ideals of leisure and freedom. With the growth and expansion of technology, he believed, capitalism in spite of itself would create disposable or non-work time, thus reducing work time to a minimum and giving everyone free time for his own development. Up to this point, he does not differ much from J. S. Mill, save in degree. Human freedom, he states, has as its fundamental premise the shortening of the working day. He goes further, in generalizing that the realm of freedom is beyond the realm of material production. Free time, he says in his notebooks, which means both leisure time and the time for higher activity, naturally transforms those who dispose of it into a different type of agent. Marx, too, confuses free time and leisure, of course — he even has them upside down — but he recognizes a higher type of activity, and this we may take to mean the activity of men of leisure.

The interesting thing is that Marx seems to have been groping for a fresh expression of the classical concept. (This should not surprise us too much: Marx's doctoral thesis was on Epicurus.) He maintained that only as one passes into the realm beyond work and production does one become free; in leisure one is transformed into a different kind of person. But *who* is transformed — anyone at all? Here Marx goes back again to the democratic ideal, or rather here Marx is one of the precursors and advocates of the ideal. Some former societies gave leisure to a few. Capitalism and technology (unwittingly) and socialism (consciously) will give it to all, eventually. Then the free development of individuality will correspond to the artistic and scientific education of all individuals, thanks to the free time made available. And in the future communist society, he writes in the *German Ideology*, he, Marx (who spent his life in libraries), will do "this today, and that tomorrow, hunting in the morning, fishing in the afternoon, raising cattle in the evening, and even be a critic after dinner . . . just following my fancy." So, even though Marx has subtleties in his writing that do not appear among the doctrinaires, for all practical respects the ideals of democracy and socialism in regard to free time are twins, similar if not identical.

Let us set apart for the time being the historical evidence on the fate of leisure under democracy and socialism. Instead, let us ask ourselves a central question, a dangerous question, outright. Few writers seem to want to tackle it in the affirmative. Most think it prudent not to raise it, not even obliquely. The question: Are democracy and leisure compatible? The answer: No. In democracy today free time does exist, though in less quantity than is thought; of leisure, there is none.

Swiftly the train of discourse has again moved over onto the terrain of the political. Most people find it difficult to realize that leisure and politics are related. The reaction stems naturally from the idea that leisure is fun and political matters are not. The political bearing that they can see more easily appears in legislation affecting free time and its activities. A government agency exercises powers over radio and TV — clear enough. Government subsidies go to farmers and agricultural schools, but not to musicians and music schools — another clear case. The government controls passports, which in turn determine where or whether one can travel abroad; Congress appoints committees to study recreation — all these are clear instances of politics. Clear, surely, but minor instances. Politics and religion, too, stand in a more fundamental position to leisure. Their significance appears upon asking a single question, logical and simple enough. Why can't the present idea of free time be modified so that it comes closer, at least, to the classical concept?

Suppose we take any one of the eight or ten characteristics of free time discussed above and try to transform them. What would be necessary to carry out the change? In every case, democracy, as it is conceived today, would have to retreat.

To take the time-ridden quality out of free time one would have to take it away from work and machinery. It would be equivalent to saying to people: You can come to work or not and at whatever time you please; it really doesn't matter; we assure you enough to live on. Who has the authority to say this in a democracy? An ideology not based on time and work could not support an industrial system. If in certain quarters we can find a different time schedule — say, restaurants open all night — the reason is usually that there are night shifts at work in the vicinity. Greenwich Village in New York makes one of a few exceptions: many shops are closed on Monday and normally open from noon to 9 P.M. or 10 P.M. or midnight. Elsewhere we may find a few little islands supported by small groups of persons, artists and writers, some of them in good faith living off the margins of the business world while ideologically revolted by it. The millions of other Americans cannot afford this luxury.

To take the improvement, the ethicizing, the busily active, the always-chasing-something quality out of free time would mean stealing the doctrine of progress away from democracy, of melioration, of optimism, of the very mobility it prides itself on: that anyone can rise from bottom to top (and, less proudly, skid from top to bottom). A second's reflection would make it appear doubtful that social climbing and the struggle for status can lie down peacefully with leisure. Striving means you want something badly, that you are in a state of necessity, the state opposed to leisure.

To take the passivity or uncritical spirit out of free time would be as difficult as to take away its craving for fun too. If they are essentially relief reactions to a workaday life, they apply to Americans universally, for in America work is universal. In the old days of sociology, when a scholar wanted to determine whether a given species showed instinctive behavior, he would ask himself, what activities do all members of the species do without exception? Using such logic, he might have been led to believe that job-holding is an instinct of *Homo americanensis*. The only way to rid the race of its free-time traits would be to relieve workers of work, something that no one can do unless another way of acquiring a livelihood is given in return. The same applies to free time's base of operations — commodities. To keep Americans away from things one would have to eliminate advertising and offer them another authority to guide their free time. Advertising interests are formidable in themselves. And, of course, in back of them stands business.

Industry had found advertising and marketing techniques necessary to keep a capricious market from playing hop, skip, and jump. As more and more production is based on so-called leisure items, industry's dependence on advertising (for all that advertising cannot completely cure its marketing troubles) becomes greater and greater. The American economy has as its ultimate purpose to produce more commodities. It would come as no surprise to hear an economist say that this is the goal, the object of everything that we are working at: producing things for consumers. To try even to put a tax on advertising would raise fears of the economy's collapse, as well as make an issue of the extent to which a democratic, professedly antisocialistic government can itself operate in restraint of trade. The luxury taxes the United States now has exist only because World War II made it possible to push them through.

CONTENDERS FOR AUTHORITY

Whatever measures are tried to break the grip of commercialism implicate the substitution of authority, of government direction for commercial direction. Immediately some would say that this would then be socialism, not direction. Others, however, will be reminded that J. S. Mill, too, thought of the government as a teacher, and he by now is no longer regarded as a socialist by anybody. Still others might remember that Venice passed sumptuary edicts, and she was never regarded as socialist by anybody. In that magnificent commercial power, you could have a gondola of any color you wished, as long as it was black. Of course it wasn't long before Venetians took to brightening their colorless vehicles with fine silks and satins profusely displayed. The gondola today is still black and retains the same height and length, but an expression from a gayer epoch survives also. As applied to a woman — "She's all decked out like a gondola!"

We are again at the impasse common to educators and democratic theorists. The government as educator has been an ineffective teacher, evidently. Mill thought it couldn't help teaching men about politics and, by giving them a sense of participation, make them feel a solidifying common interest. It is doubtful, though, that the ordinary citizen knows any more about politics than any of Shakespeare's characters from the lower ranks, and doubtful that he is better informed or feels a deeper sense of participation in national events.

Mill didn't go much further than believing that political participation would bring about better government. Since the original government had to be good enough to enact the laws permitting people to participate, it had to be good to start with. Mill's problem of authority was easy. He believed implicitly in a superior class, a class of taste, education, wealth, and breeding. So if he never got much beyond the problems of suffrage, representation, and administration, it was because he took for granted that if things began to look up, and workers had free time on their hands, they would follow the guidance of their betters. To a limited extent, and for England, not the United States, he was right. One can see the slight difference by comparing private radio and TV programs in the United States with those of the BBC. To the new democracy in the United States after the eighteenth century this kind of authority was unacceptable. For this very reason educators have always had to insist that one man's taste in anything was as good as another's and that everyone is entitled to leisure.

What makes anyone think that if the government instead of business set up entertainment programs they would be any better than they are? Can the government find men of better taste than industry can, or artists of greater stature? The trouble is that such men are not to be found in any camp. A national shortage of them exists, has existed for a century and a half or more. Government officials on the whole have had a more general education than business executives, but not enough to raise hopes. Remember that the schools, apart from those few older universities, have done an efficient job in denying the leisure tradition. Suppose everyone by the next generation has a college education. Will they spend their free time differently from that described by the contemporary free-time ideal? Not at all. Indeed advertisers and marketing men are only too glad that college enrollments are on the increase. It's a kind of audience they like to get: one with the itch for status and things. They buy commodities as fast as anyone else, and usually faster.

So far, in the tension between government and private industry, the government's role in free time has been restricted to supplying certain facilities gratis, or at a nominal price, without giving them enough publicity to compete with commercial facilities. The government confines itself (with the exception of museums) chiefly to the outdoors — parks, forests, and playgrounds, offerings that are not accessible on a daily basis to working adults and that require enough energy to get up out of the armchair. The health and morale of the poorer classes of children has often guided the government in providing outdoor recreation; by the same token such efforts are noncontentious because noncompetitive. These children have little to spend on private facilities. Criticism that the government has not done enough has always existed, and alongside it the criticism that it does too much. Recently critics have taken to comparing expenditures for education and other services with those of private industry for advertising. One of the points they make is that by looking at advertising costs one can see that the country needs to spend more money on education. The logic, of course, is far from invulnerable. Why must advertising and education have a seesaw relation to each other?

On the other hand, of course, government and business work together in many ways and hold the same beliefs. Without what I have described as its allies, advertising's influence would go down almost to the level of a peddler; the on-foot salesman, the advertiser before the days of mass media, would again come into his own as in the days of Babbitt. These quiet allies — consumer credit, installment purchasing, obsolescence and disappearance of commodities, and so on — are not only part of business, but also by now part of government legislation. The government, too, acts as an ally. The whole scene has given rise to economic theories that if the consumer does not continue to buy commodities, the economy will soon give the healthy appearance of weeds growing high in abandoned railroad tracks. Until a new economics comes along basing itself on new facts, every government is at the mercy of economists who tell it that without consumption the end is near. Actually with the economics that exists (it is surprising that no one has noticed it) free time in quantity is unhealthy and would quickly lead to ruin.

The maze may have an earlier exit — government support of recreation. Since the person is hit on all sides by shrapnel, striking him with contradictory fragments — one, that he should buy things; two, that he should enjoy them in his free time — and since he can't work to buy and have free time simultaneously, he is left dissatisfied no matter what he does. His recourse is to use his other vote — the ballot. If the only way to enjoy life is to have these things, and if everybody should have them — these are both themes of advertising — then the government should make them part of its services. Indeed, another of the claims of the critics mentioned above is that the vast amounts spent on advertising could be better spent by government in services to the public. So, curiously enough, advertising, which at first leads to greater spending and a less capricious market, eventually leads to government support of recreation facilities. The role of advertising in laying the basis for the welfare state would be a study well worth doing.

Once the government enters the field a number of different things may happen. If it dips into the pool with but its little toe, which it has done so far, the situation is one of the tension already described as existing between government and business. If the government is in a stronger position and moves in more confidently, as it did during the depression, then advertising has less to advertise, titillation of the consumer decreases, the demand for commodities goes down and free time increases. At the same time, if the government sinks money into longer-range expenditures, such as buildings for the arts, then the less material kinds of free time may show a spurt of activity. The problem of government interference in the arts is just as serious as business interference, since there is no difference in the education of their personnel, but the government is not interested in selling things commercially. If anything, it is interested in selling programs wrapped — at the present rate — in two- to four-year packages. The electoral term gives it a slight edge over the shorter-run approach of advertising. Government can allow a wider margin in the recreation area than immediate popular approval on sales charts. If, furthermore, it confines itself to grants of permanent character — like buildings, squares, and city planning — the possibility of its interference in recreational and cultural activities is cut down. The same would be true if business made grants through foundations. Once the money is in foundations the control of business diminishes; once the foundation puts the money in bricks and mortar, then its control possibilities diminish too. All to the good. Architecture then seems to be a key to the kind of government or foundation intervention that would lead to a break in advertising and business control of free time and yet would not involve excessive direct control over choice. Still every step is a step affecting choice, this cannot be denied.

Undoubtedly the government's entry into recreation, as in all welfare and service functions, means more technical government, which in turn means more bureaucracy. (The implications this has for the pace of life is a subject we shall return to in the last chapter.)

Contemporary practices in state welfare took shape at the beginning of the twentieth century, in England perhaps in Parliament's National Insurance Act of 1911, in the United States about 1913 with the national revenue made possible by Federal income tax law. Ever since the Beveridge report of 1945 (where the phrase does not occur) English, American, and Scandinavian governments have sometimes been dubbed with the ambiguously flavored title of "welfare state." Such a government arranges by law for insurance, medical care, pensions, and other bureaucratic services for the citizenry. Doubtless these services can be increased, and commodity spending can be decreased, by taxes on consumer goods or on advertising or on incomes generally. Apart from the effects, calculable and incalculable, that this would have on the economy, the reduction of commodities and advertising and the increase in government services would not solve the problem of what citizens are supposed to do in their free time. They all work and have need of recreation. As part of its services the government would have to go into the entertainment industry. The problem of who chooses what entertainment shall be offered in the evening hours remains the same, except that the authority to choose has been shifted from business and advertising executives to government officials. Since the need for recreation comes from work, and work will not have changed character, the public's tastes (in so far as they can be expressed) will remain the same.

Thus, no sooner does one begin to think of changing the present idea of free time than the charge arises that democracy is being undermined. At first "socialism" is the charge — but only because to eliminate advertising and substitute government for business influence is the first solution many persons think of. They believe that the government has or can have something different in mind with which to entertain the people. Actually, the change counts for little. Work and its consequences remain: therefore the people will need their recreation. We cannot believe that work will be eliminated, for then how should we live? The solution, let some work, some not, runs against both the democratic and socialistic grain.

The charge now becomes aristocracy, and this strikes closer to the core. For in both cases above — the advertiser versus the government official — the people were considered as the arbiter of taste.

Or rather, the question of taste did not appear onstage. What the people like in entertainment — as in services, as in commodities, as in free time — whatever they like is what they shall have. The businessmen and advertisers count dollar-sales as votes; the government official counts ballots. The authority, the shaper of choice, remains the people. In theory. And one step removed. If we say that this one step removed makes all the difference, we are wrong. It merely replaces an advertising account executive with a bureaucrat. There is no evidence that in the United States the one has notably better taste than the other. Besides, the public will be no more communicative of its preferences than before, since the mass media of entertainment will remain in force, still holding their audience in uncritical attention. The argument for leisure belongs on another plane. One barrier is work. The other is equality. The plane is aristocracy.

Educators take their sides, as they have since the last century, some insisting that everyone should have an emphatically liberal education, some wanting everyone to have a chiefly vocational or technical or scientific education. To see that ideological barriers dictate the sides they take, we need simply note that both say "everyone" and neither says "impossible." With their horns thus locked, it is empty rhetoric for them to say, as a respectable report on American education does say, that there must be a rigorous re-examination of our present methods, and bold experiments with new ones. The reappraisal will try to put education more in tune with the latest technological and military requirements. The "bold experiments" will amount essentially to suggesting the use of the latest technological methods again, like TV, to reach new masses of students and adults, thereby reducing education to a lower level of critical attention than that to which it has hitherto sunk.

Do those educators who talk about liberal education ever advise the methods of Socrates or the Academy or the Peripatetic School or the Kepos? The siesta in the country, walking or stretched out on the grass, under a tree, near fountain or stream — these are the particulars of the *beata solitudo* that reach us from Plato's *Phaedrus,* after the seduction, or the way of uncounted poets and philosophers. A liberal education cannot be given over TV or in lecture halls seating hundreds. Education is the discovery and drawing out of the best that is in a person. How can it be done in crowds? Mass education is a contradiction in terms. There must be a one-to-one or at least one-to-a-few relationship. Out of Socrates came one Plato, and out of Plato one Aristotle. If we are willing to assign such a man-power ratio to education, then we can have a liberal education right here. But how can we? We have to work (work, again) and we cannot discriminate, can we, by selecting a few (equality, again)? Is it any surprise that advertisers greet the prospect of a college-graduate population of 100 per cent as good news?

Far from being unrelated to politics, the issue for anyone interested in leisure today is political. The way in which leisure and the political got separated is instructive. It bears, for one thing, on the tension between government and business. For political theory, the event is of interest, for in much the same manner the political sphere, which for the Greeks embraced all of life, dried up to a shriveled pea called government.

In the breaking away from the feudal, monarchical, and aristocratic regimes that dominated Europe until the end of the eighteenth century, the increasingly powerful commercial and industrial interests took sides with any definitions of liberty that aided them in their struggle. Liberty to speak against the state was called freedom of opinion and nicely juggled to include freedom of the press. Given the existing state of military and industrial technology, arms and hands were needed for armies and factories, and also as allies in the struggle against aristocratic privilege. Voting equality was extended to men and called part of their liberty. Thus all those who had lived in previous centuries under kings were automatically indicted as slaves, or at any rate unfree men. The artistic and cultural parts of freedom as yet were ignored. Marx, as we saw, verged on recognizing them, but then couldn't get away from the necessity of work, except in a faraway time when machines produce by themselves. The present of Marx's day of course was the nineteenth century, the time of great industrial development. The purpose of the state seems to have been to insure political liberty, considered as freedom of the press and equal voting rights. Once these were granted, then what? This was a question that did not seem to trouble political thinkers or economists. For the latter, goods got cheaper and cheaper and people could get more and more of them: this was all that mattered.

Here the *laissez-faire* economists did their share in implanting the commodity mentality. When they began their discourses, however, the idea was not so objectionable, since they were talking mainly about clothing and foodstuffs and the like, of which at the time there was little enough. For the economist too, it seems, the question of "Then what?" never was answered. Work, it is true, got one justification from the reformed churches. One from the state, also, for once the military power of technology was recognized, work and production received credit for making the nation strong. What place had art and beauty in this scheme of things? They began to be things apart, existing by themselves, divorced from political life — if ever they had been falsely united.

Contemplation, which plays so great a part in Plato, Aristotle, Epicurus, even in Roman thought and certainly in the Middle Ages and the Renaissance, and which belongs to a life of leisure, takes on a specifically nonpolitical and nonreligious cast. Leibniz took a first step by distinguishing one mode of apprehending that needed no reasons or grounds. It characterized knowledge obtained through the senses, and in it was the feeling of beauty. But, scientifically, only the intellect could go beyond the indistinct form of things to their true essence. So though the senses bring us beauty, they separate us from the intellect. This distinction fathered esthetics, the science of the beautiful, but a second-rate science, since intellect was foreign to it. Later Kant reasoned his way to further distinctions in which the beautiful with its *a priori* character pleases without need of a conception. But therefore doctrine in esthetics cannot exist; only a critique of taste is possible. Hence in matters of taste nothing would be gained by proofs of logic or conceptions.

Schiller even more positively relates contemplation to esthetics. With an unusual philosophic interest in art and the beautiful, of which there are intimations in his "Die Künstler," he concludes that contemplation apprehends the object without subjecting it to cognition or understanding. The enjoyment of the beautiful is independent of the practical and the theoretical reason both. Schiller went on to the educating of man through the esthetic life. Art eventually promotes morality and science. Greatly inspired as he was by Shaftesbury, he developed the ideal of the *schöne Seele*. But Schiller and then even Goethe, though they succeeded in fusing the divisions that Leibniz and Kant had cut, left an emphasis that remains to this day, through the influence of German poets and philosophers, on "the beautiful soul," on living life as a work of art, on leisure as the way to esthetic sensibility.

Enthusiasm was what Shaftesbury had, enthusiasm for the true, the good, and the beautiful. As the Greeks would live the life of leisure, life was to be lived in science, virtue, and art. Shaftesbury glorifies the world poetically, and he sings the whole world, not one with intellect and beauty apart.

The distinction between political liberty and cultural liberty, or taste, worked out well when the issue arose of government control over any of the mass media. Since the political supposedly had nothing to do with the cultural, business interests could in effect say to the government: "Mind your own business! The vote that elected you to office was for political matters. For cultural things the people themselves decide. They use another vote to express their choice, and their candidate is whatever they spend their dollar for." Since the mass media have been defended not only as economic enterprises and therefore entitled to be let alone, but also as instruments of political liberty — freedom of opinion and the press — the government even by mandate of the people could not interfere with the cultural liberty of the mass media: upheld by businessmen and advertisers, they too were equipped with a mandate from the people.

The degradation of aristocratic authority meant that aristocratic taste had to be defamed, too. This was not an easy accomplishment. It has succeeded less well than the attempt to nullify aristocratic political competence and morality. Yet the assertion of esthetic relativism, *de gustibus non disputandum,* did make headway and prepared the ground for the succeeding dogma — majority taste, a militant doctrine asserting that what people like they have a right to, and no one can tell them they are in bad taste. Aggressive though it may be, the doctrine has never gone so far as to say that what the majority likes makes good taste. It has shied away from the word *taste.*

Leisure became apolitical. Liberty took on a restricted reference to free press and the suffrage, and later to labor association. The mass media took over entertainment, keeping the government out in the name of titles they freely appropriated — communication and a free press. Thus political theorists are confronted with the doctrine whereby the ballot box expresses political choice, and the market takes care of cultural choice.

The political and the religious spheres as well are slighted in studies of free time also for the reason given above and for another one. This latter reason, also, has a special interest: it involves two concepts that often have confused the ideal of leisure. One is time (quantitative); the other is activity (visible). After the discussion of time in the previous chapter, it should be evident that the importance of an activity cannot be judged by the time it consumes. In any given day, month, or year the amount of time a person devotes to religion is small compared, say, to that he spends in transportation or work or shopping. One of the surveys cited in an earlier chapter indicated that on Sundays outdoor "leisure" increased noticeably for the young and old alike. The one-hour difference was due chiefly to the mass of people who go out to church on Sunday. This, though, seems to be about the only inch of time that can wholly be assigned to religion, except for small amounts spent in church socials or receiving visits from one's pastor, Bible reading, listening to church services on radio or television.

The same time-pettiness is true of politics. A man may not give any time whatever to the elections even in election year. Yet for his country — a political entity — he will make great sacrifices, perhaps give his life in war, something he would not do for a television program or be asked to do even for his job. Recent studies of electoral campaigns indicate that three out of every four voters voted, that one out of three tried to persuade others to his political views, and that another one out of that three did not care how the elections came out at all. Perhaps one in ten attended political rallies, only a few in every hundred donated time or money to parties or candidates, and about one in fifty belonged to a political club. This is the score once every four years. The average amount of daily time so spent would have to be measured by a stop watch.

There is something to add, though, to these figures. A citizen in a democracy is supposed to keep himself informed of what goes on in the world. The above tallies do not include the time spent on the news sections of the newpaper, radio, and television, or in reading books with political implications, or in earning the money to pay taxes. Certainly in the election heat it is almost as hard to escape the campaign as it is each year to escape taxes. Still, even if the political aspects of reading, listening, and viewing be added, the time spent is much less than that given in the evening to musical variety programs. There is no educational or news program, for example, that reaches the top ten on television.

Thus, by using the strictly quantitative assembly-line conception of time — time as a moving belt of equal units — one ignores the significance of much activity. A moment of awe in religion, or ecstasy in love, or orgasm in intercourse, a decisive blow to an enemy, relief in a sneeze, or death in a fall is treated as equal to a moment of riding on the bus, shoveling coal, or eating beans. As a matter of fact in most research the former kind of moments get left out altogether. In the search for the meaning of activity neither the quality of time nor the inner share of action can be ignored without damage. They go together, each lending significance to the other. The importance of activity without visible movement — reflecting or meditating, for example — escapes most Americans. Traditionally America is the land where action (meaning bustling activity) wins the day. For Plato and Aristotle, not horse racing, money-making, or fighting, but meditating, reflecting, speculating — these, the activities of the mind, were the ones by which men, old and young everywhere, distinguished themselves from the animals and placed themselves in relation to God. The United States in its short history among the nations of the world has gone straight ahead of everyone in rewarding bustle. This premium, I have tried to show at several points, affects not only the reporting of activity but each person's definition and description of it.

Religion is not merely going in and out of church doors. It is also a way of life, a standard for conduct, a morality, and more still. All of Sunday is a religious day, a holy day. All activity falls into its context. We saw earlier how it affects the day's character. Should the whole twenty-four hours be considered religious?

No more is politics merely going to the polls once every four years. The American as a political being has standards that regulate his conduct, or, to continue the usage here, his activities. Actually, "activities" as applied to religious and political conduct is not the right word. For activities does not connote the standard that "conduct" does. A person on free time engages in activities, but these are contained within a framework of the permissible, the moral, the framework of conduct. A strictly quantitative reckoning of time cannot take this into account. Studies and perspectives based on it will always underestimate the political and the religious action.

So, more than we have been led to believe, free time, as well as leisure, maintains close contact with politics. To the examples cited earlier — legislation affecting education and mass media, national parks, forests and museums, subsidies and taxes affecting occupations and commodities, congressional committees on recreation, passport control — we can add a most obvious one: government regulation of hours of work. At best, though, these measures reflect an underlying relationship.

What is the state for? This is the real question. In contemporary times the answer has been to provide order and a variety of liberty that gives all persons formal access to political choice (for example, universal suffrage and education). In more recent years, this liberty has been extended to provide security against certain misfortunes, like illness, old age, and unemployment — in a phrase, the welfare state. The acceptance by the government of unemployment insurance signifies that it accepts a role as the guarantor of work. Beyond this, the passing of years has seen little change in the state's part in free time; it provides a bit of space and houses a few collections of paintings or natural history. The local level, especially city governments, often offers greater variety. Since a congressional commission administers the District of Columbia, the activities of the Federal government there resemble those of an ordinary municipality. If there are summer band concerts in New York City, there are United States Marine Band concerts in Washington, D. C.

Because of the conflict with private interests, of the mix-up in the mass media of news and entertainment, and of the accepted theory that the market is the arbiter of free-time choice, the question of the role of the state goes begging for study and reflection. The democratic state therefore has no position to take, and, without a reasoned and strongly felt position, no authority to act.

THE MANY PLEASURES OF THE MANY

Any real passage from free time toward leisure cannot be made, we have seen, without leaving the confines of the present-day democratic credo, in particular its ideas of work and equality. There thus seems little chance of rapid change in the ways people have of spending their free time. But one shouldn't lay the blame at the door of democracy alone. What does Russia offer its citizens for their hard work? Free time and commodities, if not now, sometime soon. How do Russians spend their free time now? Less in overtime, none in moonlighting, more for cultural uplifting, more in collective undertakings, less with commodities, more in political readings, but, all told, everyone looks ahead to the goal apparently reached by Americans — much more free time.

All that need be added is consumers' goods in quantity for the pattern to move up toward identity. Not long ago the clerical employees of a Western oil company in North Africa went on strike, though their pay stood among the best on the continent and their working conditions included air-conditioned offices. The reason for the strike was clearly stated and comprehensible. The company's offer of a cost-of-living pay increase made no provision for the inflated costs of entertainment. Being entertained was not a luxury, the union had said, but a necessity now in order to break the monotony of employment. This little story neatly fits some aspects of the contemporary rationalized work style. The point to be made, though, is limited neither to democratic governments nor to industrial patterns of work.

No civilization has ever seen all or even a majority of its people participate in the best standards of taste, or those highest activities of the mind that reveal the presence of leisure. The majority typically presents a spectacle of free-time activities resembling today's. There are important differences of time, space, and taste in these activities, but I shall save discussion of them for a later moment. Ancient Greece, where the ideal was brought to its pinnacle, ancient Rome with its centuries of peace, the Republic of Venice which was called the Serenissima, Brunelleschi's Florence, the eye of the Renaissance — all present us with only a few capable of enjoying leisure. There is no point in saying this is bad, or that popular pleasure in free time is reprehensible. Why be a spoilsport? It is what it is. About the only thing that can be done is to rephrase things so that they sound better. The mandarin Khanh-du once improvised a moving poem on selling coal.

The contemporary American's attitude toward the theory and practice of leisure might present itself now somewhat like this: For convenience, he keeps work and leisure running on the same time schedule; he takes pleasure in moderation so that work does not suffer; freed from basic fear by the security provisions of his government, he stands ready to take the most out of life, little caring what happens afterward; an optimist, he is proud of his fellow man's progressive conquest of nature, of his country's resources, of the appliances he can buy with the work he puts in; he uses these appliances as they should be used: as means to the end of saving time and labor and of having fun; he constantly and actively seeks ways to improve his position; unimpressed by the dullness of politics and the sobriety of religion, he is not averse to raising hell every now and then; he finds social pleasure in doing what others do, being a strong believer in teamwork and team play; he is convinced that one man is as good as another, if not a damn sight better, and deserves as much as another, specially if he's a practical man; once the day's work is done he is content to relax in the humble diversions offered by the home and its accessories. Why is anything wrong with any of this? It sounds no worse than the circuses of Rome, the Parisian worker and wife's Saturday night outing at the old café-concert, the periodic fisticuffs in Venice at the Ponte dei Pugni, the cockfights of Mexico, the possession-dramas of Ghana, or the Englishman's crowded beach at Brighton.

We have seen at least two good reasons why people might not take leisure though the opportunity existed: first, there may be no strong tradition of leisure; second, in its absence, forces opposed to leisure, unless stopped, may intervene to bring not a new tradition but a follow-the-piper, day-to-day pattern for work, free time, and money-spending. There is a third reason: leisure may be beyond the capacity of most people. If history shows no people in any quantity ever enjoying its delights, perhaps we are dealing with something that only a few can enjoy in any case.

Persons democratically inclined immediately react to such a possibility with an environmental explanation: No wonder only a few can have or enjoy leisure; the rest of humanity has been brought up in such squalor as to prevent their ever arriving at leisure. Yet we can point to cases — Rome is one — where the mass of the citizenry had no need to work, being supported by the foreign tributes exacted by their government, where libraries and literacy flourished, where health and hygiene were as good as they've ever been, and still we meet the same kind of popular pursuits. Socrates needed little to find leisure; Epicurus the same, Diogenes even less. Undoubtedly, the American's work can unfit him for leisure, but what can we say of times when it was not necessary to work? Aristotle had pointed out that the Spartans could have no leisure as long as the Helots might be expected to rise up and massacre them. The *plebs* had no such fears. Is it temperament, then, that fits only a few for leisure?

Greek thinkers had set up a different ideal, granted, in making leisure the state of being free of everyday necessity. For them this meant that a man should do nothing, or very little, in order to attend to his appetites. By and large they understood by appetites the carnal or material ones — hunger, thirst, sex. Here and there in this book we have touched on sex in relation to time, work, and leisure, but a word on its place as a necessity is still in order. (I hope to be given credit here not for what I write but for what I refrain from writing.) Natural appetites should be satisfied naturally. The Greeks believed in giving the body its due. Its due should not cost much. The government, though other costs might have risen, kept the price of flute girls at two drachmas. They liked wine with grace and bodies with grace, which, however, were not spiritual things. At most they were imitations of spiritual things. Once you move from the natural appetites and the pleasures of Bacchus and Aphrodite into other lands of desire, like power or fame or riches, the ground begins to get shaky.

Take away all desire from a man, he is no longer alive. Man is a desiring creature. Love for family, particularly for one's children, was recognized as natural, once the family existed. Beyond this Plato and Aristotle recognized a love for justice and for the state and, of course, for God and the gods. Epicurus put little stock in the *polis* or the gods, but admitted a desire for philosophical fame. These then were natural or at least naturally understood desires, even in a state of leisure.

For theory's sake appetites and desires had to have an acknowledged role. They defined necessity. If you were free of the necessity of food and shelter, for instance, you did not have to work — unless you were prey to false desires such as those for riches or power. If you had no desires save natural ones naturally satisfied, then whatever you did was free of obligation. You did it for its own sake.

Now in admitting natural desire and the love for virtue, the Greeks avoided trying to make a man without passions, a paper man. In letting in desire, however, they opened the door to something it was not easy to keep an eye on. They were probably right in treating corporeal desires in a natural fashion, but other desires cannot be treated so casually. Man's make-up and situation conspire to complicate all his desires. They become difficult to trace or to reduce to their origin. What appears as love of God may be a desire for riches, and a seeming drive for power may be a passion for justice. Perhaps again they were right in ignoring such subtleties. After all, given the absence of everyday necessity for toil, of sycophanting to superiors, of taking it out on inferiors, of seeking only what is needed to advance one's ends — having got rid of imperfections as gross as these, the smaller defects will not cause great harm. (Early in the next chapter, I shall come to the customary ways of being free of necessity.)

The Greeks may seem to have underestimated the twists and turns personality can take, even when free of everyday necessity. Actually, they did not. They neglected such facets because they were talking about persons whose background they took for granted. What might they have said if confronted by this businessman? He was asked whether, if he had an independent income assuring him of his present standard of living, he would continue to work. He replied, "I am sole heir to four million. Does that answer you?" Some might say that the reply proves that for this man his business is his leisure; he does it for its own sake. But the Greeks would have reasoned differently. Their idea of freedom from necessity itself is foreign to most of us. Instead, "We all have to work" seems to us a self-evident law of the universe. Since we work, we have no necessity. This is the way we reason. But it is the work that creates the un-freedom. Illogically, we start from the premises of work when we try to prove our freedom from necessity, thus tying ourselves to necessity before we begin to reason.

One of the ideas the monks of the Middle Ages had was that by monotonous manual labor the mind was freed for thought and contemplation. The argument has been advanced in recent times, too, apropos of factory work. Surely a man can be spiritually free of his work, if while he is at it he can forget it. If he prefers another place for his reflections, however, and another time, and another activity — in other words, if he were doing other than what he is, and were free to choose any time and place for it — then he is unfree, and the product of his mind and hands will show it. To write poetry one man may need the clean air and solitude of wide open spaces; another may compose best in a small smoke-filled back room. This is a different matter, reflecting a choice of place only, while present-day work involves a time schedule and specified activities, too. If one is subject to a boss who says, "You work in the room filled with blue smoke over there," it will be hard not to suspect necessity. Any case where one is subject to the orders of another would raise the suspicion. It may be that some persons like to work under direction, or that some wouldn't know what to do with themselves if they didn't have to go to the office or factory in the morning, or that others would prefer a clean orderly air-conditioned office to a hot house and unkempt wife. In each instance, work, though they may like it, remains a means to particular ends. The heir to millions presents a different situation.

Perhaps these Greek thinkers did not make clear enough that a man could be unfree and not know it, that like a life-sentence prisoner suddenly pardoned, he could be too long subject to necessity ever to leave the prison once the gate was opened. In any case, their first response might be that the man was educated improperly. As we said a moment ago, the Greeks had in mind persons whose educational tradition they understood. Even in castigating Sparta, Aristotle was singling out its aristocracy. Education consisted in being brought up in an aristocratic family and being tutored privately. It formed character, developed mind and body. If a man didn't have this education there was little he could do to obtain it later in life: the impressionable years for character, mind, and body had long passed. Culture is *paideia,* something you absorb as a child.

Youth is not free in practice, law, or custom from parents, teachers, and others who tutor and watch over minors. Hence, the young can be neither free of necessity nor capable of leisure. The term *minors* expresses their inferior station. They cannot yet have formed standards for themselves; only a good upbringing will give them the proper foundation.

Bouvard et Pécuchet is the story of two men who acquire the income to do what they want but fall heir to it at too late an age for their adult studies to do them much good. As for a man brought up to like work, what chance would he have? If he didn't work, he wouldn't know what to do with himself. So Aristotle, probably, would have taken a bet that the man, if truthful, would have given the answer of one of his most famous forefathers, Abraham Lincoln. When elected to Congress, it is told, Lincoln was given a form requiring him to describe his education. He wrote one word, "Defective."

The Greek's second response might well have been that the man simply didn't have the stuff it takes to enjoy leisure. There is such a thing as intelligence. Bouvard and Pécuchet, though towering over the people around them, may have lacked some of the necessary amount of it, and perhaps also of another requisite — the leisure temperament. To any other temperament, the delights of leisure are not so delightful. Some of them can be appreciated by almost anyone, perhaps. The banqueting, the dallying, the friends chosen for their own sake, conversations about anything — love, politics, the gods — music and poetry, gambols, wining and dining, all the way through the night. "No songs can please nor yet live long," says Horace, "that are written by those who drink water."

A man of leisure cannot work in the sense of earning daily bread, but he can play — if play is what he wants to do. Generally play for him will be a distraction; the mind, after long pursuing a line of thought, may need to run playfully along a different line. In another sense, the man of leisure is always at play — since his delight is in the play of the mind. This may seem an unwarranted extension of *play*, and can only be used in the English, not the Greek, sense of the word, yet it is justified not only by long usage but also by the detachment which, we have shown, appears in leisure. This detachment and objectivity is related to the lack of seriousness in play, for the mind seems to play without disturbing a flower.

Actually the detachment is more fundamental than this. What is meant by unseriousness is that play ceases when at the player's shoulder pallid necessity appears. If starvation or death is the outcome of a contest, then it is neither game nor play. For the professional boxer, the tightrope walker, the gladiator, the contest is a matter of bread and butter or of life and death. For the spectators it may be a game. They suffer the excitement of siding with contestants in agony; they feel joy of victory or humiliation of defeat. But behind them there does not stand *chlōra anankē*.

In a true game, one without such high stakes, the players' tension does not come from fear of necessity, but from imagining that the play is serious. This is play's set of mind, acting as if the outcome counts for something vital. The idea of fair play and being a good loser belongs to the same quality of unseriousness. If absorption goes too far, it becomes a trance or ecstasy or leads to breaking the rules of the game. A justified and common complaint of players is that one or another person takes the game too seriously. But if the game loses too much of its power of illusion and absorption, it becomes uninteresting or frivolous.

In English *game* is often used metaphorically for *contest,* since both have the element of striving. Yet a contest can be to the death; a game cannot. People sometimes say that business is a game, and certainly it can be one, if not taken seriously. But for those who work at it, business is usually in earnest and counts for what it is supposed to.

Play's relation to leisure lies more on the side of pleasure. The joy of the game comes from voluntarily exciting oneself to maximum strength and skill, or acting as if the stakes are the highest, while remaining all the time aware that it really doesn't count. The duel is a contest and yet a game if both fencers stop the moment a drop of blood is drawn. The joy of the game, then, is pretending to battle or acting out a danger situation, a play of skill and risk, within a situation really without peril. The player leaves his everyday world and enters one in which for the moment he is free of necessity, namely in his free time, his time of recreation. Symbolically he does battle with necessity, knowing that he cannot lose; indeed, if he plays and acts well, he may win.

In ordinary life, of course, if a man works he is not free of necessity, and on the next day or hour returns to the workaday world. But play has lifted him out of it for a moment and made him a free man, one who could choose or not to play, one who, keeping faith with all the rules, faces the bull in the arena. So, for the ordinary man, play is a taste of leisure. The festivity and the holidays are playdays, out of this world, moments when the ordinary is suspended and all rejoice in a common unconcern for everyday cares, to celebrate this and other wonders of the cosmos.

The man of leisure, we said earlier, is always at play or (as

Plato would say) on the hunt, in the exercise of the mind. And in another sense also: in his freedom from necessity. Plato, who understood play better than Aristotle, may well have meant this when as an old man he wrote in the *Laws* that the right way to live is at play, in games, in giving the gods their due, in singing and dances. The philosopher concludes this remark significantly: Then, he says, a man will be able to propitiate the gods, defend himself against enemies, and win the contest. Note that he separates play and games from contest, here. Play and games can be considered in terms of social function as preparation for work tasks in later life. This we mentioned in a previous chapter. But the significance here is not sociological function. With leisure comes detachment and objectivity. In play too, since the game doesn't count, there is also detachment. The player plays without the passion of a real struggle. The quality of dispassion and objectivity in play is what leads to the recommendation not infrequently heard to do a given task or job as if it were a game. Talleyrand's advice in diplomacy was *surtout, pas de zèle*. In nations where honor is a dominant virtue, the aristocrat acts as if everything others live in terror of were to him a game. Thus he is always prepared for quick and true decision. Cool and collected, he sees that all life is a game. An extreme example of this occurs in polite Japanese speech, where the speaker speaks as if his hearers did whatever they did because they wanted to, not because of necessity. On hearing that a man's father had died, one would say to him, "I hear that your father has played dying." The one who can look on life as a game, the man free of necessity, has the advantage of detachment, of the objectivity of leisure, that graces play in its brief moment. A world with leisure supports a world with play.

Whether we accept Xenophon's or Plato's description of a symposium, both of them describe pleasures that have a wide appeal. But underneath it all, moving it along and lifting it to unequaled heights, is delight in the play of the mind. These men of leisure came to the banquet well prepared in the exercise of the speculative faculty. They led a life of theory, and for them that life was the only one worth living. The businessman's job, as can be seen at once, ought to be useful for many ends — the pleasure of commanding, of a game, of outfoxing a competitor, of prestige, of carrying on a family tradition, fulfilling one's responsibilities toward employees, and so forth. The job can be a means toward any of these ends, but nowhere is it reputed to open up vistas for contemplation. One interested in the exercise of the mind gets out of a narrow field that offers no prospect of it.

The world is divided into two classes. Not three or five or twenty. Just two. One is the great majority; the other is the leisure kind, not those of wealth or position or birth, but those who love ideas and the imagination. Of the great mass of mankind there are a few persons who are blessed and tormented with this love. They may work, steal, flirt, fight, like all the others, but everything they do is touched with the play of thought. In one century they may be scientists, in another theologians, in some other bards, whatever the category may be that grants them the freedom to let their minds play. They invent the stories, they create the cosmos, they discover what truth it is given man to discover, and give him the best portion of his truth and error. It is a select, small world of thinkers, artists and musicians — not necessarily in touch with one another — who find their happiness in what they do, who can't do anything else, their daemon won't let them. The daemon doesn't depend on environment. You have it or have not. The pleasures of this handful of persons differ sharply from those of the rest. It cannot be otherwise. The ordinary person must buy his pleasures with the time and income of his occupation, while this class is actually occupied in its pleasures. That is why no matter how much the class is underpaid, it is a luxury class and will always have its select spirits as members. As long as it has leisure. Its felicity is assured in each act and at the very moment. The others, moreover, need to re-create themselves from their occupation, whereas this class has, if anything, only a need of distraction.

The others have their mass or popular or folk cultures; the leisure kind create culture. Culture doesn't necessarily make a person happier than folk culture (it depends on the person), but it is more profound, truer, highest in skill, artistic, beauti-ful. Those of the non-leisure class are formed by others. The man of the leisure class may be poor or rich, noble or commoner, of the strong or the weak, but he is always powerful in that he is the only one who, by his daemon, forms himself.

Veblen thought the rich and the aristocratic made up the leisure classes. The rich, specially the newly rich, buy com-modities and ape the manners and taste of the noble. The noble and the anciently rich have quite constant spare time pleasures, at best like those of Pliny. They ride and hunt and go to the theater, they make love, they converse, dance, and drink. They also work, or at least the real ones did, to keep their estate in order, to see the crops distributed, or they fight to enlarge and protect it. Some of their pleasure has its origin in the battling of land aristocracies. Thus it bears a relation to the nobleman's work, and can be called recreation. They read, too, though some may have the literary taste of the ante-bellum plantation where the fondness for Sir Walter Scott was excessive. Since that author helped feed the Southerner's idea of himself, perhaps reading in the South too was recreation. (I have been using the modern sense of work here, which, of course, does not apply to an aristoc-racy, as it does not to the vocational categories mentioned in an early chapter.) Of all these rich and aristocratic activities, be they work, play, or something else, none show a great love for the cultivating of the mind.

Class is linked to Marx, since he taught the class struggle. *Leisure class* is linked to Veblen, since he wrote *The Theory of the Leisure Class*. Both these thinkers are so far from the ideas of this book that it would be only fair to disassociate them from our use of *the leisure class*. *Class,* moreover, when applied to groups usually involves some communication among class members; this is not necessarily true of the class we intend. They may neither know of nor care for one another's existence. The preferable term in many cases is *the leisure kind.* The word *kind* allows more room for a temperamental element and suggests a deeper environmental imprint than class. Yet the phrase *leisure class* should not be discarded, if only because popular reaction to it is significant.

To use the phrase *the leisure class* kindly today invites hostility and envy. The phrase rubs against the grain of equality. In recent centuries the envy must date from around the time of the French Revolution. Equality was probably not the first concept to raise the war cry against the leisure class. More probably "work" antedated "equality," work in its newer factory form, with an idea of production as whatever comes out of machines.

Sometimes it is as hard to convince people that everybody does not want leisure as it is to convince them that in the days of domestics, servants pitied their masters' lot. Much of Plato's *Republic* is devoted to the simple proposition that we cannot all be philosophers. If we can't be philosophers, we'd be bored with leisure.

The practical man, in relation to thought, can take it or leave it (he thinks). Shakespeare, Bach, Cézanne, mystery stories, comic books, western films — to him it's only a question of how you want to spend your free time. But for this same practical man the question of a leisure class boils down to a privilege: there are some people around who take it easy and live in luxury. This, highly simplified, is Veblen's idea too. The non-leisure class nowadays believes that a leisure class is one that leads an enviable life. We have just agreed that we cannot all be philosophers, gentlemen, musicians, or scholars, and that most of us would not want to be.

Then what is it the non-leisured envy in their false picture of the leisured? Above all they envy the thought that the others take it easy. This element of envy brings us to another difference between the two classes. The majorities of peoples have never sought the delights of leisure. For them "delights" is a misnomer. There is another mass of evidence to be brought in. It resides in two bodies of literature, each corresponding to one of these two great classes that distinguish mankind.

Leisure's Future

THERE's a far land, I'm told, where cigarette trees and lemonade springs abound; the hens lay soft-boiled eggs; the trees are full of fruit, and hay overflows the barns. In this fair and bright country there's a lake of stew and of whisky, too. "You can paddle all around 'em in a big canoe." There ain't no short-handled shovels, no axes, saws or picks. It's a place to stay, where you sleep all day, "where they hung the jerk that invented work." It's called the Big Rock Candy Mountain, but its ancient name is the land of Cockaigne.

And they say there's an isle deep in clover. Only a few have ever found it. Atlantis is its ancient name; the one it has gone by in recent centuries is Utopia.

Both lands have their literary genre. Utopia is a possessor of culture; Cockaigne is possessed by the folk. Both express how the world should be reshaped to heart's desire. So both are linked to the myths of the Golden Age, Paradise, and the Elysian Fields, where man lives among the gods. There is a difference. Utopia's world is for the leisure kind, Cockaigne's for the whole of humanity. Their importance to us is that the different shapes of their emerging worlds show that leisure is for a few and free time for the many. They also show how fundamental is the error that the many pine for leisure when what they dream of is ease and abundance.

Utopia's significance for us lies less in its content than its form. It is a literary invention designed to take the problems that disturb mankind and propose a solution in a complete way, a way that takes account of the complexity of human affairs where statesmen so often go wrong. They propose a remedy that sets in motion forces which neutralize the remedy or make things worse. In the matter of work and leisure, Chapter II showed briefly how the utopias could leap centuries ahead of their time. From Plato to William Morris, each utopia takes problems that have been handled by piecemeal reforms, or not at all, and tries to bring them together for solution. The distinctive mark of utopias is just that — they try to give a full yet harmonious picture. Complex, yes, searching for truth, profound, artistic, and sometimes poetic.

The land of Cockaigne, a less familiar genre, transmits itself by verses sung or cheaply printed and illustrations stamped on broadsides or sometimes glued on crude paper fans. Its special significance lies less in literary form (of which it has little) than in substance. In utopias there is work for everybody and 4-hour days or 8-hour days; free time is spent in walking, in reading, or at the theater; a variety of things will be found, not all by any means conducive to a life of leisure. The lands of Cockaigne instead are much the same. From the verses of blind storysingers to the Big Rock Candy Mountain comes a simple theme, running so uncompromisingly on one track it is often funny. Whoever is caught working has both his legs broken. Hunger doesn't exist, nor thirst, nor old age, nor pain. The law is eat, drink, and no work. Otherwise there is no law. Nor policemen to make you work. In the Big Rock Candy Mountain, the cops all have rubber legs. Cake-lands vary in the kinds of food or drink preferred and how it grows or is served up to them (often falling off trees, or to be picked off the ground), and how drastic the penalty for working may be: they are the products of different climates, times, and places.

In topographical maps of the land of Cockaigne printed in the seventeenth century, there are illustrated captions, such as a mountain labeled "the mountain of gold where the more you dig away the more it fills up," or a river of muscatel, or cows that give birth to calves every day, a traditional lake of milk and honey, musicians singing and playing, a hill made of grated cheese, a prison for whoever but talks of work, people sleeping in bed under the sign, "The more you sleep the more you earn," birds and fish that hop into your hand at your call, a table always set and laden with delicacies. In some verses, links of sausages hold the bulging grapes tied to the vine, in others pheasants fly right into your mouth, already roasted. But ease and abundance are the terms that characterize them all.

While bread and work was the slogan of many uprisings in the nineteenth century, the driving force behind the larger, more dangerous revolts was the thought of ease and luxury, the twin sirens of all cake-lands. Anyone trying to reach the seat of power needed the help of the people — with factories and mass armies people's help was needed — and had only to promise them some form of Cockaigne land. Indeed, for the newly rich businessmen what else in this world was there to offer? It was what they themselves had in mind when they thought of how the ruling classes lived. Cases in point are the socialist manifestoes and proclamations of this period and the democratic ones that preceded them by a half-century or so. The growth of *invidia* can be clearly seen. Veblen saw the cream of the business groups of his time trying to enjoy what they had struggled all their life to reach — the land of Cockaigne. They had thought, and so did Veblen, that ruling and noble classes lived there. They wouldn't have understood Marcus Aurelius's reflection that a person can be happy even in a palace. In trying to get there themselves, they had offered their bid for popular support in the only way they knew how, and they were right. The slogans of Louis-Philippe's Revolt of 1830, the great bourgeois revolution, had been *"Enrichissez-vous!"* The entrepreneurs in Anglo-Saxon lands also invited everybody to get rich.

Of course, the rules had changed somewhat since the captains of industry had earned their four stripes, but this, for us here, is not as important as to recognize that the land of Cockaigne, of take-it-easy, of *commodité,* is the best that commercial societies can offer in the way of the good life. Get rich, reads the invitation, enjoy life the way the rich do, have ease and luxury, but first work hard. Equality proclaimed as a liberty, in this scheme of things becomes the instrument of the envious element. For if I must work hard to have my cake, you shall not have it unless you work hard too. Privilege is an outrage. The leisure class becomes the symbol standing for those who have idleness and luxury without having to work for it like the rest of us poor suckers.

The genius of the present industrial world is that it has given everybody, even the most unsuccessful of the lowest workers, those who instead of going onward and upward have gone backward and downward, the skidders — has given even them the sense of having almost reached the land of Cockaigne. Ease and abundance are always nearly at hand. People shall have everything they want, and leisure too. Actually the singers of Cockaigne take themselves less seriously. They play on a world where you live without working, where you see with your stomach's eyes, and they know it's a dream, perhaps a lie. Sometimes they use the satiric style, or else a comic tone that shows they are laughing at themselves. Not so for the cake-land of today. The industrial world has been able to keep alive the sense of being almost within Cockaigne's borders by the wide distribution of so-called laborsaving devices.

In the United States, in spite of what is often said to the contrary, it is not true that manual labor earns respect. Toil here has always been reserved for slaves, indentured servants, bondsmen, and the latest wave of immigrants. Non-manual labor has always been preferable to and a social step far above, indeed in a different caste from, manual labor. (Note that though *work* is a word we apply to almost anything, yet we say manual *labor,* not manual *work.*) I have already indicated the American worker's notion that if he has a machine between his hands in his work, it raises his own estimation of himself to another kind of being, a non-manual worker; it separates him from the laboring slobs. Labor-saving, or rather effort-saving, devices for free time come highly prized too. The owner of the new car with push-button windows feels (for three or four months) like a pasha and looks down on the guy who still has to crank his windows up and down like a sweating peasant. If he thinks about it, he's sure that St. Peter's gates open by photoelectric beam. The American abroad applies this notion wherever he sees work being done without an array of power tools. A peasant is a farmer without farm machinery. An artisan is a poor manual laborer making quaint irregular products. And he fondly recalls his own country, where anyone who would work that way deserves to have his legs broken, and his employer's, too.

There are other Americans, we know, who contrariwise buy these quaint products as paragons of beauty. Abroad they are apt to write of the nonindustrial country they are visiting as a land of leisure. They make the mistake of believing that a country with a less precise time than their own is a place of sweet indolence. This may not be so. A different time sense from ours is a necessary condition for leisure; it is by itself nothing but that. In a hot agricultural zone, Yucatan, let us say, the tourist who looks around at midday finds nobody working until three or four o'clock and then dwells on how nice it must be to loaf and take a siesta every day. (Chapter IV caught our own northern farmers cat-napping, hard to believe though it may have been.) The people the tourist sees drowsing have been up while he was still in the arms of Morpheus, long before dawn. Peasants everywhere work hard. The difference is that they work more according to the natural limits of light, climate, and appetite. This is enough to give us the idea they have leisure. Corn for tortillas and a place to swing a hammock, that's all they need and want. No wonder they have a leisurely life.

Rural peoples have games, a religion, government, and custom, and an art of song, story, dance, and decoration. Nothing wrong with such a life. Far from it. But they have no leisure. Once we go from the rural to the urban, from the tortillas and hammocks of rural Yucatan to the ruins of Chichen Itzá, we have to change our minds. We can no longer believe that the ancient Mayas were content with hammocks and tortillas. Neither do art and temples assure us that when they were built there was leisure. Something more is needed. The world is divided into two, I ventured, the leisure and the non-leisure kinds. Therefore, it would seem, a leisure kind always exists. If so, it would exist in rural as well as urban areas. If so, the form of government or religion would make no difference either. The leisure kind, a class based on temperament, could not increase or decrease in number by good or bad treatment under varying forms of government. In this light the political system seems irrelevant to leisure.

What does always exist is a rudimentary leisure class. The small-town boy who likes to speak in verse (his two brothers have nothing to distinguish them), the shaman trying to work out a perpetual calendar, the city shipping clerk who can't hold a job (he's always forgetting things, but fascinated by dream books), the painter who paints portraits (to keep alive and painting), the philosopher who becomes a professor (isn't it curious that all philosophers today have to be professors, else they are not philosophers?) — we cannot go into all the subterfuges that scientists have to devise or all the double-dealing that scholars have to learn, or the sycophanting that painters have to go through, in order to get a semblance of a leisurely life. Persons like these may need leisure and are to be considered part of the leisure kind, but since they are without leisure, since they live under the shadow of necessity, they remain rude and unwrought.

For men of leisure to exist, persons who by disposition delight in cultivating the mind and are free of the state of necessity, a country must have built up at least a small surplus. This is not so rare an accomplishment. Almost all communities, even the most primitive, have enough margin to support a class of priests. If ever there was a stage in the life of mankind where each and everyone had to grub all day long for food, that time must be lost in a geological past. A leisure class, in order to develop, must also live where existing political and religious beliefs set store by the cultivation of ideas. If contemplating, study, meditating, and speculation are held to be the pastimes of incompetents, the community will be hostile in ways flagrant and subtle, as we have seen and shall see again, to those who live for these things.

The next step is vital: neither political nor religious doctrines must insist that everybody work for a living. Every form of government has a doctrine of equality, much as every religion has. In some one sense all members of the country are recognized as of the same stripe, and therefore equal at least in that one important particular. An ideology does not stop there but goes on to prescribe other equalities before the law of God or man. If a doctrine of equality is extended to work, however, it stunts the growth of a life of leisure. The pursuit of happiness, which we saw originates as the free and various pursuits of men of leisure, comes to mean, in the hands of the courts, the pursuit of work. No matter how we come to think of work as the mark of a free man, in the ideal of leisure it becomes prostitution, the bending of mind and body for hire.

In writings on the life of leisure, the wherewithal achieves little or no notice. Since the well-off and the noble were the main groups in which the leisure kind customarily found its fellows, the problem often does not appear. History reveals three or four main ways of keeping alive without work. Property in land or buildings is one. A system of tenant farming or of renting may call for little effort on the part of the owner. Tenant farming supported the Florentine villa as well as the *villula* in the Sabine countryside where Horace lived and ruled, and where so many leading colonial Americans from New England down to New Orleans set their dreams on location. Property in persons (slavery) was another means to avoid work as such. This was

Aristotle's chief resource for a life of leisure. Slaves were either a source of income in working farms and shops, or servants in the household or to the person, thereby freeing the master of tasks that would otherwise clutter up his life. Property in quantity in stocks and bonds can also provide for an adequate income without work. The method proposed by Plato, that the state provide the necessities for a class of philosophers, draws upon a wider base. He secures his rulers' room and board by having the ruled provide for it in tribute or taxes, as you will.

We might mention lastly the case which the Greeks, in contrast to the Orientals, were not much interested in, except in moderation — asceticism. Man can keep alive on very little, practically nothing but water and a few nuts or grains. Given a country sympathetic to both thought and asceticism, you can stay alive by eating wild plants or begging a bowl of cereal when hungry, as priests still do in Southeast Asia. Even for the Greeks, it was all right to reduce your desires and get along the best you could, perhaps with a handout from friends or strangers every now and then. Diogenes is the celebrated Greek example: Diogenes lived in a tub and when Alexander the Great, in gratitude for a profitable talk with him, told him to name his wish, he simply asked the emperor to move out of the way, he was blocking the sunlight. The story also exemplifies the importance of climate and reminds us that leisure is a Mediterranean discovery. Since the Greeks, in general, did not believe in the mortification of the flesh, the possession of what would today be called unearned income was almost essential.

We can agree that the mortification of the flesh is unnatural and perverts the senses. Yet real property sufficient to provide an income on which to live is becoming scarce. Indeed, property, except in small parcels, is disappearing, at least in the classical and the seventeenth- and eighteenth-century sense. In Roman law the owner had full power over his lands and possessions. In Continental law, modeled after the Napoleonic civil code, the proprietor has the right to enjoy and dispose of things in a full and exclusive manner. Locke had united property and liberty indissolubly. Blackstone had kept away from a man's property all control or diminution. And Kant had laid the foundation of jurisprudence on proprietorship.

Compared to this solidly personal ownership, the proprietors of today's large properties, particularly industrial, are faceless. Nobody owns what they own. Ownership and control has been split. The fragmentation of ownership into stocks has returned the owner a share of the profits while leaving him with the smallest influence over the property. The managers control it, and profit from it, also. So large are their incomes from it that we could say they have the usufruct of the property. But to have this they must work. The president of a corporation works.

Certainly property as a base for income is no longer as important as it used to be (Table 17). Moreover, taxes on inheritance and unearned proceeds, designed to equalize income, help see to it that a revenue from real estate is rarely enough. Church and state both refuse to admit chattel. Although property in cattle remains a way of obtaining income or services, the tax agent considers income from livestock to be *earned,* a word that implicates work. And accurately so. For a man to run his farm as a "gentleman farmer" is generally held to be inefficient and somewhat disreputable. The dairy farmers surveyed as a group in an earlier chapter were not gentleman farmers. That breed is almost extinct. A considerable number of the executive class today could quit work to live off the income of its stocks and bonds, but has little desire to do so. How many stockholders hold enough to afford forgoing their paychecks?

I have not gone into how property may be acquired and retained. Laws of inheritance and primogeniture are of capital importance. The dowry is another custom once of service in permitting a life of leisure, now out of service. The Talmud, for example, says that a rabbi should not be paid for his teachings and should have, instead, a rich wife. In Europe it is still not unusual for a professor to be supported by his wife's dowry.

Lastly, the idea of using taxes to support the leisured appears unworkable. Taxes are collected to finance public purposes. The American form of the separation of church and state keeps public funds from being used to support a body of theologians. At one time if a family had a son who showed signs of intellectual or artistic gifts, he was marked for the clergy. Today but a few are so channeled. More go into scientific work. Science can be supported by public funds, but the scientist is supposed to work, to put in at least the ordinary 9:00 to 5:00 that clerks do, at the office or lab. Tax money cannot go to any class without some prospect of the public weal being served. And the only accepted way of serving it is by work. What benefit does the leisure kind bring, a class that doesn't work? If we had been able to see any benefit in the first place, we would not have had to go through this series of traditional ways of maintaining a life of leisure. If a community sees benefit in the leisured, it will try to provide support instead of putting legislative and tax barriers in its way. At present no one sees a benefit. If a person today lives off unearned income from property or stocks and bonds, he is not likely to call himself a capitalist or a *rentier*. The most passive word he dare use in referring to himself is "investor." The government officially stigmatizes his income as unearned. The people are growing fewer daily who, to the blunt question, "What do you do?" can answer, "I don't do anything. I *have* money."

Ultimately I shall turn to the question of leisure's benefits. At present, let's continue with these political factors to see whether there may be others that can induce an unwrought leisure class to develop its potentialities so as to become a real one. Some such factors have been discussed earlier; now that the concepts of free time, leisure, and the leisure kind appear more distinctly, their significance may have changed. An economic depression oddly enough may turn people away from the acquisition of commodities into devising less costly ways of spending free time. The general effect may be a wider appreciation of nonmaterial forms of production — the theater, for example. While the entertainment of the mass media seems inexpensive in prosperous times, in hard times just the constant repairs and electricity to run the things makes them a drain on resources, like tires with a slow leak, always in need of being pumped up. The government may take action to relieve want, not excluding starving artists and intellectuals, some of whom are accustomed to half-starving anyway. By and large, the income of the leisure class in proportion to the others rises because it was so low to begin with. The classic example might be the philosophy professor's salary. Even in good times, he never is called on for fat consultantships as his colleagues in physics or mathematics are today; and in a depression he suffers the happy fate of those with fairly fixed dollar incomes.

Commercial ages often go hand in hand with nationalistic ages. A country's size or military power increases. The rapid expansion of industry finds favor and support among nationalist groups. American industry served to build the country and to make it strong. To deny this political element in commerce and industry would distort history and in particular the history of the idea of work. In the United States work has a religious strain, certainly, but also a political one. Work, the work of everyone's muscles, was needed to make this country great. The picture drawn earlier wherein the easy life of Cockaigne is the only one a commercial world can offer must be similar for all commercial ages. Prosperity may not necessarily be the country's sole aim, though. The size of a nation or *polis* depends on many factors such as its population's age and racial composition, on communication and transport and the legal system, but once it gets involved in political, religious, or commercial dominance over other communities, it acquires other purposes besides order, security, the good life, other purposes that may extend its size or prosperity. Usually, it is difficult to judge what the motive for expansion may be. It often takes place under the guise of preserving or extending goals like those just mentioned. For this reason an expansion of size or power or range of control, when it steps into the national program, may take its place with hardly a clear head in the nation having thought about empire.

Hand in hand with the growth of strength, like a boy learning to box, goes a growth in the image of oneself as someone to be respected. Little by little the nation takes over from less powerful ones, often for reasons of pride that would have been quietly swallowed or not even raised by countries not busily engaged in flexing their biceps. All the time the only national purpose it openly proclaims may be advancing the dignity of the individual. Of course, there's no denying that the greatness of a nation enhances the dignity of individual citizens. Anyway, where a political entity is in the process of growing — whether it has set its destiny consciously or not — its energy pours into military, commercial, applied scientific, and administrative tasks.

Nations in an expansionist mood are places where spare time is hard to find. Time becomes important. Haste and energy (visible activity) and practicality prevail. These periods are generally unfavorable for leisure, and their benefits are not to be seen in beauty, grace, art, literature, or leisureliness of life. Individuality, doing things for one's own sake, is hard to find, no matter how much proclaimed. Collective purpose dominates the scene.

Whether visible energy spends itself, whether the life of commodities leads to a love of creature comforts and softness, whether setbacks bring pain and withdrawal, whether an optimal national size is reached — at a certain time expansion may stop. People no longer have a sense of great national purpose or destiny. They straighten up their backs from work and begin to ask why they should work, who they are, what their country is, and where it is going. Military designs are often the first to falter. Once one gave one's life for one's country; now voices begin to be heard. Why die for Mr. X's speeches? Why go to war for the liberals? . . . or the conservatives? Without the sense of do-or-die, a vast bureaucracy may build up, lazy, comfortable, making it impossible to do anything in a hurry, enforcing a slower pace of life, and possibly reaching the refinements of Byzantium. With the urgent sense of collective purpose gone, at least in international affairs, with consequent reduction in military, commercial and administrative tasks, energy and prosperity rushes into the arts and sciences — based, as usual, on a sense of individuality. The liberal arts and the free, unapplied sciences — these are not attuned to national goals but to the enjoyment of what life offers in beauty and wonder. Since the energy carried over from the reduction of collective tasks is greatest at the time of the reducing, a great sweep of culture may appear just before the decline (whether rapid or gradual) right at the apogee of a state's power — Pericles, Caesar, Lorenzo, Elizabeth. Then if the decline is gradual and pacific, there follows a gentle period of cultivation and refinement and a leisurely pace. Augustus freezes the frontiers of the Roman Empire, stopping its expansion, and the Augustan Age begins.

Perhaps because of this coincidence, leisure has a bad name with the militarists. Wherever they see refinement in a country they conclude it has already given up expansion. Sometimes such a belief has proved embarrassing to the attackers, in particular when they calculated that a country with which they were about to join battle, having lost its expansionism, had also lost all fighting virtues. The Mayans against the Spaniards makes a good example; most recently, the English against the Germans; and of course the Egyptians against the Hittites. Perhaps military men keep in mind the fate of Hannibal who after a victorious campaign set up quarters in Capua. His soldiers — wild Iberians, Gallic mercenaries, and Numidian horsemen — had never known the comforts of urban life. They slept in a real bed until midday. The roofs on stone and brick buildings along with the charcoal braziers kept them dry and warm. They drank wine, took warm baths, and reveled in the best bumpkin style. But that was just it. The Romans, too, had such comforts, were used to them and took them in their stride. In this case, the stride was a long firm one toward Capua.

Refinement is not enough to bring a sharp decline in military valor. Neither is it enough that a country go into expansion and then stop, for it to produce a great culture. "Nor does the Muse when called come to the savage Goths," says Ovid. A country must also have been exposed to a great tradition of faith, for one thing. When great expansions are associated with great cultural growth, it may have been not only the contact with new nations that was stimulating but also, and often overlooked, the strong faith that in the first place brought the confidence and courage for expansion. An age of faith, by itself — the Dugento is an example — can produce a magnificent culture. Perhaps culture and leisure live together on either side of commercial ages. Beauty and security of faith may give rise to a spirit of risk and adventure which in turn brings a dedication to commerce and expansion, war, money, and comfort. Faith might support a life of leisure in parts of a priesthood, or among nobles and artisans. Subsequently, the wealth of a commercial age with its surpluses and cities may encourage the leisure kind to emerge and evolve. There must be other matters too that either call or frighten away the Muses. Across the cities, surely, they have often blown their inspiration, but their mode of invocation is yet imperfectly known. As some men are kings by grace of Zeus, said Hesiod, other men are poets by grace of the Muses.

Great culture or not, when a nation, having reached the stage of halt, proceeds in its slow decline, it may take on the character of what can be called a disengaged or uncommitted state. People from the expansionist, rigidly-purposed, stoical, ugly, or dull nations will go there for beauty, time, and individuality. Their quest must not be confused with the rustic's awe of the city, the small town American's gawking at New York's skyline, or the central Asian's being overcome at the sight of Moscow's turrets. Instead, it is what Romans felt for Athens, what our fathers felt for Paris, and what we feel for Venice. Small nations in a world of sweating giants sometimes remain cool, live on a horizontal rather than a vertically inclined plane, and develop a kind of unhurried life undisturbed by great purposes and upheavals. Today we have as examples Switzerland, the Scandinavian countries, even England with its welfare state and the gradual retirement of the army and Her Majesty's Royal Navy.

ON FALSE AND TRUE POWER

I have used the word decline to make myself understood. I could just as easily have spoken not of the fall of a nation but of its rise. For what purpose is a nation? Where would you prefer to live, in a nation of drums, marches, and steel helmets, of smoke, metal, and commodities, of rigidity, ugliness, and haste — or in a land of flowers, squares, unhurriedness, and beauty? The musings I have given way to in this chapter are not intended to be taken as historical laws. In the fashion they were presented, if they resemble interpretations of history, it is because I wanted to illustrate in the history of leisure a complex interplay of small and large things both, an interplay not only of consumers' goods, the working week, and overtime, but also of faith, commerce, nationalization, and wealth.

A state's history of art and letters may be plotted as a curve of heights and depths, just as could (and is) its history of might, its industrial and military strength. If we laid the two curves one atop the other they might bisect each other, intertwining like a panorama of Tuscan hills. The question I am leading up to, though, is, Which of these two curves do we wish to call real power and which one false power?

GNP is a familiar abbreviation of the last decade or so, standing for Gross National Product, usually written reverently in capitals. American businessmen, economists, and politicians use it constantly to refer to the country's industrial and military strength and potential, and often as a measure of our well-being. An economist cannot object that the measure refers only to our industrial and military strength and capacity. He knows that economists have for some time been in the habit of equating GNP and welfare. As a measure of welfare, the GNP has gross limitations. It takes no account, for example, of morale in industry or in war (factors related to both industrial and military potential). It is important not only to know a battalion's fire power, but also whether the men in it will squeeze the trigger. Leaving aside the question of work and military morale, we should like to ask whether beauty, sun, and purple beds of flowers are irrelevant to well-being. Is there well-being in the person who spends days watching lesser white-throats creeping up and down a nettle? If so, where is it reflected in the GNP?

The efforts of a person who spends his time in conversation are never entered in that ledger. A page of the GNP devoted to Socrates' whole life would have been a blank, pure white, unstained by numerals except perhaps for the government's expense at his trial. The American seems sociable enough, indeed is known for his affability and first-name calling on short notice, but good conversation plays little part in this sociability. It may be that conversation at best is prized by a minority in any time or place, yet in the United States it is hard not only to find this minority, but to find the activity honored. In eighteenth-century France and England, good conversation was an art to be cultivated and admired. Beverages, like tea and coffee, and the coffeehouses that served them, owed their fame to the power they had of stimulating conversation. How many Johnsons are there who never had a Boswell, who never wrote plays or dictionaries, who give their best in a drama of ideas and persons, whose thoughts alight here and there, some on rocky ground, others on rich soil? They are not counted, for they are people who just talk and talk and never get anything done.

Instead, the organizers of men and workers in factories are heroes of the GNP, comparable to the inventors of new production-increasing machines. There is no page in the GNP for subtracting whatever is lost when men are organized, lost in the efficiency of style, grace, taste. Of course, it is a mere hypothesis that style, grace, and taste affect the health and well-being of the worker, whereas it is a widely accepted fact that electric razors and mixers and quick-drying paint make him stronger, quicker, and handsomer.

The history of the notion of production and efficiency contained in the GNP, like that of revenue in our income-tax laws, would make an uproarious study. Henry Ford had a dual accounting system, in which there were only two main kinds of costs — production costs (the only real ones) and "burden." Not long ago at the Ford Company burden was changed to overhead. Adam Smith preceded Henry Ford, we have noted, and Saint-Simon did, too. And the utopias were there before any of them. In Thomas More's famous land, machines hadn't been invented yet. How was it, then, he could reduce work to a 6-hour day? By putting to work all the idle and unproductive people like princes and others of their ilk.

Once upon a time energy and power were not concerned with things to be measured only by a head of steam, in weight of coal, or bars of steel. The discovery of iron and carbon alloys does improve ax and spear heads. It has brought about great changes in the world but it has not steelified the power of *caritas* or the energy of love. After all, what moves men? Brandishing a steel-headed ax might, but so does charity. Love, it has been said, makes the world go round. Unless we abandon the idea that men can be moved by women, we must admit that women have some horsepower at their disposal. If, as one study shows, today's housewife has the energy of ninety-nine servants at her disposal, energy contained in motors and labor-saving equipment of one kind or another, there must be something lacking in the kinds of energy measured, for whoever has been lucky enough to have had one live servant of the pre-World War I type would prefer that one to the fictitious ninety-nine.

Aristotle's irony has been wasted on many persons who have cited him in defense of machines and automation. We quoted the passage earlier, the one about imagining machines not simply for weaving but also for strumming the lyre. Now why should it be less desirable to have a luting machine than a lutist? The fact is we have a kind of luting machine today in the juke boxes, instruments of culture that emanate from the United States to the farthest corners of the world. Perhaps for most persons a juke box is better than nothing. (That there was ever nothing, however, is doubtful.) A juke box permits the choice of the songs you want. Almost everyone has a private one at home in his gramophone. Now, imagine that you could have any disks or tapes you wished to play. For one thing you are limited by your own choice; later you may want something you forgot to order or you didn't know about. All right, suppose then you owned all that have ever been recorded. You are still limited by the choice of whoever chose to record the records. You may wish to hear a lullaby only your grandmother remembered, or a tune you heard children singing while playing in the streets. Apart from these limitations (some of which the musician cannot remove either) the lutist has the distinction of being a person. You can hum a tune to him and perhaps he'll catch it; you can make subtle choices — "Play me the last one you played last night, but tonight play it in a lower key"; you can droop wearily in a chair and he will try to divine the mood and what music will bring you out of it, or permit you to luxuriate in it; you can be sure he won't play one tune too often, for it will stale for both of you; you can hear new ones he has composed, or a serenade for your love, a lullaby for your new child, a lament for your death; and you can develop in taste without realizing it, under his guidance, until both audience and lutist have achieved a rare perfection.

Well, you say, rare is right. Find me such a lutist. The answer is, I can't. Such a lutist does exist, but there are only two or three like him. I might be able to substitute a guitarist for you, but in such perfection perhaps there are only a dozen or two alive. Once there were many more for both the guitar and the lute; they have been chased off the market. At the moment we have the juke box.

It would be wrong to take such talk as the celebration of a previous, simpler life. A person can put himself in your place; crude machines have no empathy. We ignore this when we talk of machines as replacements for domestics, or when we speak of service occupations as substitutes for servants. A good lutist, person and skill together, is more complicated than a good juke box. For one thing, there are more ways of influencing him than by being the possessor of a quantity of small change — all the ways in which men and women influence one another. It is a mistake to regard other ages as simpler, in any case. The primitives were and are no simpler than we are. Nor am I here expressing a preference for a golden age in contrast to today's barbarism, though Orpheus did civilize the ancient world with his music. I wish not to celebrate but merely to remind of other standards.

Perhaps these remarks should be directed primarily to those who pronounce with solemnity, affected mild regret, and not so secret smugness: you can't turn back the clock. The industrial world is not stable. Indeed, its instability is often cited by its advocates as something precious: it is not a static society. If a society is dynamic, it merely means that it is moving, but the direction is not necessarily a right one, as recent connotations to the word dynamic would have us believe. The twentieth century has seen a great depression, and the use of commercial ballyhoo in an effort only partially successful to stabilize the capricious demand for commodities. Further mechanization will bring the problems already mentioned under the name of automation. The twentieth century has also witnessed terrible wars and a world growing ever bigswoln with population. To believe that no one of these sad sights could precipitate our world of cities into darkness is precisely to believe that you can't turn back the clock.

Why is it the people who say that you can't go back are also the ones who nowadays are most fearful of the future? Perhaps because they are ignorant of history, perhaps they believe that with the cities destroyed, *après nous,* everything is destroyed.

But after the city dwellers are buried, the rural world goes on. It is an urbanite's prejudice, too, to think that in the rural world there is no activity of mind. Not alone the rural but also the primitive, not only the illiterate but the preliterate worlds have their thinkers, their seekers after and finders of truth, their philosophers. If not squeezed under the thumb of massive cities, they can bring forth music and theater and a literature, if not written, then oral. Before the scribe there was another who neither toiled nor spun — the bard. We can see the roots of art in the human nucleus that planted the culture of cities. Pindar stood on the shoulders of the Bard and was no greater a poet than whoever composed Homer's lines, but poetry is Homer and Pindar, and Sappho too, and where do we hear of them but in the cities?

Without the cities, I do agree we shall have gone backward. Though a nonurban culture is possible, great art and civilization depend on cities. Cultures flower in plots at least the size of the Greek *polis,* which for us would be a fair-sized country town. And to be able to use leisure, men must at some time in their life, preferably, like Boswell, in youth, have lived in the city. Great religious discoveries can be made by men who have had the least of contacts with cities, by desert nomads like the Jews (and even they were often in contact with the cities), but for art and science the *polis* is a teacher, one, like all teachers, to excel if possible, to be able to do without later. Only in the towns is there conversation, and if one does not converse, he must at least listen and look at the conversing of men and watch what they do. The dialogue, that which the broadcasting media cannot provide, is the best foil for the mind, not because we must convince our adversary and give proof of our rhetoric but because only the praise and criticism, the give-and-take of conversing and of human contact, can lead to higher standards.

The Greeks in their development of the ideas of leisure gave a fair share to the part played by the city. They knew it was essential. They were aware also that it could become so large that its conversation would turn into babbling. When, in Magna Graecia, they thought that Cumae was getting too large, they stopped expanding, moved over and began anew with Neapolis. What happened later to the Neapolitan city to change it into the still beautiful but oversized Naples, was none of their doing. A city which, as it was said of Babylon, could be invaded at one end two days before the other end heard of it, was not a *polis*.

For Plato, the city is already becoming a physical burden. Though essential for the education of a man of leisure the city can become a threat to his peace by overwhelming him with false necessity. Doubtless the man of proper background will never succumb. He can draw back into himself, be alone even in the middle of the market. You can touch him, but he isn't there. Even so, it is easy to fall into social life and be caught in the net of the thousand-things-to-do. We shall refer to the dangers of the city later, in an encounter with Epicurus. Yet leisure needs the city for education. Athens was the school of Hellas, as Pericles said. Those who are properly educated can later take the city or leave it — they are strong enough to make the choice — but those of imperfect background stand to fall to the city's lures.

Cities are fragile things. When built to towering heights by commerce they are more fragile still. Alas, alas that great city, Babylon, that mighty city! Even without the city's bursting to smithereens, or dissolving to dusty heaps of mortar, or returning to the oxcart and puddles in dirt streets, there are still ways the clock has of going backward. What makes the clock go ahead, as we have seen, is not the pendulum or a coiled spring or an electric impulse, but the machine. It is not impossible that the machine will be given up gradually. Nothing points in this direction now, it might seem. Actually, technology and industrialism as an ideology pull ahead of democracy. If a dictator says his country needs dictatorship in order to industrialize itself, he is excused for being a dictator. All countries have an inalienable right to technology. Their real hero is not Marx or Adam Smith but one of whom they may never have heard — Saint-Simon.

Today a democratic or socialist leader, if he does not believe wholeheartedly in technology and does not make the country undergo great sacrifices to industrialize itself — I have Nehru in mind but there are lesser examples — is considered a fogy.

The decline of machines is a chance not to be overlooked. No decision may be needed to turn back the clock. It will falter when our faith in machines falters. That faith may quail in the face of military defeat. Athens and Sparta did not run at the approach of Xerxes but a faint heart at the sign of superior power is not a rarity. A loss of morale, whether the GNP measures it or not, in itself may be suicidal for machinery. Not having been able to win with it, we may spit on machinery and its offspring, production. Mathematical supremacy did not save Babylon, and after Babylon mathematics spiraled into a slow, deep decline. Victory in turn may bring too great a faith in machines, and then, betrayed by it into false confidence, the country sinks into defeat and despair. But let us cite a more cheerful way as well. A world government, reached by conquest or agreement, would by eliminating the threat of war, decrease the pressure for technical improvement in arms. The removal of military pressure alone would cause a decline in the prestige of machinery and of industrial production, which as we noted has always been associated with military power as well as with commodities. If industrial progress is no longer needed to keep us strong, then its only ground for existence is commodity production, a ground not strong enough to forestall questioning. People might ask why give the best part of life to work, the hours of light and sunshine, the prime of our years? Indeed, some signs of questioning are with us already.

It all has to do with the prowess of machines. When economists, businessmen, and labor leaders worry that increased automation may cause unemployment, one of the dangers in the back of their minds is that machines will produce too much, that what they produce will not be absorbed by consumer demand. Were this not a fear, the question of unemployment would be simpler, a matter largely of readjusting and shifting personnel. Thus everybody would work the same hours, produce more, get more pay, and buy more things. The note of doubt remains: machines produce too much. Then, the consumer's most heartening contribution to prosperity would be to step up his purchases of homes and cars. Economists would be cheered were he more enthusiastic over the appliances that choke the warehouses of electrical manufacturers. "And the merchants of the earth shall weep and mourn over her, for no man buyeth their merchandise any more."

More important as a possibility, still, is the effect the prowess of machinery may have on the ideal of work. We have seen work grow out of toil, take on a religious and a patriotic cast. We have seen the religious coloring grow thin, while the military and patriotic significance persists: work builds a strong and great nation. Yet, as the utility of the mass army diminishes in warfare, so may the utility of mass labor diminish. If automation offers work for only a small class of specialists, the concept of a labor force is on the way out. For the mass of workers, then, work will have little significance. If machines, tended by a few machine-herders, do the work, why should men work? The heat is off. Though we may deny that the gospel of work ever extended to miners and factory workers, the sense of national purpose work gave to all classes cannot be so easily disputed. Though we were disposed to argue, along the lines of those who say that after all the only thing the worker works for is the many mouths at home, even this motive for work is gone.

In the West, escape from poverty as an excuse seems to justify the industrial system no longer, nor does funneling into it the best brains (for example, scientists), talent (for example, advertising), and resources (for example, landscapes). The workers in this country have been able to use their political force to get government to guarantee them either jobs or pay without jobs. If the worker needs activity guided by a strong purpose, work, it seems, will not supply that purpose. Then who or what is going to create it and how? Machines and machine-tenders will do the work; men in masses will not be needed for factory or army; free time will be wide open. The big question appears once more: What to do with it?

So far, as I have remarked time and again, work shows no signs of collapse. Religiously, politically, economically, militarily, and mentally it is still thought better to work than to do what you please. Although all these justifications have weakened, the habits of work and its prestige in the world persist. Moreover men prefer to work not because they don't know what to do with their free time — we, like the Greeks and Romans, enjoy boxing and wrestling matches and horse races — but because the job still gives a sense of participation in the affairs of the city, the country, the world. Whatever enjoyment they might get out of more free time, they cannot give up their place in the scheme of things without gaining another place. Retirement, for example, does not offer them another, nor does it offer the social satisfaction that many jobs have today, specially in the white-collar range. If work ever loses its significance in the way I have laid out above, then these parts of a job not included in the job description will lose much of their pleasure too.

The men who go to work in the morning and come home at night are still the pillars of society, and society is still their pillar of support. If an eroding work ethos causes these pillars to crumble, must the new pillars of purpose be found in leisure? This evidently is the hope of many who speak of education for leisure. They foresee that free time is on the increase. They fear that empty free time is idleness (and in Old English they can find support: "idel" probably meant empty). They fear that free-time activities today are vain and useless (and in Anglo-Saxon they can find that etymological meaning). They would like to fill these empty, vain, and useless hours, days and weeks and years with something good, something that would turn it into leisure. Really they are still using the old word, idleness. Unfortunately for their hopes, leisure has nothing to do with idleness or free time, nor are the mass of men easily attracted to its joys.

If the work ethos changes, the political ethos, of which it is part, changes also. Democracies decline when armies cannot use citizen-levies and factories don't need labor forces. Before long the politician does not need their votes. Characteristically, American political writings in the nineteenth and twentieth centuries do not stop to consider the possibility of democracy's passing. Characteristically, current books on the future omit the possibility, too. Political or ideological change is so inconceivable that writers do not have it in mind, even as a remote chance. They are being less realistic than the Founding Fathers, who, though amateurs, were better political scientists than graduate schools turn out today. They had one rule of politics firmly in mind, a rule they learned from the Greeks. Democracy degenerates into tyranny. The many tyrants in Hellas's short span helped Greek students of politics as much as clear cloudless skies helped Egyptian students of the stars. But we choose to act as if the possibility that we could concur in any form of government but democracy did not exist.

Perhaps it would be more accurate to say that republics lead to democracies, which then degenerate into tyranny. The Founding Fathers raised many safeguards; barriers to democracy, they might be called. Some still stand, others have been washed away. One evidence of the change is that the word republic is rarely used any more to refer to the government of the United States, except in the school child's obligatory pledge of allegiance. The preferred and nearly universal usage is democracy. Yet to come upon Thomas Jefferson, for example, using the word democracy in his pile of papers is a task to give a proofreader. Furthermore we have made history to read as though the great Western cultures — Periclean Greece, Laurentian Florence, Elizabethan England — rode to their heights on the back of democracy. The first was an aristocratic republic, the second a benevolent despotism, the third a monarchy with a fair, firm hand and a good measure of aristocracy, too. If we take a later England, the eighteenth or nineteenth century, we have a monarchy limited constitutionally by an oligarchy. Spain's golden age was monarchical. The eighteenth-century United States was an aristocratic republic. In all these times, liberty was highly thought of. Not the same can be said for equality.

A government that tries to legislate equality, we seem to forget, interferes with ability just as a college program available to everyone restricts the intelligent student's opportunity to get an education that will carefully draw out the best in him. From this kind of democracy that blindly believes liberty and equality are compatible, but if in doubt, the latter is the surer policy — from this leveling or radical democracy to another kind of ideology needn't take long. Pericles dies and Athenian democracy, so-called, is finished. Alexander follows. The Augustan empire moves right in almost while Caesar's corpse is still warm. Lorenzo dies, and Elizabeth dies, and all coherence dies with them. A change great enough to be visible may take two hundred years or one hour. In both cases it would seem less than an hour to those who believe that democracy is the final and immutable form of government on this earth.

A compromise is already noticeable today when educators begin to talk of an impossibility as though it were possible, to say that the educational system should not founder over whether to provide quantity or quality; it obviously should provide both. The next step is to admit that perhaps in some cases it is better to have quality than quantity. The "some cases" become more frequent and "perhaps" turns into "probably" when specialized and elite forces are called for in military and labor corps. What's in these conventional political tags, anyway?

As far as leisure is concerned, little. As far as creating a culture is concerned, a lot. If as I intimated the free-time activities of men do not change as much throughout history as the games of children today from those of Peter Brueghel's time, the form of government matters not much. But both in their search for entertainment and in their building and work, men imitate whatever is around them. Therefore it is important that their environment be fitting and beautiful. In a leveling democracy, standards that are not coarse are hard to find, for it asks men who are all right as learners to wear the hats of creators. School learning and book learning, specially on a mass scale, must be superficial things. As a result, at those times when the cultural level of the people is to be brought up to the highest point, it brings down instead whatever standards exist to the level of mediocrity, a level so low that the work of artisans — wherever they have managed to survive — is regarded as art.

By contrast, monarchic or aristocratic systems, which make little to-do about raising the popular level of culture, succeed in doing so by conserving and creating standards of taste and beauty. Like an Egyptian painting that shows the queen in greater size than her handmaidens, yet in the same human proportions, so the masons of Tuscany built houses smaller than those that the master masons created for the Florentine villa, but in the same architectural proportions. If the neighboring Tuscan peasant or workman of the last generation has a greater vocabulary and precision in his choice of words than anywhere else in Italy and perhaps in the West, the fact is not due to his learning them in school, but to his Tuscan forefathers, who included masters of poetry and prose — Dante, Boccaccio, and Machiavelli.

I have chosen this last example in the cultural field to show that an objective esteemed by mass education — range of vocabulary and precision in its use — can be achieved universally in nondemocratic times. Shakespearean England may be another instance, but this case is clearer in that living examples still exist of the older stamp of Florentine. We do not have to ask whether this cultural superiority makes him happier, since the skill is conceded to be a good thing today. The only thing that might not be considered good is that the one who spoke even better was the polished Florentine. Here again we touch the *invidia* of equality. It is the very fact that some talked and wrote not merely as well as but better than he did that enables him to talk as he did and does.

The depreciation of man power in army and factory, a decline in the prestige of the machine, the intrusion of inegalitarian ideas in education and politics, not to mention the leveling of cities — these are all things that in themselves or in their consequences would turn back the clock. I admitted that the disappearance of cities would turn back the clock, figuratively. I have also hinted, however, that the other instances, while necessarily slowing down the clock literally, might not turn it back figuratively. At all events the effect they would have on leisure would not necessarily be the same they would have on free time or on culture. They are all political factors, and our concern with them has been to give an idea of how, whenever we think of change in free time, culture, or leisure, we come up against the prospect of political change as well, a kind of change that many declare they would not wish to see come about.

LEISURE AND POLITICS

At this point it should be possible to clarify the relation of leisure and free time to political beliefs. Taking free time first, its duration appears to have bottom limits in fatigue, which itself varies with such things as the intensity of working purpose, the amount of communication permitted by the work situation, or the worker's freedom to start and stop according to his state of mind and body. In a settled condition, without crisis, personal or political, actual working hours seem to run about 45 to 50 a week. By hiding laborers and labor under one roof, by binding them to machines and the clock, by lightening toil until it became work, our own world concentrated free time into off-the-job time. Much off-the-job time was not free but work-related.

Because it was taken in a lump, officially after 5:00 P.M., let's say, it seemed to be larger than it was and also more than any other peoples or times had ever enjoyed. The conviction, though wrong, was held by all classes of persons, so that workers, employers, and advertisers all believed together that there was a great mine of free time to be exploited.

We can speak, then, of loose natural limits to work time and to its obverse, free time. Other factors put other limits on the quantity of free time. Since work has purpose it dominates the work/free time relation. Free time, without purpose of its own except as related to work, has no separate existence. If it increases, it brings the worker a sense of uneasiness; he doesn't know what to do with it if there is too much, and underneath it all he fears there lurks a lack of purpose to his whole life. If offered the choice, then, he readily accepts the alternative of more work, specially if it is sugared with the promises of a higher standard of living or the enjoyment of free time through easy-to-buy merchandise.

The state, since it usually considers work essential, usually considers free time essential too. Free time restores men to work; its duration must be protected. Sometimes part of a political ideology may hold that free time should be spent in political activities. We saw J. S. Mill as advocate for this brief. The political system also defines who is to get free time. In an industrial democracy, and in socialism, we noted, the deserving are those who work. Free time is one of their rewards. A man unable to work is a man unable to have free time. He is either sick, old, unemployed, or imprisoned. Democracy and socialism combine the universal duty of work (or the paradoxical "right" to it) with the doctrine of equality, thereby making everybody not alone a worker but a beneficiary of free time as well. All workers get it, no one gets it without work (no leisure class), and no one has a right to more of it than others. The distribution of free time thus cannot change without a change in the doctrine of work and equality.

The present doctrine of freedom, as it applies to commerce and the extended family of the press, affects free time chiefly in its activities. Inasmuch as free time depends on work, it has no purpose of its own to guide activity. Given the view that government should keep hands off the press and market, except to make them freer, which is difficult to do if you lay hands on them, business through its various channels succeeds in guiding much of the spending of free time. It must keep its guidance within the bounds of law and morality, to be sure.

Free-time activities are not divorced from moral concern, or at least are not oblivious of it. Torture and killing, shoplifting and incest form no part. It comes as somewhat of a surprise to hear that primitive tribes make war in their free time, just as it is a shock to hear young delinquents say that they killed or tortured a boy because they had nothing else to do. This is not free time, somehow, it is . . . what? . . . idle time? the devil's time? Only a rare person would answer an interviewer's question about what he does in free time with the reply, "Fornicate." Not that the activity doesn't occur. Perhaps the answerer did not even think the activity was immoral; he may just have feared that the interviewer might think it was. In using the word, though, one brings in a moral and also a legal tone. The time becomes not free time but a special kind of underworld, a vice time. Anyone who wanted to avoid it would have used another phrase, like "Make love" or "Look up some willing girls." In this language the activity seems much more possible as a free-time pursuit. Of course, you will find local variations. A study of a slum in a large foreign city once found that several men in answer to the question, What do you do in your free time? reported, "I go out and steal." The place was a hangout for thieves. On the subject of incest, one might also find expected deviations, in fact if not in reply, in isolated farming communities. And in history's vast range many other variations appear. "If you're not doing anything now, let's go down to Tyburn. I just saw a cartload of women and little girls going by to be hanged." These words would once have been considered an invitation to spend a few hours in the big city in capital entertainment.

These are local variations. On the national scale certainly, open attempts to guide free time, like government announcements or advertising, do not admit such deviations. Advertisers cannot push heroin across the counter like cigarettes, and, at the moment, cigarettes themselves come under scrutiny.

Thus is the dilemma resolved that has troubled us so often in these chapters — activities that are done during free time but with a sense of obligation, are they really free-time activities? Activities that fall in free time are by definition free-time activities. It is only when a man raises a subjective objection, namely, that he feels as though he *has* to do the activity, that he doesn't *feel* free, only then does the dilemma appear. The problem arises when free time is first used in a strict time-off-the-job sense and then mixed with the sense of felt freedom. If we say that free-time activities must satisfy both senses of the idea, we then bump up against another part of the paradox, to wit, that free-time activities cannot be immoral, and yet if moral they are often not considered fun. This puzzle I shall come back to shortly.

While work may have individual justifications today — work is good for you — individualism is part of the philosophy of the state. So this part of the work ethic is political too, along with the idea that work is good for the nation, making it rich, strong, and great. What's good for you is good for the country, and vice versa. For free time to take an independent position, the dogma of work and of its helper, time, too, would have to undergo change. If work and time change form and conception, then the activities of free time change also. The *plebs* were not in the kind of rat race that afflicts many sectors of the city today; their time system had not had synchronized machines to speed it up. The manner of our work affects free-time activities in many ways, spreading over them the same qualities of machine-time that govern the factory, so that while the lump of free time seems large, control by the clock drops it into the vortex of haste and hurry, production and efficiency, into a race with time.

By winning its independence from work, free time would not cease to be a political concept. It is inevitably political in any land or age because, like work, it implicates the question what to do with one's life here and now. With work dominant, free time raises no such question: work takes care of the answers. Should free time rival work, as in any one of the possibilities this chapter has touched on, then up comes the question again looking for a fresh answer. This, too, I shall deal with later, as the problem of shifting to the second stage of political life. To finish the summary now of free time's political nature, the role of temperament seems to lie outside of politics. If, as it seems, the majority of people enjoy much the same kind of free-time activities, and if much of the variations in cities and towns throughout history can be explained by custom and the availability of time and space, then the political ingredient must be small. Yes, except that the political ingredient in custom, time and space, as we have seen, is not at all small. Lastly, the political system which lays down the fundamental order and time system influences taste. Free-time activities may be similar, but some are in better taste than others. In this matter the doctrines of equality and freedom, as our contemporaries understand them, deserve fair responsibility.

Leisure's relation to the state is more complex. I have already spoken of the ways the state could affect leisure, and more at length of the difficulty of transforming free time into leisure even for a few persons, without basic changes in political beliefs. But of the manner in which leisure may affect the state I have merely suggested a few possibilities or given a few hints, mostly while discussing how an unwrought leisure class may develop.

Now of what use is leisure after all? My efforts throughout have shown, I should hope, that while current usage of the word leisure may run through many definitions in the dictionaries, in political philosophy and the realm of ideas, generally, it has a specific meaning. Nor should we be too hard on dictionaries. One of the best in the world, and not a lengthy one either, gives as the definition of leisure: "1. Freedom afforded by exemption from occupation or business." "Exemption from necessity" would be sounder historically and conceptually. But occupation, broadly taken, covers a lot of necessity. There is little to quarrel with. Note that leisure is defined as a state, the state of freedom. This is the important thing. Time doesn't appear until the next version of the definition: "2. Time free from employment." This, for us, has always been free time. The volume could almost be given the title of official dictionary for the study. Common usage has these two terms, then, with different senses, free time and leisure, as well as recreation, play, distraction, amusement, and pastime. We can discriminate among them without trying to cut down their richness and variety in ordinary speech. Even more in the realm of ideas do we want to keep leisure's classic lines clean.

But why? Why preserve this ideal? If it forecasts changes in our political system what do we stand to gain from it? The benefits of leisure are the benefits of cultivating the free mind. Here and there through the book, and especially in these last chapters, we have touched on them. The great benefits to man are three: creativeness, truth, and freedom. Being interested now in its relation to the community, we can add two more — a political benefit and a religious one. We are not adding two benefits so much as specifying where the benefits fall, and why they can be considered benefits. We can discuss the political benefit first, and since it contains a few important philosophical twists, it will take longest to describe. I can, as a matter of fact, introduce the subject of creativeness and political benefit both by returning once more to the Founders. Though we set apart the beauty and power of their literature or the courageousness of their fight and consider only those ideas of theirs that lost out, there still are things to make us marvel. They were afraid of the consequences of big cities, for example, an idea that came to them too, with their Greco-Roman heritage.

Bigness is one of the great problems today. The Greeks tried to solve it by building new small cities; the Romans by roads, bridges, and a deified emperor to hold things fast. So far we have built on the press, the radio, and TV — the broadcast media. We have literally built on air. The price has been high. In the substituting of sound and visual images and symbols for human contact the community has lost much of its concreteness. The dialogue, whether of buying and selling, of politics or of art and the theater, has turned into a monologue, a transmission. The problem that the Fathers saw ahead, though they based their prognosis on the past, is now a current problem, and remains unsolved.

For the makers of the country, the good life was the life of leisure. They believed in it, and they themselves led such a life as long as they could. What does it matter to us that Jefferson, as some said, threw away his patrimony? We should be grateful he did. Some others may wish to say that their greatness depended not at all on the leisureliness of their life. Be that as it may, after them a leisure class could flourish no longer. They were first-class by any standard. Men with a thousand ideas, a bit radical, antidemocratic, men with a thousand interests and interesting lives, they, the fathers of the country, had no sons. American statesmen after them do not distinguish themselves by their mental gifts. Compared to them, Lincoln, a man of principle and open heart, is a great speaker only. Up to the present day, though we have given birth to many genial tinkerers, we have produced no great theoretical scientist. The foreigners have taken the seven-league steps. The brilliant theoretical capacity of the Founders disappeared along with the leisure they had.

Creativeness in politics, if it is to come, will come from leisure. It must be the real thing — not something else, like free time, rest, or recreation. We saw earlier that while the first settlers drew much in law and custom from the Middle Ages, the Revolutionary generation chose many of its ideas from an even more remote past. Concerning leisure, they were closer to Greece than to Rome, to Plato and Aristotle than to Cicero. If anyone among the Romans, Seneca would have been their model. The other Romans thought too often, though charmingly, of leisure as a rest or retirement from active public life. This is not *otium* or *scholē* or *theoria* or *sophia* for its own sake. It is rest for work's sake, repose earned by work, a retreat better to fill the front line. Cicero, Loyola, Thoreau, all seem to have conceived of retreat as preparing one better to cope with the city. Perhaps Thoreau should not be included. "I left the woods," he said, "for as good a reason as I went there." He had made an experiment; having made it, he returned unobtrusively to his ordinary life. The life of leisure may allow compromises — the exile banished from the *polis,* the hobo working only enough to eat, even the naturalist who wishes to test himself out by changing a style of life — but it offers none to the man who goes for a rest in the country, who needs a change of pace, whose aim has to be a return to work and the city. Not that a change of scenery does no good for the city-dwelling worker. Not that the life of leisure can be isolated from the everyday world — it cannot — but it can see this and any other world plainly only if it is not enslaved to the everyday world.

At another point the stand of the Founders differed neither from the two great Greeks nor from the Romans. Chapter I noted that the ideal of leisure went into Rome borne not only by Plato and Aristotle but also by Epicurus. In his hands a change took place which the Founders would have shied away from. The vexing question of free time's relation to obligation, duty or responsibility, comes into it. Originally the "free" in free time referred primarily to freedom from work. As factory work grew out of its worst abuses and demonstrated the power machines had to lighten toil, as office work became brighter and less and less something out of Dickens's gloomier pages, work gradually declined from the high place it held as an aversion, and settled in a position much closer to, yet always remaining above, other obligations like family, improving oneself, religious rites and political observances. Concerning the latter matters, the decline in the sense of obligation has been less, but it has been enough to raise the question.

The punitive and prohibitive limits set by politics — its laws against activities that are also against morality — are generally adhered to in free time. Earlier I spoke of theft and incest in this regard. Yet politics, we have also seen, is not widely held to be fun, or what one would choose to do were one free of work, family, and church. The more visible and positive aspects of political life like voting or keeping informed or joining in meetings do not usually fall within the wide net the American in his free time casts out for fun. If one *has* to go vote, or if one doesn't go to political rallies unless he *has* to, the element of obligation is there. In one sense, free time is political (it adheres to the law); in the other, it is antipolitical (it avoids political obligation).

Epicurus in his writings tried to eliminate these obligations, along with the others. The life of leisure has no obligation to benefit the state. Keep away from political activity, was his injunction. Ultimately it leads to indifference toward political allegiance. The wise man lets the state founder without lifting a hand, if doing so would disturb his calm. Anaxagoras, accused of neglecting kinsfolk and country, points to the sky. "There is my country." Any place in the world or out of it is the wise man's home. This answer approaches the stoic's cosmopolitanism, without having its political connotations. As Seneca remarked, this philosophy puts the citizen outside the state. Plato and Aristotle, who esteemed the life of leisure above all others, never let the injunction pass. For them the political life has the final say on earth. They never denied their political mission. Those in Plato's *Republic* who do pass every test and trial with honor and in contemplating and leisure succeed in seeing the good in its essence, "are to take it as a model for the rest of their life and must use it in giving order to the *polis* and private persons and themselves in turn. Most of the time they will occupy themselves with philosophy, but when their turn comes they one at a time for the sake of the *polis* take over rulership, looking on it not as a gentlemanly activity but as if it were labor done out of the necessity of making a living." In the *Apology* Socrates warned of the dangers of the political life. Far from being so gentle as merely to disturb one's calm, it could cut a man down in short order. With Plato and Socrates ringing in his ears, the reader of Epicurus might feel that somewhere there is a fearful shrinking from the right path. It is the just act of a virtuous man, the philosopher's giving up his life of contemplation and leisure to go down to the depths to help his former fellow prisoners.

The philosopher's independence of the state is dubious. He may wish to forget home and country and deny that they have ever given him anything good, but the claim can be disputed and a respectable invoice from them presented instead. Put just two things onto the balance, nurture and language — the life of leisure has already a heavy debt to pay to family and country. Man is ever in duty bound to country. His very ideas about contemplating and leisure, even what he sees atop Mount Fuji, are influenced by his land, no matter how far away it may be in miles. Awake, asleep, or a-dreaming, his freedom is of the community. Should he but stay physically alone too long, he becomes spiritually alone, which signifies losing his human faculties. Plato made an argument much like this when he portrayed the philosopher who must tear himself away from the supreme good of contemplation in order to put on the onus of office. All the philosopher is he owes to the *polis;* and he pays it back by guiding the state as it once guided him. Aristotle would remind us that the state is a sign of man's humanity. Anyone who can live without it is either subhuman or divine. In this case there is no doubt which.

Epicurus became famous for his pleasures, and one might be tempted to associate with him the fun-seeking, responsibility-avoiding view of freedom in free time. This would be an error as grievous as the first, and would only make it proper to insist that no one is less epicurean than Epicurus. The Epicurus of leisure, contemplation, peace, and quiet did not slough off political and other ties in order to have fun. The real and permanent pleasure is serenity. Continuous drinking and revelry are illusionary pleasures. Marriage and children too. And whoever goes into politics or business or military affairs is headed for frustration. Ambition in any of these fields is sure to lead to the orders or influence or money of others. Accepting money from anyone, Socrates had said, is to create a boss and a slavery for yourself. Epicurus went further: the wise man should not even beg for his bread. If you engage in social life you become dependent on others, get attached to them, come under their influence, wrapped up in hundreds of activities for them, activities that seem so important — and then all tumbles in disillusion. These activities and desires for the most part do not originate in yourself anyway. They originate in the others who put you into the whirlpool of false sensations, hopes, struggles, disappointments. When you seek their approval and respect, you fall into their power.

The only solution is to withdraw from activity and people of this kind into yourself where you alone are the one to command. Nothing, says Epicurus, generates quiet in the soul like doing but a few things, not giving a hand to unpleasant enterprises, and not exceeding one's own strength. All these things cause disturbances in human nature. Once you have detached yourself from persons and activities, your troubles will diminish and over you will steal a calm that is healthful and lasting, unlike the fluttery pleasures of Aphrodite or the violent ones of power. The country is ideal, with its minimum of activities, far from politics and wars, from business, intrigue, the noises and temptations of the city. Here the lover of pure knowledge freed of the chains of personal and political activity will find in the life of leisure what he could never achieve by riches, political glory, a royal crown, an elegant tenor of life, the luxuries of the table, love's delights, or any others.

It would be wrong to suppose that Epicurus encouraged playing the ascetic. He could not have got his name associated with pleasure had that been the case. Man is not different from other creatures. The flesh makes fugitive but recurrent demands and must be satisfied. Give the flesh its due, the spirit is freed of insuperable carnal obstacles. The life of leisure as Epicurus saw it is not interested in fighting for justice. The country and justice, virtue and the common life, run together. The wise man cares not for the social good. He is an individual, like the gods if gods there be, unmoved and unmoving, self-contained, indifferent.

It would be wrong here, too, to associate this individual with the American political version of individualism or with the frontier's don't-give-a-damn-for-nobody. The serenity reached in leisure, like the tranquillity that for Jefferson was the *summum bonum,* brought with it a sensitivity to wisdom. Again Epicurus does not stray far from classical Greek tradition. Though you may disagree with his belief that man owes no debt to the *polis* you must acknowledge that the attempt to separate the two was for a worthy cause. The life of leisure leads to wisdom. Note that Epicurus does not say that politics would not benefit from leisure. Not at all, but if you engage in politics, you will lose your leisureliness and with that your perspective. It will break up your peace and weaken your desire for truth.

Nothing, not even politics, should deflect the discovery of truth. At the beginning of the book I presented the theory of objectivity that supports this claim. Leisure's benefit to science comes from the detachment of a life free of necessity. ("Science" is used here in its original sense of knowledge, and "benefit" in the sense of enabling to discover knowledge.) If you look on the world with intent, you can see little or but partially. You are observing, not contemplating. You are taking a slice, not the whole. In cutting off intent on the world there is implicated not only a regimen of practice but a theory of action or motivation. Eliminate the pursuit of material and corporeal indulgence, of family, marriage, and children, of the respect of others, the compulsion to do well in their eyes — eliminate them, and you have eliminated many of the motives that push men to manipulate the world and its creatures. You are getting near a Stoic autarchy. But even before the Stoics, many philosophers, major and minor, had pointed to the need to curb appetites and desires. Socrates, says Xenophon, "could be conquered neither by bodily pleasures nor by those of riches." In the *Apology* Socrates proudly proves his disinterest. "Here is the witness that I speak the truth — my poverty."

Design on the world, then, fractionizes your view. Not only that, it unsettles the mind. The crowding of desires, one upon the other, can shake a man's head until it rattles. In the end he has not only bias but confusion to contend with. To be objective, you must be tranquil.

We are in the presence of a radical theory of detachment that looks on Galileo, Newton, and Einstein as technicians or specialists. If you have a problem you are no longer objective. Your autarchy, your capacity to be your own company, is gone. Knowledge now has to pertain to the problem. You cannot contemplate, you can only intently observe the problem you are slicing. The problem approach that opens doors to modern science walks into a gate barring the path to the life of leisure. No discipline today dares set up such standards of objectivity. All sciences talk of objectivity as desirable. Some say they have it, at least in comparison with others. Why it should be more possible in the sciences than in any other field of learning is not made clear. Awareness of bias is supposed to help, but the only painless way to objectivity seems to be teaching by bad examples, namely giving students historical cases of partiality and superstition. The idea of freedom from necessity or of "for its own sake" implies no purpose, exploitative or utilitarian or otherwise, on objects or persons in sight. Compared to this detachment, modern science seems not really serious about objectivity.

There is a contrast here, containing divergent ideas of change in man and nature. Theories entwined with intent or practice look on the world as needing some change, believe that it can be changed at least in part as desired, hold that man can accomplish such change with — or else without — the help of the gods. They are bound up with the idea of work that cut a victorious path from the Dark Ages to the nineteenth century. With change a terrestrial life can be worth while, the winning of earthly happiness and justice is possible, and political action is a means of obtaining them. The theorist of the contemplative life does not quite agree. Politics is to be looked at *sub specie aeternitatis*. A measure of happiness and justice might be possible but it cannot be won. Remolding the world to desire turns out to be a desire for something else. Anyway, try to remold it and see what happens. *Plus ça change, plus c'est la même chose*. The world is to be received, marveled at, not subdued.

The theory of theory-plus-practice looks on man and earth as malleable objects, whereas the theory of knowledge for its own sake has no such active intent; it is more at peace with the world. Hardly can the world be called an object. The flower is there but can you feel its fragrance? The bird, yes, but do you burst to sing its song? With understanding, the line between subject and object begins to fade. As all mediating interests go, so goes that line. The life of leisure leads to a greater sensitivity not to truth alone, but also to beauty, to the wonder of man and nature, to its contemplation and its re-creation in word or song, clay, colors or stone. The artist as well as the thinker is a child of slow time. He must be able to detach himself from the everyday world else ideas and images will never come into his mind.

In so far as it is given men to learn about themselves and their relation to the universe, this is the way they will learn about it. Truth is a moral matter, and beauty too. He who seeks them is

Of Time, Work, and Leisure

on a religious quest, and what he finds or creates matters for religion *and* for politics. Hence I said that the benefits of leisure were three, but five if one wished to consider more than one man, men living together, in possible community, with political and religious law to discover, to live up to, and rediscover.

The ideal of leisure, though it require a disengagement from workaday ties, offers the chance of discovery and creation. Its desire to be free of obligation is of another sort than that of free time. Its purpose is to be able to be serene, serene not simply as a guide for living, but to clear the way to truth, to be serenely objective. Thus morality and obligation are built into leisure by the truth that rules over it.

Time, though, is often considered free when it is free of obligation. In this meaning, a demand for free time could well signalize the deterioration of the sense of community. A community without a periodic feeling of being and living concertedly may not be a community for long. At various times, I may have gone into the wish for free time as if it were a bad omen for common life. The demand for freer time may be a wish to unravel particular threads in the fabric. How many are unraveled determines whether the fabric falls apart or breaks under strain.

I have warned against making too facile an interpretation. A demand for free time may be a demand for something else, as we have seen in the case of unions or of men wishing they had time to repair a leaky faucet or even to do more paid work. Moreover, suppose people want more time free of the obligation of work, or free of family, church, and political responsibilities. Such demands may signify no more than a desire to shift obligation, a desire to loosen home ties, let's say, in order to be freer to take a foreign assignment somewhere, to undertake one obligation for another. This would indicate a shifting of substrata, not necessarily the collapse of the city gates. In addition to work, the American acknowledges responsibilities of husband and father, of head of the family, of church, of duty to his country. Asked what he needs more time for, he typically gives priority to house and home. Religion and politics are held to be serious matters and as such not part of the fun of free time. Perhaps the fun part of the free-time concept does not merit much emphasis; it does lose much of that quality with advancing age when the goal of self-improvement establishes itself more firmly. Yet fun and freedom often seem almost synonymous: when you're having fun, you're free and only if you're free can you have fun.

Consider the mixed feelings involved in relating family and free time. Many events combined in the first half of the twentieth century to produce an enormous child-consciousness in the United States. Among these events were the spread of psychoanalytic theories, the fear and guilt over excessive geographical mobility, the increase in working mothers and delinquency, and the two world wars. Of these factors perhaps the one least appreciated in population studies is that having children gives a sense of stability and responsibility even in a trailer, and that people living increasingly in ever-growing jungles of asphalt seem to search for roots somewhere. Where children are, the hearth is, at least figuratively. Another point is that advertisers, aware of the at-homeness of American weekday free time life and of their own excellent means of penetrating the house and its purchasing power, have in recent years taken to demonstrating that being and doing things with the family is fun.

Certainly mothers always have given the infant of themselves, cradled it, caressed it, warmed it with their own bodies, and fathers have protected it before, sometimes felt responsible for it, and been proud of it (specially of the sons) and fallen in love with it (specially with the daughters). To see the happiness of the family and its importance stressed is no novelty. Among eighteenth-century French engravings, for instance, there are many entitled *La Famille Heureuse*. In the United States an old quip has it that no politician would ever go on record as being in favor of anything more controversial than home and mother. Half-true, surely, but no politician ever went so far as to claim that home and mother were fun.

In any case, family activities today stand a better chance than politics or religion of being considered fun. There seems to be little deterioration in the family. Nor does there seem to be much in political and religious obligation. The citizen spends little time on politics and religion, but as we saw time-quantities often aren't good measures. It would be more accurate if we added the time the citizen spends working to earn his income-tax money, but even this would include in the accounting none of the years of his life or the blood he gave to the armed forces.

Not so much the overarching ideology of politics seems to be deteriorating as the grass-roots kind of busyness, the get-out-the-vote routine that goes by the name of politics. Just as the *Homo Economicus* of the classical economists was a man built by themselves, so the *Homo politicus* is a man invented by democratic theorists, and the role seems to be boring him. "Man is a political animal" never meant that he should be put to work licking envelopes.

Oh, we can put all these obligations in different terms easily enough, thus making them seem more acceptable as free-time projects. Family responsibility becomes the joys of parenthood, of seeing one's youngsters grow up, of playing with them, and so on. Religious obligation becomes the joy of singing in choir, the warmth of the congregation, the way the church looks in springtime or covered with snow in winter. Politics is the crackle of cracker-barrel argument, the fellow feeling of Americans after the campaign is over, the zest of accomplishment in community service. Morality and fun needn't be opposites, of course.

Yet, specially for the young or rebellious, free-time activities may play on the edge of morality. Work has restraints that men react against; living in society involves restraints, too. Like petting, you might say, free-time activities sometimes have to fall on that narrow strip where fun exists and morality maintains a border in the law and the mores broadly conceived in their letter, spirit, application, history, or anthropology. The word leisure came into English through French from the Latin *licere*, meaning to be allowed. Thus it has something that involves the idea of permission, lawfulness, and morality. But the word license, meaning excessive or lawless liberty, comes from the same root, reminding us thereby of the difficulty of hanging a social meaning onto a term having the sense of personal freedom.

The question of boredom enters here. To be bored a person must believe, I think, that something both interesting to do and permissible exists somewhere. Either he hasn't the external means (the juvenile without enough money to buy a motorcycle), or is prevented by morality (the nice young typist who dreams of an orgy), or hasn't the knowledge of what to do but believes that the knowledge exists somewhere (the child saying to the parent, "I don't know what to do with myself"). Some believe that rural communities do not experience boredom. This is doubtful. The mind of man must be exercised. If he has no problems — a rare situation — he seems to create them for himself. Small communities do contain bored persons. The community's adaptation to them proceeds gradually, later becoming institutionalized so that the bored are hard to find from the outside looking in. An institutionalized example is the game, usually called *passatella,* played with variations, in some rural areas of southern Europe. Its purpose is obviously to spark antagonisms and to make players take sides in the conflict. Since the game tends to break into violence, the law often prohibits it.

Adults too sometimes say, "I don't know what to do with myself." This can refer to their lack of education, their ignorance of the possibilities that exist, or — on the contemporary scene — to the uselessness, given nothing but small pieces of time, of heading in a new direction. But if their saying "with myself" reflects a concern with the self, it indicates that at the time no purpose or danger exists capable of absorbing them. Americans do not seek more time for what is commonly conceived of today as politics. Nor do they seek more time for worship. They want more time for home and family and more time to enjoy themselves. Both aims seem to require purchases; therefore both require more time and more work. Does the American ever resent dancing this jig that goes on and on? We see the appropriateness of saying that if people don't know what to do with themselves in peace, in war they may have activities that absorb them. This may be related to what Aristotle meant when he said the Spartans didn't know what to do with themselves when prosperous and at peace. He may seem unfair to the Spartans, for at least at one time in all Greece there was nothing to equal them in the field of music. But (and this supports Aristotle's point) that time was before the Spartans became exclusively militaristic. We are interested here, however, in whether the philosopher's statement might possibly have any bearing on the United States.

Recently the country has had an educational crisis. Why? Because in military research and invention another country beat it to the punch. Thereupon the whole educational system that most Americans had conceived to be good and efficient, if not the best in the world, is called in for questioning. After soul-torturing examination by leading representatives in the fields of business, government, labor, and education (including the reputable foundations), a committee issues a report, or perhaps a leading educator will take on the assignment and publish a book. The usual conclusion calls for more science and more mathematics (for the world is moving into a new era of technology) and more foreign languages (for America's position in the world today requires a knowledge of foreign cultures). For both these justifications, the translation reads: education for military purposes, defense or offense.

Of the three (or five) benefits that leisure could possibly bring, I have spoken of all but freedom. The cultivation of the mind in leisure can occur only in a person who is free of everyday necessity. The great debates on freedom and liberty in the nineteenth century were over political and economic liberties. We saw earlier how the idea of leisure was divorced from all political and religious significance. It was isolated from debates on the ideal of freedom in the contemporary world. Leisure became the time or the life in which to contemplate the beautiful. Yet, just as science has much to learn from leisure's detachment, so politics has much to learn from leisure's freedom.

Faced by all the problems and profits of urbanism and industrialization, the leaders of the nineteenth century could think only with difficulty of any freedom except that which could be granted to everyone. Towns and cities teemed. Originally, the right to vote had power in small councils. Now those who had it and those who didn't fought over it, and only as each step to extend the right was taken did they dimly recognize that they were no longer fighting over the original thing: the power given by the right to vote — in small council. The right to be educated also was a power once. It now dwindled to minute proportions as the numbers to educate increased, and the numbers who could educate decreased. The fight to organize into unions was fought on both sides by persons who believed that the right to work was a liberty. Neither one saw that they had fallen into a society where one was so dependent on a job that without it he starved. With many alarms, these were the burning issues of freedom, the so-called political and economic liberties.

Democratic society could not and cannot offer the kind of freedom that one has in leisure. Too many intelligent persons believed, and still believe, that that freedom is a luxury. Therefore, if one takes it from the few and gives it to the many, the result is a clear gain. Leave to one side the question of the restraint of freedom involved in taking it away. What is it you are giving to the many? Surely not the same freedom from necessity. No more the same freedom than the vote won by the barons of the Magna Charta is the same vote we enjoy today. No more the same than the time and space of the villager is the time and space of the suburbanite. You have taken away the possibility of cultivating the mind, of eying the world with some clarity, of being receptive to inspiration and sensitive to beauty. You have taken it away — and this must be to your regret — not from a few who don't count, but from everyone.

A bit more to show how deeply the benefits of leisure penetrate. The lack of freedom from the workaday world, we shouldn't forget, means a dependence on that world. Anyone who depends on it — and who today does not? — is intent on it. The fault this leads to, I have pointed out, is that he cannot then lift his head up to look around freely. Even could he do so, he couldn't speak out to say what he sees. Dependent as he is in his workaday world, let him stand on its lowest or highest rung, he always has good reason to keep his mouth shut. Speaking one's mind declines when property holding declines, and with it those who are free of necessity disappear from sight. Boasting of freedom of speech and opinion in democracy means little if the conditions don't exist for anyone's finding out any but trivial truths and for his speaking anything but whatever fits his practical or workaday world.

THE LIFE OF LEISURE

What is practical to the free and to the unfree is different. The question of action plays no part. If you can decide who was free — Thales of Miletus or the little maid who laughed to see him fall — you can tell that the free are not against action or practice itself. They see people all about them who merely think they are doing something. Unimportant practice is simply uninteresting. They are not fleeing real life but making their way toward it. On the way they may trip over their own feet, not recognize their neighbor, be ignorant of feminine wiles or where the shopping center is, or what the boys in the back room are saying about machines, but what they know would make them all dizzy, all those whose time is not free for learning, including the maids of Thrace. Action, then, is not the point. Contemplation is the sheerest of acts. To try to avoid all action would be unnatural and futile. Reducing intent on the world does seem to reduce activity to a minimum, but only because present standards push it to an artificial maximum.

To justify the life of leisure to the state, any state, not simply the democratic state, is a formidable task. An eminent economist had something like this in mind in saying that it is almost impossible for the scholar to be a true patriot and to have the reputation of being one in his own time. The man of leisure cultivates the mind and may find the truth in his furrow, but he cannot say, when or if he finds it, or some of it, that it will be good for the state today, or next year, or in five hundred years. Besides, the state may appreciate it never. Furthermore, if he finds it, who knows whether he will communicate it? Epicurus wrote three hundred works, of which forty-one were said to be excellent; but he might just have decided to write none. Someone less concerned than he to save a few good souls might not have written them. Nothing says that whatever one learns in leisure must be communicated to others.

The state may ask why men of leisure engage in talking and writing at all. In writing books or teaching they may be accused of resorting to persuasion, rhetoric, recruiting, or publicity. There are, it seems to me, acceptable explanations. A man's writing apart from letters can be considered a mnemonic device, or a way of reining in runaway thoughts, or else a celebration, an expression of immanence, an overflow of well-being, a richness, a song. "Verily — may the Lord shield me! — Well do I write under the greenwood." At all events it is solely the Epicurean version of the ideal that forswears politics. For the others politics is the only field important enough to pull a man away from his leisurely activities.

Such we saw to be the attitude of the Founding Fathers, as well as that of Plato. There is no doubt in them. The benefits of their life are for their country, if ever it needs them. They would communicate what they know, they would teach or write what they have learned; they would fight, too. Remember that while Aristotle does not admit work into a life of leisure, he will admit war. His logic is simple. Of course war takes you away from leisure and contemplation, but wars are fought to have peace, and peace is good because it offers leisure. Violent action, it seems, is acceptable so long as it is for the purpose of leisure, and not, as the Spartans had it, for training in the interval between wars. If the enemy won the war, leisure would be lost. Aristotle never questions this. It seems to be part of the belief that only Greeks are civilized, and so only they are capable of understanding what kind of state one needs. That state would be best that could create the life of leisure. It could have no higher purpose. Even Epicurus admits that the state's laws might be of some service by keeping wise men from being treated unjustly.

With this as background, perhaps we can further reason about the good state. The desire for tranquillity in the life of leisure leads toward a politics of peace both internally and externally. The convenience of tolerance leads toward a program of politics without crisis or great national efforts, perhaps a form of conservatism. The choice of stability as a criterion for truth and pleasure leads also to a preference for hereditary forms in government and property holding.

This, perhaps, would be the state that could reap most of the benefits leisure has to offer. Under other circumstances a country may consider the ideal of leisure dangerous and actually subversive. A regime whose support is not too steady may fear that truth seeking for itself may take a political turn. The seeker himself admits he does not know where his search will take him. A regime may also take the line that the ideal, especially its nonpolitical version, sets a bad example. By saying that patriotism is a hindrance, it affects loyalty. A bad example might not affect the many, but the few is already too much. Or if a regime is committed to great economic or military enterprises, the vaunting of a life of leisure in the country is a hostile doctrine. Teachings and writings do exist, and if they happen to persuade large numbers of persons to adopt the contemplative life, are they not political tracts?

Perhaps the life of leisure could be made easier everywhere if only the modern state could see something positive in it. Seneca in *De otio* said, "In brief, this is what we can expect of a man:

that he be useful to other men; to many of them if he can; to a few, if he can but a little; and if he can but still less, to those nearest him; and if he cannot to others, to himself." Today this being useful by being useful only to oneself cannot be widely understood because the wise man is not a model, nor does heaven smile upon his protection. Otherwise his usefulness could be seen in his living his daily life.

Isn't it easier to hear a contemporary biologist or sociologist or even a political theorist asking, What function do such persons serve in the organism, in society, or in the state? Where is the benefit? On the contrary, there is harm. In this contemporary view the life of leisure is antidemocratic, antisocial, against organization, opposed to work and to most of the things men work for, and indifferent to home, mother, and perhaps even country. One can see why the man of leisure is a rare bird. Not all lands are as amiable as Ionia.

There will be those who retort that though many people hold the above opinion of leisure, yet we must not forget that the advocacy of leisure is permitted nonetheless; for opinion in a democracy is kept free. Anyone can think, write, and speak as he wishes, even if one has nothing but bad to say. The state withholds its interference from any but illegal acts, and to think, write, and speak are not such acts. Still the question arises, is inactivity illegal? If a man does not want to work, but to contemplate, is he a madman? If, to be free from the Lilliputian threads of society, he wants to beg for his bread, should there be a law against it? If he leaves his wife, is he a deserter? By refusing to join the armed forces, is he a criminal? Should there be laws refusing him entrance to certain parts of the country because he has no visible means of support? What do the laws of vagrancy aim at? What is loitering? Omission can sin more than commission. Opinion may be free, yet the laws conspire against a way of life.

There is another defense of the life of leisure that seems to have a special attractiveness today. It has recently become commonplace to look for benefits from those whom the shoe of society habitually pinches, in particular artists and scientists. I have mentioned it here as the benefit of creativeness. As pointed out previously, nonfiction books on the future don't spend many pages on art in the future except to say that with more free time will come more art. Perhaps the lover of leisure can be tolerated or even appreciated for the benefit he brings to society in the long run through his creativeness in science, literature, or art. The argument is by no means absurd. Some will say, though, that it follows that the life of leisure should somehow be worked into workaday life. Then everybody could be creative. An alternating of work and leisure is the usual proposal. At most their solution falls into the formula the Romans expressed as *otium/ negotium*. It splits up time, thus again becoming the wrong formula for leisure. For contemporary use it translates well in the duality, free time/work time. As far as leisure goes, irrelevant.

The life of leisure cannot be justified to the state and perhaps also it has exaggerated its independence of the state. It still makes little difference. If it could be justified in terms of the state, then we could speak of its function. If we could do this, the life of leisure would no longer be free. It would have a determined relation to the state. It would become a state functionary. The same subservience would strain leisure were it to be justified in terms of any other society. Should it be possible to confine philosophers and artists in a retreat and say to them, Produce? The life of leisure may accomplish many things; it can promise nothing. Freedom, truth, and beauty is its religion. Let who will go whoring after commodities, and money, fame, wars, and power, too.

We shall go back a little now to bring some of the things we have already discussed in these chapters to bear on the matter of the benefits leisure offers. The phrase "the leisure problem" crops up often these days. Though many use it, they use it with several different views in mind. Many people, indeed most of those who use the phrase, worry that there is too much free time nowadays or that there will soon be too much. This, for the present and for the near future, is wrong. There is not much free time, nor likely to be much.

Many other persons not only believe there is too much free time but also that it is badly spent. In their ranks we should not only include those critics of culture who wish for an uplift in the common man's pleasures, but we should also include the many men, common or not, who are dissatisfied, perhaps without knowing why, with the way their life goes.

Little can be done for the improvers and the culture critics and for all those who, like them, see the problem as too much free time, badly spent. The ideas of work and equality block their way. Seen in this light, things can't get better until they get worse. If things get worse, it will not be their fault as much as that of uneasy people. The worn-out fringe of the Cockaigne dream shows up in the farewell salute familiar in American cities, "Take it easy," and its return, an equivalent of "O.K., I'll try to," or "Yeah, you do the same," both given with the ritual or cynical or resigned but unbeaten air of never, ever, making it. Life in happyland can be improved for them, but not by changing their activities. Work being what it is, the time machine also, and the make-up of most of us being what it is, free-time devices cannot move to a different plane. They can rely less on commodities and purchases, however; they can slow down to a walk in a less hurried setting; they can achieve better taste. But these changes will not come in a vacuum. Changes in political beliefs will take place, too.

Change may be calm or fierce, gradual or swift. Just as it is impossible to keep men from knowing there is widespread unemployment, no matter how dictatorial the press control, no more can people be kept from learning that they don't have lots of free time, don't have a chance of getting it so long as they run after shiny lures into the horizon, and won't have a good life if their cities and towns are the ugliest in the world. It may take a while for these facts to register; it may come suddenly like the click of a door — so suddenly that the words *production* and *efficiency* sour even as we say them.

The third group of people, a handful, believe we need a new texture to our life and that the only hope for it is leisure in the classical manner. They think we need more than processed food and tricky machines and cleverly designed products. They think we need ideas, that all of us need to live in beauty. Without doubt, leisure at times has woven a new texture. It doesn't always succeed, though. There is no way men can say that light and beauty will come to them. Certainly if they try by working harder and harder they only get farther and farther away. Leisure prepares the ground; the rest comes from somewhere beyond man.

If we cannot justify the followers of leisure, more's the pity: we stand to lose more than they. The hope (not the function) that the leisure kind offer politics is that they can learn (and that what they learn they may reveal) about men and politics and their relation to the cosmos. They also offer leisure as the ideal of freedom. All this the state can hope for. A man can hope for more, that through leisure he may realize his ties to the natural world and so free his mind to rise to divine reaches. Man's recognition of himself and his place in the universe is essentially a religious discovery. As such it transcends politics.

The leisure kind themselves are not much interested in justifying their life, and why should we press them? Truth is their justification. There is, they say, something beyond the state that comes to a man in a life of leisure that can come in no other way. The detachment I have already spoken of, and the perspective that a man gains from being able to pull back into himself and, yes, the inspiration. What such a man can do is produce himself. Cultivation of the mind distinguishes him. He shows his godlike nature. Inasmuch as the state too should know its place, it is a good state if it fosters leisure. Just as a good church will try to see that everyone comes to know what contemplation is and will help not only the few who are born to it but everyone to experience it by encouraging retreat and meditation with beautiful stillness — something that architects should remember — so the good state in its support of the life of leisure will try to see that all come to benefit from incorporating some of that life's maxims into their daily world.

The Emperor Justinian built a garrison city on Mount Sinai to protect hermits and desert saints. That is one way. Another is to conceive of leisure as a way of life that is healthier and more satisfying, as an *ars vitae*. The state can expect numerous minor good results from leisure. They are by-products. It can expect bad results too. Out of the situation, traditions, and social arrangements of different countries will come a variety of ways of approaching leisure. For leisure is an ideal. One can only try to get as close to it as possible. The closer to the ideal, the purer the air.

Every great discovery that man makes of his relation to God, to the universe, to his fellow humans, to himself, is so wonderful it calls for celebration. Religion marks it with a holiday. The state too has its holidays. A holiday is universal. It is celebrated not by the discoverers alone, but by all who share the wonders it reveals. It joins the two classes, the great majority and the leisure kind, and all those who have strayed and separated into society's many crannies. The holiday heals whatever rifts exist and reminds men that they are bound together by the one equality with which they came into this world and with which they bow out. So for the few who love leisure and for the many who need free time, the holiday is a day to celebrate the wonder of life.

Leisure, given its proper political setting, benefits, gladdens, and beautifies the lives of all. It lifts up all heads from practical workaday life to look at the whole high world with refreshened wonder. The urge to celebrate is there.

Felicity, happiness, blessedness. Certainly the life of leisure is the life for thinkers, artists, and musicians. Many of the great ones, though seldom attaining it, have throughout their lives given signs of their passion for it. Throughout their biographies runs an attempt to get more free air than the surrounding atmosphere held for them. For that matter, though none of us may ever have been able to live this way, most of us too, perhaps, have had moments when we felt close enough to get glimpses of a truth — that could we have more of the way of life, we would also have more of the truth.

The unwrought leisure kind struggles on. No one can turn them away easily. Their kind of life is too tough. Yet signs appear even now that their day may come, that the United States is moving toward a life where leisure may be possible, that there is a great hunger throughout the land, after so long a life in poverty of spirit. The man invented by the economists has disappeared; *Homo politicus* is bored with precinct politics; the consumer, alone in the furrow scratched by advertising and its allies, noses ahead.

The last fact is what confounds observers of the work ethic. They saw off-work time in the nineteenth century condemned as idleness, they saw workers seeking in free time their rest and, in vain, their old pleasures. They saw work become a calling and then lose its meaning. Free time is no longer idleness, and to play on Saturday and Sunday is no longer a sin. Yet men work as much as before; they must somehow. Work still remains in the lead. Free time is still but the parenthesis. At the moment both are marking time. The question is, will the next step be back to work or forward? And if forward, where to? To the circuses, of course, but to anywhere else?

A great fracture in the ethos has taken place. The resultant fault will bring work and time under survey. The American will have to question his identity and ask about his destiny. Why does he work and rush? For bread? To stay alive? Why stay alive? Because he is like all other animals? Because he was taught to stay alive? Anyway, does it matter? What really does matter? A great shifting of substrata is going on, a whole pattern of duties and pleasures seeking to come to rest on something new. Work and time's displacement will bring a fresh inclination. Were our tradition of leisure stronger, we could be more confident that it would settle us where we should have been long ago — in the second stage of political community, the living of a life of good quality. Perhaps this long siege under garrison conditions will enable us to dream better, and dreaming better to build with art and intelligence.

We of the twentieth century may not be here to enjoy the fruits of this questioning and to savor many of the changes. We shall be here now to encourage whoever wants to, to build beautiful things; and to know that in so far as those few succeed, tomorrow's city, slightly mad, not too neat, human, will become a place to stroll, to buy and sell and talk of many things, to eat and drink well, to see beauty and light around.

Those who do not like the way this future looks can "do ye nexte thynge," in whatever way they may choose, to block it. Work, we know, may make a man stoop-shouldered or rich. It may even ennoble him. Leisure perfects him. In this lies its future. For those who do like that future, the next thing is to lean back under a tree, put your arms behind your head, wonder at the pass we've come to, smile, and remember that the beginnings and ends of man's every great enterprise are untidy.

Appendices

Table 1

LENGTH OF AVERAGE WORK WEEK IN AGRICULTURE AND IN NONAGRICULTURAL INDUSTRIES, 1850–1960

Year	All Industries	Agriculture	Nonagricultural Industries
1850	69.7	72.0	65.7
1860	67.8	71.0	63.3
1870	65.3	70.0	60.0
1880	63.8	69.0	58.8
1890	61.7	68.0	57.1
1900	60.1	67.0	55.9
1910	54.9	65.0	50.3
1920	49.4	60.0	45.5
1930	45.7	55.0	43.2
1940	43.8	54.6	41.1
1941	44.2	53.2	42.2
1942	45.2	55.3	43.1
1943	47.3	58.5	45.1
1944	46.2	54.4	44.6
1945	44.3	50.6	43.1
1946	42.4	50.0	41.1
1947	41.7	48.8	40.5
1948	40.8	48.5	39.6
1949	40.2	48.1	39.0
1950	39.9	47.2	38.8
1951	40.4	47.9	39.4
1952	40.5	47.4	39.6
1953	40.0	47.9	39.2
1954	38.9	47.0	37.9
1955	39.7	46.5	38.9
1956	39.5	44.9	38.8
1957	39.1	44.2	38.6
1958	38.6	43.7	38.1
1959	38.5	43.8	38.0
1960	38.5	44.0	38.0

Sources:

1850–1930: agriculture and nonagricultural industries from J. Frederic Dewhurst and associates, *America's Needs and Resources: A New Survey*, Twentieth Century Fund, New York, 1955, Appendix 20–4, p. 1073; all industries is average of other two columns weighted on the basis of percentage of gainfully occupied in agriculture and in nonagricultural industries as shown in *Historical Statistics of the United States, 1789–1945*, U. S. Bureau of the Census, 1949, Series D6–7, p. 63.

1940–1952: Dewhurst and associates, *op. cit.*, Appendix 20–1, pp. 1064–1069.

1953–1960: U. S. Bureau of the Census, *Current Population Reports: Labor Force*, Series P–50, Nos. 59, 67, 72, 85, and 89; Bureau of Labor Statistics, *Employment and Earnings*, Annual Supplement, Vol. 6, No. 11, May 1960, plus preliminary unpublished data for 1960 from B.L.S. The averages published by the Census were adjusted downward to reflect zero hours of work for those "with a job but not at work."

Table 2
CHANGE IN LENGTH OF WORK WEEK FOR ALL EMPLOYED, THOSE AT WORK AND THOSE AT WORK 35 HOURS OR MORE, IN AGRICULTURE AND IN NONAGRICULTURAL INDUSTRIES, MAY OF EACH YEAR, 1948–1960
(Average Weekly Hours)

Year	All Employed[a]	At Work	At Work 35 Hours or More
All Industries			
1948	42.1	43.4	47.7
1949	42.3	43.5	48.1
1950	41.3	42.5	47.2
1951	41.9	43.2	47.6
1952	41.1	42.6	46.7
1953	40.8	42.1	46.4
1954	40.8	41.6	46.3
1955	40.6	41.9	46.5
1956	40.3	41.6	47.0
1957	39.8	41.1	46.3
1958	39.8	41.0	46.6
1959	39.9	41.1	46.5
1960	39.5	40.8	46.4
Percentage decline, 1948–1960	6.2	6.0	2.7
Agriculture			
1948	51.1	52.5	63.2
1949	52.5	53.3	62.6
1950	48.9	50.1	60.7
1951	52.0	52.6	62.4
1952	50.0	50.9	60.0
1953	48.1	50.0	62.5
1954	48.2	49.3	60.6
1955	48.4	49.5	59.7
1956	48.7	49.6	61.1
1957	45.1	46.3	58.1
1958	48.8	49.6	61.9
1959	47.0	47.9	59.9
1960	47.3	48.0	60.0
Percentage decline, 1948–1960	7.4	8.6	5.1

Table 2 (Continued)

Year	All Employed[a]	At Work	At Work 35 Hours or More
	Nonagricultural Industries		
1948	40.6	41.9	45.6
1949	40.4	41.7	45.6
1950	40.1	41.3	45.3
1951	40.6	41.9	45.7
1952	39.9	41.5	45.1
1953	39.9	41.2	44.9
1954	39.1	40.6	44.7
1955	39.5	40.9	45.1
1956	39.3	40.7	45.4
1957	39.2	40.5	45.2
1958	38.8	40.0	45.1
1959	39.1	40.4	45.2
1960	38.8	40.1	45.2
Percentage decline, 1948–1960	4.4	4.3	0.9

Sources: U. S. Bureau of the Census, average weekly hours of "all employed" and "at work" from *Current Population Reports: Labor Force,* Series P–50, Nos. 13, 19, 31, 40, 45, 59, 67, and 72 and Series P–57, No. 203, U. S. Dept. of Labor, *Monthly Report on the Labor Force,* May 1960. Average hours for those "at work 35 hours or more" from a special tabulation.

a. Average weekly hours for all employed represents the average for those actually at work plus those with a job but not at work because of vacation, illness, bad weather, etc. The latter group is counted as having zero hours of work during the week.

Table 3

AMOUNT OF TIME BETWEEN 6 A.M. AND 11 P.M. DEVOTED TO VARIOUS ACTIVITIES, MEN AND WOMEN 20–59 YEARS OF AGE, SPRING 1954[a]

(Hours)

Activity	Average Weekday		Saturday		Sunday		Average Day[b]	
	Men	Women	Men	Women	Men	Women	Men	Women
Total	17.0	17.0	17.0	17.0	17.0	17.0	17.0	17.0
Away from home:								
At work	7.2	2.0	4.3	0.8	1.2	0.3	6.0	1.5
Traveling	1.4	0.6	1.4	0.7	1.3	1.0	1.4	0.7
Shopping	0.1	0.4	0.3	0.8	0.1	—	0.1	0.4
At restaurant, tavern, barber, etc.	0.3	0.1	0.3	0.2	0.1	0.1	0.2	0.1
At friend's or relative's home	0.4	0.8	1.2	1.2	1.4	1.4	0.7	1.0
Leisure (games, sports, church, etc.)	0.3	0.4	0.6	0.4	1.4	1.1	0.5	0.5
At home:								
Leisure (other than reading)	2.1	2.7	2.8	2.8	4.0	3.5	2.4	2.8
Reading	0.8	0.8	0.9	0.9	1.1	1.1	0.9	0.8
Miscellaneous work at home	0.6	1.2	1.0	1.1	0.8	0.7	0.7	1.1
Household chores or housekeeping	0.2	3.0	0.2	2.6	0.2	1.7	0.2	2.7
Eating or preparing food	1.2	2.5	1.2	2.5	1.3	2.5	1.2	2.5
Dressing, bathing, etc.	0.6	0.9	0.7	0.9	0.7	0.9	0.6	0.9
Asleep	1.8	1.8	2.1	2.1	3.4	2.7	2.1	1.9
All leisure activities[c]	3.6	4.7	5.5	5.3	7.9	7.1	4.5	5.1

Source: Derived from unpublished data in *A Nationwide Study of Living Habits*, a national survey conducted for the Mutual Broadcasting System by J. A. Ward, Inc., New York, 1954.

a. Based on diaries covering every quarter-hour period from 6 A.M. to 11 P.M. during March and April 1954.

b. Represents average of all seven days of week.

c. Includes visiting at friend's or relative's home; games and sports, etc., as a spectator or participant, as well as other forms of leisure such as church, where one is part of an audience; and reading and any other activity at home that is not work (playing cards, listening to the radio, watching television, talking on the telephone, visiting

[444]

Brief Description of Sample Used in the J. A. Ward Study

The sample upon which these data are based is a subsample of a national sample of approximately 7,000 separate households. The full sample included all individuals over the age of 5 in these households — a total of approximately 20,000 individuals. The subsample covered every fifth individual in these households. The sample is what is commonly called a probability sample of the area type — i.e., it was so drawn that mathematical projections to total population data are practical and possible. Each individual in the sample maintained a complete diary of activities for a specific two-day period during March–April 1954, for each quarter hour of the day from 6 A.M. to 11 P.M.

The total sample was made up of seven interpenetrating samples, each statistically identical to each of the others and each covering a different two-day period. By overlapping the seven separate two-day samples of 1,000 families each, data were developed on a sample base of 2,000 families and approximately 6,000 individuals for each day of the week. The subsample from which the data in our analysis were developed covered 1,770 individuals for each weekday, 1,619 for Saturday, and 1,521 for Sunday.

By all tests, the sample appeared representative of the population of the country. The distribution of the respondents in the sample by geographic area, by number and make of cars owned, by home ownership, by color, by income, and by telephone ownership — all the distributions were extremely close to independent estimates for the United States. By limiting the period for which diaries had to be maintained to two consecutive days, some of the usual objections to the diary approach were met. In addition, following the personal visit during which the diaries were left with the respondents, a reminder telephone call was made the next day. Apparently the elaborate system of cross-checks that was possible not only enabled the editors and coders to achieve a high degree of accuracy but also revealed a high degree of accuracy in the original entries.

Table 4

CONSUMER EXPENDITURES FOR RECREATION IN CURRENT AND 1959
DOLLARS AND AS PER CENT OF NATIONAL INCOME AND
TOTAL CONSUMER EXPENDITURES, 1909–1959

| | Amount | | Per Cent of:[b] | |
Year	Current Dollars	1959 Dollars[a]	National Income	Total Consumer Expenditures
1909	$ 860	$ 3,598	2.8	3.0
1914	1,000	3,861	2.8	3.0
1919	2,180	4,977	3.0	3.7
1921	2,055	3,952	3.8	3.7
1923	2,620	5,209	3.6	4.1
1925	2,835	5,559	3.6	4.0
1927	3,120	6,058	3.9	4.2
1929	3,840	7,356	4.4	4.9
1931	2,877	5,543	4.8	4.7
1933	1,871	3,803	4.7	4.0
1935	2,259	4,610	4.0	4.0
1937	2,940	5,731	4.0	4.4
1939	3,000	5,650	4.1	4.4
1940	3,284	6,081	4.0	4.6
1941	3,722	6,646	3.6	4.5
1942	4,100	6,997	3.0	4.6
1943	4,263	6,713	2.5	4.2
1944	4,651	6,616	2.5	4.2
1945	5,278	7,210	2.9	4.3
1946	7,639	10,104	4.3	5.2
1947	8,320	10,335	4.2	5.0
1948	8,670	10,236	3.9	4.9
1949	8,913	10,151	4.1	4.9
1950	10,018	11,489	4.1	5.1
1951	10,340	11,514	3.7	4.9
1952	10,819	11,994	3.7	4.9
1953	11,380	12,492	3.7	4.9
1954	11,730	13,004	3.9	4.9
1955	12,593	14,008	3.8	4.9
1956	13,476	14,793	3.8	5.0
1957	14,205	15,016	3.9	5.0
1958	14,845	15,086	4.0	5.1
1959	16,180	16,180	4.0	5.2

Sources and notes on following page.

Sources: Table 7a; *National Income, 1954 Edition* (Supplement to the *Survey of Current Business*), Table 30, pp. 206–207; *U. S. Income and Output*, Tables I–1, I–8, and II–4, pp. 118–119, 126, 127, and 150–151; *Survey of Current Business*, July 1960, Tables 1, 2, and 15, pp. 8, 9, and 16; J. Frederic Dewhurst and associates, *America's Needs and Resources: A New Survey*, Twentieth Century Fund, New York, 1955, Appendix 4–2, Table A, p. 958; *Historical Statistics of the United States, 1789–1945*, U. S. Bureau of the Census, 1949, Series L–1, p. 231 and L–47, p. 236; *Economic Indicators* (1957 Historical and Descriptive Supplement), U. S. Government Printing Office, 1957, p. 53; *Statistical Abstract*, 1960, p. 336.

a. Estimates in current dollars adjusted by price series computed from price indexes in sources linked in overlapping years and shifted to 1956 base.

b. Based on expenditures and income in current dollars; estimates of national income and total consumer expenditures for 1909–1927 based on estimates in Dewhurst and associates, *loc. cit.*, adjusted to estimates for 1929 in *National Income* (*1954 Edition*).

Table 5

AVERAGE HOUSEHOLD EXPENDITURE FOR GOODS AND
SERVICES BY TYPE OF EXPENDITURE, 1956

Type of Expenditure	Amount	Per Cent
All goods and services	$4,110	100
Food, beverages, and tobacco	1,203	29
Clothing and accessories	494	12
Medical and personal care	222	5
Home operation and improvement	763	19
Home furnishings and equipment	346	9
Recreation and recreation equipment	215	5
Automotive	591	14
Other goods and services	276	7

Source: *Life Study of Consumer Expenditures*, Time, Inc., New York, 1957, Vol. One, pp. 17 and 20.

Table 6

PERCENTAGE DISTRIBUTION OF EXPENDITURES OF HOUSEHOLDS WITH DIFFERENT CHARACTERISTICS, BY TYPE OF EXPENDITURE, 1956

Classification of Households	All Goods and Services	Food, Beverages, and Tobacco	Clothing and Accessories	Medical and Personal Care	Home Operation and Improvement	Home Furnishings and Equipment	Automotive	Other Goods and Services	Recreation and Recreation Equipment
All households	100	29	12	5	19	9	14	7	5
By annual household income									
Under $2,000	100	36	11	7	17	7	11	6	5
$2,000–2,999	100	33	11	5	20	8	13	5	5
3,000–3,999	100	30	13	6	18	8	15	6	5
4,000–4,999	100	29	12	5	19	8	14	7	6
5,000–6,999	100	28	11	5	19	8	16	7	5
7,000–9,999	100	26	13	5	18	9	15	9	5
10,000 and over	100	24	14	6	18	10	15	7	6
By level of education attained by household head									
Some grade school or less	100	34	12	6	16	8	13	6	5
Finished grade school	100	32	11	5	18	8	14	7	5
Attended high school	100	31	11	5	18	8	15	7	5
Finished high school	100	29	13	5	18	9	14	7	5
Some college or beyond	100	25	13	5	21	9	14	7	6
By occupation of household head									
Professional, semiprofessional	100	26	13	5	21	8	14	7	6
Proprietor, manager, official	100	27	12	6	19	9	14	8	5
Clerical, sales	100	27	13	6	19	8	16	6	5
Craftsman, foreman	100	32	10	5	17	9	15	6	6
Operative	100	32	12	5	18	8	15	5	5
Service worker	100	32	13	5	20	8	11	6	5
Farmer, farm laborer	100	26	10	5	17	10	18	9	5

Under 30 years	100	27	11	5	20	10	16	5	6
30–39 years	100	29	11	5	20	8	15	6	6
40–49 years	100	29	13	5	17	8	15	8	5
50–64 years	100	31	13	6	17	8	14	6	5
65 years and over	100	31	12	6	17	8	12	8	4
By household stage in the "life cycle"									
No children and head under 40	100	26	12	4	19	10	17	5	7
Some children under 10	100	30	12	5	20	8	14	6	5
Children between 10 and 19 only	100	30	13	6	15	8	15	8	5
No children and married head over 40	100	29	11	6	18	9	14	8	5
No children and single head over 40	100	28	13	6	23	7	10	8	5
By market and geographic location									
All metropolitan markets	100	30	13	5	19	8	13	7	5
Northeast region	100	33	13	5	19	7	11	7	5
Central region	100	28	13	5	20	9	14	6	5
Southern region	100	30	12	5	19	8	15	6	5
Western region	100	27	12	6	19	9	15	6	6
All nonmetropolitan areas	100	28	11	6	17	9	17	7	5
Northeast region	100	30	12	6	18	7	16	6	6
Central region	100	28	10	5	18	9	17	8	5
Southern region	100	29	12	6	16	9	17	6	5
Western region	100	25	10	6	17	9	18	9	6

Source: *Life Study of Consumer Expenditures*, Time, Inc., New York, 1957, Vol. One.

Table 6a

AVERAGE EXPENDITURES BY HOUSEHOLDS WITH DIFFERENT CHARACTERISTICS, BY TYPE OF EXPENDITURE, 1956

Classification of Households	All Goods and Services	Food, Beverages, and Tobacco	Clothing and Accessories	Medical and Personal Care	Home Operation and Improvement	Home Furnishings and Equipment	Automotive	Other Goods and Services	Recreation and Recreation Equipment
All households	$4,110	$1,203	$ 494	$222	$ 763	$346	$ 591	$276	$215
By annual household income									
Under $2,000	1,933	689	223	139	327	132	206	119	98
$2,000–2,999	2,924	976	311	153	588	229	375	154	138
3,000–3,999	3,839	1,167	495	209	698	286	554	238	192
4,000–4,999	4,363	1,271	518	225	843	354	621	298	233
5,000–6,999	5,016	1,417	566	262	932	458	797	328	256
7,000–9,999	6,063	1,622	778	286	1,086	523	925	521	322
10,000 and over	7,946	1,913	1,082	444	1,463	809	1,156	566	513
By level of education attained by household head									
Some grade school or less	2,807	962	325	166	447	216	375	173	143
Finished grade school	3,576	1,124	386	191	656	296	500	257	166
Attended high school	4,032	1,238	460	201	724	331	606	266	206
Finished high school	4,612	1,324	571	240	851	392	671	315	248
Some college or beyond	5,442	1,351	718	302	1,124	480	795	364	308
By occupation of household head									
Professional, semiprofessional	5,626	1,432	741	265	1,156	474	797	404	357
Proprietor, manager, official	5,437	1,455	648	384	1,045	495	757	446	257
Clerical, sales	4,845	1,295	651	269	914	398	757	314	247
Craftsman, foreman	4,572	1,453	484	240	778	404	677	280	256
Operative	4,002	1,269	473	193	747	310	594	211	205
Service worker	3,577	1,156	476	169	696	304	394	222	160
Farmer, farm laborer	3,187	826	335	177	589	308	563	276	163

By age of household head

Under 30 years	$4,193	$1,139	$467	$203	$834	$404	$676	$220	$250
30–39 years	4,703	1,371	504	240	962	382	682	299	263
40–49 years	4,872	1,396	650	253	814	415	710	384	250
50–64 years	3,930	1,207	498	224	691	317	551	254	188
65 years and over	2,405	736	285	158	451	194	291	182	108
By household stage in the "life cycle"									
No children and head under 40	4,332	1,111	536	183	845	419	726	210	302
Some children under 10	4,607	1,379	531	236	895	386	655	280	245
Children between 10 and 19 only	4,881	1,442	652	267	745	385	747	379	264
No children and married head over 40	3,639	1,069	415	217	653	325	525	273	162
No children and single head over 40	2,350	667	305	149	537	159	246	181	106
By market and geographic location									
All metropolitan markets	4,652	1,387	584	245	893	383	607	307	246
Northeast region	4,852	1,593	632	248	898	363	511	356	251
Central region	4,892	1,353	632	235	985	439	699	292	257
Southern region	3,883	1,156	451	206	758	311	571	245	185
Western region	4,658	1,256	545	301	874	408	700	297	277
All nonmetropolitan areas	3,318	934	361	186	574	291	194	161	172
Northeast region	3,647	1,091	409	215	672	238	576	232	214
Central region	3,458	964	332	186	642	298	592	268	176
Southern region	2,948	850	358	160	473	277	504	178	148
Western region	4,026	1,013	409	251	687	368	740	340	218

Source: Life Study of Consumer Expenditures, Time, Inc., New York, 1957, Vol. One.

Brief Description of the Sample Used in the Life Study of Consumer Expenditure

The data for this survey were collected from a sample of all individuals who were 20 years of age and over (and a subsample of individuals 10–19 years of age) living in households within the continental limits of the United States. A multistage probability sample of the area type was used. In such a sample, the probability of each person's inclusion in the sample is associated with the probabilities of the sampling unit in which he is located being selected at each stage of the sampling process. The results of such a sample may be projected to the total population. The sample data were collected in a series of four-week interviewing periods known as "waves." Each household was interviewed once during each "wave" with four-week intervals between interviews. Thus a household remained in the study for a period of 13 weeks. The four "waves" of interviews corresponded to a "cycle." During the fourth wave, the household kept a daily record of its purchases. As a result of the wave technique, new households entered the sample each week for an entire year. Likewise, each set of households completed its cycle including the daily record of its expenditures in systematic sequence, one week after another, thereby representing expenditures in the sample every day for a full twelve months. The total reporting group in each cycle was equivalent to an independent representative sample of U. S. households. In total there were 13 separate but overlapping cycles or samples. The first cycle began on October 3, 1955, and the thirteenth cycle was completed on December 26, 1956. A total of 110,314 interviews were made with 34,825 individuals in 15,003 households. Of these 15,003 households in the "total" sample in which at least one individual was interviewed in at least one wave, 10,243 households and 24,112 individuals were interviewed in each of the four waves. All of the expenditure findings in the report are based on these 10,243 households.

Table 7

| Year | Total | Theaters & Entertainments | | | | Clubs and Fraternal Organizations[d] |
		Total	Motion Picture Theaters	Legitimate Theaters, Opera, etc.[b]	Spectator Sports[c]	
1909	100.0	19.4	—	—	—	14.1
1914	100.0	19.1	—	—	—	14.0
1919	100.0	15.4	—	—	—	11.1
1921	100.0	18.6	14.6	4.0	1.5	11.8
1923	100.0	18.4	12.8	5.6	1.8	9.2
1925	100.0	19.1	12.9	6.2	1.7	9.7
1927	100.0	23.1	16.9	6.2	1.5	9.1
1929	100.0	22.0	18.7	3.3	1.7	7.9
1930	100.0	23.4	20.7	2.7	1.8	8.3
1931	100.0	27.7	25.0	2.7	2.0	9.6
1932	100.0	27.7	25.0	2.7	2.2	11.5
1933	100.0	28.0	25.8	2.2	2.7	11.1
1934	100.0	26.8	24.8	2.0	3.1	9.5
1935	100.0	26.5	24.6	1.9	3.2	8.7
1936	100.0	25.8	23.9	1.9	3.2	7.6
1937	100.0	24.8	23.0	1.8	3.0	6.9
1938	100.0	25.6	23.5	2.1	3.4	7.1
1939	100.0	24.1	22.0	2.1	3.3	6.6
1940	100.0	24.6	22.4	2.2	3.0	6.2
1941	100.0	23.8	21.7	2.1	2.9	5.5
1942	100.0	27.1	24.9	2.2	2.2	5.0
1943	100.0	32.7	29.9	2.8	1.4	5.1
1944	100.0	31.9	28.8	3.1	1.7	5.1
1945	100.0	30.3	27.5	2.8	2.2	5.3
1946	100.0	24.4	22.1	2.3	2.6	4.7
1947	100.0	21.4	19.1	2.3	2.7	4.8
1948	100.0	19.4	17.3	2.1	2.7	5.1
1949	100.0	18.3	16.2	2.1	2.7	5.1
1950	100.0	15.5	13.6	1.8	2.2	4.7
1951	100.0	14.4	12.6	1.8	2.1	4.7
1952	100.0	13.2	11.4	1.8	2.0	4.7
1953	100.0	12.1	10.3	1.8	2.0	4.6
1954	100.0	12.2	10.3	1.9	1.9	4.7
1955	100.0	11.7	9.7	2.0	1.8	4.6
1956	100.0	11.2	9.1	2.0	1.8	4.8
1957	100.0	10.0	7.9	2.1	1.7	4.8
1958	100.0	10.0	7.9	2.1	1.7	4.9
1959	100.0	10.0	7.9	2.1	1.6	4.6

Continued on following page.

Table 7 (Continued)

Year	Total	Commercial Participant Amusements[e]	Pari-Mutuel Net Receipts	Reading[f]	Gardening[g]
1909	2.6	—	—	12.1	8.1
1914	2.5	—	—	13.1	5.6
1919	2.5	—	—	9.4	6.2
1921	6.2	—	—	11.6	6.2
1923	5.6	—	—	10.3	6.7
1925	5.1	—	—	11.2	6.4
1927	5.1	—	—	11.2	5.9
1929	5.6	5.4	0.2	9.3	5.8
1930	5.9	5.7	0.2	9.2	5.4
1931	6.3	6.1	0.2	10.7	4.7
1932	6.5	6.3	0.2	11.6	4.2
1933	6.8	6.5	0.3	12.8	4.8
1934	7.4	6.5	0.9	12.2	5.6
1935	7.4	6.2	1.2	11.9	5.8
1936	7.4	6.3	1.1	11.2	6.1
1937	7.9	6.6	1.3	10.9	6.3
1938	7.4	5.8	1.6	11.0	6.2
1939	7.5	6.1	1.4	10.9	6.4
1940	7.7	6.0	1.7	10.5	6.1
1941	7.4	5.7	1.7	10.0	6.2
1942	6.9	5.2	1.7	10.2	5.9
1943	6.9	5.0	1.9	11.9	6.4
1944	8.0	5.2	2.8	12.0	7.1
1945	8.3	5.4	2.9	11.8	7.2
1946	8.1	5.0	3.1	9.3	5.9
1947	8.0	5.0	3.0	9.0	5.7
1948	8.0	5.0	3.0	9.5	5.6
1949	7.7	4.9	2.8	9.8	5.7
1950	7.0	4.6	2.4	9.1	5.2
1951	7.2	4.7	2.4	9.5	5.6
1952	7.7	4.7	3.0	9.6	5.9
1953	8.0	4.8	3.2	9.6	5.9
1954	7.9	4.8	3.1	9.4	5.9
1955	7.9	4.9	3.0	9.4	5.7
1956	8.0	5.0	3.0	9.2	5.7
1957	8.1	5.1	3.0	9.6	5.8
1958	8.2	5.2	3.0	9.7	5.5
1959	8.0	5.0	2.9	9.5	5.6

Table 7 (Continued)

| Radios, Television, and Musical Instruments | | | Sports Equipment[h] | | | |
Total	Radio and Television Receivers, Records, and Musical Instruments	Radio and Television Repair	Total	Nondurable Toys and Sports Supplies	Wheel Goods, Durable Toys, Sports Equipment, Boats, and Pleasure Aircraft	Other[i]
19.3	—	—	16.6	—	—	—
19.3	—	—	18.6	—	—	—
30.6	—	—	17.3	—	—	—
21.4	—	—	16.4	—	—	—
24.3	—	—	17.4	—	—	—
26.1	—	—	14.5	—	—	—
22.9	—	—	15.1	—	—	—
27.0	26.3	0.7	14.5	8.8	5.7	6.2
26.8	26.0	0.8	12.8	7.9	4.9	6.4
17.4	16.6	0.8	14.8	9.3	5.5	6.8
13.6	12.7	0.9	15.1	9.9	5.2	7.6
11.2	10.4	0.8	14.6	9.6	5.0	8.0
11.7	10.9	0.8	15.2	9.6	5.6	8.5
11.9	11.0	0.9	15.6	9.6	6.0	9.0
13.5	12.7	0.8	15.8	9.3	6.5	9.4
13.9	13.1	0.8	16.3	9.2	7.1	10.0
12.9	12.0	0.9	17.0	9.5	7.5	9.4
14.9	14.0	0.9	17.1	9.5	7.6	9.2
16.0	15.0	1.0	17.0	9.3	7.7	8.9
17.3	16.3	1.0	18.1	9.7	8.4	8.8
16.6	15.5	1.1	17.3	9.8	7.5	8.8
10.9	9.5	1.4	15.6	9.2	6.4	9.1
8.2	6.7	1.5	16.8	9.9	6.9	9.2
8.2	6.5	1.7	18.0	10.4	7.6	8.7
16.5	15.0	1.5	21.6	11.0	10.6	6.9
18.9	17.2	1.7	22.6	10.9	11.7	6.9
19.1	17.1	2.0	23.7	12.4	11.3	7.0
21.4	19.1	2.3	23.7	13.1	9.5	6.7
27.3	24.5	2.8	22.7	13.9	8.8	6.3
25.3	21.9	3.4	24.8	16.1	8.7	6.3
25.5	21.9	3.6	25.0	15.8	9.2	6.4
26.7	22.9	3.8	24.5	14.9	9.6	6.6
27.4	23.4	4.0	23.9	13.8	10.0	6.7
26.3	22.2	4.1	25.7	14.6	11.1	6.9
25.7	21.3	4.3	26.6	14.9	11.7	7.1
25.7	21.1	4.6	27.1	14.7	12.4	7.2
25.5	20.7	4.9	27.2	14.6	12.7	7.3
26.5	21.6	4.8	26.9	14.7	12.2	7.3

See Table 7a for sources and notes.

Table 7a
CONSUMER EXPENDITURES FOR RECREATIONAL GOODS AND SERVICES, BY TYPE, 1909–1959[a]
(Millions)

Year	Total	Theaters & Entertainments				Clubs and Fraternal Organizations[d]
		Total	Motion Picture Theaters	Legitimate Theaters, Opera, etc.[b]	Spectator Sports[c]	
1909	$ 860	$ 167	—	—	—	$121
1914	1,000	191	—	—	—	140
1919	2,180	336	—	—	—	242
1921	2,055	382	$301	$ 81	$ 30	242
1923	2,620	482	336	146	46	242
1925	2,835	541	367	174	47	275
1927	3,120	721	526	195	48	283
1929	3,840	847	720	127	66	302
1930	3,540	827	732	95	65	294
1931	2,877	797	719	78	57	277
1932	2,105	584	527	57	47	242
1933	1,871	523	482	41	50	208
1934	2,090	560	518	42	65	199
1935	2,259	600	556	44	72	197
1936	2,615	676	626	50	83	198
1937	2,940	729	676	53	89	203
1938	2,815	721	663	58	95	200
1939	3,000	723	659	64	98	199
1940	3,284	806	735	71	98	203
1941	3,722	888	809	79	107	203
1942	4,100	1,114	1,022	92	90	205
1943	4,263	1,393	1,275	118	62	217
1944	4,651	1,483	1,341	142	80	236
1945	5,278	1,598	1,450	148	116	281
1946	7,639	1,866	1,692	174	200	359
1947	8,320	1,782	1,594	188	222	399
1948	8,670	1,685	1,503	182	233	438
1949	8,913	1,628	1,445	183	240	458
1950	10,018	1,552	1,367	185	223	467
1951	10,340	1,487	1,299	188	221	483
1952	10,819	1,425	1,235	192	221	506
1953	11,380	1,372	1,172	200	222	525
1954	11,730	1,435	1,210	225	225	549
1955	12,593	1,468	1,217	251	232	582
1956	13,476	1,504	1,228	276	240	642
1957	14,205	1,416	1,120	296	246	681
1958	14,845	1,481	1,168	313	255	724
1959	16,180	1,617	1,278	339	265	744

Table 7a (Continued)

| | Participant Recreation | | | | Radios, Television, and Musical Instruments | | |
Total	Commercial Participant Amusements[e]	Pari-Mutuel Net Receipts	Reading[f]	Gardening[g]	Total	Radio and Television Receivers, Records, and Musical Instruments	Radio and Television Repair
22	—	—	$ 104	$ 70	$ 166	—	—
25	—	—	131	56	193	—	—
55	—	—	204	135	667	—	—
128	—	—	239	128	439	—	—
148	—	—	270	176	637	—	—
145	—	—	318	182	739	—	—
159	—	—	349	183	713	—	—
215	$207	$ 8	356	221	1,038	$1,012	$ 26
210	203	7	326	190	948	921	27
181	175	6	307	134	502	478	24
136	132	4	244	89	287	268	19
127	121	6	240	90	209	195	14
154	135	19	255	116	246	229	17
167	141	26	268	130	269	248	21
194	165	29	293	159	354	333	21
232	194	38	320	186	408	385	23
208	164	44	309	176	364	339	25
224	183	41	328	191	448	420	28
252	197	55	346	201	526	494	32
275	210	65	374	229	643	607	36
282	213	69	417	241	680	634	46
294	215	79	506	274	463	403	60
372	241	131	559	327	383	311	72
437	284	153	624	378	432	344	88
620	379	241	711	447	1,258	1,143	115
670	415	255	747	475	1,569	1,429	140
692	436	256	824	483	1,653	1,479	174
686	440	246	875	504	1,905	1,704	201
700	463	237	912	524	2,738	2,457	281
743	490	253	987	582	2,614	2,264	350
833	510	323	1,041	634	2,762	2,373	389
912	545	367	1,095	675	3,036	2,608	428
927	565	362	1,105	687	3,216	2,741	475
990	615	375	1,178	721	3,314	2,792	522
981	673	408	1,243	770	3,457	2,872	585
56	725	431	1,359	824	3,652	3,000	652
19	772	447	1,434	815	3,787	3,067	720
89	816	473	1,538	905	4,281	3,497	784

Continued on following page.

| | | Sports Equipment[h] | | |
Year	Total	Non-dura-ble Toys and Sports Sup-plies	Wheel Goods, Durable Toys, Sports Equipment, Boats, and Pleasure Aircraft	Other[1]
1909	$ 143	—	—	—
1914	186	—	—	—
1919	377	—	—	—
1921	338	—	—	—
1923	455	—	—	—
1925	411	—	—	—
1927	470	—	—	—
1929	555	$ 336	$ 219	$ 240
1930	453	281	172	227
1931	425	266	159	197
1932	317	207	110	159
1933	274	181	93	150
1934	318	200	118	177
1935	352	216	136	204
1936	413	242	171	245
1937	479	269	210	294
1938	478	268	210	264
1939	513	285	228	276
1940	560	306	254	292
1941	676	362	314	327
1942	710	404	306	361
1943	664	393	271	390
1944	782	459	323	429
1945	953	553	400	459
1946	1,652	843	809	526
1947	1,882	910	972	574
1948	2,059	1,079	980	603
1949	2,019	1,172	847	598
1950	2,274	1,396	878	628
1951	2,567	1,663	904	656
1952	2,703	1,709	994	694
1953	2,787	1,694	1,093	756
1954	2,798	1,624	1,174	788
1955	3,239	1,842	1,397	869
1956	3,583	2,008	1,575	956
1957	3,854	2,094	1,760	1,017
1958	4,045	2,162	1,883	1,088
1959	4,358	2,378	1,980	1,183

Sources and notes on following page.

urces and notes to Table 7a

Sources: Estimates for 1909–1927 based on J. Frederic Dewhurst and associates, *America's Needs and Resources: A New Survey,* Twentieth Century Fund, New York, 1955, Appendix 4–4, pp. 974–*. Estimates for 1929–1959 based on *National Income, 1954 Edition* (Supplement to the *Survey of Current Business*), Table 30, pp. 206–207, *United States Income and Output,* Table II–4, p. 151, *nd Survey of Current Business,* July 1960, Table 15, p. 16.

a. Estimates of total recreation expenditures for 1909–1927 based on the trend of the sum of the individual categories of expenditure (including estimates of outlays on spectator sports for 1909–1929) derived from expenditures for "admissions to amusements, total" in Julius Weinberger, "Economic Aspects of Recreation," *Harvard Business Review,* Summer 1937, Table II, p. 454; the trend is linked to the Commerce estimate for 1929. Estimates for the individual categories for 1909–1927 are based on trends in Dewhurst and associates, *loc. cit.,* linked to estimates for 1929 in *National Income, 1954 Edition.*

b. Also includes entertainments of nonprofit institutions (except athletics).

c. Comprises professional baseball, football, and hockey, horse and dog race tracks, college football, and other amateur spectator sports.

d. Comprises gross receipts less cash benefits of fraternal, patriotic, and women's organizations except insurance; and dues and fees of athletic, social and luncheon clubs, and school fraternities; excludes insurance.

e. Comprises billiard parlors, bowling alleys, dancing, riding, shooting, skating and swimming places, amusement devices and parks, daily fee golf course greens fees, golf instruction, club rental, and caddy fees, sightseeing buses and guides, and private flying operations.

f. From 1929 to 1959, 42 per cent of Commerce estimates for "books and maps" and "magazines, newspapers, and sheet music." The remaining 58 per cent is considered an expenditure for education.

g. Flowers, seeds, and potted plants.

h. Includes games, toys, sporting, athletic, and photographic goods, and related products, divided roughly between the two subgroups on the basis of durability.

i. Comprises photo developing and printing, photographic studios, collectors' net acquisitions of stamps and coins, hunting dog purchase and training, sports guide service, veterinary service, purchase of pets, camp fees, nonvending coin machine receipts minus payoff, and other commercial amusements.

Figures for "other" for 1921–1927 could be computed by subtraction; but they would not be statistically significant since a relatively small error in the estimates of total recreation expenditures could cause a relatively large error in the residual or "Other" category.

Table 8

PER CENT OF POPULATION ENGAGING IN VARIOUS LEISURE ACTIVITIES "YESTERDAY,"a BY PERSONAL CHARACTERISTICS

Rank	Activity	Per Cent of All Respondents	Years of Age						Sex and Employment Status			
			15–19	20–29	30–39	40–49	50–59	60 and over	Men	Women		
										All	Employed	Not Employed
1	Watching television	57	56	57	56	61	56	53	56	57	56	58
2	Visiting with friends or relatives	38	46	41	40	36	33	37	32	42	42	43
3	Working around yard and in garden	33	20	24	33	39	38	42	36	34	27	38
4	Reading magazines	27	31	29	25	25	23	27	25	27	26	28
5	Reading books	18	21	19	17	15	15	21	17	18	16	19
6	Going pleasure driving	17	25	21	18	14	11	11	15	16	16	16
7	Listening to records	14	35	16	14	10	6	6	9	13	15	11
8	Going to meetings or other organization activities	11	11	9	10	11	11	12	10	11	11	11
9	Special hobbies (woodworking, knitting, etc.)	10	11	9	10	10	12	11	8	12	9	14
10	Going out to dinner	8	7	10	8	8	8	6	7	9	12	7
11	Participating in sports	8	26	8	8	7	3	2	8	4	5	3
12	Playing cards, checkers, etc.	7	12	7	6	7	5	6	6	7	6	7
13	None of those listed	7	3	7	8	7	8	9	8	8	10	6
14	Spending time at drugstore, etc.	6	20	7	5	5	3	1	5	3	5	3
15	Singing or playing musical instrument	5	10	5	5	5	3	3	4	4	4	4
16	Going to see sports events	4	7	4	4	4	4	2	5	2	4	1
17	Going to movies in regular theater	3	9	4	3	3	2	1	2	3	4	2
18	Going to drive-in movies	2	6	4	2	2	1	0	2	2	2	1
19	Going to dances	2	8	4	1	1	1	0	1	1	2	1
20	Going to a play, concert, or opera	1	1	2	1	1	0	1	0	1	1	1
21	Going to lectures or adult school	1	1	1	0	2	1	1	1	1	0	1

Table 8 (Continued)

Rank	Activity	Car Ownership		Rural-Urban				Region			
		Own Car	Do Not Own Car	Rural	Urban Below 100,000	100,000–999,999	1,000,000 & over	North-east	North Central	South	West
1	Watching television	59	48	56	56	59	56	60	60	51	56
2	Visiting with friends or relatives	39	38	40	42	37	35	36	38	40	41
3	Working around yard and in garden	35	26	43	34	31	23	26	39	32	38
4	Reading magazines	28	20	27	31	28	22	30	24	23	34
5	Reading books	18	19	18	18	18	18	18	16	18	20
6	Going pleasure driving	19	8	15	20	17	15	17	17	16	16
7	Listening to records	13	15	11	13	15	17	14	14	12	17
8	Going to meetings or other organization activities	11	9	11	12	11	9	10	9	13	9
9	Special hobbies (woodworking, knitting, etc.)	11	9	11	11	13	9	11	10	9	12
10	Going out to dinner	8	8	9	8	8	10	8	8	6	12
11	Participating in sports	9	5	7	10	8	8	11	9	6	8
12	Playing cards, checkers, etc.	7	7	7	8	6	7	7	7	6	7
13	None of those listed	6	11	7	6	7	8	6	6	10	7
14	Spending time at drugstore, etc.	6	7	6	5	5	9	9	5	5	6
15	Singing or playing musical instrument	6	7	6	5	5	9	9	5	5	6
16	Going to see sports events	5	5	6	5	5	4	5	4	5	7
17	Going to movies in regular theater	4	2	3	4	5	4	3	4	5	3
18	Going to drive-in movies	3	4	2	3	3	5	4	2	4	2
19	Going to dances	2	1	3	1	3	3	3	3	2	1
20	Going to a play, concert, or opera	1	1	1	1	1	1	1	0	1	1
21	Going to lectures or adult school	1	1	1	1	1	1	1	1	1	0

Continued on following page.

Table 8 (Continued)

Rank	Activity	Educational Attainment of People 20 Years and Older					Annual Family Income			
		Less than 8th Grade	8th Grade	High School, Incomplete	High School, Complete	College	Under $3,000	$3,000–4,999	$5,000–6,999	$7,000 and over
1	Watching television	51	56	59	61	55	47	60	59	59
2	Visiting with friends or relatives	38	35	40	38	36	39	38	38	39
3	Working around yard and in garden	35	36	34	35	37	35	30	33	34
4	Reading magazines	12	19	24	29	40	23	25	27	33
5	Reading books	12	15	15	15	30	20	16	18	20
6	Going pleasure driving	10	11	17	18	18	13	17	18	17
7	Listening to records	8	8	11	11	13	13	12	14	15
8	Going to meetings or other organization activities	11	8	9	11	14	11	10	10	11
9	Special hobbies (woodworking, knitting, etc.)	9	9	11	11	11	8	12	11	11
10	Going out to dinner	5	6	7	9	12	6	7	7	12
11	Participating in sports	3	4	5	7	9	3	8	10	11
12	Playing cards, checkers, etc.	5	7	7	6	7	5	6	8	8
13	None of those listed	13	9	7	6	5	10	8	5	6
14	Spending time at drugstore, etc.	3	3	6	4	4	5	6	7	7
15	Singing or playing musical instrument	3	3	4	4	7	5	4	5	4
16	Going to see sports events	1	3	4	4	4	3	4	5	5
17	Going to movies in regular theater	3	2	2	3	3	3	3	2	4
18	Going to drive-in movies	1	1	3	2	1	1	3	3	2
19	Going to dances	2	1	1	2	2	2	2	1	1
20	Going to a play, concert, or opera	1	1	0	1	1	1	1	1	1
21	Going to lectures or adult school	1	0	1	1	1	0	1	1	1

Source: "The Public Appraises Movies," A Survey for Motion Picture Association of America, Inc., Opinion Research Corporation, Princeton, New Jersey, December 1957, Vol. II.

ef Description of Sample Used in
inion Research Corporation Study

his report is based on personal interviews with a national probability sample of 5,021
ons, representing the total United States population, aged 15 and over, living in private
seholds.

SAMPLING METHOD

ndividuals with whom interviews were conducted were selected entirely by area prob-
ity sampling procedures. Through a series of sampling steps, a known probability of
ction was assigned to each person in the survey universe. Mechanical devices predesig-
ed both households to be included in the survey and specific individuals to be inter-
ved, removing such choices from the hands of interviewers.

nterviews were taken in 86 widely scattered sample areas (primary sampling units) as
ows:

The entire area of the United States was divided into about 1,800 primary sampling
units. With a few minor exceptions, a primary sampling unit consists of a county or a
group of contiguous counties.

All primary sampling units were allocated to 86 strata. Each stratum consisted of a set
of primary sampling units as much alike as possible with respect to such characteristics
as geographical location, size of central city, rate of population growth, and economic
characteristics.

Because of their size, 22 large metropolitan areas were in strata by themselves and
were automatically included in the sample as "self-representing" areas. One sample
area was selected in a random manner from each of the remaining 64 strata. Within a
stratum the probability of selection of any one primary sampling unit was proportionate to its estimated population.

total of approximately 450 sample segments, or interviewing locations, were allocated
he 86 sample areas.

Vithin a sample area the probability of selection of a sample segment was proportionate
ts estimated population. Several sources were used in estimating the size of each seg-
t. These included Bureau of the Census block statistics and mapping materials as well
pecial field visits to subdivide Census enumeration districts into segments.

or each sample segment the interviewer was provided with a detailed map and instruc-
s for listing a specific group of households in which interviews were to be conducted. No
iation from the specified procedures was permitted.

Vithin sample households, probability procedures were used to predesignate the specific
son to be interviewed. All members of the household, aged 15 and over, were first listed
prescribed manner on a form provided for the purpose. Random numbers, in a mathe-
ical sense, were used to designate one specific person in the sample household to be in-
iewed.

o attain maximum control of non-response, interviewers made up to four calls at house-
ls where designated respondents were not at home on the interviewer's first or subse-
nt calls.

he sampling tolerances estimate the limits, in percentage points, of possible sample
ation at the 95 per cent confidence level.

Table 9

FREQUENCY OF SHOPPING TRIPS TO SELECTED TYPES OF STORES BY MEN AND WOMEN, JUNE 1952

	Type of Store							
	Grocery or Supermarket		Drugstore		Department Store		5 and 10¢ Store	
Frequency of Visits	Men	Women	Men	Women	Men	Women	Men	Women
	Per Cent							
In last week:								
5 times or more	19	26	4	4	1	4	[a]	3
3–4 times	18	23	4	8	2	8	6	8
2 times	15	24	16	15	5	13	8	15
1 time	27	20	38	35	27	28	19	33
No visits	20	7	35	35	60	43	63	40
Don't know or not reported	1	0	3	3	5	4	4	1
	Number							
Average (median) times in last month	8	8	4	4	4	4	4	4

Source: "The Drug Topics Survey of Consumer Buying Habits, June 1952," conducted for Drug Topics by Opinion Research Corporation, Princeton, N. J., July 3, 1952 (Verifax).

a. Less than 0.5 per cent.

Table 10

DAY OF WEEK AND TIME OF DAY OF USUAL TRIPS TO
GROCERY STORE BY MEN AND WOMEN, JUNE 1952[a]

(Per Cent)

Day and Time	Men	Women
Day of week:		
Monday	1	5
Tuesday	2	3
Wednesday	3	3
Thursday	4	8
Friday	26	38
Saturday	29	34
Sunday	1	0
Every day	3	3
No special day	30	13
Don't know	9	1
Time of day:		
Morning	19	34
Afternoon	19	37
Evening	29	18
No special time	27	11
Don't know	6	1

Source: "The Drug Topics Survey of Consumer Buying Habits, June 1952," conducted for *Drug Topics* by Opinion Research Corporation, Princeton, N. J., July 3, 1952 (Verifax).

a. Percentages add to more than 100 because of multiple answers.

SUPPLEMENT TO TABLES 9 AND 10

Brief Description of Sample Used in the Drug Topics Survey of Consumer Buying Habits

Tables 9 and 10 are derived from data based on a national cross-section of 505 cases. Interviewing was conducted in respondents' homes during the period June 7–15, 1952 by members of the resident interviewing staff of Opinion Research Corporation.

Since women do more shopping than men, three women were interviewed for every two men interviewed. The sample was then weighted so that men would be represented in the total results in the same proportions as they exist in the actual adult population.

Table 11

PERCENTAGE DISTRIBUTION OF PASSPORTS ISSUED AND RENEWED, BY
OCCUPATION AND BY AGE OF RECIPIENT, 1958, 1959, AND 1960

Occupation or Age	1958	1959	1960
Occupation: total	100.0	100.0	100.0
Housewife	25.7	24.4	23.8
Student	9.0	9.7	10.6
Retired	5.4	6.2	6.3
Clerk-secretary	5.4	4.5	4.4
Teacher	4.0	4.4	5.1
Other	50.5		
Skilled-technical or sales worker	n.a.	26.8	16.2
Independent business or profession	n.a.	10.9	20.3
Military	n.a.	2.0	2.6
Religious	n.a.	1.4	1.5
Transportation and travel industry	n.a.	1.0	1.4
Entertainment	n.a.	1.1	1.1
Unskilled worker	n.a.	1.5	0.2
Civilian government	n.a.	0.9	1.1
Journalism	n.a.	1.0	0.9
Sports	n.a.	0.1	0.1
None stated		4.3	4.4
Age: total	100.0	100.0	100.0
Under 20 years	13.0	10.6	9.7
20–29	19.1	17.5	17.4
30–39	17.1	17.6	16.7
40–49	15.9	16.2	16.0
50–59	17.6	18.2	18.3
60–76	16.7	18.9	20.7
Over 76	0.6	1.1	1.3

Source: "Summary of Passport Statistics," U. S. Department of State, Passport Office, Jan. 1959 and Jan. 1961, Tables 3 and 7 (mimeo.).

Table 12

NUMBER AND PER CENT OF EMPLOYEES ON VACATION,
ANNUAL DAILY AVERAGES, 1946–1960

(Numbers in Thousands)

Year	Civilian Employment	Employees on Vacation	
		Number	Per Cent
1946	55,050[a]	662	1.20
1947	57,812	834	1.44
1948	59,117	1,044	1.77
1949	58,423	1,044	1.79
1950	59,748	1,137	1.90
1951	60,784	1,073	1.76
1952	61,035	1,130	1.85
1953	61,945	1,171	1.89
1954	60,890	1,361	2.24
1955	62,944	1,268	2.01
1956	64,708	1,346	2.08
1957	65,011	1,447	2.22
1958	63,966	1,479	2.31
1959	65,581	1,494	2.28
1960	66,681	1,576	2.36

Source: Economic Report of the President, Jan. 1961, Tables C–18, and C–19, pp. 148 and 149.

a. Estimate adjusted to new definition of employment so as to be roughly consistent with estimates for subsequent years.

Table 13
ECONOMIC STATUS AND INTERESTS OF COLLEGE AND NON-COLLEGE WOMEN, OCTOBER 1956
(Per Cent)

Economic Status and Interests	College-Educated Women	Non-college Women
1. Employment status:		
A. Full time	17	12
B. Part time	41	21
C. Total employed	58	33
2. Married	77	92
3. Home owners	69	63
4. Types of music enjoyed:		
A. Religious	85	89
B. Light opera or musical comedy	85	54
C. Popular or jazz	83	77
D. Symphony	81	44
E. Folk music	80	65
F. Grand opera	59	28
G. Hillbilly	27	54
5. Types of conversation best liked:		
A. Educational problems	50	34
B. Personal chit-chat	37	47
C. Cultural subjects	31	11
D. Homemaking	31	61
E. Politics and international affairs	27	10
F. Entertainment	22	35
6. Sports engaged in:		
A. Swimming	13.5	6.4
B. Golf	7.6	1.0
C. Tennis	4.0	0.5
D. Bowling	3.9	5.1
E. Basketball, softball, volleyball	3.4	1.2
F. Ice skating, skiing, tobogganing	2.9	1.5
G. Fishing, boating	2.6	3.2
H. Miscellaneous	7.9	4.4
I. Net participating in one or more sports	33.8	17.8
7. Membership in civic and cultural clubs:		
A. Parent-Teacher Association	38	19
B. American Red Cross	34	12
C. College sorority	15	—
D. Book-of-the-Month Club	15	7
E. Literary Guild	6	1
F. League of Women Voters	4	2

Table 13 (Continued)

Economic Status and Interests	College-Educated Women	Non-college Women
8. Travel outside U.S.A.:		
A. Canada	50	26
B. Central and South America	12	5
C. Europe or Mediterranean	10	4
D. Caribbean and Bermuda	8	3
E. Far East	2	1
F. Net travel outside U.S.A.	58	32
9. Duration of vacation:		
A. One week or less	31	46
B. Two weeks	39	37
C. Three weeks or more	30	17
10. Nature of two or more week vacations:		
A. Traveling	47	31
B. Stayed put	53	69
11. Income:	Dollars	
A. Median family income	5,950	4,172
B. Median independent income	2,468	1,465

Source: *A Study of the College Educated Women of America* (Street & Smith Publications, Inc.), conducted for *Mademoiselle* by J. A. Ward, Inc., New York, 1956.

SUPPLEMENT TO TABLE 13

*Brief Description of Sample Used in a Study
of the College-Educated Women of America*

The procedure used in this survey was based firstly on the selection of 7,500 households on an area probability basis, in each of which a count was made of ages and educational levels of all women over 18 years of age.

Successful interviews were obtained from 799 women who had been college trained and 1,043 who had never been to college.

In order to avoid any deficiency in the number of working women interviewed, two thirds of all the household counts were conducted weekends or after 6 P.M. on weekdays, and to compensate for the fact that the other interviews were unlikely to be with working women, a proportionate weight was applied prior to tabulations, bringing each sample into proper proportions as between working and non-working women.

Table 14

HOBBIES, INTERESTS, AND ACTIVITIES OF STEELWORKERS
AND OTHER MANUAL WORKERS, MARCH 1956

(Per Cent)

Interest	Steelworkers	Other Manual Mfg. Workers in: Steel Communities	U. S.
A. Main hobbies and recreations			
1. Competitive sports and games			
a. Spectator	36	41	27
b. Participant	17	26	20
c. Indeterminate	3	2	5
2. Noncompetitive sports	32	31	38
3. Noncompetitive athletics	8	8	11
4. TV, radio, theater, movies	12	11	9
5. Craft hobbies	5	4	5
6. Church activities	5	3	3
7. Gardening	5	1	6
8. Outings and picnics	2	4	7
9. No hobbies or recreations	13	13	13
B. Belong to church	72	76	66
C. Wives belong to Parent-Teacher Association	18	15	16
D. Belong to social, recreational, political, or athletic clubs	18	12	7
E. Belong to fraternal organization			
1. Masons	6	4	5
2. Knights of Columbus	1	2	1
3. Eagles	3	2	2
4. Elks	1	3	2
5. Moose	2	3	2
6. Other	4	5	4
F. Hold office in club or organization	6	8	5
G. Hold public office	*	1	*
H. Vacation away from home lasting one week or more	52	56	58
1. Within past 12 months	33	31	37
2. Not within past 12 months but within past 5 years	19	25	21

Table 14 (Continued)

Interest	Steelworkers	Other Manual Mfg. Workers in:	
		Steel Communities	U. S.
I. On last vacation trip (within past 5 yrs.)[b]			
1. Traveled by car	90	84	86
2. Took along one or more members of family	91	80	91
3. Went to another state	71	71	74
4. Cost of vacation			
a. Less than $100	21	27	28
b. $100–199	38	38	28
c. $200–299	15	9	16
d. $300 and more	17	18	17

Source: "How the Industrial Worker Lives, March 1956," Opinion Research Corporation, Princeton, N. J., May 23, 1956 (Verifax).

a. Less than ½ per cent.

b. Percentages shown in this section relate to those who did take vacations within the past five years.

SUPPLEMENT TO TABLE 14

Brief Description of Sample Used in a Study by Opinion Research Corporation of How the Industrial Worker Lives

Findings in this study are based on a sampling of approximately 8,000 households which resulted in personal interviews with 651 steelworkers and 555 other manual workers in manufacturing in 14 steel-producing areas and with 445 other manual workers in manufacturing in 82 different urban areas in every geographic section of the country. In the latter group, the sampling plan provided for dependable coverage of every manufacturing industry grouping and manual workers at all economic levels.

To provide for a sampling of steelworkers of sufficient size for separate analysis, sampling ratios in "steelworker areas" were higher than in other areas. Varying weights were used in the tabulation to give proportionate representation to all manual worker groups in the final results of the survey.

Table 15
HOURS WORKED PER WEEK BY PERSONS AT WORK, BY MAJOR OCCUPATIONAL GROUP, ANNUAL AVERAGES, 1960

Major Occupational Group	Total	Per Cent Working:			Average Weekly Hours
		Under 35 Hours	35–40 Hours	Over 40 Hours	
Total	100.0	21.0	46.6	32.5	40.5
Professional, technical, and kindred workers	100.0	16.6	51.0	32.3	41.3
Farmers and farm managers	100.0	21.5	12.1	66.4	52.0
Managers, officials, and proprietors (excl. farm)	100.0	8.7	30.3	61.1	49.5
Clerical and kindred workers	100.0	18.8	66.3	14.9	37.6
Sales workers	100.0	28.0	35.0	36.9	38.2
Craftsmen, foremen, and kindred workers	100.0	13.0	57.1	29.9	41.0
Operatives and kindred workers	100.0	17.5	55.6	27.0	40.3
Private household workers	100.0	60.7	20.1	19.1	26.6
Service workers (excl. private household)	100.0	26.5	41.4	32.1	38.7
Farm laborers and foremen	100.0	41.9	15.9	42.3	39.3
Laborers (excl. farm and mine)	100.0	29.4	50.1	20.5	35.9

Source: Bureau of Labor Statistics, *Employment and Earnings,* May 1961, Vol. 7, No. 11.

Table 16

Percentage Distribution of Manpower by Industry Division, Selected Years, 1870–1957

Industry Division	Gainful Workers			Experienced Civilian Labor Force			
	1870	1900	1930	1930	1940	1950	1957
Total	100.0	100.0	100.0	100.0	100.0	100.0	100.0
Agriculture	50.3	37.3	22.1	21.5	18.0	11.9	8.8
Forestry and fishing	0.5	0.7	0.6	0.3	0.3	0.2	0.2
Mining	1.6	2.6	2.4	2.5	2.2	1.4	1.1
Construction	5.9	5.8	6.4	6.4	7.0	6.2	6.5
Manufacturing	17.6	22.1	23.1	22.8	23.9	25.8	27.3
Transportation, communication, and public utilities	4.8	7.1	9.6	9.6	7.7	8.6	8.5
Trade (incl. business and repair services)	6.1	8.6	12.7	13.1	14.4	18.5	18.1
Finance, insurance, and real estate	0.3	1.1	3.0	3.1	3.1	3.2	4.0
Government	2.0	2.8	5.1	5.3	6.1	7.9	8.2
Professional service (incl. amusement)	1.6	2.5	4.9	4.8	5.9	6.3	7.2
Personal and domestic service	9.3	9.4	10.1	10.7	11.4	10.1	10.2

Sources: 1870–1940 based on Daniel Carson, "Change in the Industrial Composition of Manpower since the Civil War," *Studies in Income and Wealth*, Vol. 11, National Bureau of Economic Research, New York, 1949, Table I, p. 47: 1950 and 1957 based on unpublished estimates of the Bureau of the Census derived from its current population sample for April of each year, and independent estimates of the percentage of the experienced civilian labor force attached to "eating and drinking places" (2.9 per cent in 1950 and 3.0 per cent in 1957) which were shifted from "trade" to "personal and domestic service" for comparability with Carson's classification.

Table 17
PROPERTY INCOME[a] AS PER CENT OF PERSONAL INCOME
EXCLUSIVE OF TRANSFER PAYMENTS, 1850–1960

Year	Per Cent	Year	Per Cent
1850	19	1941	15
1860	23	1942	12
1870	19	1943	10
1880	27	1944	10
1890	22	1945	10
1900	21	1946	12
1910	23	1947	12
		1948	12
1929	22	1949	13
1930	23	1950	13
1931	23	1951	12
1932	25	1952	12
1933	23	1953	12
1934	20	1954	13
1935	18	1955	13
1936	19	1956	13
1937	18	1957	13
1938	18	1958	13
1939	17	1959	14
1940	16	1960	14

Sources:

1850–1910 — Simon Kuznets, *Uses of National Income in Peace and War,* Occasional Paper 6, National Bureau of Economic Research, New York, March 1942, Table 9, p. 38; property income as per cent of national income was raised to next higher percentage point to allow for the fact that personal income in those years was slightly lower than national income.

1929–1960 — *Economic Report of the President,* Washington, Jan. 1961, Table C–12, p. 141; for consistency with earlier years when transfer payments and personal contributions for social security were inconsequential, the former were excluded from personal income as estimated by the U. S. Department of Commerce and the latter were added back in.

a. Property income consists of rental income of persons, dividends and personal interest income; other personal income consists of labor income (wages and salaries) and proprietors' income (entrepreneurial income or withdrawals).

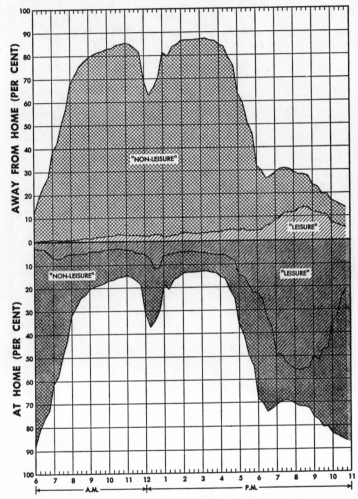

SOURCE: Derived from unpublished data in *A Nationwide Survey of Living Habits,* a national survey conducted for the Mutual Broadcasting System by J. A. Ward, Inc., New York, 1954.

NOTE: The total percentage at any particular point on the time scale may exceed 100 because individuals may engage in more than one activity during a given 15-minute period.

NOTES

CHAPTER I: The Background of Leisure

In spite of the importance of leisure and contemplation in ancient culture, relatively few studies on ancient civilization examine the problem with any care. Of the works that do treat it, most have passing references but do not go into the subject.

The Greek ideal of leisure is discussed by Jacob Burckhardt, *Griechische Kulturgeschichte,* Vol. III, Neunter Abschnitt, Stuttgart, 1952; Cecil Deslisle Burns, *Greek Ideals: A Study of Social Life,* Bell, London, 1917; Ernest Barker, *Reflections on Leisure,* National Council of Social Service, London, n.d.; Arnold Toynbee, *A Study of History,* Oxford U. Press, London, Vol. IX, 1954; and William A. Newman, *The Politics of Aristotle,* Clarendon Press, Oxford, 1887–1902.

Definitions of pertinent Greek concepts can be found in R. Arnou, Πράξις et Θεωρία — *étude de détail sur le vocabulaire et la pensée des Ennéades de Plotin,* Paris, 1921.

A discussion of *otium* in the thought of the Church Fathers is found in Adolphe Alfred Tanquerey, *Compendio di teologia ascetica e mistica,* Rome, 1927.

Christian views in general are reviewed by J. Clark Murray, "Idleness," in *Encyclopaedia of Religion and Ethics,* James Hastings, ed., Scribner, New York, 1908–26, Vol. VIII, p. 100. A small but penetrating modern Catholic work is Joseph Pieper, *Leisure, the Basis of Culture,* tr. by Alexander Dru, Faber, London, 1952.

On contemplation, see Franz Boll, *Vita contemplativa,* Festrede zur zehnjährigen Stiftungsfeste der Heidelberger Akademie der Wissenschaften, C. Winter, Heidelberg, 1920; André M. J. Festugière, *Contemplation et vie contemplative selon Platon,* Vrin, Paris, 1936; Rodolfo Mondolfo, "Origen del ideal filosófico de la vida," *Revista de Estudios Clasicos,* U. Nacional de Cuyo, Mendoza (Argentina), I, 1–34, 1944. Alberto Grilli, *Il problema della vita contemplativa nel mondo greco-romano,* Bocca, Rome, 1953, is mainly concerned with the positions of Epicurean and Stoic philosophers on contemplation, and deals with most of their relevant passages, but traces their origin from Aristotle and the thinkers that followed him. However, the author has not realized the significance of the concept of time in the Epicurean position. Essential to the Epicurean notion of good life is the condemnation of the connection between time and human life: time is an accident of cosmic movements, whereas the time of the soul is different. The relevant passages are quoted in the booklet by Jean Fallot, *Le plaisir et la mort dans la philosophie d'Epicure,* Julliard, Paris, 1951. For the Stoic, an essential element of ethical life was the adjustment of the time of human life to cosmic time. See Victor Goldschmidt, *Le système stoïcien et l'idée de temps,* Vrin, Paris, 1953.

A treatment of Christian views of contemplation is found in the article "Contemplation" by Charles Baumgartner in *Dictionnaire de spiritualité ascétique et mystique, doctrine et histoire,* Marcel Viller, ed., Beauschesne, Paris, 1937–57, Vol. II, pp. 1643–2193. Contributions can be found also in Marcel Viller, *La spiritualité des premiers siècles chrétiens,* Bloud et Gay, Paris, 1930; Edward C. Butler, *Western Mysticism: the teachings of SS Augustine, Gregory and Bernard on contemplation and the contemplative life,* Constable, London, 1922; and Gustave Bardy, *La vie spirituelle d'après les pères des trois premiers siècles,* Bloud et Gay, Paris, 1935.

The following works deal with contemporary Catholic attitudes: Jacques and Raïssa Maritain, *Liturgy and Contemplation,* tr. from French by Joseph W. Evans, Kenedy, New York, 1960; Jacques Maritain, "Action et contemplation," *Revue Thomiste,* XLIII, 1937, pp. 18–50; Reginald Garrigou–Lagrange, *Christian Perfection and Contemplation,* Herder, St. Louis, 1946; Thomas Merton, *The Ascent to Truth,* Harcourt, Brace, New York, 1951, and *Bread in the Wilderness,* 1953.

Other discussions of contemplation can be found in Edward I. Watkin, *A Philosophy of Form,* Sheed & Ward, London, 1950; William James, *The Varieties of Religious Experiences,* Riverside Press, Cambridge, 1903; James H. Leuba, *The Psychological Origin and the Nature of Religion,* Constable, London, 1909; Emile Bréhier, *La philosophie en Orient,* Presses Universitaires de France, Paris, 1948; and Douglas Van Steere, *Work and Contemplation,* Harper, New York, 1957. For a notable fictional account, see Herbert Read, *The Green Child,* Eyre and Spottiswood, London, 1947.

Some helpful works on the history or culture of the various periods discussed in this chapter are: for Sumer, Samuel Kramer, *History Begins at Sumer*, Doubleday, Garden City, 1959; for Egypt, W. M. Flinders Petrie, *Social Life in Ancient Egypt*, Mifflin, Boston, 1923; for Greece, Fustel de Coulanges, *The Ancient City*, Doubleday, Garden City, n.d.; Emile Mireaux, *Daily Life in the Time of Homer*, tr. by Iris Sells, Macmillan, New York, 1959; and Alfred E. Zimmern, *The Greek Commonwealth*, Clarendon Press, Oxford, 1911; for China, Fung Yu-lan, *A History of Chinese Philosophy*, tr. by Derk Bodde, Princeton U. Press, Princeton, 1952; and Marcel Granet, *Chinese Civilization*, Knopf, New York, 1930; for India, Sarvepalli Radhakrishnam and Charles Moore, eds., *A Source Book in Indian Philosophy*, Princeton U. Press, Princeton, 1957; and Joseph Campbell, ed., *Philosophies of India*, Pantheon, New York, 1951; for Rome, Jerome Carcopino, *Daily Life in Ancient Rome*, Penguin, Harmondsworth, 1956; Edith Hamilton, *The Roman Way*, Norton, New York, 1932; and Grant Showerman, *Rome and the Romans*, Macmillan, New York, 1931; for the Middle Ages, Eileen Power, *Medieval People*, Doubleday, Garden City, 1954, and G. C. Coulton, *Medieval Panorama*, Macmillan, New York, 1946; for scholasticism, Etienne Gilson, *Reason and Revelation in the Middle Ages*, Scribner, New York, 1938. On Venice, Pompeo G. Molmenti, *Venice, Its Individual Growth from the Early Beginning to the Fall of the Republic*, tr. by Horatio F. Brown, McClurg, Chicago, 1906–08. On the transition to the Renaissance, Eugenio Garin, *Dal medioevo al rinascimento*, Sansoni, Florence, 1950. On Florence, J. Lucas–Dubreton, *La vie quotidienne à Florence au temps des Médicis*, Hachette, Paris, 1958. On Christianity and classical culture, Charles Cochrane, *Christianity and Classical Culture*, Oxford U. Press, New York, 1957, and Umberto Fracassini, *Il misticismo greco e il cristianesimo*, Il Solco, Gubbio, 1944, p. 347. On Greek and Roman education, see William Barclay, *Educational Ideals in the Ancient World*, Collins, London, 1959, and Werner Jaeger, *Paideia: The Ideals of Greek Culture*, tr. by Gilbert Highet, Oxford U. Press, New York, 1945. For the relations of Islam, Greece, and Christianity, Gustave von Grunebaum, *Medieval Islam*, U. of Chicago Press, Chicago, 1956. On Egyptian education, Pierre Montet, *Everyday Life in Egypt*, tr. by A. Maxwell–Hyslo and Margaret S. Drower, Arnold, London, 1958; for the life of the Sumerian scribe, Kramer, *History Begins at Sumer*; for the life and material of Greek and Roman writers, Moses Hadas, *Ancilla to Classical Reading*, Columbia U. Press, New York, 1954; for scribes, schools, students, and professors in the whole ancient world see Henri Marrou, *Histoire de l'éducation dans l'antiquité*, Editions du Seuil, Paris, 1948; for the Christian scholar, Elmore H. Harbison, *The Christian Scholar in the Age of the Reformation*, Scribner, New York, 1956.

PAGE

11 The quotations from Aristotle are located as follows: on the fall of the Spartans because of leisure, in *Politics*, II, 1271b;

13 on leisure as freedom from labor, *Politics*, II, 1269a.

14 On the etymology of words connected with leisure, such as work, labor, and activity, see Hannah Arendt, *The Human Condition*, Doubleday, Garden City, 1959. The quotation from Martial is from the *Epigrams*, X, 58. Seneca's remark about the barber and ringlets occurs in *de otio*. His paradigm for Lucilius (*Vaco, Lucili, vaco*) appears in *Epistulae*, 62, 1.

15 The quotations from Aristotle are located as follows:
on silly work, *Ethics*, X, 1176b;

16 on the happiness of the leisured as well as the activities of leisure, *Politics*, VIII, 1337b.

18 The remark on the Spartan army's music appears in the story of Lycurgus in Plutarch's *Parallel Lives*. In his "Life of Pericles," Plutarch presents an extreme view of activity in leisure. He quotes the philosopher Antisthenes as saying in reply to a remark about an "excellent" piper, "It may be so, but he is but a wretched human being, otherwise he would not have been an excellent piper."

21 One can see the lack of reflection on leisure as freedom in Mortimer J. Adler's compendium on *The Idea of Freedom*, Doubleday, Garden City, 1958.

ALL HANDS SET TO MOTION

29 For another early or pre-Renaissance view of leisure, quiet, and the city, see Petrarch's *De Vita Solitaria* (1346). In "Petrarch's Views on the Individual and His Society," *Osiris*, 1954, Charles Trinkhaus concludes that "Petrarch's ideal was that of a perpetual vacation enlivened by flights into the past and into eternity through the power of inner fantasy" (pp. 186–187).

In Japan's Muromachi Period, about this time, Yoshida Kenko was writing *Essays in Idleness* (1340). His "trifling thoughts" would easily have suited an earlier day in the West. "One should not write unskillfully in the running hand, be able to sing in a pleasing voice and keep time to music; and lastly, a man should not refuse a little wine when it is pressed upon him." Portions of this medieval work (*Tzurezure–Gusa*) can be found in Donald Keene, ed., *Anthology of Japanese Literature,* UNESCO collection of representative works, Grove, New York, 1955.

30 For the imaginary dialogue between Lorenzo and Alberti, see Christoforo Landino, *Disputationes Camaldulenses, Liber primus, de vita activa et contemplativa,* Florence, ca. 1486. Origenes, *In Ioan,* II, 18, frag. 80 (ed. Klostermann, Heinrich, Leipzig, 1932, IV, p. 547), seems to have been the first to identify Mary with contemplative life and Martha with active life, on the basis of Luke 10 : 31. St. Thomas identifies as pertinent to this distinction: Matthew 5 : 8, 6 : 21; Romans 1 : 20; II Corinthians 3 : 18. For the Old Testament in regard to the contemplative life, see the Book of Ecclesiastes, XXXVIII, 24–25.

Two Spanish poets should be singled out in the sixteenth century: Fray Luis de León, author of "Vida retirada," and San Juan de la Cruz, of "Noche obscura del alma" and "Coplas hechas sobre un extasis de alta contemplación."

31 The text of Sir Thomas More's *Utopia* (1516) and a translation of Tommaso Campanella's *Città del sole* (1602) can be found in *Famous Utopias,* Dunne, Washington, 1901.

33 Some of the results of the modern attitude toward work, the world and nature can be seen in William L. Thomas, Jr., ed., *Man's Role in Changing the Face of the Earth,* U. of Chicago Press, Chicago, 1956.

CHAPTER II: Toward the Work Society

The condemnation of labor is general in ancient writers. See, for instance, Plato, *Republic,* VI, 54; *Laws,* V, VII, VIII; Aristotle, *Politics,* III 3, IV 13, V 2, VII 8; Xenophon, *Economics,* IV. The view is summed up by Cicero, *de officiis,* I, 42: *opifices omnes in sordida arte versantur: nec enim quidquid ingenuum habere potest officina.*

The only ancient praise of labor is found in Hesiod, *Works and Days,* lines 298–321; and Vergil, *Georgics, Bucolics.* "Sweat is the ornament of virtue's face," says Hesiod.

For modern general studies on historical attitudes toward work, labor, and slavery, see Adriano Tilgher, *Homo faber, storia del concetto di lavoro nella civiltà occidentale,* Libreria di Scienze e Lettere, Rome, 1929; Enzo Cataldi, *Il lavoro umano,* Jandi Sapi, Rome, 1958;

and again Arendt, *The Human Condition.* In addition to works cited in Chapter I, see for antiquity Henry A. Wallon, *Histoire de l'esclavage dans l'antiquité,* Paris, 1879, who connects the attitude toward labor with the institution of slavery; William L. Westermann, *The Slave Systems of Greek and Roman Antiquity,* American Philosophical Society, Philadelphia, 1955; Reginald H. Barrow, *Slavery in the Roman Empire,* Methuen, London, 1928; Gustave Glotz, *Ancient Greece at Work,* Knopf, New York, 1926; Humfrey Michell, *The Economics of Ancient Greece,* Heffer, Cambridge, 1957; A. E. E. McKenzie, *The Major Achievements of Science,* Vol. II, Cambridge U. Press, London, 1960; and Benjamin Farrington, *Greek Science,* Penguin, London, 1953.

Farrington, writing from a Marxist position, contends that concern with contemplative life began only with Plato and Aristotle, because their political conception of society was based on slavery. Earlier Greek thinkers would have been concerned with doing and with changing the world. This view may be compared with Willi Zimmermann, *Arbeit als Weltanschauung: eine kulturpolitische Grundlegung,* Panverlagsgesellschaft, Berlin, 1937, who, writing from a national-socialist standpoint, claims that only Nazism following Germanic ideals established labor as a supreme value.

For the Middle Ages, see Marc Bloch, *Lavoro e tecnica nel medioevo,* Laterza, Bari, 1959; Prosper Boissonnade, *Le travail dans l'Europe chrétienne au moyen âge,* Paris, 1921. For the Christian view of labor, see, besides Boissonnade above, Salvatore Talamo, *Il cristianesimo e il lavoro manuale,* Rome, 1885. For the transition from classical culture to Christianity and the relation of one to the other, see Cochrane, *Christianity and Classical Culture.*

The philosophers of antiquity and Christianity gave much attention to distinguishing and ordering the several ways of life. Plato distinguishes two types of science, *gnōstikē* and *praktikē* (*Politicus,* 258, 259), but in *Philebus,* 61 C, points to a mixed life including study and activity. Aristotle distinguishes (*Ethics,* I, 1095; X, 1177) three forms of moral life: *apolaustikós* (voluptuous), *politikós* or *praktikós* (of practical affairs), and *theōrētikos* (contemplative). Augustine (*City of God,* XIX, 19) distinguishes three types of life, *otiosum, actuosum, ex utroque composito.* Thomas Aquinas makes the same distinction as Aristotle: in III *Sententia Distincta,* 35 quest. a.l., *Summa Theologica,* 2a–2ae, quest. 179 a.l., *Ethicorum Aristotelis expositio,* I. lect. m-58–59.

PAGE

39 On the Lord in relation to *play* rather than *work,* see Book of Proverbs, viii, 22–23, 20–21, in the Douay translation, based on the Vulgate, quoted by Johan Huizinga in *Homo Ludens,* Beacon Press, Boston, 1950, p. 212.

THE MEDIEVAL FRONTIER

41 For an English translation of the Rule of St. Benedict, see Henry Bettenson, ed., *Documents of the Christian Church,* Oxford U. Press, New York, 1947.

44 On imitation by the great artists of the Renaissance, see K. E. Maison, *Art Themes and Variations: Five Centuries of Interpretations and Recreations,* Abrams, New York, 1961.

45 For the influence of the Reformation and the Industrial Revolution on attitudes toward work see Max Weber, *The Protestant Ethic and the Spirit of Capitalism,* tr. by Talcott Parsons, Scribner, New York, 1950; Werner Sombart, *The Quintessence of Capitalism,* Dutton, New York, 1915; Richard H. Tawney, *Religion and the Rise of Capitalism,* Harcourt, Brace, New York, 1926; Bertrand de Jouvenel, "The Treatment of Capitalism by Continental Historians" and other papers in Friedrich A. von Hayek, *Capitalism and the Historians,* U. of Chicago Press, Chicago, 1954; and Robert L. Calhoun, *God and the Day's Work,* Reflection Books Association, Princeton, 1957.

46 An analysis of psychological studies of unemployment can be found in Sebastian de Grazia, *The Political Community,* U. of Chicago Press, Chicago, 1948.

   For the percentages given of the United States labor force by age and sex, see Gertrude Bancroft, *The American Labor Force,* Wiley, New York, 1958, Table B-3, adjusted to decennial census levels by means of adjustment factor shown in Table A-15, *ibid.,* and applied to population shown in U. S. Bureau of the Census, *Current Population Reports, Population Estimates,* Series P-25, No. 187.

47 The reference to Italian unskilled workers is based on Sebastian de Grazia, *Borgata Urbis,* 1954, unpublished. Some of the data appear in Hadley Cantril, *Politics of Despair,* Basic Books, New York, 1958.

THE WORKLESS

47 For labor legislation protecting women, children, the aged, and the health of workers generally, see W. S. Woytinsky *et al., Employment and Wages in the United States,* Twentieth Century Fund, New York, 1953.

48 On age and work participation see *Employment and Earnings,* May

1960, U. S. Dept. of Labor, Tables SA-6, SA-27, pp. 60, 80; and in general Robert W. Kleemeier, ed., *Aging and Leisure,* Oxford U. Press, New York, 1961. On proportion of the labor force not working because of illness, see references for Chapter V.

49 For females in the labor force see Robert W. Smuts, *Women and Work in America,* Columbia U. Press, New York, 1959. For the "nonemployed adults" and other data on stockholders see Lewis H. Kimmel, *Share Ownership in the U. S.,* Brookings Institution, Washington, 1952. See also J. A. Livingston, *The American Stockholder,* Lippincott, New York, 1958.

For a recent expression of anti-playboy attitudes, see Adlai E. Stevenson, "America Under Pressure," *Harpers,* August 1961, p. 21.

50 On the hobo, tramp, and bum, see Nels Anderson, *The Hobo,* U. of Chicago Press, Chicago, 1923, and specially for modern types of the Wino, the Beat, the Angry, the Delinquent, and the Hipster, see Paul Goodman, *Growing Up Absurd,* Random House, New York, 1960. For a historical and social analysis of vagabondage, see Alexandre Vexliard, *Introduction à la sociologie du vagabondage,* Rivière, Paris, 1956.

51 Saint Simon's proposal for toning up the nation can be found in F. M. H. Markham, ed., *Henri Comte de Saint-Simon, 1760–1825,* Macmillan, New York, 1952.

MONKS IN THE FACTORY

54 On the inaccessibility of the working and slave classes, see Erich Auerbach, *Mimesis,* tr. by Willard Trask, Doubleday, Garden City, 1957. There is much statistical information on these classes today, but not much reliable data on their sentiments. See *Characteristics of Low-Income Population and Related Federal Programs,* Joint Committee on the Economic Report, Subcommittee on low income families, 84th Congress, U.S.G.P.O., Washington, 1955.

For studies of working men and women's attitudes, see Lee Rainwater, *And the Poor Get Children,* Quadrangle Books, Chicago, 1960; Richard Hoggart, *The Uses of Literacy,* Penguin, Harmondsworth, 1958; Ferdynand Zweig, *The British Worker,* Penguin, Harmondsworth, 1952, and *Labour, Life and Poverty,* Gollancz, London, 1949; Lee Rainwater, Richard P. Coleman and Gerald Handel, *Workingman's Wife,* Oceana, New York, 1959. Critiques and studies of mass production and the assembly line are numerous. For a recent one, see Charles R. Walker and Robert H. Guest, *The Man on the Assembly Line,* Harvard U. Press, Cambridge, 1952. On contemporary work see also Georges Friedmann, *Le travail en miettes,* Gallimard, Paris, 1956, and *Où va le travail humain?,* Gallimard, Paris, 1950; J. Fourastié, *Machinisme et bien-être,* Minuit, Paris, 1951; and J. Folliet *et al.,*

Civilisation du travail? civilisation du loisir?, Arthème Fayard, Paris, 1956. For a statement by a pioneer, see Henry Ford, "Mass Production" in *Encyclopaedia Britannica,* 14th ed., 1929. On *Henry Ford,* see Roger Burlingame, Knopf, 1955, and Allan Nevins, *Ford: The Times, The Man, The Company,* Scribner, New York, 1954.

Studies of white-collar workers also exist in quantity. See, for example, C. Wright Mills, *White Collar, The American Middle Classes,* Oxford U. Press, New York, 1956; Carl Dreyfuss, *Occupation and Ideology of the Salaried Employee,* tr. by Eva Abramovitch and E. E. Warburg, 2 vols., Columbia U. Press, New York, 1938; Roy Lewis and Angus Maude, *The English Middle Class,* Knopf, New York, 1950.

For examples of fictional and literary accounts of men and machines see Harvey Swados, *On the Line,* Bantam, New York, 1957; Sherwood Anderson, "Machine Song" in *Perhaps Women,* Liveright, New York, 1931.

Charles A. Dana's story, date-lined Paris, June 29, 1848, can be found in Louis L. Snyder and Richard B. Morris, *A Treasury of Great Reporting,* Simon and Schuster, New York, 1949.

55 First-hand observation of the "underground life" of factory workers can be found in William F. Whyte *et al., Men, Money and Motivation,* Harper, New York, 1955. On "personal delay" and restriction of output, see also Adam Abruzzi, *Work Measurement: New Principles and Procedures,* Columbia U. Press, New York, 1952. For public attitudes in general toward work, see *Big Business from the Viewpoint of the Public,* Survey Research Center, Institute for Social Research, U. of Michigan, March 1951.

For an example of the importance of ethnic or racial differences in work attitudes, see John Kenneth Morland, *Millways of Kent,* U. of North Carolina Press, Chapel Hill, 1958, a study of mill, farm, and town people in a southern Piedmont area; for comparison see Erskine Caldwell's *God's Little Acre,* Duell, New York, 1949. For rural-urban differences see Michael P. Fogarty, *Personality and Group Relations in Industry,* Longmans, New York, 1956. For factory and professional worker differences, see Robert Dubin, "Industrial Workers' Worlds," *Social Problems,* January 1956, and Louis H. Orzack, "Work as a Central Life Interest of Professionals," *Social Problems,* Fall 1959.

56 Pin-making appears on what was possibly the first page of Adam Smith's manuscript, but exists as page 4 in the Modern Library edition of *The Wealth of Nations,* Random House, New York, 1937.

The casting of Perseus is told by Benvenuto Cellini himself in his autobiography, *Memoirs of Benvenuto Cellini,* Ernest Rhys, ed., Dent, London, 1906.

57 The figures showing the decline in the ratio of self-employed to em-

ployed are derived from U. S. Bureau of the Census, *Sixteenth Census of the United States: 1940,* Vol. III: *The Labor Force,* Part I, Table 2, p. 16, and U. S. Bureau of Labor Statistics, *Monthly Report on the Labor Force, April 1960,* Table 9, p. T-5. C. W. Mills, *White Collar,* estimates that in the early nineteenth century four fifths of the employed were self-employed entrepreneurs and by 1870 only about one third.

For varied views of the growth of corporateness and bureaucracy in American business and government, see: J. K. Galbraith, *American Capitalism,* Houghton Mifflin, Boston, 1956; James Burnham, *The Managerial Revolution,* Indiana U. Press, Bloomington, 1960; David E. Lilienthal, *Big Business,* Harper, New York, 1953; E. S. Mason, "The Apologetics of 'Managerialism,' " *Journal of Business,* January 1958, p. 1; Richard Eells, *The Meaning of Modern Business,* Columbia U. Press, New York, 1960; Edward S. Mason, ed., *The Corporation in Modern Society,* Harvard U. Press, Cambridge, 1959; and Carl Kaysen, "The Social Significance of the Modern Corporation," *American Economic Review,* May 1957, p. 311.

THE JOB: TECHNICAL AND SOCIAL

58 For various aspects of job description see N. C. Kephart, *The Employment Interview in Industry,* McGraw–Hill, New York, 1950. An example of a book lauding the job for its sociability is Henri de Man's *Joy in Work,* tr. by E. and C. Paul, Holt, New York, 1929; and one reporting the disagreeableness of the job's work requirements is Simone Weil, *La condition ouvrière,* Gallimard, Paris, 1951. For the thought that work can be made as satisfying as leisure, see Glen U. Cleeton, *Making Work Human,* Antioch Press, Yellow Springs, Ohio, 1949. For the importance of the non-work or social aspects of the job, see the study based on a national sample, Nancy C. Morse and Robert S. Weiss, "The Function and Meaning of Work and the Job," *American Sociological Review,* April 1955. For similar aspects of the job today, see also Eugene A. Friedmann and Robert J. Havighurst, *The Meaning of Work and Retirement,* U. of Chicago Press, Chicago, 1954.

60 For American studies concerned with the human relations and the social side of work, see the list of studies done under the influence of Elton Mayo in *The Social Problems of an Industrial Civilization,* Harvard U. Press, Cambridge, 1945; and George C. Homans, *The Human Group,* Harcourt, Brace, New York, 1950. For a critique of the Hawthorne researches, see Georges Friedmann's *Industrial Society,* Free Press, Glencoe, Ill., 1955. See also Burleigh Gardner, *Human Relations in Industry,* Irwin, Chicago, 1950, and Everett C. Hughes, *Men and Their Work,* Free Press, Glencoe, Ill., 1958. The impetus

given by Marx to studies of human relations on the job is usually overlooked by writers on the subject.

For Taylor and Taylorism see John Dos Passos, *The Big Money*, Harcourt, Brace, New York, 1936; Daniel Bell, *Work and Its Discontents*, Beacon Press, Boston, 1956; Ralph M. Barnes, *Motion and Time Study*, Wiley, New York, 1937; and Abruzzi, *Work Measurement*.

CHAPTER III: Time Given, Time Taken Away

Contemporary works on free time include Max Kaplan, *Leisure in America*, Wiley, New York, 1960; Eric Larrabee and Rolf Meyersohn, eds., *Mass Leisure*, Free Press, Glencoe, Ill., 1958; Bernard Rosenberg and David White, eds., *Mass Culture, The Popular Arts in America*, Free Press, Glencoe, Ill., 1957; Wilma Donahue *et al.*, *Free Time*, U. of Michigan Press, Ann Arbor, 1958; Ida Craven, "Leisure" in *Encyclopedia of the Social Sciences*, Macmillan, New York, n.d.; David Riesman, Reuel Denney, and Nathan Glazer, *The Lonely Crowd*, Yale U. Press, New Haven, 1952; Eugene Staley, ed., *Creating an Industrial Civilization*, Harper, New York, 1952; Harold L. Wilensky, *Labor and Leisure in the Urban Community* (forthcoming); John W. Riley, Jr., *Social Leisure: Dynamics of Non-family Group Leisure*, Doctoral Dissertation, Harvard U., 1937; Martin H. and E. S. Neumayer, *Leisure and Recreation*, Ronald, New York, 1958; C. D. Burns, *Leisure in the Modern World*, McGraw–Hill, New York, 1932; Benjamin S. Rowntree and G. R. Lovers, *Life and Leisure*, Longmans, New York, 1951; B. S. Rowntree, *English Life and Leisure*, Longmans, London, 1951; George A. Lundberg *et al.*, *Leisure: A Suburban Study*, Columbia U. Press, New York, 1934; Kleemeier, ed., *Aging and Leisure;* Henry Durant, *The Problem of Leisure*, Routledge, London, 1938; Nels Anderson and F. K. Karrenberg, *Leisure: By-product of Industrial Urbanism*, UNESCO Institute for Social Sciences, Cologne, June 1957. With rare exceptions these works deal with free time rather than leisure. For some contemporary works closer to the concept of leisure, see Ernest Barker, *Reflections on Leisure;* Pieper, *Leisure;* Arnold Toynbee, *A Study of History*, Vol. IX, Oxford U. Press, London, 1954; T. S. Eliot, *Notes Towards the Definition of Culture*, Harcourt, Brace, New York, 1949; and Miguel de Unamuno, "En defensa de la haraganeria," in *Ensayos*, Aguilar, Madrid, 1942, Vol. 2.

Some special journal issues on the subject are: "Le Loisir," *Esprit*,

Paris, No. 274, June 1959; "The Uses of Leisure," *American Journal of Sociology*, LXII, No. 6, May 1957; "Recreation in the Age of Automation," *Annals* of the American Academy of Political Science, September 1957; and "Sociological Aspects of Leisure," *International Social Science Journal*, UNESCO, XII, No. 4, 1960. See also the magazine *Homo Ludens* (*Der Spielende Mensch, Die Zeitschrift für Musse und Spiel*), published in Stuttgart, Germany. A growing number of documentary films are pertinent to the study of work, free time, and leisure. See, e.g., "Nice-Time," British Film Institute, London, and "The Assembly-Line," National Film Board of Canada.

Among recent European educational and empirical studies dealing with free time, see Viggo Graf Blücher, *Freizeit in der industriellen Gesellschaft,* Enke, Stuttgart, 1956; Enrich Reigrotzki, *Soziale Verflechtungen in der Bundesrepublik,* Mohr, Tübingen, 1956; Ferdinand Böhny, *Die Freizeit des Städter,* Zürich, n.d.; Erwin Jeangros, *Lehrtochter und Lehrling in der Erziehung zum Beruf,* Bern, 1950; Eduard Spranger, "Zur Psychologie der Bildsamkeit des Erwachsenen — Eine Skizze," in *Bildungsfragen der Gegenwart,* Klotz, Stuttgart, 1953; Heinrich Hanselmann, *Vom Umgang mit sich selbst,* Rotapfel, Zürich, 1931, and *Andragogik,* Rotapfel, Zürich, 1951; Karlfried Graf Dürchkheim, *Durchbruch zum Wesen,* Niehand, Zürich, 1954; Anna Anflossi *et al., Ragusa, comunitá in transizione,* Taylor, Torino, 1959; Sebastian de Grazia, *Borgata Urbis;* Magda Talamo, ed., "Caratteri e problemi del tempo libero a Ivrea," Gruppo Tecnico per il Coordinamento Urbanistico del Canavese, Ivrea, No. 7, 1954; Delfino Insolera, ed., "La famiglia, il lavoro, il tempo libero in Ivrea," Gruppo Tecnico per il Coordinamento Urbanistico del Canavese, No. 6; C. Cottone, *Il Tempo libero,* Giuntini, Florence, 1956; Erik Allardt, Pentti Jarttl, Faina Jyrkllä, and Yrjö Littunen, "On the Cumulative Nature of Leisure Activities," *Acta Sociologica,* III, 1958; John and Dorothy Keur, *The Deeply Rooted,* Van Gorcum, Assen, 1955; A. Blonk, J. P. Kruijt, and E. W. Hofstee, *De besteding van de vrije tijd door Nederlandsche arbeiders,* Amsterdam, 1936; Netherlands Central Bureau of Statistics, *Leisure in the Netherlands* (*Vrije-tijdsbesteding in Nederland*), De Haan, Zeist, 1957; and Ivan Gardourek, *A Dutch Village,* Leiden, 1956.

Ronald P. Dore, *City Life in Japan,* U. of California Press, Berkeley, 1958, gives some particulars of free time in present-day urban Japan. For other American and European works, see the following bibliographies: for the United States, Larrabee and Meyersohn, in *Mass Leisure;* and Reuel Denney and Mary Lea Meyersohn, "A Preliminary Bibliography on Leisure," *American Journal of Sociology,* LXII, No. 6, May 1957; for England and Holland, Asher Tropp, "The Study of Leisure in Great Britain," T. T. ten Have, "Research on Leisure in the Netherlands," both mimeographed, Fourth World Congress of Sociology, Stresa, Italy, September 1959; for France, J. Dumazedier and F. de Charnacé, *Les sciences sociales du loisir — Bibliographie française et guide d'orientation documentaires,* Centre d'Etudes Sociologiques, Paris, n.d., mimeographed; and "Some Bibliographical Notes on Leisure," Youth Institute, UNESCO, Gauting, Munich, June 1958.

For representative collections of pertinent statistical data see, for the United States, J. Frederic Dewhurst *et al., America's Needs and Resources: A New Survey,* Twentieth Century Fund, New York, 1955; for England, A. M. Carr–Saunders *et al., A Survey of Social Conditions in England and Wales,* Clarendon Press, Oxford, 1958, and Goeffrey Brown, *Patterns of British Life,* Hulton Press, London, 1950. For studies currently under way in Europe, see R. Hennion, "Coordinated Research on Leisure in Various European Countries," *International Social Science Journal,* XII, No. 4, 1960, pp. 585–595.

PAGE

65 Aristotle's remark about machines that could do their own work, like the statues of Daedalus or the tripods of Hephaestus, is from the *Politics,* I, 1253b.

66 Estimates of number of paid vacations, holidays, etc., can be found in *Fringe Benefits, 1955,* Chamber of Commerce of the United States, Washington, 1956. See also Table 12 in Appendix above.

   On longevity and working life, see S. L. Wolfbein, "The Changing Length of Working Life," *Proceeding of the Seventh Annual Meeting of the Industrial Relations Research Association,* Detroit, December 1954; on the complexities of associating age with leisure, see Sebastian de Grazia, "The Uses of Time" in Kleemeier, ed., *Aging and Leisure.*

67 On youth, free time, and leisure, see August Heckscher, "The New Leisure," in Eli Ginzberg, ed., *The Nation's Children,* 3 vols., Columbia U. Press, New York, 1960, Vol. I; A. de Belmont Hollingshead, *Elmstown's Youth,* Wiley, New York, 1949; David Potter, *People of Plenty,* U. of Chicago Press, Chicago, 1954; Eleanor H. Bernert, *America's Children,* Wiley, New York, 1958; and Goodman, *Growing Up Absurd.*

A MAN'S JOB FULL TIME

68 The number and per cent of males by occupation at work full time as of May 1960 are as follows:

Males Working 35 Hours or More, May 1960

Occupation	Working 35 Hours or More (*Thousands*)	As Per Cent of All at Work
Males working 35 hours or more, all occupations	37,514	86.5
Professional, technical, and kindred workers	4,223	92.1
Farmers and farm managers	2,300	85.9
Managers, officials, and proprietors, except farm	5,465	92.6
Clerical and kindred workers	2,718	89.8
Sales workers	2,183	81.5
Craftsmen, foremen, and kindred workers	7,209	89.4
Operatives and kindred workers	7,389	87.5
Private household workers	15	55.6
Service workers, except private household	2,223	81.2
Farm laborers and foremen	1,179	68.7
Laborers, except farm and mine	2,612	70.7

Source: Bureau of Labor Statistics, U. S. Department of Labor.

70 The official figures on moonlighting come from Gertrude Bancroft, "Multiple Jobholders in December 1959," *Monthly Labor Review,* October 1960, *Current Population Reports: Labor Force,* Series P-50. For information on Akron and rubber workers, see Harvey Swados, "Less Work – Less Leisure," in Larrabee and Meyersohn, *Mass Leisure;* and Woodrow L. Ginsburg and Ralph Bergman, "The Worker's Viewpoint," in *The Shorter Work Week,* Public Affairs Press, Washington, 1957.

72 Some aspects of the effect moonlighting has in complicating the calculation of the work week are treated by Joseph S. Zeisel, "The Workweek in American Industry 1850–1956," in Larrabee and Meyersohn, *Mass Leisure.*

The figure used for the time of the work journey is confirmed by various other surveys. The local character of these studies makes it difficult to unify their results. But see Fortune, *Exploding Metropolis,* Doubleday, Garden City, 1958; Kate Liepmann, *The Journey to Work,*

Paul, Trench, Trubner, London, 1944; Sir George Thompson, *The Foreseeable Future,* Viking, New York, 1955; Pitirim A. Sorokin and Clarence Berger, *Time-Budgets of Human Behavior,* Harvard U. Press, Cambridge, 1939; American Society of Planning Officials, "The Journey to Work: Relation Between Employment and Residence," May 1951, No. 26; and Jean Gottmann, *Megalopolis,* Twentieth Century Fund, New York, 1961.

The engineer and architect Buckminster Fuller in a personal communication (1958) said that within ten years, a man may leave his home, travel to the furthermost point in the world, and return to his home to sleep that night. If we define a town as a place where we both sleep and work, he added, 1968 will see a *"one town world."*

73 The five-day work week as a phrase has an official ring, but as a week it has little factual support. The figures in Table 3 dispute it openly. The following data reveal what proportion of workers have either no agreement or no provisions for the five-day week.

SCHEDULED WORK DAYS PER WEEK IN MAJOR COLLECTIVE BARGAINING AGREEMENTS, 1956–57

	Agreements		Workers	
	Number	Per Cent	Number (*Thousands*)	Per Cent
Total studied	1,813	100.0	8,025	100.0
No provision	297	16.4	1,926	24.0
Five-day week	1,408	77.7	5,548	69.1
Six-day week	18	1.0	40	0.5
Other[a]	90	4.9	511	6.4

Source: Monthly Labor Review, Feb. 1958, Table 2, p. 137.

a. Includes agreements in which number of scheduled work days varies by season, by occupation; those which provide 5 days or equivalent thereof (4 full days and 2 half days in communications); etc.

See also the tabular data in notes below for Chapter VI, p. 220, on per cent of full-time workers by age and sex.

74 Fortune, *Exploding Metropolis,* indicates that for both drivers and riders the journey to work is mostly unpleasant; Bill Longgood and Ed Wallace, *The Pink Slip,* McGraw–Hill, New York, 1959, use ways men spend time on their journey to work to create amusing hypothetical work types.

75 59.4 per cent of all non-farm owner-occupied dwelling units are mortgaged. See *Statistical Abstract of the United States, 1960.*

77　For a recent collection of data on pioneer experiences, see Harriette S. Arnow, *Seedtime on the Cumberland,* Macmillan, New York, 1960.

　　For the extent of do-it-yourself activities, see "Summary of Information on the Do-It-Yourself Market," *Business Service Bulletin,* U. S. Department of Commerce, No. 84, November 1954; and "The Do-It-Yourself Market," Research Department, Curtis, Philadelphia, May 28, 1953.

WOMAN'S WORK

78　Evidence for the decline in household size from 1930 to 1959 can be found as follows: 1890–1950 in *Statistical Abstract, 1957,* pp. 5 and 45; 1958 in *Current Population Reports, Population Characteristics,* Series P-20, No. 88, November 17, 1958, and *Current Population Reports, Population Estimates,* Series P-25, No. 188, November 7, 1958; 1957 in *Current Population Reports, Population Estimates,* Series P-25, No. 187, p. 16 (Series II adjusted to exclude Armed Forces overseas), and *Current Population Reports, Population Characteristics,* Series P-20, Nos. 90 and 106, December 29, 1958 and January 9, 1960.

　　For data on age at first marriage see *Current Population Reports, Population Characteristics,* Series P-20, No. 90, December 29, 1958.

　　For data on marital status of women in the labor force, and labor force participation rates by marital status and age, 1890 and 1950, see Special Labor Force Report No. 13, "Marital and Family Characteristics of Workers," March 1960, U. S. Bureau of Labor Statistics. See also Bancroft, *Labor Force;* Smuts, *Women and Work;* National Manpower Council, *Womanpower,* Columbia U. Press, New York, 1958; and Madeleine Guilbert and Viviane Isambert–Jamati, *Travail féminin et travail à domicile,* Centre National de la Recherche Scientifique, Paris, 1956.

81　On work and life fifty to one hundred years ago, see Arthur M. Schlesinger, *The Rise of the City 1878–1898,* Macmillan, New York, 1933; James M. Williams, *The Expansion of Rural Life,* Crofts, New York, 1931; David Lewis Cohn, *The Good Old Days,* Simon, New York, 1940; Oscar Handlin, ed., *This Was America,* Harvard U. Press, Cambridge, 1949; and Edgar W. Martin, *The Standard of Living in 1860,* U. of Chicago Press, Chicago, 1942.

　　For literary accounts, see Thornton Wilder, *Our Town,* McCann, New York, 1938; and Eugene O'Neill, *Ah, Wilderness!,* Random House, New York, 1933.

83　On the increase in the category of operatives and kindred workers, see Bancroft, *Labor Force.*

　　On quit rates, absenteeism, etc., on time-stress jobs, see Walker,

Assembly Line, and the study by R. M. Belbir and Antonio M. N. Sewell reported in Industrial Relations Research Association, *The Aged and Society,* I.R.R.A., Champaign, Ill., 1950.

84 Bertrand Russell, *In Praise of Idleness and Other Essays,* Allen and Unwin, London, 1935, makes the point that modern men, if they worked less, would be able to spend their free time less passively.

85 On American geographical mobility, see *Automobile Facts and Figures,* 1959–60 edition, Automobile Manufacturers Association, Detroit, which reveals that Americans today in intercity travel alone average about 5,000 miles per capita. See also Franklin M. Reck, *A Car Traveling People,* Automobile Manufacturers Association, Detroit, 1942; Marion Clawson, *Statistics on Outdoor Recreation,* Resources for the Future, Inc., Washington, April 1958; Gottmann, *Megalopolis;* and Conrad and Irene Taeuber, *The Changing Population of the United States,* Wiley, New York, 1958. See also note below for p. 239.

A TALE OF THE TIMES

86 Examples of the free-time myth are common. See, for instance, Marion Clawson, *The Dynamics of Park Demand,* Park, Recreation and Open Space Project of the Tri-State New York Metropolitan Region, RPA Bulletin No. 94, April 1960; "Reasons for Increased Leisure Time," *Information Section Report,* February 1952, Research Department, Curtis, Philadelphia, much of which is based on the *Monthly Labor Review;* and Morris Ernst, *Utopia 1976,* Rinehart, New York, 1955. Examples are specially common in books foretelling the future. See Chapter VII for references.

For the unfree things Americans would want to do had they more free time, see note below for p. 147.

88 For modern Greece, see William H. McNeill, *Greece: American Aid in Action, 1947–1956,* Twentieth Century Fund, New York, 1957.

89 For small-town life in this century, see Albert Blumenthal, *Small Town Stuff,* U. of Chicago Press, Chicago, 1932.

For calendars and holidays from antiquity to the Reformation, see Burns, *Leisure;* Paul Lafargue, *The Right to Be Lazy,* tr. by C. H. Kerr, Kerr, Chicago, 1917; Arendt, *Human Condition;* Oskar Seyffert, *Dictionary of Classical Antiquities, Mythology, Religion, Literature and Art,* Macmillan, New York, 1891; "Holidays" and "Feasts and Festivals" in the *Encyclopaedia Britannica.* For a close study of the celebration of an American holiday in one city, see W. Lloyd Warner, *American Life: Dream and Reality,* U. of Chicago Press, Chicago, 1953. For *The Englishman's Holiday,* see John A. R. Pimlott, Faber, London, 1947; and for that of the Dutch, Gardourek, *Dutch Village,* and Bureau of Statistics, *Vrije-tijdsbeteding.*

CHAPTER IV: Free Time and Its Uses

92 For a recent study of the costs and demand for medical care see Herman M. and Anne R. Somers, *Doctors, Patients, and Health Insurance,* Brookings Institution, Washington, 1961. On cosmetics, see Murray Wax, "Themes in Cosmetics and Grooming," *American Journal of Sociology,* May 1957.

95 For other data on the day's activities, see George A. Lundberg *et al., Leisure, A Suburban Study,* Columbia U. Press, New York, 1934; Sorokin and Berger, *Time-Budgets of Human Behavior;* and Tables 9 and 10 in the Appendix.

THE THINGS BOUGHT

97 For comparison of data with the 1955–56 *Life Study of Consumer Expenditures* (Table 5), see the 1950 *Consumer Expenditures Study* of the Wharton School of the University of Pennsylvania, 18 vols., 1956.

103 For some of the complications in using expenditure data to test hypotheses about free-time spending, see George Fisk, "Toward a Theory of Leisure-Spending Behavior," *Journal of Marketing,* October 1959; Kaplan, *Leisure in America,* points out the discrepancies in different sources of total recreation expenditure calculations. Little has been done on comparing recreation expenditures internationally.

104 The report of the Outdoor Recreation Resources Review Commission (O.R.R.R.C.) is entitled *Outdoor Recreation for America,* U.S.G.P.O., Washington, 1962.

THE THINGS DONE

105 For some problems and experiments in time-budget and time-allocation studies, see Nelson Foote, "Methods for the Study of Meaning in Use of Time," in Kleemeier, ed., *Aging and Leisure;* Richard L. Meier, "Human Time Allocation: A Basis for Social Accounts," *Journal of the American Institute of Planners,* XXV, 1959, 1, 27–33; Sorokin and Berger, *Time-Budgets of Human Behavior;* and Edward L. Thorndike, "How We Spend Our Time and What We Spend It For," *Scientific Monthly,* XLIV, 1937.

108 For "Youth and the Automobile," see the article by Ross A. McFarland and Roland C. Moore in *Values and Ideals of American Youth,* Eli Ginzberg, ed., Columbia U. Press, New York, 1961, and Gene Balsley, "The Hot Rod Culture," *American Quarterly,* II, 1950.

For age and tempo of daily activities, see Robert J. Havighurst, "The Nature and Values of Meaningful Free-Time Activities," in Kleemeier, ed., *Aging and Leisure.*

109 Estimates of automobile mileage for various purposes can be found in *Automobile Facts and Figures* and in Franklin Reck, *A Car Traveling People.*

    Lundberg *et al., Leisure,* made estimates in 1934 of 1 hour and 45 minutes weekly of pleasure driving. For recent reduction in the activity, see "Leisure Time Activities," Table R-17, Study 685, Economic Behavior Program Survey Research Center, U. of Michigan, December 1959 (unpublished). For the 1958 estimate of work vs. non-work automobile travel, see Frank B. Curran and J. T. Stegmaier, *Travel Patterns in 50 Cities,* Division of Highway Transport Research, Bureau of Public Roads, Department of Commerce, Washington, 1958.

111 For an outdoor recreation figure of under half a billion yearly visits, see Clawson, *Statistics on Outdoor Recreation.* A figure for municipal and county parks is not included because it could only be approximated roughly. For recent data on national and state parks and outdoor recreation generally, see National Park Service, "Public Use of National Parks and Related Areas," December 1960, and "State Park Statistics — 1959," June 1960, U. S. Department of the Interior; and *Progress Report,* Outdoor Recreation Resources Review Commission, Washington, January 1961. For the history of parks and playgrounds, see C. E. Rainwater, *The Play Movement in the United States,* U. of Chicago Press, Chicago, 1922.

112 For overseas travel, in addition to Table 11 above, see O.R.R.R.C., *Study Report 18, A Look Abroad,* by Pauline Tait.

113 For the number of "Households with Television Sets in the U. S.," see *Current Housing Reports, Housing Characteristics,* May 1960, U. S. Bureau of the Census.

114 The ambiguity of results obtained in researches on TV viewing is discussed by Rolf Meyersohn, "An Examination of Commercial Entertainment," in Kleemeier, ed., *Aging and Leisure.* The figures Meyersohn uses (Tables 9.7, 9.8) from the Television Bureau of Advertising 1957 for per capita viewing — about 105 minutes daily average — fit within the weekday free-time margins for adults calculated in this chapter from Tables 3, 9, and 10. For the top-ranking place of TV in free-time activities, see Table 8 above. See also L. Bogart, *The Age of Television,* Ungar, New York, 1956.

PARCELS OF TIME

115 On the napping of American farmers, see John E. Ross and L. R. Bastian, *Time-Use Patterns and Communications Activities of Wisconsin Farm Families in Wintertime,* U. of Wisconsin Department of Agricultural Journalism, Bulletin 8, March 1958.

    On vacations see Table 12 above and "Reasons for Increased Leisure Time," Research Department, Curtis, Philadelphia.

117 For the data given on vacation trips and the money spent thereon, see "The Travel Market among U. S. Families with Incomes of $5,000 or More," Research Department, Curtis, Philadelphia, 1955, and Federal Reserve Bank of Philadelphia, "On Vacation, Part I, The Findings," and "Still on Vacation, Part II, The Problems," in *Business Review* (Philadelphia), April 1958, pp. 3–11, and May 1958, pp. 3–8. For further information on distance traveled on vacation, see O.R.R.R.C., *Outdoor Recreation for America,* Table 14, p. 217.

118 For today's "The English Weekend," see *Holiday,* April 1958. Since there are no national legal holidays, the term "bank holiday" is still significant. See *Holidays 1960,* Manufacturers Trust Company, International Banking Department, New York, 1959.

122 For what exists that resembles sabbaticals, see Stern Family Fund, *Recognition of Excellence,* Free Press, Glencoe, Ill., April 1960.

CATEGORIES OF PERSONS

127 For studies touching on the effect of TV on visiting and entertaining, see *Rhode Island Rural Housing and Family Leisure,* Bulletin 315, U. of Rhode Island, April 1953; and Alice C. Thorpe, *Patterns of Family Interaction in Farm and Town Homes,* Technical Bulletin 260, Michigan State U., April 1957.

131 Among the many studies of the executive, see "1700 Top Executives," *Fortune,* LX, November 1959; Melvin T. Copeland, *The Executive at Work,* Harvard U. Press, Cambridge, 1951; E. P. Learned *et al., Executive Action,* Andover Press, Andover, 1951; Chris Argyris, *Executive Leadership,* Harper, New York, 1953; Fortune, *The Executive Life,* Doubleday, Garden City, 1956; and Mabel Newcomer, *The Big Business Executive,* Columbia U. Press, New York, 1955. For the government executive in the United States, see Marver H. Bernstein, *The Job of the Federal Executive,* Brookings Institution, Washington, 1958; and in plant and office in the Soviet Union, David Granick, *The Red Executive,* Doubleday, New York, 1960.

134 The survey containing the data presented on the executive is August Heckscher and Sebastian de Grazia, "Executive Leisure," *Harvard Business Review,* July–August 1959.

137 The statistical part of the present work is largely based on national and general surveys, but local and particular researches, of course, have also been consulted. Small studies, sometimes intensive, exist not only for particular locations or types of workers (e.g., B. M. Berger, *Working-Class Suburb,* U. of California Press, Berkeley, 1960) but also for particular activities (e.g., Rolf Meyersohn and Robin Jackson, "Gardening in Suburbia," in William Dobriner, ed., *The Suburban Community,* Putnam, New York, 1958; and Irving Crespi, "The Social

Consequences of Card Playing," *American Sociological Review*, December 1956). For examples of related studies with some historical span, see Georges Hardy, "Ethnologie et jardins," *Revue de psychologie des peuples*, 1960, pp. 9–32, and Catherine Perry Hargrave, *A History of Playing Cards*, Houghton Mifflin, Boston, 1930.

CHAPTER V: In Pursuit of Time

139 For union views on leisure, shorter hours, overtime, and related matters, see *The Shorter Work Week*, Public Affairs Press, Washington, 1957. For average overtime hours currently in manufacturing industries, see U. S. Bureau of Labor Statistics, *Monthly Reports on the Labor Force*.

140 For the opinion polls mentioned, see Press Releases of July 31 and August 2, 1957, American Institute of Public Opinion, Princeton, N.J., and Elmo Roper *et al.*, "Four Day Week . . . Boon or Menace," Roper Public Opinion Research Center, Williamstown, Mass., 1957. For numerous public opinion polls relating to questions of work and free time, see Hadley Cantril, ed., *Public Opinion, 1935–1946*, Princeton U. Press, Princeton, 1951. See also the international study in progress under Cantril's direction for the Institute for International Social Research.

143 For examples of the thesis that the American has taken much of his productivity gains in the coin of free time, see Dewhurst *et al.*, *America's Needs and Resources; The Shorter Work Week*; Woytinsky *et al.*, *Employment and Wages*; and Editors of Scientific American, *Automatic Control*, Simon and Schuster, New York, 1955. The usual expression is that American labor has taken recent gains in productivity in the rough proportion of one third more free time to two thirds more pay.

INDUSTRIAL ESCAPE

144 On the difficulties of living without work today, see Edmund G. Love, *Subways Are for Sleeping*, New American Library, New York, 1956. For historical aspects of vagabondage, see Vexliard, *Sociologie du vagabondage*; A. Compton–Rickett, *The Vagabond in Literature*, Dutton, New York, 1906; Helen Waddell, *The Wandering Scholars*, Doubleday, Garden City, 1955; and Nels Anderson, *Men on the Move*, U. of Chicago Press, Chicago, 1940. See also the significance of these and related phenomena as forms of protest in Goodman, *Growing Up Absurd*.

145 On days lost to medical care, see Rollo H. Butten *et al.*, "The National
Health Survey: Some General Findings as to Disease, Accidents and
Impairments in Urban Areas," *Public Health Reports*, March 15,
1940. Days of disability average about 10 per capita per annum. The
following figures give an indication of the incidence of illness on work
time.

NUMBER AND PER CENT OF EMPLOYEES NOT WORKING
BECAUSE OF ILLNESS, ANNUAL AVERAGES, 1946–1959

Year	Civilian Employment (*Thousands*)	Employees Out Sick	
		Number (*Thousands*)	Per Cent
1946	55,050[a]	819	1.49
1947	57,812	847	1.46
1948	59,117	844	1.43
1949	58,423	719	1.23
1950	59,748	718	1.20
1951	60,784	782	1.29
1952	61,035	775	1.27
1953	61,945	827	1.34
1954	60,890	776	1.27
1955	62,944	835	1.33
1956	64,708	901	1.39
1957	65,011	962	1.48
1958	63,966	882	1.38
1959	65,581	907	1.38

Source: Economic Report of the President, January 1960, Tables D-17 and
D-19, pp. 174 and 177.

a. Estimate adjusted to new definition of employment so as to be roughly
consistent with estimates for subsequent years.

See also Somers and Somers, *Doctors, Patients and Health Insurance,*
and Dewhurst *et al., America's Needs and Resources.* Perhaps more
numerous as a loss to free time are the days lost because of mental dis-
order or neurosis. For estimates of the number of persons affected, see
G. Gurin *et al., Americans View Their Mental Health,* Basic Books,
New York, 1960, and Sebastian de Grazia, *Errors of Psychotherapy,*
Doubleday, New York, 1952.

146 On suburbia as a vision, see Robert C. Wood, *Suburbia, Its People and
Their Politics,* Houghton Mifflin, Boston, 1959; Fortune, *Exploding*

Metropolis. For nostalgic aspects see Ima H. Herron, *The Small Town in American Literature,* Duke U. Press, Durham, N. C., 1939; Blumenthal, *Small Town Stuff;* J. M. Williams, *The Expansion of Rural Life,* Crofts, New York, 1931; and Cohn, *Good Old Days.*

147   For what auto workers would do, had they more leisure time, see Matthew Radom, "A Comparison of Attitudes Toward Work, Leisure and Retirement," mimeographed, August 1960. In rank order: (1) "Work around the house," 96.8%; (2) "Spend more time with family," 76.8%. For additional material on auto workers see Berger, *Working-Class Suburb;* and Eli Chinoy, *Automobile Workers and the American Dream,* Doubleday, New York, 1955. For the population at large, where "Working around the house" also takes first place, see Elmo Roper *et al., The Public Pulse* of June 16, 1957.

148   The portal-to-portal pay issue raised by coal mining is related to that raised by the work journey: where and when does working time start? *The Shorter Work Week* touches on this point. For general consideration of the unaccounted costs of private industry, see John M. Clark, *Social Control of Business,* McGraw–Hill, New York, 1939, and K. W. Kapp, *The Social Costs of Private Enterprise,* Harvard U. Press, Cambridge, 1950.

150   On the reception in the U.S.S.R. of Khrushchev's policy of reducing working hours, see *Repatriate Reports,* April 10, 1958, Office of Research and Intelligence, U.S.I.A. For a list of the lengths of the official work week in various countries, see American Newspaper Guild, *The Guild Reporter,* June 27, 1958.

152   For seniority questions and the greater attentiveness to work of old persons, see "The Older Worker," *Factory,* Vol. 116, No. 3, March 1958; for some of the implications of the age composition of the population, see Frank G. Dickinson, "The Younging of Electorates," *Journal of the American Medical Association,* March 1958. For some of the financial obligations, such as marriage, house, and car, assumed by the young, see Arno H. Johnson, "The Economic Outlook for Shopping Centers in 1958–59," J. Walter Thompson Company, New York, February 19, 1958, mimeographed.

MIGRATORY TRAILS

154   In the great migration from Europe 1800–1950, 60 million persons left the continent; 40 million of these came to the United States; see W. S. Woytinsky and E. S. Woytinsky, *World Population and Production,* Twentieth Century Fund, New York, 1953. For data on the generations of residence in America of Americans, see Alfred de Grazia, *The American Way of Government,* Wiley, New York, 1957, Table 20. For the occupations of *Immigrants and Their Children, 1850–1950,*

see Edward P. Hutchinson, Wiley, New York, 1956. For foreign white stock in New York City, see Oscar Handlin, *The Newcomers,* Harvard U. Press, Cambridge, 1959.

155 The different ways immigrant groups have of spending free time may introduce new pastimes to the new country but also give rise to irritation, fear, and anger; see Clarence Senior, *Minority Group Leisure Patterns as Community Irritants,* paper to the Society for Study of Social Problems, December 1959, unpublished.

156 For recent works on jazz and its origins, see H. O. Bunn, *The Story of the Original Dixieland Band,* U. of Louisiana Press, Baton Rouge, 1960; André Hodeir, *Jazz, Its Evolution and Essence* (tr. by D. Noakes), Grove Press, New York, 1956; J. S. Slotkin, "Jazz and Its Forerunners as an Example of Acculturation," *American Sociological Review,* VIII, 1943; R. A. Waterman, "African Influence on the Music of the Americas," *International 29th Congress of Americanists Proceedings,* 1952; Nat Shapiro and Nat Hentoff, eds., *Hear Me Talkin' to Ya,* Rinehart, New York, 1955; and Wilder Hobson, *American Jazz Music,* Norton, New York, 1939. For *Indian Art of the United States,* see Frederic H. Douglas and René d'Harnoncourt, Museum of Modern Art, New York, 1941.

For the question of how travelers are changed by foreign visits, see Harold D. Lasswell, *World Politics and Personal Insecurity,* McGraw–Hill, New York, 1935. For recent studies, see Harlan Cleveland, Gerard J. Mangone, and John Clarke Adams, *The Overseas Americans,* McGraw–Hill, New York, 1960, and Ithiel de Sola Pool, "What American Travelers Learn," and the other articles in "The American Abroad" issue of the *Antioch Review,* Vol. 18, 1958.

IDEAS AND DISBELIEF

158 On the education of businessmen, see Robert A. Goldwin, ed., and Charles A. Nelson, consultant, *Toward the Liberally Educated Executive,* Fund for Adult Education, White Plains, N. Y., 1957; and Leonard S. Silk, *The Education of Businessmen,* Committee for Economic Development, New York, 1960. The subject is treated at greater length in Chapter VII above.

160 On the resources credo as part of American abundance, see Potter, *People of Plenty,* and Samuel H. Ordway, *Resources and the American Dream,* Ronald, New York, 1953.

161 Time-saving equipment apart, the hidden costs of labor-saving equipment have rarely been systematically investigated. One cost may well be physical fitness, both in youth and manhood. The steps taken to remedy the poor test showing of American compared to European children in 1955 have so far not gone into the role of labor-saving ma-

chinery except in urging youth, "Walk, don't ride." The problem is touched on, however, by Shane MacCarthy, "Fitness and the Future," an address at the Second Annual Conference of the President's Council on Youth Fitness at Fort Ritchie, Cascade, Md., September 8, 1958.

HUMAN NATURE VERSUS WORK

163 For some indication of regularity's long-run effect on the organism, see Alexis Carrel, *Man, the Unknown,* Harper, New York, 1935.

165 Particulars on unemployment compensation in the United States can be found in Dewhurst *et al., America's Needs and Resources,* and in Woytinsky *et al., Employment and Wages,* which includes a brief history of the legislation.

167 The estimate given of discretionary spending power was derived, for 1940, from *National Income, 1954 Edition* (Supplement to the *Survey of Current Business*); and, for 1959–60, from *Survey of Current Business,* February 1961 (for disposable personal income less consumer expenditures for food, clothing, and housing); and, for July 1940 and July 1959, from *Statistical Abstract of the United States, 1960,* Table 2. July 1960 from *Current Population Reports, Population Estimates,* Series P-25, No. 219, August 17, 1960 (for population).

For similar estimates of discretionary spending power, see A. H. Johnson, "Shopping Centers," and Sanford S. Parker *et al.,* "The Decade of the 'Discretionary' Dollar," in Editors of Fortune, *The Markets of the Sixties,* Harper, New York, 1960.

CHAPTER VI: Shapers of Choice

170 For some of the more exotic settings in the climate, diet, custom, and topography of free time, see *Elephant Bill* by J. H. Williams, Doubleday, Garden City, 1950; Petrie, *Social Life in Ancient Egypt;* Jack C. Drummond, *The Englishman's Food,* J. Cape, London, 1940; Charles T. Seltman, *Wine in the Ancient World,* Routledge, London, 1957; H. E. Jacob, *L'épopée du café,* tr. from German by Madeleine Gabelle, Editions du Seuil, Paris, 1953; and the anthropological collections of the *Human Relation Area Files.*

For the settings for the use of alcohol in the United States, see B. Roueché, "Annals of Medicine," *New Yorker,* January 9, 16, and 23, 1960. For tobacco, see George Arents, *Tobacco, Its History . . . ,* 5 vols., Rosenbach, New York, 1937. See also the English studies on *The Pat-*

tern of Smoking Habits by J. W. Hobson and H. Henry, Hulton Press, London, 1948, and *The Pub and the People,* by Mass Observation, London, 1943.

172 On the decline of outdoor activities with age see Survey Research Center, Table R-14-B, and O.R.R.R.C., *Outdoor Recreation for America.*

On the "younging" of the population, see Dickinson, "Younging of the Electorate." See also Henry D. Sheldon, *The Older Population of the United States,* Wiley, New York, 1958.

On the gallantry of the West, see Philip A. Rollins, *The Cowboy,* Scribner, New York, 1936.

173 For the population problem of sewage, still with the cities, see Luther Gulick, "The City's Challenge in Resource Use" in Henry Jarrett, ed., *Perspectives on Conservation,* Johns Hopkins Press, Baltimore, 1958.

Underestimating the possibility of free time because of lack of "leisure facilities" is related to the problems economists have in estimating the income of non-industrial countries, and their welfare or "ecfare." See S. Herbert Frankel, *The Economic Impact on Under-developed Societies,* Harvard U. Press, Cambridge, 1953.

For the effect of population density on outdoor recreation, see O.R.R.R.C., *Outdoor Recreation for America.* For the difference the availability of space can make, see the recreational activities described in Hollingshead, *Elmstown's Youth.* Frank Lloyd Wright maintained that every person should have a space of at least 4,000 square meters. The disappearance of space has created enormous handicaps in architecture and urbanistica. See Bruno Zevi, *Storia dell'architettura moderna,* Einaudi, Milan, 1955.

174 For Walden's downfall see "Our Great Outdoors," *Vital Issues,* Center for Information on America, Washington, Conn., November 1957.

On the attitudes toward Nature's beauties in America see Edward Eggleston, *The Transit of Civilization from England to America in the Seventeenth Century* (1900), Beacon Press, Boston, 1959; and J. W. Krutch, ed., *Great American Nature Writing,* Sloane, New York, 1950.

175 For the chair and leisure, see Herbert Collins, "The Sedentary Society" in Larrabee and Meyersohn, *Mass Leisure.*

For an example of the introduction of technology to a culture, see Alfred Metraux, "The Ax that Cut the Centuries," tr. by Elaine P. Halperin, *Diogenes,* Spring 1959.

176 Some of the effects of urban architecture on leisure and free time can be seen in G. E. Kidder Smith, *L'Italia costruice,* Comunità, Milan, 1955. For the dullness of zoned areas, see Jane Jacobs, *Death and Life of American Cities,* Random House, New York, 1961. Contrast the poverty in perspectives in most towns in the United States with

the richness in a poor Honduras village, seen in Witlin's photograph for United Fruit, reproduced in the Twentieth Century Fund's *Newsletter*, No. 34, Winter 1959.

178 For the at-homeness of farm vs. town families, see Thorpe, *Patterns of Family Interaction in Farm and Town Homes.* The Boston study referred to is Sorokin and Berger, *Time-Budgets.*

179 The dairy farmers study is Ross and Bastian, *Time Use Patterns and Communications Activities of Wisconsin Farm Families in Wintertime.*

180 The figures for "walking for pleasure" given in O.R.R.R.C., *Outdoor Recreation for America,* as used in their text (pp. 25–26) and as presented in charts (pp. 34, 36) and in Tables 1 and 5, may be somewhat misleading. The rankings reflect what Americans do chiefly while on vacations, overnight trips, and outings. (See O.R.R.R.C., *Study Report 19, National Recreation Survey,* U.S.G.P.O., Washington, 1962.) As a result, even cycling appears as the sixth highest activity. Usually, walking and cycling do not appear in tables of free-time activity, for the simple reason that their percentages are too small. Whereas in the O.R.R.R.C. interviews, respondents were presented with a list of activities to select from, the Survey Research Center Study reported (Table R-17) that 2 per cent of its sample spontaneously mentioned "going for walks" in their "leisure time." Part of this study, though not this particular section, is contained in O.R.R.R.C., *Study Report 20, Participation in Outdoor Recreation,* by Eva Mueller and Gerald Gurin; see Table 27. On the dangers of walking today, including arrest by the police, see Lois Balcom, "The Best Hope for Our Big Cities," *Reporter,* October 2, 1957.

183 For "home" in Victorian times, where we "cease the struggle in the race of the world and give our hearts, leave and leisure to love," see Morton M. Hunt, *The Natural History of Love,* Knopf, New York, 1959, who quotes the above phrases of James Froude, the Victorian historian, on p. 315. See also H. V. Routh, *Money, Morals and Manners,* Nicholson and Watson, London, 1935.

184 Margaret Mead has opposed the tendency toward male at-homeness as debilitating for foreign policy. See also the article by Caroline Brown, a part-time social worker, "Now Father Is at Home," *The Guardian,* October 12, 1960.

185 For sociological usage of "customs and mores," see William G. Sumner, *Folkways,* Ginn, Boston, 1907.

186 Baudelaire's remarks on the dandy are from "The Painter of Modern Life." See Charles Baudelaire, *The Essence of Laughter,* Meridian Books, New York, 1956. Contrast his remarks with the change made by one James Plumptree of Shakespeare's lyric from "Under the green-

wood tree / Who loves to lie with me" to "Under the greenwood tree / Who loves to work with me," quoted in Hunt, *The Natural History of Love*, p. 298.

Gaius Valerius Catullus' fault-finding occurs in his "Farewell to Lesbia."

For *l'amour c'est l'adultère* among the Baluchi, see Rosalie Wax, "Free Time in Other Cultures," in Donahue, *Free Time*. See also Nelson N. Foote, "Sex as Play," *Social Problems,* April 1954. Bronislaw Malinowski in *Sex and Repression,* Meridian Books, New York, 1955, speaks of the type of young male Trobriander who scorns the unmarried for the married women, tries to have an intrigue especially with a chief's wife or else with a member of his own clan. He may be called "Oh, thou exogamy breaker!" but the joking tone means, "Oh, you gay dog!" Malinowski is also the anthropologist who noted the bellicose free time of the Trobrianders.

188 For the statistics on Americans killed by automobiles and in battle, see U. S. Bureau of the Census, *Historical Statistics of the United States: Colonial Times to 1957,* Washington, 1960.

189 Said Aristotle in the *Politics* (VII, 1329b), "Leisure is needed both for the developing of virtue and for active participation in politics." For the Greeks' political activity, see Coulanges, *Ancient City;* Zimmern, *Greek Commonwealth;* Livio C. Stecchini, *The Constitution of the Athenians by the Old Oligarch and by Aristotle,* Free Press, Glencoe, Ill., 1950; and American School of Classical Studies at Athens, *The Athenian Citizen,* Princeton U. Press, Princeton, 1960.

For political apathy among American citizens, see Angus Campbell *et al., The Voter Decides,* Row, Peterson, Evanston, Ill., 1954, and *The American Voter,* Wiley, New York, 1960; Elmo B. Roper, *You and Your Leaders 1936–1956,* Morrow, New York, 1957; Elihu Katz and Paul F. Lazarsfeld, *Personal Influence,* Free Press, Glencoe, Ill., 1955; Alfred de Grazia, *The Western Public,* Stanford U. Press, Stanford, 1954; and Robert Lane, *The Political Life,* Free Press, Glencoe, Ill., 1959.

The political information of those who graduated at least from high school is surveyed in *Look Magazine Educational Survey,* Audience Research, Inc., Princeton, 1957. 38 per cent gave the correct answer within 10 per cent for the population of the United States. No interest in local politics: 68 per cent; no interest in state politics: 75 per cent. These give some idea of the responses.

191 The cowboy, incidentally, did not work: he *rode.* For his free-time activities, including the fireside reciting by heart of the print on condensed milk cans, see Rollins, *The Cowboy.* The first popular lending

library in England (1842) is described in Monica Stirling, *The Fine and the Wicked,* Coward–McCann, New York, 1958.

192 For Lord Byron, see Lord Macaulay's *Essays, Critical and Historical,* Houghton, Boston, 1901. For Gabriele d'Annunzio, see Sir Osbert Sitwell, *Noble Essences,* Little, Brown, Boston, 1950.

WORKERS OUT OF VILLAGERS

192 Among the works on English social and economic history of the nineteenth century, see John L. and Barbara Hammond, *The Bleak Age,* Longmans, Green, New York, 1934; and *The Town Labourer, 1760–1832,* Longmans, New York, 1920; T. C. Barker and J. R. Harris, *A Merseyside Town in the Industrial Revolution: St. Helens, 1750–1900,* U. Press, Liverpool, 1954; Charles Booth, ed., *Life and Labour of the People in London,* Macmillan, New York, 1892–97; T. H. S. Escott, *England: Her People, Polity, and Pursuits,* Holt, New York, 1880; Guy Chapman, *Culture and Survival,* J. Cape, London, 1940; C. F. G. Masterton, *The Condition of England,* 1906; Henry Mayhew, *London Characters,* Chatton, London, 1881; G. M. Young, ed., *Early Victorian England, 1830–1865,* 2 vols., 1934; R. Nettel, *Seven Centuries of Popular Song,* Phoenix, London, 1956; W. H. Hutt, "The Factory System of the Early Nineteenth Century" and T. S. Ashton, "The Standard of Life of the Workers in England 1790–1830" in Hayek, *Capitalism and the Historians.* For a picture at the end of the Middle Ages of English town life with its "townfields," George M. Trevelyan, *English Social History,* Longmans, New York, 1946.

The new concern of the overdeveloped with the underdeveloped countries reveals that much of the English experience in industrialization is being repeated in the unmodern parts of the modern world. See Bert F. Hoselitz, "The City, the Factory and Economic Growth," *American Economic Review,* May 1955; Simon Marcson, "Social Change and Social Structure in Transitional Societies," *International Journal of Comparative Sociology,* September 1960; and Wilbert E. Moore, *Industrialization and Labor,* Cornell U. Press, Ithaca, 1951.

194 The remark on "the cost of living and a little more" appears in Chapman, *Culture and Survival.*

201 Hannah Arendt in *Human Condition* discusses the history of the idea of property here described as held by the villager. The riots over the loss of commons are documented by Eggleston, *Transit of Civilization.*

The remark about the English linking of soap and civilization is Chapman's.

202 The quotations of the Commissioner of Police and the traveling millwright appear also in Chapman's *Culture and Survival.*

The gloomy holiday strategy reappears on this side of the ocean in legislation the remnants of which still exist in various parts of the country as "Blue Laws." See Carl N. Degler, *Out of Our Past*, Harcourt, Brace, New York, 1959. For the religious and cosmological significance of the holiday see Pieper, *Leisure;* and Roger Caillois, *L'homme et le sacré: "La fête est le chaos retrouvé et façonné à nouveau."* See also Strabo as cited in note for p. 435 below.

203 On drink and alcoholism in Europe, see Henry Carter, *Europe's Revolt against Alcohol*, Kelly, London, 1915, and Hermann Levy, *Drink: An Economic and Social Study*, Routledge, London, 1951.

204 For the "tertiary stage" concept in economics, see Allan G. B. Fisher, *Economic Progress and Social Security*, Macmillan, London, 1945; for a more recent concept of stages in which "the age of high mass consumption" appears as the parallel, see W. W. Rostow, *The Stages of Economic Growth*, Cambridge U. Press, London, 1960. For criticism of current trends in the manufacturing of goods and wants in the United States, see John K. Galbraith, *The Affluent Society*, Houghton Mifflin, Boston, 1958.

206 London did get some fine examples of squares and crescents from Christopher Wren and after him from James and Robert Adam. The advocacy of squares and piazzas is sustained by Camillo Sitte in *Der Städe-Bau*, Vienna, 1899; in the English version, *The Art of Building Cities*, tr. by C. T. Stewart, Reinhold, New York, 1945.

NEW GUIDES FOR NEW TIMES

209 On the history of the movements for ten-hour and eight-hour work days in the United States, see *History of Labour in the United States* by John R. Commons and Associates, 4 vols., Macmillan, New York, 1918–35; S. Perlman, "Shorter Hours Movement," *Encyclopedia of the Social Sciences;* and *The Thirty-Hour Work Week*, Hearings before a Subcommittee of the Committee on the Judiciary, U. S. Senate, January 1933, Washington, 1933.

For the history of advertising in the United States as well as England, see Henry Sampson, *A History of Advertising from the Earliest Times*, Chatto and Windus, London, 1874; Frank S. Presbrey, *The History and Development of Advertising*, Doubleday, Garden City, 1929; E. S. Turner, *The Shocking History of Advertising!*, Dutton, New York, 1953; and Edgar R. Jones, *Those Were the Good Old Days*, Simon and Schuster, New York, 1959. For more recent decades in the United States, see Martin Mayer, *Madison Avenue, U.S.A.*, Harper, New York, 1958; Editors of Fortune, *The Amazing Advertising Business*, Simon and Schuster, New York, 1957; Herbert Marshall Mc-

Luhan, *The Mechanical Bride,* Vanguard, New York, 1951; and Otto Klepper, *Advertising Procedure,* Prentice–Hall, New York, 1952.

211 "Status panic" is what Mills calls the exceptional need for status in the *White Collar* class. In discussing the attitudes of professional classes toward consumption, a distinction must be made between the old and the new (the bureaucratized) professional class. See Emil Lederer and Jacob Marschak, *The New Middle Class* ("Der Neue Mittelstand," *Grundriss der Sozialökonomik,* IX Abteilung I, 1926), tr. by S. Ellison, Columbia U., WPA Project, New York, 1937; Hans Speier, "The Salaried Employee in Modern Society," *Social Research,* February 1934; Lewis and Maude, *The English Middle Classes;* Dreyfuss, *Salaried Employee;* T. H. Marshall, "The Recent History of Professionalism in Relation to Social Structure and Social Policy," *Canadian Journal of Economics and Political Science,* reprinted in *Readings in American Social Classes,* Robert C. Angell, ed., U. of Michigan Press, Ann Arbor, 1945; A. M. Carr–Saunders and P. A. Wilson, *The Professions,* Clarendon Press, Oxford, 1933; and Harold D. Lasswell, "The Moral Vocation of the Middle-Income Skill Group," *Ethics,* January 1935.

The subject of workingmen's consumption has a long history in sociology and economics beginning with Quetelet and Le Play's studies, moving through Engels' formulation of the ratio of luxuries and necessities into "Engels' Law," to Keynes's concern with the business cycle. A brief history of consumer expenditures can be found in Woytinsky and Woytinsky, *World Population and Production.* The workingman's attitude toward consumption can be studied from statistical breakdowns in the Wharton or *Life* (Table 6, above) expenditure surveys. In addition to studies already cited, such as Hoggart, *Uses of Literacy;* Rainwater *et al., Workingman's Wife;* Whyte, *Men, Money and Motivation;* Zweig, *British Worker;* Chinoy, *Automobile Workers;* and Berger, *Working-Class Suburb,* see Carl C. Zimmerman, *Consumption and Standards of Living,* Van Nostrand, New York, 1936; R. Centers and Hadley Cantril, "Income and Income Aspiration," *Journal of Abnormal and Social Psychology,* XLI, 1946; Hazel Kyrl, *A Theory of Consumption,* Houghton Mifflin, Boston, 1923; Herman P. Miller, *Income of the American People,* Wiley, New York, 1955; David Riesman and Howard Roseborough, "Careers and Consumer Behavior" in *Consumer Behavior,* Lincoln H. Clark and Nelson N. Foote, eds., New York U. Press, New York, 1954–1961; George Katona, *Psychological Analysis of Economic Behavior,* McGraw–Hill, New York, 1951; Pierre Martineau, "Social Classes and Spending Behavior," *Journal of Marketing,* XXIII, No. 2, October 1958; and *Characteristics of the*

Low Income Population and Related Federal Programs, Joint Committee on the Economic Report.

218 For the confusion caused at the inauguration of the seven-hour day in Moscow, see Osgood Caruthers, "Rubles and Free Time," *New York Times,* January 7, 1961. For some other aspects of "How Russians Relax," see Fred R. Bellmar, *Employee Recreation,* XX, No. 7, July–August 1959.

219 On old age and the desire to continue working, see Margaret S. Gordon, "Work and Patterns of Retirement" in Kleemeier, ed., *Aging and Leisure,* and Sheldon, *Older Population.*

220 The image of women in the dilemma of Buridan's ass can be seen in such works as Alva Myrdal and Viola Klein, *Women's Two Roles, Home and Work,* Routledge, London, 1956; Lorine Pruett, *Women and Leisure,* Dutton, New York, 1924; Margaret Mead, *Male and Female,* Morrow, New York, 1949; Virginia Woolf, *A Room of One's Own,* Harcourt, New York, 1929; Simone de Beauvoir, *The Second Sex,* tr. by H. M. Parshley, Knopf, New York, 1953; Ferdinand Lundberg and Marynia Farnham, *Modern Woman: The Lost Sex,* Harper, New York, 1947; National Manpower Council, *Womanpower,* and *Work in the Lives of Married Women,* e.g., in the opening addresses by Erwin D. Canham and James P. Mitchell.

The higher proportion of females in part-time jobs at almost all ages can be seen in the following figures:

PER CENT OF ALL PERSONS AT WORK WHO WERE WORKING
FULL TIME, BY AGE AND SEX, MAY 1960

Age	Male	Female
Both sexes, 14 years and over	81.0	
14 years and over	86.5	69.9
14 to 17 years	19.1	12.8
18 to 19 years	62.9	65.7
20 to 24 years	86.7	78.9
25 to 34 years	91.8	74.7
35 to 44 years	93.2	72.0
45 to 64 years	90.5	73.2
65 years and over	65.4	49.0

Source: Bureau of Labor Statistics, U. S. Department of Labor.

221 On the motives for women's buying, see National Manpower Council, *Womanpower;* Katz and Lazarsfeld, *Personal Influence;* and Editors of Fortune, *Why Do People Buy: A Close Look at Selling,* McGraw–

Hill, New York, 1953. Lord Bryce, in explaining why American women have higher literary taste and influence than European women, mentioned the leisure they possess as compared with men. Many women do go into social, community, charitable and political activities because of free time available to them. The proportion made up by such volunteers is small compared to that of women who "have to" go to work for the money. For female literary taste, see Helen Papashvily, *All the Happy Endings,* Harper, New York, 1956.

For an example of the heat generated in discussions of women's proper role, compare Eve Merriam, "Are Housewives Necessary? . . . ," *Nation,* January 31, 1959, with Jerome L. Toner, O.S.B., "Married Working Women," address to the Catholic Economic Association, December 28, 1957, dittoed. The prominence of appeals to women by advertising in the mass media often leads foreigners to think that the United States is a matriarchy.

CHAPTER VII: The Fate of an Ideal

225 For some of the effects of advertising on demand curves, see R. Triffin, *Monopolistic Competition and General Equilibrium Theory,* Harvard U. Press, Cambridge, 1940.

John Wanamaker is credited with the remark on waste in advertising; see Mayer, *Madison Avenue, U.S.A.*

226 For J. M. Keynes's point, see his Galton Lecture, "The Economic Consequences of a Declining Population," *Eugenics Review,* XXIX, No. 1, 1937.

227 For advertising posters and signs based on presidential encouragements and using such slogans as "Buy Now; Bye, Bye Recession!" and "The President says, BUY!" and "Buy Your Way to Prosperity," see *New York Times Magazine,* May 25, 1958.

228 For the effect on the size of enterprise of efforts to stabilize market power, see Joan Robinson, *The Economics of Imperfect Competition,* St. Martin's, London, 1933.

PEDDLERS OF DYNAMISM

229 Some scientists are willing to say publicly that the more science knows, the less it knows. See the remarks of Otto Hahn, "La vendetta di Otto Hahn," in *La Nazione,* Florence, August 20, 1961. For a criticism of modern innovation along political lines, see Hans Morgenthau, *The Purpose of American Politics,* Knopf, New York, 1960.

230 For *6000 Years of Bread,* see H. E. Jacob, Doubleday, Doran, New York, 1945.

231 For the varying attitude toward cars in the last few decades, compare Reck, *A Car Traveling People;* Ken W. Purdy, *The Kings of the Road,* Little, Brown, Boston, 1952; and John Keats, *The Insolent Chariots,* Lippincott, Philadelphia, 1958.

  Fashion changes have long interested men and women. For an example of concern over it in the early Middle Ages, see the *Quinze joyes de mariage,* Bibliothèque Elzévirienne, 2nd ed., Paris, 1857; in the Renaissance, Niccolò Machiavelli, "Belfagor" in *Opere complete,* Parenti, Firenze, 1843, p. 585, "*Io voglio lasciar le grandi spese, che per contentarla faceva, in vestirla di nuove usanze, e contentarla di nuove fogge, che continuamente la nostra città per sua natural consuetudine varia";* and for contemporary concern, see Eva Merriam, *Figleaf,* Lippincott, New York, 1960.

232 For an example of the arguments of the advertiser, see A. H. Johnson, "Shopping Centers." For a vigorous defense of advertising, see the address by James A. Farley at the Adcraft Club of Detroit, January 9, 1959, U.S.G.P.O., Washington.

236 An interesting aspect of some utopias like William D. Howells, *A Traveler from Altruria,* Harper, New York, 1894; Bellamy's *Looking Backward, 2000–1887,* Houghton Mifflin, New York, 1929; and especially Simon Berington, *Memoirs of Signor Gaudentio di Lucca,* Faulkner, Dublin, 1738, is the desire therein reflected to keep people in their free time from staying too much at home and losing touch with society. Home therefore is comfortable enough yet so simply arranged and equipped as to encourage the individual to go out to mingle with his fellows. For a theoretical statement of man's place in the public and private realms, see Hannah Arendt, *The Human Condition;* and also in this connection Frank R. Cowell, *Culture in Private and Public Life,* Praeger, New York, 1959.

239 On the history of geographical mobility in the United States, see Hutchinson, *Immigrants and Their Children;* Woytinsky and Woytinsky, *World Population and Production;* Charles and Mary Beard, *The Rise of American Civilization,* 4 vols., Macmillan, New York, 1927–42; Frederick L. Paxson, *A History of the American Frontier 1763–1893,* Houghton Mifflin, Boston, 1924; Alexis de Tocqueville, *Democracy in America,* Langley, New York, 1841; and Stewart H. Holbrook, *Yankee Exodus,* Macmillan, New York, 1950. Recent data appear in "Mobility of the Population of the United States, April 1958 to 1959," *Current Population Reports, Population Characteristics,* Series P-20, No. 104, September 30, 1960.

242 For a touch on the American smile, see the note "Cheerful" in the

New Yorker, April 18, 1959, recounting the efforts of the U. S. Passport Office to get "passport photographers and new passport holders to go in for smiles, smiles, smiles."

243 C. H. Currier's photograph of the kitchen of the 90's appears in *Image of America, Early Photography, 1839–1900, A Catalog,* Library of Congress, Washington, 1957.

John Locke's thoughts on suspending judgment appear in "An Essay Concerning Human Understanding."

244 For a discussion of Plato's view of democracy and spending, see Alexandre Koyré, *Discovering Plato,* tr. by Leonora Gohen Rosenfield, Columbia U. Press, New York, 1945. Arendt, *Human Condition,* also treats ancient and modern consumption in a political context.

In regard to contemporary spending for status, see Potter, *People of Plenty;* Katz and Lazarsfeld, *Personal Influence;* and also the comments of Eric Larrabee, *The Self-Conscious Society,* Doubleday, New York, 1960, on opinion surveys relating mobility to consumption. A reference to the practices of the Kwakiutl may be in order: see Helen Codere, *Fighting with Property,* Augustin, New York, 1950, and Margaret Mead, ed., *Cooperation and Competition among Primitive Peoples,* McGraw–Hill, New York, 1937.

TRACES OF THE TRADITION

249 For an idea of the difference between the cowboy's liberality and consumer spending today, contrast Rollins, *The Cowboy,* with the remarks of Ralph Cordiner, "Testimony on Automation, Before the Subcommittee on Economic Stabilization, Joint Congressional Committee on the Economic Report," Washington, October 26, 1955, General Electric Company: "I think the demands of the citizens everywhere are so insatiable . . . ," p. 15.

On the leisureliness of the Plains Indian, see Rosalie Wax, "Free Time in Other Cultures," in Donahue, ed., *Free Time.* For some aspects of Latin American culture, see George Valliant, *The Aztecs of Mexico,* Doubleday, Doran, New York, 1944; Emilio Cecchi, *America Amara,* Sansoni, Florence, 1946; Miguel León–Portilla, *The Mind of Ancient Mexico,* U. of Oklahoma Press, Norman, 1961; George M. Foster, *Culture and Conquest: America's Spanish Heritage,* Wenner–Gren, New York, 1960; Melvin M. Tumin, *Caste in a Peasant Society,* Princeton U. Press, Princeton, 1952; Oscar Lewis, *Life in a Mexican Village: Tepoztlán Restudied,* U. of Illinois Press, Urbana, 1951; and the *Texas Quarterly,* II, No. 1, Spring 1959.

250 For details of the colonial and early Republican days of American culture, see Thomas J. Wertenbaker, *The Golden Age of Colonial*

Culture, Cornell U. Press, Ithaca, 1949; Carl Bridenbaugh, *Cities in the Wilderness,* Ronald, New York, 1938; Gilbert Highet, *The Classical Tradition,* Oxford U. Press, New York, 1957; Howard Mumford Jones, *America and French Culture 1750–1848,* U. of North Carolina Press, Chapel Hill, 1927; Degler, *Out of Our Past;* Eggleston, *The Transit of Civilization;* Harvey Wish, *Society and Thought in Early America,* Longmans, New York, 1950; Vernon Louis Parrington, *Main Currents in American Thought,* Harcourt, Brace, New York, 1930; and Edward N. Saveth, ed., *Understanding the American Past,* Little, Brown, Boston, 1954.

252 Not only the leading men who first came over but those of a hundred and more years later, too, were well-dipped in the culture of the Old World. The Roman origins of *Senate* and *Capitol* are well known. Less familiar is the motto "the New Order of the Ages," taken along with two other quotations from an ancient poet (Vergil), symbolized by the pyramids, and inscribed in a dead language on the Great Seal of the United States, and through it on every modern dollar bill.

255 On Merry Mount, see William Bradford, *History of Plymouth Plantation 1630–1650,* Massachusetts Historical Society, Boston, 1856; and Thomas Morton, *New English Canaan* (publ. 1637), Charles Francis Adams, ed., Prince, Boston, 1883. Merry Mount was turned into a story by Hawthorne and an opera by Howard Hanson. See also Henry W. Lawrence, *The Not-Quite Puritans,* Little, Brown, Boston, 1928. Even in Puritan New England there were large numbers of non-Puritans — sailors, fugitives, and others — who with difficulty could be kept from swearing, drunkenness, and fornication. On swearing in New England, see H. L. Mencken, *The American Language,* Supplement I, Knopf, New York, 1945.

After the War of 1812, a number of notable Americans chose German rather than English universities: George Ticknor, Edward Everett, William Emerson, George Bancroft.

260 On the culture of the South, see Willard Thorp, *A Southern Reader,* Knopf, New York, 1955; Parrington, *Main Currents;* and W. J. Cash, *The Mind of the South,* Knopf, New York, 1941.

267 For a discussion of American expatriates see R. P. Blackmur, "The American Literary Expatriates" in *Foreign Influences in American Life,* David F. Bowers, ed., Princeton U. Press, Princeton, 1944; Van Wyck Brooks, *The Dream of Arcadia; American Writers and Artists in Italy, 1760–1915,* Dutton, New York, 1958; and for some of the writings of the earlier American visitors to Europe, Philip Rahv, ed., *Discovery of Europe,* Houghton, Boston, 1947.

Adolf A. Berle, in *Power Without Property,* Harcourt, Brace, New York, 1959, though somewhat more sanguine in estimating the present strength of universities, gives them perspective and future by identifying them as today's Lords Spiritual.

In regard to study vs. research, it may be noted that the professor goes no longer to his study, but to his office. On the incongruity of the notion of "research without purpose," see Renzo Sereno, *The Rulers,* E. J. Brill, Leiden, 1962.

268 For questions related to liberal education today in the United States, see A. Whitney Griswold, *Liberal Education and the Democratic Ideal,* Yale U. Press, New Haven, 1959; Earl J. McGrath, *The Graduate School and the Decline of Liberal Education,* Columbia U. Press, New York, 1959; James B. Conant, *The American High School Today,* McGraw–Hill, New York, 1959; Mortimer J. Adler and Milton S. Mayer, *The Revolution in Education,* U. of Chicago Press, Chicago, 1958; John W. Gardner, *Excellence,* Harper, New York, 1961; President's Commission on Education Beyond the High School, *Second Report to the President,* Washington, 1957; Mortimer Smith, *The Public School in Crisis,* Regnery, Chicago, 1956; Gordon Keith Chalmers, *The Republic and the Person,* Regnery, Chicago, 1952; A. J. Nock, *The Theory of Education in the United States,* Harcourt, New York, 1932; Arthur Bestor, *The Restoration of Learning,* Knopf, New York, 1955; William H. Kilpatrick, *Philosophy of Education,* Macmillan, New York, 1951; Howard Mumford Jones, *One Great Society,* Harcourt, Brace, New York, 1959; Horace M. Kallen, *The Education of Free Men,* Farrar, Straus, New York, 1949; Alfred North Whitehead, *The Aims of Education,* New American Library, New York, 1929; Robert M. Hutchins, *The Conflict in Education: In a Democratic Society,* Harper, New York, 1953; and William Lloyd Warner, Robert J. Havighurst, and Martin B. Loeb, *Who Shall Be Educated? The Challenge of Unequal Opportunities,* Harper, New York, 1944.

For the opinions and actions of executives and businessmen in regard to leisure and free time, and for some of the questions involved, see August Heckscher and Sebastian de Grazia, "Executive Leisure"; Fortune, *The Executive Life,* and "1700 Top Executives"; Reuel Denney, "The Leisure Society," *Harvard Business Review,* XXXVII, No. 3, May–June 1959; A. C. Spectorsky, *The Exurbanites,* Lippincott, Philadelphia, 1955; and Ralph J. Cordiner, "Long-Range Planning — New Dimension in Our Economy," address before the Economic Club of New York, *General Electric,* March 5, 1956.

269 For a recent survey of employee recreation activities sponsored by various firms, see "Study of Company Expenditures," Organization and Administration of Employee Recreation Programs, *Employee Recreation,* New York, August 1959. See also J. M. Anderson, *Industrial Recreation,* McGraw–Hill, New York, 1955.

The need for association in free time which the mobility and impersonality of much of contemporary life often leads to, is treated in Sebastian de Grazia, *The Political Community,* U. of Chicago Press, Chicago, 1948.

271 As part of the present book, Thomas C. Fichandler did a series of personal interviews with union leaders on the subject of leisure and free time. In general the results paralleled the opinions expressed in *Shorter Work Week.* For an example of management's interpretation of union views, see the speech by Joseph M. Bertotti, *Daily Labor Report,* Washington, October 15, 1957.

272 On programs and aims for educating the executive, see *The Liberally Educated Executive;* Robert A. Gordon and J. E. Howell, *Higher Education for Business,* Columbia U. Press, New York, 1959; F. C. Pierson *et al., The Education of American Businessmen,* McGraw-Hill, New York, 1959; and Leonard S. Silk, *The Education of Businessmen.*

273 A religious examination of the problem of leisure and free time is reported in "Problems and Challenges of The New Leisure," prepared by the Planning Committee of the 2nd Session of the Spiritual Statesmanship Conference convened by the Jewish Theological Seminary of America, Boston, March 14–15, 1956.

A summary of the influence of time-sense on mental patients can be found in Otto Fenichel, *Psychoanalytic Theory of Neurosis,* Norton, New York, 1945. The American Psychiatric Association, as evidence of its interest in the problem of leisure, has occasionally distributed reprints of articles, e.g., Fyfe Robertson, "Leisure Unlimited," *Picture Post,* April 2, 1955.

275 For state constitutions, see Francis N. Thorpe, *Federal and State Constitutions,* U.S.G.P.O., Washington, 1909.

277 For the significance of the *Pursuit of Happiness,* see Howard Mumford Jones, Harvard U. Press, Cambridge, 1953. See also Carl Becker, *The Declaration of Independence,* Harcourt, Brace, New York, 1922; Charles Beard, *An Economic Interpretation of the Constitution of the United States,* Macmillan, New York, 1923; and Robert M. MacIver, *The Pursuit of Happiness,* Simon and Schuster, New York, 1955.

278 Franklin's blast appeared in his "The Interests of Great Britain Considered with Regard to Her Colonies" (1760), cited in Jones, *Pursuit of Happiness.*

The idea of property here described seems essentially that which A. Whitney Griswold finds in Jefferson's conception: see *Liberal Education.*

For Colonel William Byrd of Westover in Virginia, Esq., see W. K. Boyd, ed., *William Byrd's Histories of the Dividing Line Between*

Virginia and North Carolina, 1929. James B. Bryce's remark is taken from his *Modern Democracies,* Macmillan, New York, 1921.

279–81 The relation of colonial and revolutionary generations to Epicurus is generally overlooked because of their more obvious connections with the Enlightenment, Rome, Plato, and Aristotle. See Norman Wentworth De Witt, *Epicurus and His Philosophy,* U. of Minnesota Press, Minneapolis, 1954. Otis, Washington, and Adams are quoted in Jones, *Pursuit of Happiness,* as are the subsequent passages from court cases.

LIBERALS AND LEVELERS

283 For the intellectual setting preceding J. S. Mill, see Elie Halévy, *The Growth of Philosophic Radicalism,* tr. by Mary Morris, Beacon Press, Boston, June 1960.

285 For Mill's remarks on Greece, see *On Liberty,* Oxford U. Press, London, 1940, p. 197.

On Athenian schools and education, see Marrou, *Histoire de l'éducation dans l'antiquité;* and Barclay, *Educational Ideals in the Ancient World.*

286 An Aristotelian analogy is that not the builder of a house but the inhabitant knows whether it is suitable (*Politics,* III, 1282a). Plato is more subtle, distinguishing the arts of the user, the maker, and the imitator (*Republic,* X, 601 D).

289 Implications of political apathy are also discussed in Chapter IX.

290 James Fenimore Cooper's comment on men of "great leisure and large fortunes" appears in *Notions of the Americans,* Philadelphia, 2 vols., 1828, Vol. I, p. 64. His distillation of the "purest democrat" is offered in *The American Democrat* (first published 1838), Vintage Books, New York, 1959, p. 96. For related judgment on aristocracy in relation to art and taste, see Tocqueville, *Democracy in America.*

On Jackson and Jacksonianism, see Parrington, *Main Currents;* Arthur Schlesinger, Jr., *The Age of Jackson,* Little, Brown, Boston, 1945; Joseph Dorfman, *The Economic Mind in American Civilization 1606–1865,* Viking, New York, 1959; Marvin Meyers, *The Jacksonian Persuasion: Politics and Belief,* Knopf, New York, 1957; Walter Hugins, *Jacksonian Democracy and the Working Class,* Stanford U. Press, Stanford, 1960; Joseph L. Blau, ed., *Social Theories of Jacksonian Democracy,* Liberal Arts Press, New York, 1954; and Herbert W. Schneider, *A History of American Philosophy,* Columbia U. Press, New York, 1946.

291 "The common judgment in taste, politics and religion is the highest authority on earth," wrote George Bancroft in *Literary and Historical Miscellanies,* Harper, New York, 1855.

Mill's attack on the false American creed wherein "any man (with a white skin) is as good as any other" appears in *Representative Government.* See *On Liberty,* Oxford U. Press, London, 1940, pp. 288–289. His reliance on leisure and the better elements for taste is more clearly seen in *Principles of Political Economy,* Longmans, Green, Reader & Dyer, 1873, p. 140, where he hopes for "a great multiplication of persons in easy circumstances, with the advantages of leisure, and all the real enjoyments which wealth can give, except those of vanity; a class . . . [capable of rendering those] services which a nation having leisured classes is entitled to expect from them, either by their direct exertions or by the tone they give to the feelings and taste of the public."

292 For the roots of the free-market theory of voting, see Alfred de Grazia, *Public and Republic,* Knopf, New York, 1951. For a recent example of its use: "When we get to 1965, and then for the ensuing decade, I said I thought the American people at the market place would make the decision as to whether they wanted more services, more products, or a shorter work week . . ." Cordiner, "Testimony on Automation," p. 15.

294 The military justification for recreation can be clearly seen in O.R.R.R.C., *Outdoor Recreation for America.* In fact, apart from the work justification ("the individual returns to his work with a sense of renewal"), the only other concrete benefit that the study could think of was military: "Even in this era of electronic warfare, men are still the key to vigilant defense. In many situations a fit man with a rifle in his hand is the only effective defense, and in those where machines are the combatants, fit men must direct them. The increasingly high rate of men rejected by the Army for physical reasons . . . " (p. 23). For military justification underlying education too, see p. 426 above.

On sports and the state, see José Ortega y Gasset, *Toward a Philosophy of History,* Norton, New York, 1941. On American sports, see John Durant and Otto Bettman, *Pictorial History of American Sports,* A. S. Barnes, New York, 1942, and for an examination of one of them in particular, see David Riesman and Reuel Denney, "Football in America," *American Quarterly,* III, 1951.

CHAPTER VIII: Time Free of Machines

295 An illustration of how close Flaubert in *Bouvard et Pécuchet* came to the present world can be found in Leone Diena, *Gli uomini e le masse,* Einaudi, Torino, 1960, on p. 96, where two workers take nearly the same positions about the future.

296 The following are samples of works that deal with the more or less remote future: Fortune, *Markets of the Sixties;* Thompson, *The Foreseeable Future;* Editors of Scientific American, *Automatic Control;* "Man and Automation," Report of the Proceedings of a Conference, Technology Project, Yale U. Press, New Haven, 1956; and Harrison Brown, *The Challenge of Man's Future,* Viking, New York, 1954.

A MECHANIZED TOMORROW

300 On the crucial role of machines and technology, see, in addition to the works just cited, C. P. Snow, *The Two Cultures and the Scientific Revolution,* Cambridge U. Press, Cambridge, 1959; Siegfried Giedion, *Mechanization Takes Command,* Oxford U. Press, New York, 1948; and Dewhurst *et al., America's Needs and Resources.* For the prediction of a group of Russian scientists, see Mikhail Vasiliev, *Reportage aus dem 21. Jahrhundert, so stellen sich sowjetische Wissenschaftler die Zukunft vor,* Nannen, Hamburg, 1959.

The works on the future referred to above are avowedly nonfiction. Science fiction books often look on art and leisure more imaginatively, although still with a technical eye. See Isaac Asimov, *The Living River,* Abelard–Schuman, New York, 1959; Arthur C. Clarke, *The Challenge of the Spaceship,* Harper, New York, 1959; and Benjamin Appel, *The Funhouse,* Ballantine, New York, 1959. One must not forget Aldous Huxley's *Brave New World,* Harper, New York, 1932. For public amusements in a technocratic world, see Harold Loeb, *Life in a Technocracy,* Viking, New York, 1933. An example of a nonfiction book on the future that contains essays on art, writing, music, manners, and morals is Bruce Bliven, ed., *Twentieth Century Unlimited,* Lippincott, New York, 1950.

302 For water and sun clocks and the time-telling of priest, soldier, and civilian in ancient Egypt, see Montet, *Everyday Life in Egypt.* The hourglass could be made small enough to measure a patient's pulse and was so used by Erofilus of Alexandria in the third century B.C. and Nicholas of Cusa in the fifteenth century A.D. Diderot's *Encyclopédie* is interesting here also for the section on *"horlogerie."*

THE STORY OF TIME PIECES

303 On the history and significance of the clock, see Lewis Mumford, *Art and Technics,* Columbia U. Press, New York, 1952; François Le Lionnais, *Le Temps,* Robert Delpire, Paris, 1959; and Frederick Klemm, *A History of Western Technology* (first published 1954), tr. by Dorothea W. Singer, Allen and Unwin, London, 1959.

For philosophical, religious, scientific, literary studies of time, see Joseph Campbell, ed., *Man and Time,* Eranos Yearbooks, Bollingen

Series 30, III, Pantheon, New York, 1957; W. R. Inge, *Mysticism in Religion,* U. of Chicago Press, Chicago, 1948; Harold F. Blum, *Time's Arrow and Evolution,* Princeton U. Press, Princeton, 1955; W. T. Stace, *Time and Eternity,* Princeton U. Press, Princeton, 1952; Pierre Lecomte du Noüy, *Biological Time,* Macmillan, New York, 1937; John F. Callahan, *Four Views of Time in Ancient Philosophy,* Harvard U. Press, Cambridge, Mass., 1948; Hans Reichenbach, *The Rise of Scientific Philosophy,* U. of California Press, Berkeley, 1951; Wyndham Lewis, *Time and Western Man,* Beacon Press, Boston, 1957; George Poulet, *Studies in Human Time,* tr. by Elliot Coleman, Johns Hopkins Press, Baltimore, 1956, and Goldschmidt, *Le système stoïcien et l'idée de temps.*

304 On the *campanile,* "the signal of the plains," see Piero Bargellini, *Volti di pietra,* Vallechi, Florence, 1943.

310 For concepts of time in other cultures, see Margaret Mead, ed., *Cultural Patterns and Technical Change,* UNESCO, Paris, 1953; Robert J. Smith, "Cultural Differences in the Life Cycle and the Concept of Time," with contributions by Allan R. Holmberg, Charles C. Hughes, Colleen Rustow, and William Rower, in Kleemeier, ed., *Aging and Leisure;* and Edward T. Hall, *The Silent Language,* Doubleday, New York, 1959.

311 The poem of Ciro di Pers, "L'orologio da ruota" appears in Benedetto Croce, ed., *Lirici Marinisti,* Laterza, Bari, 1910. On the age-sense of Europeans until the modern epoch, see John U. Nef, *Cultural Foundations of Industrial Civilization,* Cambridge U. Press, Cambridge, 1958.

CLOCKED FREEDOM

313 On time-claustrophobia, see Fenichel, *Theory of Neurosis.* On time-conditioning today, see Jean Piaget, *Le développement de la notion de temps chez l'enfant,* Paris, 1936; Philipp Frank, *Philosophy of Science,* Prentice–Hall, Englewood Cliffs, 1957; George Woodcock, "The Tyranny of the Clock," *Politics,* October 1944; and John Seeley *et al., Crestwood Heights,* Basic Books, New York, 1956.

314 For recent thinking on conformity and individualism, see William H. Whyte, *The Organization Man,* Simon and Schuster, New York, 1956; Sebastian de Grazia, "What Authority is *Not,*" *American Political Science Review,* June 1959; Henry A. Murray, "Individuality" in Elting E. Morison, ed., *The American Style,* Harper, New York, 1958; and Alpheus T. Mason, "American Individualism: Fact and Fiction," *American Political Science Review,* March 1952.

315 For a current example of the popularization of Baxter's time morality, see Godfrey M. Lebhar, *The Use of Time,* Chain Store, New York,

1958, which calculates that by sleeping six hours instead of eight, one's life will be lengthened by two years.

316 For criticism of the time-and-motion idea of the one "best way," see Abruzzi, *Work Measurement*.

317 Among moderns, Gabriel Marcel discloses a musical time-sense similar to that of the Greeks. Music reveals man to himself because it touches the point of breakthrough where man communes with the essence of others and where he unites interiorly with all those who participate in the human adventure. See Bernard G. Murchland, "The Philosophy of Gabriel Marcel," *Review of Politics*, XXI, No. 2, April 1959.

OTHER PLACES, OTHER TIMES

318 An idea of the proliferation of time notions can be seen in Max Knoll, "Transformations of Science in Our Age," in Campbell, ed., *Man and Time*.

321 For Friedrich Nietzsche on time, see *Thus Spake Zarathustra*, tr. by Thomas Connon, Macmillan, New York, 1911. For Oswald Spengler, see *The Decline of the West*, tr. by Charles F. Atkinson, Knopf, New York, 1926–28. For Henri Bergson, see *Time and Free Will*, tr. by F. L. Pogson, Allen and Unwin, London, 1921.

TIME ON AN UPWARD PLANE

321 For Augustine on time, see the eleventh book of *Confessions*.

On the ideas of progress and the millennium, see Karl Löwith, *Meaning in History*, U. of Chicago Press, Chicago, 1949; John B. Bury, *The Idea of Progress*, Macmillan, New York, 1932; Albert Salomon, *The Tyranny of Progress*, Noonday Press, New York, 1955; Mircea Eliade, *The Myth of the Eternal Return*, tr. by Willard R. Trask, Pantheon, New York, 1954; Norman Cohn, *The Pursuit of the Millennium*, Harper, New York, 1961; Benjamin Nelson, "Community — Dreams and Realities," and Jacob Taubes, "Community — After the Apocalypse" in Carl J. Friedrich, ed., *Community*, Liberal Arts Press, New York, 1959; and see also Norbert Wiener, *The Human Use of Human Beings*, Houghton Mifflin, Boston, 1950.

324 On inner clocks, see Karl Buhler, "The Skywise and Neighborwise Navigation of Ants and Bees," *Acta Psychologica*, VIII, 1951–52; and C. S. Pittendrigh, "Clock System Controlling Emergence Time in Drosophila," *Proceedings of the National Academy of Sciences*, XL, October 1953. For "The Relation Between the Time of Psychology and the Time of Physics," see *British Journal for the Philosophy of Science*, II, August 1951.

325 On fears of retirement, see August Heckscher and Sebastian de Grazia, "Executive Leisure"; Matthew Radom, *A Comparison of Attitudes*

Toward Work, Leisure and Retirement, August 1960, unpublished; Opinion Research Corporation, *Preparing Older Workers for Retirement,* O.R.C., Princeton, N. J., XIV, No. 2, February 1956; and Sebastian de Grazia, "The Uses of Time" in Kleemeier, ed., *Aging and Leisure.*

John Locke's exhortation to proper time-thinking appears in *An Essay Concerning Human Understanding.*

CHAPTER IX: Transforming Free Time

329 For the equipment in the average American household today, see Dewhurst *et al., America's Needs and Resources,* and Coleman, *Workingman's Wife.*

TODAY'S FREE TIME

331 Many writings today examine American life for its free time, leisure, and culture. See Larrabee, *The Self-Conscious Society;* Clyde Kluckhohn, "Have There Been Discernible Shifts in Values During the Past Generation?," *The American Style,* E. Morison, ed.; and Lee Coleman, "What Is American," *Social Forces,* XIX, 1940–41, which cover some aspects of American traits related to free time.

332 Meyersohn in "Commercial Entertainment" discusses which of the mass media requires the most mental and physical energy. On "Immobility as Leisure" see Kaplan, *Leisure in America.*

334 Dancing to music is a different matter, of course, and has been discussed before, in Chapter V. Accordingly, if recordings are danced to, the activity can no longer be classified as merely listening to music.

335 Expenditures of time and money on sports, music, theater, etc., were presented in Chapter IV. For *The Play of Animals* and *The Play of Man,* see Karl Groos, Appleton–Century, New York, 1898 and 1901.

338 For an example of Olivetti's political writings, see his *L'ordine politico delle comunità,* Edizioni di Comunità, Rome, 1946.

As for prisons, much depends on their location and type. In the Auburn system, long accepted in the United States, conversation called for summary punishment. The "congregate but silent" method has now given way to other methods of control. See Richard A. Cloward *et al., Theoretical Studies in Social Organization of the Prison,* Social Science Research Council, Pamphlet 15, March 1960; Richard McCleery, *Policy Change in Prison Management,* Michigan State U., East Lansing, 1957; and also Gresham M. Sykes, *The Society of Captives,*

Princeton U. Press, Princeton, 1958, where an actual sequence of guards' duties is given, in which appears after the 6:00 P.M. dinner: "the evening recreational program begins. When an evening move, such as TV takes place, check to determine how many attend and check on double-ups. . . . 9:30 P.M. Men return from TV or other evening movements. Lock men in their cells, secure Wing and take Check Count of entire Wing." (Pp. 142–143.)

341 It is not only marble cutters who disappear. R. Denney, "The Leisure Society," *Harvard Business Review*, May–June 1959, and Kaplan, *Leisure in America*, discuss the decline in numbers of artists and musicians.

342 On lack of inward attentiveness, see R. M. MacIver, *Pursuit of Happiness*. Foreign visitors rarely note contemplation, reflection, and meditation as a characteristic of the United States. See Franz M. Joseph, ed., *As Others See Us*, Princeton U. Press, Princeton, 1959; also Allan Nevins, ed., *American Social History*, Holt, New York, 1923.

For Central Park and several other areas of Manhattan, see Marya Mannes, *The New York I Know*, J. B. Lippincott Co., New York, 1961.

RESISTANCE TO CHANGE

344 Most American writers on American democracy write little democratic sermons. Or else in light of the misunderstandings of foreign critics they offer a slightly altered version of the *sermo sublimis,* but never a real shaking up of concepts. The misunderstandings are treated on the plane of what democracy hopes for, or is in transition toward, not what has happened to it, nor what goes on today in the living rooms and bedrooms, streets and public places — or what goes into them or is built for them. Three different approaches to democracy can be seen in Russell Davenport, *The Dignity of Man*, Harper, New York, 1955; Anthony Downes, *An Economic Theory of Democracy*, Harper, New York, 1957; and "The Pursuit of Excellence: Education and the Future of America" in *Prospect for America:* The Rockefeller Panel Reports, Doubleday, New York, 1961. For the effects of American abundance and prosperity on the American outlook, see Potter, *People of Plenty*.

For newspaper reading, as well as at-homeness, see Louis Halsey's poem "Home Is Where." The man of the city "then read his daily letter from the world / to which he never wrote."

On American newspaper reading over a hundred years ago, see Jane L. Mesnick, *The English Traveler in America, 1785–1835*, Columbia U. Press, New York, 1922. Henry David Thoreau in *Walden* (1854) notes that, "Hardly a man takes a nap after dinner, but when he wakes he holds up his head and asks, 'What's the news?' " See also

August Heckscher, "Reading in America — Its Social and Cultural Background," paper to Conference on the Undergraduate and the Lifetime Reading Habit, Ann Arbor, Michigan, mimeographed, February 1958; and James D. Hart, *The Popular Book*, Oxford U. Press, New York, 1950.

345 The rest of Rabelais' prologue to *Gargantua: "et vous, Verolez tres precieux — car à vous, non à aultres, sont dediez mes escriptz."* Thence to Plato's *Symposium*.

346 On the problem of automation and its lack of place for less intelligent employees, Thompson in *Foreseeable Future* opens a chapter with a title that most American authors would not have thought of — "The Future of the Stupid." Frederick H. Harbison chose a title with fine American touch, however, in writing on the same subject: "More Chiefs, Fewer Indians," *University: A Princeton Magazine*, Winter 1961.

For works on automation other than those cited in notes to pp. 296 and 300, see R. H. Macmillan, *Automation, Friend or Foe?*, Cambridge U. Press, New York, 1956; Georges Friedmann, *Industrial Society;* and John Diebold, *Automation: The Advent of the Automatic Factory*, Van Nostrand, Princeton, N. J., 1952.

A recent volume on the significance of the *plebs* is R. E. Smith, *The Failure of the Roman Republic*, Cambridge U. Press, Cambridge, 1955. For historical sequence, see also N. Cohn, *Millennium;* J. L. Talmon, *The Origins of Totalitarian Democracy*, Secker and Warburg, London, 1955; and Hannah Arendt, *The Origins of Totalitarianism*, Harcourt, Brace, New York, 1951.

347 The problem of obligation and commitment in free time is made a central concern in the writings of Joffre Dumazedier, "Loisir et dynamique socio-culturelle," *Cahiers Internationaux de Sociologie*, XXII, 1957; and "Loisir et pédagogie," *International Review of Education*, I, 1955: *"Le loisir est une occupation à laquelle le travailleur peut s'adonner de son plein gré en dehors des nécessités et obligations professionnelles, familiales, et sociales, pour se délasser, se divertir ou se développer,"* p. 103. The point made in the present book at various junctures is that, in free time, relaxation, diversion, and even personal enrichment are related by necessity to work, family, and society.

348 For Pindar's scorn for "those who know only because they have learned," see the *Olympian and Nemean Odes;* and also Jaeger, *Paideia*. Compare with Burke's *Appeal from the New to the Old Whigs:* "To be bred in a place of estimation; to see nothing low and sordid from one's infancy . . ."

For observations on "The Emergence of Fun Morality" see Martha Wolfenstein, in Larrabee and Meyersohn, *Mass Leisure*. See also Dulles,

America Learns to Play; Rainwater, *Play Movement;* and André Malraux, "Art, Popular Art and the Illusion of Folk," *The New Partisan Reader, 1945–1953,* Harcourt, Brace, New York, 1953.

350 For the influence of German culture on the United States, its schools and universities, see *German Culture in America, Philosophical and Literary Influences 1600–1900,* by Henry A. Pochman, U. of Wisconsin Press, Madison, 1957.

351 Karl Marx's looking forward to fishing and criticizing appears in *Deutsche Ideologie.* On the original manuscript, there is written in Marx's own hand an alternative set of occupations — shoemaker in the morning, gardener in the afternoon, and actor in the evening. This passage, like others from Marx's early works, could not have been known to communists or others generally before 1933 when the edition was first published: Karl Marx, Friedrich Engels, *Gesammtausgabe,* I, 5, Moscow, 1933, p. 22. Marx's notebooks were first published in 1953, *Grundisse der Kritik der politischen Oekonomie, 1858.* For consideration of Marx's thinking about leisure, see Maximilien Rubel, *Karl Marx, Essai de biographie intellectuelle,* Rivière, Paris, 1957.

352 For Greenwich Village time, see Kate Simon, *New York Places and Pleasures,* Meridian Books, New York, 1959. A good book guide to a city often contains illuminating information about free-time activities. See also Sam Lambert, ed., *London, Night and Day,* Architectural Press, London, 1951.

CONTENDERS FOR AUTHORITY

354 For opposing academic positions reflecting business-government tension, see Friedrich A. von Hayek, *The Road to Serfdom,* U. of Chicago Press, Chicago, 1944, and Herman Finer, *The Road to Reaction,* Little, Brown, Boston, 1945. See also Galbraith, *Affluent Society.*

356 For advertising costs in relation to educational expenditures, see Galbraith, *Affluent Society,* and Barbara Ward, as quoted by Arthur Schlesinger, Jr., "The New Mood in Politics," *Esquire,* January 1960.

357 On the government's being able to allow a wider time margin in the recreation area than in business, see Clark, *Social Control of Business,* which states that the market, discounting future values at compound interest, virtually sets no value for anything beyond two generations. For the government's role in recreation, see notes for p. 367 and p. 390 below.

358 For welfare and the Welfare State, see Hilaire Belloc, *The Servile State,* Foulis, London, 1913; Alfred de Grazia and Ted Gurr, *American Welfare,* New York U. Press, New York, 1961; Harold L. Wilensky and Charles N. Lebeaux, *Industrial Society and Social Welfare,* Russell Sage Foundation, New York, 1958; Dewhurst *et al., America's Needs*

and Resources; and Sidney Fine, *Laissez-Faire and the General Welfare State*, U. of Michigan Press, Ann Arbor, 1956.

359 For various positions on the question of popular taste, see Rosenberg and White, *Mass Culture;* John A. Kouwenhoven, *Made in America,* Doubleday, Garden City, 1948; Bernard Rudofsky, *Behind the Picture Window,* Oxford U. Press, New York, 1955; the articles by Bernard Berelson, Eric Larrabee, and others in *Understanding Public Communication,* U. of Chicago Press, Chicago, No. 3, 1961; Dwight MacDonald, "Masscult and Midcult," *Partisan Review,* XXVII, No. 2, Spring 1960; "A Theory of Popular Culture," *Politics,* I, 1944; Max Horkheimer, "Art and Mass Culture," *Studies in Philosophy and Social Science,* IX, Institute of Social Research, New York, 1941; Louis Kronenberger, *Company Manners, A Cultural Inquiry into American Life,* Bobbs–Merrill, Indianapolis, 1954; Eliot, "Definition of Culture"; T. W. Adorno, "On Popular Music," *Studies in Philosophy and Social Science,* IX, Institute of Social Research, New York, 1941; E. Van Haag, "Notes sur la culture populaire américaine," *Diogenes,* No. 17, 1957; Meyer Schapiro, "Style," in A. L. Kroeber *et al.,* eds., *Anthropology Today,* U. of Chicago Press, Chicago, 1953; B. L. Bell, *Crowd Culture,* Harper, New York, 1952; José Ortega y Gasset, *The Dehumanization of Art* and *Notes on the Novel,* tr. by Helene Weyl, Princeton U. Press, Princeton, 1948; Special Issue, "Our Country and Our Culture," *Partisan Review,* May–June 1952; Reuel Denney, *The Astonished Muse,* U. of Chicago Press, Chicago, 1957; Gilbert Seldes, *The Seven Lively Arts,* Harper, New York, 1924; Cowell, *Culture;* and Fenton B. Turck, "The American Explosion," *Scientific Monthly,* September 1952.

In the question of "popular culture" or "popular taste," as well as of "leisure activities" or "leisure time," any use of statistics should be given an unusually close scrutiny. The last article above cites many statistics (on ticket sales, e.g.) but before drawing conclusions, one should ask not simply, How many books or records were sold? but, Which ones?; not only, How many symphony orchestras? but also, By what standards are they called "symphony orchestras"? and, Do they render anything but the fifty standard war horses?

360 For examples of recent reappraisals of American education, see Daniel Seligman, "The Low Productivity of the 'Education Industry,' " *Fortune,* October 1958; Bernard Berelson, *Graduate Education in the United States,* McGraw–Hill, New York, 1960; and "The Pursuit of Excellence: Education and the Future of America," in *Prospect for America.*

The currently popular word for quality in education seems to be "excellence." The term manages somehow to blur the necessary distinctions and hide the real issue of how there can ever be a mass education. Three recent books, all containing something or other of worth, succeed in evading the question: if we insist on aristocratic standards, for everyone, how can we keep those standards high? The first book does the best job of identifying the problem (indeed it is the only one to do so), but as the book opens, it closes — without carrying out its implications — i.e., that the political system must change. The authors leave the issue, saying that after all "the aristocrats are so small in influence." The second book admits that "Reflective leisure and independence are the first things to be sacrificed in any mass program." Thenceforth it discusses the rewards and types of sabbatical to be found today for gifted students and scholars. So they win a year or two. Good! *Otium-negotium* again. The third one never diagnoses nor faces the issue except to say: Let's have all of everything good for everybody, even if it is impossible. (See Chapter X above for further discussion.) The books are, in order: Mortimer J. Adler and Milton Mayer, *Revolution in Education;* Edgar Stern Family Fund, *Recognition of Excellence,* Free Press, Glencoe, Ill., April 1960; "Pursuit of Excellence" in *Prospect for America.* The first book presents solid ideas; the second gathers substantial information; the third is encouraging. The references in the text to a re-examination of education refer principally to the third book.

361 Why do advertisers and marketing men gladly greet the news that college enrollments will be on the increase? Because studies such as the Life survey (Table 6) have led them to expect that "At every income level, there is a general tendency by the college group to spend about twice as much as households whose heads did not finish grade school." Beltrame J. Lange, *Aspects of Modern Marketing,* American Management Association, Management Report No. 15, 1958.

For the kinds of liberty, essentially political means to liberty — representation, written constitutions, removal of officials, suffrage — that animated America and Europe in the few decades leading to the French Revolution, see R. R. Palmer, *The Age of the Democratic Revolution,* Princeton U. Press, Princeton, 1959. Shortly afterward, laissez-faire economists insisted on their kinds of liberty, justified as leading to a competitive market and thus constituting the means to liberty, also. An exceptionally forthright statement of the position can be seen in Henry C. Simons, "A Positive Program for Laissez-Faire," in his *Economic Policy for a Free Society,* U. of Chicago Press, Chicago, 1948. Through such emphasis on political and economic means to liberty, the end — liberty itself — was neglected, indeed became identified with the means. See also note for page 403 below.

362 The gradual process of separating leisure from politics or religion can

be traced in Gottfried Wilhelm Leibniz's "Principles of Nature and of Grace," in *Monadology and Other Philosophical Writings*, tr. by Robert Latta, Oxford U. Press, New York, 1925; Immanuel Kant, *Critique of Judgment*, tr. by J. H. Bernard, Harper, New York, 1951; Schiller's *Artists* and the unfinished dialogue *Kallias;* and the writings of Anthony Ashley Cooper, Earl of Shaftesbury, collected in *Characteristics of Men, Manners, Opinions and Times*, 3 vols., Darby, London, 1714.

For the divorce of thought and feeling after the Renaissance, see Hiram C. Haydn, *The Counter Renaissance*, Scribner, New York, 1950.

364 For increased outdoor "leisure" on Sunday, see Table 3 above; for age breakdowns of the same data, see Tables 5.5a–5.5c in Sebastian de Grazia, "The Uses of Time," in Kleemeier, ed., *Aging and Leisure*.

365 On the history of taste in the United States, see Russell Lynes, *The Tastemakers*, Harper, New York, 1949; Aline B. Saarinen, *The Proud Possessors*, Random House, New York, 1958; Cohn, *Good Old Days;* Kronenberger, *Company Manners;* and Lewis Mumford, *The Brown Decades: A study of the arts in America 1865–1895*, Dover, New York, 1955.

366 For the electorate's campaign interest or lack thereof, see Campbell, *et al., The Voter Decides;* Alfred de Grazia, *Western Public;* and the other pertinent works cited in the notes for page 189 above.

367 The remarks about the role contemporary government has played in free time apply chiefly to the United States. France under Léon Blum had a Ministry of Leisure, but the office was short-lived. Undoubtedly other governments have made similar experiments, which altogether should warrant study. Most recently, for Great Britain, see Conservative Political Centre, *The Challenge of Leisure*, London, 1959, and Labour Party, *Leisure for Living*, London, 1959.

THE MANY PLEASURES OF THE MANY

368 The story of the North African oil company's labor troubles was reported in *Time*, February 1, 1960.

376 The example of Japanese language is from Johan Huizinga, *Homo Ludens*, pp. 34–35. A point of difference with this work should be mentioned. Contests, I would hold, are possibly, but not necessarily, games. Huizinga did not go into the relation of play and leisure. From his brief remarks on p. 161, I gather he would agree substantially with the remarks on the subject in the text above.

377 A few writers have groped for a two-class distinction in leisure. John Ruskin, in the third lecture of *The Crown of Wild Olive*, divides mankind into two races, one of workers, the other of players "proudly idle." His conception, however, puts players in the class of a military

PAGE

aristocracy like Sparta's. Somewhat nearer is Edward Bellamy's idea that "not all, nor the majority, have those scientific, artistic, literary, or scholarly interests which make leisure the one thing valuable to their possessors." See *Looking Backward.* Bellamy, though, does not explicitly divide the world in two.

378 For an example of sports and games in seventeenth-century English aristocracy, see Gladys Scott Thompson, *Life in a Noble Household 1641–1700,* U. of Michigan Press, Ann Arbor, 1959.

379 For sober questioning of the equality brought by the French Revolution, see Alexis de Tocqueville, *L'ancien régime et la Révolution,* Lévy, Paris, 1877.

CHAPTER X: Leisure's Future

381 For lands of Cockaigne, see Giuseppe Cocchiara, *Il paese di Cuccagna,* Einaudi, Torino, 1956. Lewis Mumford's *The Story of Utopias,* Boni and Liveright, New York, 1922, is still a good introduction to the subject. For the relation of cakelands and utopias to the theme of terrestrial paradise, see Arturo Graf, *Miti, leggende e superstitioni del medio evo,* Chiantori, Torino, 1925. *Pinocchio* contains a child's *Schlaraffenland.*

384 For the immigrant waves of manual labor and prejudices against it, see Degler, *Out of Our Past;* Vladimir Lenin, *A Letter to American Workingmen, from the Socialist soviet republic of Russia,* Socialist Publication Society, New York, 1918; and for the most recent wave, Handlin, *The Newcomers.*

387 For property, chattel and cattle, see (in addition to the works of Berle, Arendt, Livingston, and others cited earlier) Berle, *Power Without Property;* Richard B. Schlatter, *Private Property: The History of an Idea,* Allen and Unwin, London, 1951. Robert Schlaifer, "Greek Theories of Slavery from Homer to Aristotle," *Harvard Studies in Classical Philology,* XLVII, 1936; Raimondo Craveri, *La disgregazione della proprietà,* Feltrinelli, Milan, 1958; and Ernest Dale, "Management Must Be Made Accountable," *Harvard Business Review,* XXXVIII, No. 2, March–April 1960, p. 49.

388 De Witt, *Epicurus,* would perhaps locate the origin of the contemplative idea more precisely in Magna Graecia, which he finds to be distinguished before Plato's time by a contemplation and thinking (specially in mathematics) divorced from the practical concerns of the arts

and crafts characteristic of Greece proper in this period. In Magna Graecia thinkers seemed to have been addicted to the sitting position. In art they are represented as comfortably seated with a rod or radius in hand, drawing figures on a sanded floor. To go along with De Witt's conclusions, from these philosophers the line of contemplation and leisure reaches Greece and eventually Plato. See also Plutarch's *Lives* where Archimedes is described as being of so high a spirit that he would not condescend to leave any commentary or writings on his vast scientific knowledge and many inventions, but repudiated the whole of engineering and any art that lends itself to mere use as sordid, and put all his affection into those pure speculations that have no bearing on the vulgar needs of life.

389 Locke's quotation about property is from the *Second Treatise of Civil Government,* 1690.

Adolf A. Berle, in *Power Without Property,* makes the point that most owners of industrial property have been reduced to a "passive-receptive role."

On the belief in Jewish culture that men are not to work, see Father Giuseppe Ricciotti, *The History of Israel,* tr. by Clement della Penta and Richard Murphy, Bruce, Milwaukee, 1955.

390 For discussion of the government's role in recreation, whether in or out of a depression, see Degler, *Out of Our Past;* Dorothy I. Cline, *Training for Recreation under the WPA (1935–37),* U. of Chicago Press, Chicago, 1939; Karl Mannheim, *Man and Society,* Kegan Paul, London, 1944, and *Freedom, Power and Democratic Planning,* Oxford U. Press, New York, 1950; Eduard C. Lindeman, *Leisure — A National Issue,* Association Press, New York, 1939; R. E. McMurry and M. Lee, *The Cultural Approach,* Duke U. Press, Durham, 1947; and Ralph Purcell, *Government and Art,* Public Affairs Press, Washington, D. C., 1956.

391 For the "business liturgy" of production, see Galbraith, *Affluent Society.*

392 Doubts and questions about identity and national destiny run together. For various examples of the literature of doubt and identity, see Stuart Chase, *Goals for America,* Twentieth Century Fund, New York, 1942; Larrabee, *Self-Conscious Society;* Erving Goffman, *The Presentation of Self in Everyday Life,* U. of Edinburgh Press, Edinburgh, 1956; R. W. B. Lewis, *The American Adam,* U. of Chicago Press, Chicago, 1955; Erik Erikson, *Childhood and Society,* Norton, New York, 1950; and Edward McNall Burns, *The American Idea of Mission,* Rutgers U. Press, New Brunswick, 1957. But for the real beginnings, see Henry Adams, *Mont-Saint-Michel and Chartres,* Houghton Mifflin, Boston, 1913. Adams had already raised many of the ques-

tions in his *History of the United States of America,* 9 vols., Scribner, New York, 1889–91.

Thomas Jefferson almost explicitly applies Aristotle's proposition about the two stages of a state. Writing in 1825, he said, "Literature is not yet a distinct profession with us. Now and then a stray mind arises and, at its intervals of leisure from business, emits a flash of light. But the first object of young societies is bread and covering: science is but secondary and subsequent." Aristotle's rule is to be found in *Politics,* I, 1252b — γινομένη μὲν οὖν τοῦ ζῆν ἕνεκεν, οὖσα δὲ τοῦ εὖ ζῆιν. "While the *polis* comes into existence for the sake of life, it exists for the good life."

393 For expansion, militarism, and leisure, Philip Freneau's "To an Author," 1788, is equally to the point. "An age employed in edging steel / can no poetic raptures feel."

On the bureaucratic state, see Gaetano Mosca, *The Ruling Class,* tr. by Hannah D. Kahn, McGraw–Hill, New York, 1939. On the bureaucratizing of American industry, see in addition to the works cited in the note for page 57, Joseph A. Schumpeter, *Capitalism, Socialism and Democracy,* Harper, New York, 1950; Adolf A. Berle and Gardiner C. Means, *The Modern Corporation and Private Property,* Macmillan, New York, 1947; and Benjamin Selekman, *A Moral Philosophy for Management,* McGraw–Hill, New York, 1959; Newcomer, *Big Business Executive;* William H. Whyte, Jr., and the Editors of Fortune, *Is Anybody Listening?,* Simon and Schuster, New York, 1957.

394 Ovid's line is from ex Ponto: *Nec venit ad duros musa / vocata Getas.* For the Dugento's productiveness in one field alone — painting — see Carlo L. Ragghianti, *Pittura del Dugento a Firenze, Sele Arte,* Monografia 1.

For Greek theories of the role of mystery and madness in creativeness and culture, see E. R. Dodds, *The Greeks and the Irrational,* Beacon Press, Boston, 1957.

ON FALSE AND TRUE POWER

395 The GNP (spelled without capitals) is discussed and estimated by Dewhurst *et al., America's Needs and Resources.* For observations and queries related to the ideas of production and efficiency, see Hans B. Thorelli, "The Tantalizing Concept of Productivity," *American Behavioral Scientist,* IV, No. 3, November 1960, pp. 6–11. Writing on unproductive labor, Adam Smith, *The Wealth of Nations,* Book I, Chapter III, Modern Library, New York, 1937, p. 315, makes significant distinctions:

"The labour of some of the most respectable orders in the society is, like that of menial servants, unproductive of any value, and does not fix or realize itself in any permanent subject, or vendible commodity, which endures after that labour is past, and for which an equal quantity of labour could afterwards be procured. The sovereign, for example, with all the officers both of justice and war who serve under him, the whole army and navy, are unproductive labourers. They are the servants of the public, and are maintained by a part of the annual produce of the industry of other people. . . . In the same class must be ranked, some both of the gravest and most important, and some of the most frivolous professions: churchmen, lawyers, physicians, men of letters of all kinds; players, buffoons, musicians, opera-singers, opera-dancers, etc. . . . Like the declamation of the actor, the harangue of the orator, or the tune of the musician, the work of all of them perishes in the very instant of its production."

Adam Smith evidently did not see that some words do not die easily. His position (and also the success of his own words) should be viewed in light of John Maynard Keynes, *The General Theory of Employment, Interest and Money,* Harcourt, New York, 1936, p. 383, on "the world is ruled by little else." Smith's last remark above, about perishing in the instant of production, certainly would apply to conversation. Yet when Aristotle wished to be practical and write about productive science (*poiēsis*), he analyzed three in all, and all three dealt with talk — how to make a good argument (*Topics*), a good speech (*Rhetoric*), and a good dramatic poem (*Poetics*). For the productive sciences in Aristotle, see John Herman Randall, Jr., *Aristotle,* Columbia U. Press, New York, 1960. For the role of conversation in *Jesus' Teachings and the Use of Leisure,* see Leslie Rutledge, U. of Kansas Press, Lawrence, 1931. For an appreciation of conversation today, see Clarence R. Randall, "The Cultivation of the Mind" in Goldwin, ed., *Toward the Liberally Educated Executive.*

396   On machines, motors, and energy of "Household Operation," see Dewhurst *et al., America's Needs and Resources.* On "womanpower" see Mary Beard, *Women as Force in History,* Macmillan, New York, 1946.

397   Aristotle's irony about machines did not carry him too far. His distinction between *poiēsis* (production) and *praxis* (action) kept him from pretending that servants and slaves would not still be necessary (*Politics,* I, 1254a).

400   The civilizing importance of cities as a subject is given considerable attention by Spengler, *Decline of the West;* Frederick Pollock, *An Introduction to the History of the Science of Politics,* Beacon Press, Boston, 1960; and V. Gordon Childe, *Man Makes Himself,* New American Library, New York, 1951. See also Lewis Mumford, *The City in History,* Harcourt, Brace and World, New York, 1961; Kevin

Lynch, *The Image of the City*, Harvard U. Press, Cambridge, 1960; and Robert Moore Fisher, ed., *The Metropolis in Modern Life*, Doubleday, Garden City, 1955.

401 For the *Histoire du St. Simonisme*, see Sébastien Camille Gustave Charléty, Hartmann, Paris, 1931.

402 For the propaganda on technological progress directed at underdeveloped countries, see Frankel, *The Economic Impact*.

On Babylonian mathematics see G. A. Miller, "The First Known Long Mathematical Decline," *Science*, LXXXVII, No. 576, June 24, 1938, pp. 576–577. On the relation of politics and mathematical thought in Greece, see Livio C. Stecchini, "The History of Measures," IV, *American Behavioral Scientist*, March 1961, which summarizes his forthcoming book on the subject.

For a recent example of business worries over full warehouses, see *Economist*, October 22, 1960.

403 Economics, it seems, can no longer be persuasively defined as a science of scarcity, as, e.g., in L. Robbins, *An Essay on the Nature and Significance of Economic Science*, St. Martin's Press, London, 1946. Similarly, the doctrine of optimum allocation of resources, found in one form or other in economists so varied as Walras, Pareto, Marshall, Pigou, and in the welfare school of thought generally, seems to have lost conviction with the decline of the scarcity assumption. On welfare economics and related concepts, see Hla Myint, *Theories of Welfare Economics*, Harvard U. Press, Cambridge, 1948; Walter A. Weisskopf, *The Psychology of Economics*, U. of Chicago Press, Chicago, 1955; and for "Psychological and Economic Assumptions Underlying Automation," see H. Winthrop, *American Journal of Economics and Sociology*, XVIII, 1958. For a general examination of *Economic Thought and Language*, see L. M. Fraser, A. & C. Black, London, 1937.

404 Work as good for health is an idea with a long history. Recall the end of Voltaire's *Candide*. But the frequency with which "occupational therapy" is used today as a term and a practice indicates widespread currency. For the belief today in work's aid to physical and mental stability, see Morse and Weiss, "Work and the Job."

405 For current political studies which do not admit or consider the possibility of change in form of government — except through superior force — see *Prospect for America*. On the other hand, for a recent political work that notes the decline of democracy as a reigning political ideal, see Edward McNall Burns, *Ideas in Conflict*, Norton, N. Y., 1960. For the Greek experience with democracy see Kathleen Freeman, *Greek City-States*, Macdonald, London, 1950. Not only the Greeks but also writers like Tocqueville (*L'Ancien régime*) and Hippolyte Taine (*Les origines de la France contemporaine*, Hachette, Paris, 1899) saw

tyranny as the successor to revolution and democracy. Renzo Sereno (*The Rulers*) points out that while these men thought the French Revolution a blunder, writers such as de Bonald, Chateaubriand, von Gentz, and Balanche thought it a crime. Tocqueville and Taine were not reactionaries but "conscious libertarians" who sought in vain the freedom the Revolution had promised, convinced as they were that revolution is incompatible with freedom.

406 Another example of general high quality due to particular high quality is the theater-goer of ancient Greece.

LEISURE AND POLITICS

408 Studies of fatigue are pertinent to the question of typical working hours in settled communities. However, identifying and isolating fatigue well enough for physiological studies, while yet keeping the idea close to common sense, is a difficult task. Representative studies are S. Howard Bartley and Eloise Chute, *Fatigue and Impairment in Man*, McGraw–Hill, New York, 1947, and National Research Council, *Fatigue of Workers*, Reinhold, New York, 1941.

410 With regard to the possibility that aggressiveness appears whenever there is time to kill, two points should be made. First, aggressiveness can appear in work time as well as in free time, though its possibility of expression may be somewhat greater in free time. Second, free time without established patterns of activity may be felt as purposelessness or exclusion from society and resented, leading again to the possibility of aggressiveness. Both points can apply to adults as well as to youth. For adults, see the discussion of violence, with and without institutionalized patterns, in Chapter VI. For examples of "Recreation and Tabooed Pleasures" of the young, see Hollingshead, *Elmstown's Youth*. The study of the foreign quarter mentioned is found in Sebastian de Grazia, *Borgata Urbis*.

414 For American *Tinkers and Genius*, see Edmund Fullers, Hastings House, New York, 1955; and also Samuel Chugerman, *Lester F. Ward: The American Aristotle*, Duke U. Press, Durham, N. C., 1939; also Pearl Franklin Clark, *Challenge of the American Know-How*, Hillary, New York, 1960; Mitchell Wilson, *American Science and Invention*, Crown, New York, 1958; and Carleton Mabee, *The American Leonardo: The Life of Samuel F. B. Morse*, Knopf, New York, 1943.

In the mediation of the ideals of contemplation and leisure between Greece and Rome, Panaethius also played an important part. See Grilli, *Vita Contemplativa*.

416 The question whether a man can be free if he has to obey the law is not the same as, yet related to, Epicurus' separation of freedom and politics. Aristotle opposing the democrats of his time says that only by

life according to the constitution is there real freedom (*Politics*, V, 1310a). It is instructive to see Locke opposing Filmer on the same grounds: "Freedom is not what Sir Robert Filmer tells us, 'A liberty for everyone to do what he wants, to live as he pleases, and not to be tied by any laws.' But a freedom of men under government is to have a standing rule to live by . . ." (*Civil Government*, Ch. IV, Sect. 22). Mill would seem to go with the democrats and levelers — "Liberty consists in doing what one desires" (*Liberty*, Ch. V, Oxford U. Press, London, 1940, p. 152) — but as we know, he, as well as the others above, circumvented their definitions by many qualifications. The point to note is that none uses as a base for freedom (as Epicurus and Aristotle did for freedom and leisure both) the freedom from necessity.

Coulanges in *Ancient City* speaks of a Greek desire to be absolved of the burden of politics. This would apply to that part of the analysis in this book wherein an activity, once believed in, suffers a loss of faith and begins to be felt as the weight of obligation on free time.

420 Much of what follows on theory and practice, leisure and politics, is derived from Sebastian de Grazia, "Politics and the Contemplative Life," *American Political Science Review,* June 1960.

425 For a novel built around one version of the game *passatella,* see Roger Vailland, *The Law,* tr. from *La Loi* by Peter Wiles, Knopf, New York, 1958.

428 For a contemporary exposition of the thesis that property has a relation to leisure, freedom of speech, and scholarship, see Frederich A. von Hayek, *Constitution of Liberty,* U. of Chicago Press, Chicago, 1960.

THE LIFE OF LEISURE

429 The economist who made the observation about scholarship and patriotism is Alfred Marshall. See Arthur C. Pigou, ed., *Memorials of Alfred Marshall,* Macmillan, London, 1925.

431 For an example of the biological perspective, see Innes H. Pease and Lucy H. Crocker, *The Peckham Experiment,* Allen and Unwin, London, 1943.

435 For a book on architecture and city building that is well aware of some of the problems mentioned here, such as meditation, industry, quiet, promenades, locomotion, and squares, see Percival and Paul Goodman, *Communitas,* Vintage Books, New York, 1947.

Strabo in his *Geography* (X, 3, 9) comments on the holiday in the ancient world. "A custom common both to Greeks and Barbarians is to celebrate religious rites in connection with the relaxation of a festival. . . . This is in accordance with the dictates of nature, because the relaxation draws the mind away from human occupations (*ascholē-*

mata) and turns what is truly the mind towards the divine . . . Although it has been said that mortals act most in imitation of the gods when they are doing good to others, it could better be said, that they do so when they are happy, which means when they are rejoicing, celebrating festivals, pursuing philosophy, and joining in music."

INDEX OF AUTHORS

SUBJECT INDEX

Absenteeism, 83, 145, 269, 492–3

Action, activity, 14, 20, 92–5, 102, 114, 124–6, 136, 178–9, 181–2, 307, 332–6, 348, 364, 366, 428, 431, 480–1, 482

Activism, 5–6, 28–33

Activities: active/passive, 178, 182, 332–6, 493; indoor/outdoor, 178–80, 510; in the house/outside the house, 178–80; participant/spectator, 178, 182; sedentary/on the feet, 170, 180, 192; shared/non-shared, 179; solitary/social, 178–9; visiting at home/visiting elsewhere, 179; *see also* Free-time activities

Adult education, 268, 272, 276, 338

Advertising, 7, 244, 399; as advocate of free time, 275–6; as advocate of leisure, 271; allies of, 213–14, 217, 226–7, 230–2, 356; in ancient Rome, 235; and at-homeness, 423; beliefs of, 510; of capricious goods, 208–10, 214, 353–4; and choice, 293; and college education, 355–6, 361, 525; and commodities, 216, 353; and creation of needs, 234–5; effects on production, 227–8; failures of, 225–6, 234, 237–44, 248–9; and free choice, 228, 237; furrow of, 436; of future, 296–7; history of, 207–18, 506–7; and identity, 210–12; industry's dependence on, 353–4; influence of, 216, 255–9, 341; informative function of, 208–10; and innovation, 294; institutional, 213–14, 235; and mass media, 213; motifs in, 210–16, 218, 234–5, 238–9; and peddling, 235, 238–9; pitches, 142; press defense in, 363–4; resistance to, 229, 232; scientific research for, 227–8; and size of enterprise, 509; and suburban dream, 238; and taste, 226; talent use

in, 403; tax on, 354; time pressure in, 217–18, 237–9; waste in, 509; welfare state tendency in, 357; to women, 222; and youth, 107–9

Afghans, the, 195

Africa, 154

Age, 24, 66–7, 108, 133, 152–3, 172, 219, 273, 325, 494, 499, 502, 508

Agricultural world, 37, 116, 183

Alcohol, 74, 100–1, 121, 146, 149, 171, 184, 190, 202–3, 216, 308, 312, 341, 378, 437, 501–2, 506; *see also* Wine

American Indian, 155, 171, 223, 241, 249–52, 255, 260, 313–14

Amusement, 15, 364, 367

Anglo-Saxon, the, 154, 155, 383, 404

Appetites, 370–1

Arabs, 171, 320

Architecture, 17, 176–7, 251, 266, 357–8, 435, 502, 503, 506, 533

Aristocracy, 22, 38, 50–2, 116, 157, 204, 210–11, 215, 258, 265–7, 276–82, 284–94, 349, 359–61, 363–4, 373, 376–8, 379, 387, 405–7, 515, 516, 522, 524–5, 527

Armies, mass, 383, 402, 405, 408

Arminianism, 254

Artisans, 30, 37–8, 56–60, 183, 207, 302–4, 315, 385, 407, 485

Arts, the, and artists, 18, 52–3, 134, 155, 160, 191–2, 251, 259, 352–3, 361–4, 377, 378, 391, 392, 394–5, 400, 414, 421, 432, 435, 483, 517, 521

Asceticism, 3, 23, 50, 388, 419

Asia, 295, 394; Asia Minor, 36; Southeast, 388

Athens, Athenians, 12, 18, 35–6, 285, 290, 394, 401–2, 406

At-homeness, 183–5, 236–7, 369, 423, 503, 510

Austria, 187; Austro-Hungarians, 154

Authority, 354–66, 518

Methodology, 136–7, 496–7; *see also* Samples; Statistics

Mexico, 112, 157, 251–2, 347, 369, 385–6

Middle Ages, the, 8, 28, 40–1, 53, 89, 220, 318, 362, 372, 414, 421

Midwest (U. S.), 85, 261, 342

Migration, *see* Mobility

Milan, 187

Military, the, 391–6, 402, 426, 431; *see also* War

Mind, the, 374, 376–7, 378, 386, 400, 426–7, 434–5; *see also* Truth

Mobility, 85, 109–12, 130, 143, 146, 154–8, 195, 209, 211–12, 238–42, 269, 289, 301, 353, 423, 493, 510

Monarchy, 37, 406–7

Monasticism, 24–8, 40–4, 53–4, 483

Moonlighting, 70–2, 143, 149, 166, 368, 490

Moravians, 258, 260

Moslems, 304–5

Muses, the, 17, 22, 53, 247, 267, 394

Music, musicians, 16–19, 38, 121, 134, 156–7, 160, 251, 266, 288, 316–17, 334–5, 341, 374, 377, 398–9, 400, 426, 435, 480, 500, 519, 520, 521

Mythology, ancient, 30, 38, 176, 186, 255–6, 337, 370, 385, 394, 399, 418

Nantes, edict of, 314

Nap, 171, 495, 521–2

Naples, 401

National parks (U. S.), *see* Parks

Navaho, the, 320

Nazism, 323

Necessity, 14, 15, 20–1, 36, 38–9, 63, 246, 279, 287, 348–9, 361, 370–1, 372–6, 386–90, 427, 533

Negroes, 85, 154, 155, 157

New England, 85, 155, 220, 240, 252–7, 260–1, 387

New Jerusalem, 322

Newcastle, 198, 218

Nonconformism, 313, 339–40

North, 85, 157, 263, 342

North Africa, 368

North America, 112, 154, 213, 240

North Pole, 64

Northeast, 98

Numidian, 393

Objectivity, 20, 376, 420–2, 426, 434

Occident, *see* West, the

Occupation, 14–15, 22; *see also* Work; Job, the; Calling

Orient, Orientals, 3, 295, 388

Ottoman Empire, 309

Outdoors, 104, 111–12, 116–18, 146, 173–4, 179–80, 184–5, 273, 494–5, 502

Overtime, 139, 271, 306, 368; *see also* Moonlighting

Painting, 16–17, 529

Pakistan, 186

Paradise, 322, 381

Paris, 54, 171, 187, 258, 267, 295, 369, 394

Parks, 97, 98, 103–4, 111, 174, 342, 356, 366

Parliament, British, 194, 196–7, 200, 207, 289, 358

Part-time job, 68–70, 79–80, 221, 508

Pastime, 200

Pay, 53

Peace, 11, 12, 13

Peddler, peddling, 209–13, 235, 238–9

People, the, 281–94, 349, 359, 368–80, 381, 407–8, 435, 516

Peripatetic School, 19, 360

Persia, 3

Peru, 171, 251

Philanthropy, 358

Philippines, 171

Physicians, 273–5

Pilgrims, 5, 255, 279; *see also* Puritans

Pinocchio, 164

Pisa, 175

Play, 16, 95, 177, 246, 336, 374–7, 483, 520, 526

Pluralism, 159, 320–1

Poetry, 17–19, 160, 192, 251–2, 372, 374, 400, 505

Political science, rules of, 5, 528–9

Politics, 7, 9, 11–13, 21, 23–5, 40, 46–7, 63, 132–3, 150, 158–63, 189, 236–7, 248, 276–83, 318, 327, 349–54, 361–7, 374, 386, 391–428, 504, 532–3; *see also* Government

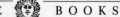